DTP'S
2025 NFL DRAFT GUIDE

DANIEL PARLEGRECO

DTP's 2025 NFL DRAFT GUIDE

Table of Contents

Introduction 1

QB's 3

RB's 17

WR's 43

TE's 69

OT's 86

Interior Offensive Lineman (Guards or Centers) 105

Edge Players (4-3 DE's and 3-4 OLB's) 123

Defensive Tackles (Includes 3-4 DE's) 149

Middle Linebackers (MIKE Linebackers in 3-4 or 4-3) 177

Outside Linebackers (Strong Side or Weak Side) 188

Cornerbacks 199

Safeties 226

Conclusion 245

Glossary of Terms 247

100 Big Board 249

Index 253

Chapter 1

Introduction

After a year off from writing a guide in 2024, I am back in 2025, bigger and better than ever! I received many questions in the last year in regard to why I didn't write a guide in 2024, and there were a number of reasons. Many of them were personal and many of them were time-oriented.

I regretted it greatly and missed the draft community and the fun interactive chats we had along the way! Make no mistake; this guide is a massive undertaking for someone who recently started a family and runs other businesses that limit my availability. I work on this draft guide and each individual evaluation every spare minute I have from October - February, and it's exhausting!

I wholeheartedly appreciate each and every one of you over the years who have purchased my guide, whether it was 1-time, 2-times, or each year I've done the guide. The draft has turned into a bigger and bigger sporting spectacle each year, and there are more and more 'draft gurus' each year who can easily become your confidant and trustee.

And while that is certainly the case, I am grateful that you trust me to be someone you read and respect. Whether I'm the only person you read or I'm the 100th draft guru you consult. I also greatly appreciate those who have never read my guide before and are picking up and reading this guide for the first time.

For those who don't know me or have read my guide in the past, who am I?

To begin with, my name is Dan Parlegreco. Around 12 years ago or so, I became popular in some internet forums for my write-ups and evaluations of draft prospects. I was tired of hearing the same cliche opinions on every single player that almost seemed cookie-cutter. No one wanted to think for themself or have a valuation of players that didn't coincide with groupthink or popular wisdom.

I realized after watching clip-up after clip-up of players that I felt differently about many players than the popular talking heads on television. Some I liked MUCH more than what I was hearing, and others I liked a lot less. After posting evaluations in forums, many readers used them and consulted with them.

But the best part of all was that months and years later, people still used them and would reach out to me and say, "I can't believe you nailed your evaluation of them! No one else was right except you!"

This led me to start the guide and make it available to everyone! While the early days of my guide saw me evaluate significantly fewer prospects, it gradually grew each year. My readership grew as people recognized me as being the only one who was as high as I was on players like Patrick Mahomes, Aaron Donald, and Fred Warner. No one else had these guys ranked as high as I did.

That doesn't mean I'm right on everyone. That's impossible! But I'm certainly not afraid to stray from common consensus based on what I see. And what I see is based solely on what I see on tape. I don't rely on the NFL combine or pro-day workouts, which have proven to be anything but accurate or a reliable indicator of future success.

Maybe you're wondering why my draft guide becomes available earlier than others. The MAIN reason is that I'm not overly concerned about the pre-draft stuff. Let players rise, and other players drop. I'm not concerned about what others have. I'm concerned about what the tape says strictly. And the truth is, the cream will always rise to the top, whether it's during their rookie seasons or shortly thereafter.

I also began evaluating prospects significantly before many of the talking heads on television who don't start until December or January, in most instances.

I encourage you to use my guide as a resource not just after the draft but also in future years, and continue to compare my thoughts with the success of every one of these players. I have a feeling you will be impressed when the dust settles on these players' careers.

But keep in mind these friends; this is entirely a sole operation as I write this guide. I can't promise it's going to be the most professional production of a draft guide, but I can promise that I have put my heart and soul into this guide each year I do it. I try to limit my time to editing as much as possible so that the primary focus of my guide can be watching film and writing up these reports.

So, if there are certain things that you feel are missing or certain technical things that would be helpful, just keep this in mind. I don't have a team or editors or designers, I have me :)

With all of that being said, let's begin! We will start with the QBs and finish with the safeties. Enjoy!

Chapter 2

QB's

1. Cameron Ward - Miami - 6'2 225 lbs

Strengths: A 2-year starter for Washington State in the Pac-12 before transferring over to play his final season with the Hurricanes in 2024. Ward has been impressive in each campaign, but he completely exploded during his final year with Miami, finishing with over 4300 yards, 39 touchdowns passing to only 7 interceptions. Ward looks the part with prototypical NFL size, showcasing NFL height and size. Ward is the definition of a big-game QB who refuses to accept defeat on any play or game. Remains in control and at his best in the biggest moments of games. As a passer, Ward displays terrific pocket awareness, feeling the pressure on all sides and knowing when to release the football. He has a tremendous ability to alter his throwing motion and trajectories to release the ball at improbable angles. Comfortable winning on designed plays or when needing to improvise and extend and turn something out of nothing. Has an impressive arm that is capable of making all the throws and understanding when to throw the fastball in tight windows. Quick release allows him to get the ball out despite defenders in his face or with minimal time. Very good touch and ball placement down the field, threatening the back half of a defense at all times. Impressive ball fakes and play-action frequently fool defenses with his deceptive trickery. Impressive off-platform, showcasing the ability to make plays on boots and waggles. A true dual-threat QB who is always a threat to a defense, showing toughness and fearlessness as a runner. Has some shiftiness to the way he moves in space, regularly making defenders whiff. Even when making a poor mistake, Ward has the mental fortitude to shake off mistakes quickly. While he can make plays on designed running plays, his instincts are always pass-first.

Weaknesses: While Ward has improved his decision-making, he can still play the position recklessly. He forces things and attempts to do too much in every single play. His ball security concerns are an issue when he takes off, leading to some poor fumbles in college. His internal clock can use some additional sophistication as he will attempt to ditch the pocket too quickly. A very rhythm-based QB who can get off for long durations of games, looking completely out of sync. He can continue to improve in the game's mental aspects, refining his pre-snap reads and looks.

Best Fit: Starting QB

Player Ranking (1-100): 90.9 - I love Ward as a prospect. He single-handedly propelled Miami to their best season in years. He's the definition of a playmaker and a gunslinger who will make some mistakes but will threaten defenses for years. He's still raw and will need continued refinement, but he has the makings of a true franchise QB. 1st round player.

2. Jaxson Dart - Ole Miss - 6'2 225 lbs

Strengths: Originally recruited to USC, Dart transferred following his freshman season with the Trojans to be the starter under Lane Kiffin for the Rebels for the last three seasons. Dart started his career with the Rebels as a heavy-running quarterback, running for over 600 yards as a sophomore before slowly transitioning to being more of a pocket passer each subsequent season. Dart has visibly improved during each campaign, both in accuracy and QBR. Dart is built with a prototypical frame to hold up at the next level. Dart is a terrific athlete, as he has shown throughout college, running on necessary and designed plays. Footwork within the pocket allows him to create additional time both within the framework and outside the pocket. Remains poised and in control on every snap, rarely looking rattled in crucial moments of games. Rarely takes unnecessary sacks, and it is incredibly frustrating for defenses how he somehow gets rid of the ball. The definition of a competitor who plays with fearlessness, refusing to go down on snaps and wiggling out of tackles routinely. As a passer, Dart is impressive when working the shorter to intermediate parts of the field, showing excellent touch and accuracy. Comfortable placing the ball in tough windows with necessary touch and ball placement. Can alter his speeds and trajectories to make more difficult throws. Trusts his receivers to make plays on the ball, sometimes in improbable situations. A high IQ QB that reads the field well, both before and after the snap. Was trusted by the coaching staff to make full-field reads, utilizing both vertical and horizontal planes. Turnover numbers have improved tremendously since his first year starting, showing improved decision-making.

Weaknesses: Dart is the definition of a gunslinger, with some good connotations and some not-so-good. While Dart certainly has an NFL arm, it isn't what you'd call an elite arm. His lack of top-end arm strength is prevalent when attempting to throw tight window throws down the field or on vertical routes. This causes some major accuracy concerns with deep balls. He has a bad tendency to throw off his back foot, leading to floated balls down the field in double coverage. His play-making abilities will cause him trouble when he attempts to do too much on every snap, some when it's completely unnecessary. His decision-making, while improved, can still be very erratic when pressure is weighing down.

Best Fit: Starting QB

Player Ranking (1-100): 85.9 - I love Dart's play style and demeanor playing the position. While he can be a risk-taker, I love how he plays the QB position. I don't think he has a bad arm, but he needs to stabilize his platform when releasing the ball, which will allow him to hit tight windows more easily and further areas of the field. Dart is impressive and worthy of a 1st round pick.

3. Shedeur Sanders - Colorado - 6'2 216 lbs

Strengths: The son of former NFL Hall of Famer Deion, Shedeur is a 2-year starter with the Buffaloes after starting an additional 2 years prior with FCS-level Jackson State. Sanders immediately impressed upon transferring to Colorado, throwing for nearly 70% completion, 3200 yards, 27 touchdowns, and only three interceptions. And he did all of this with a completely inept offensive line, getting sacked 49 times. Despite all the hits and pressures he dealt with, Sanders rarely loses the ball for the offense, displaying tremendous ball security as both a runner and passer. As a QB, Sanders displays the physical upside to be effective in the game's running and passive sides. Excels at creating additional time in the pocket, keeping his eyes downfield while turning negative plays into positive. A great decision-maker, Sanders recognizes things pre-snap, which allows him to adjust coverage and protection schemes. As a thrower, Sanders has the tools to make all of the throws, showing the arm strength to attack at all levels. He is impressive in his ability to use touch and placement when working the intermediary parts of the field, leading his receivers nicely. Has both the confidence and the velocity in his throws to make tight-window throws in small cushions. Plays the position like a playmaker, regularly altering his trajectory and arm motion on throws to make up for his lack of height to deliver improbable throws. A tough-nosed kid who shows incredible toughness and fight, showing NFL readiness.

Weaknesses: While Sanders is a good athlete, he's far better in smaller windows. When attempting to be dangerous outside of the pocket, he doesn't strike as much fear in the heart of secondaries or linebackers. Lacks the NFL prototypical frame, having more of an athlete's frame, ala Lamar Jackson. Has some major footwork concerns inside and outside of the pocket, regularly releasing the ball flat-footed. His internal clock lacks sophistication, as he routinely looks panicky when he's not under duress. Rushes throws at times to his 1st read. Quick to get into flight mode and ditch the pocket when it isn't always necessary. Attempts to do too much on every play lead to poor, negative yardage plays and sacks.

Best Fit: Starting QB

Player Ranking (1-100): 84.0 - For what Sanders had to deal with, he's had quite an impressive college career. He's used to carrying the load even when the odds are stacked against him. He has 4-years of starting QB at the college level and has seen essentially everything. I worry that Sanders has dealt with such a poor offensive line throughout college, which has caused a lot of issues in his style of play, and won't easily be taken out of his game. I don't think he's a great pocket quarterback, and factoring that in with his being undersized and a good athlete not great, it's hard for me to see a top-tier quarterback prospect with Sanders. 2nd round player.

4. Jalen Milroe - Alabama - 6'2 225 lbs

Strengths: A 2-year starter for the Tide, Milroe was a Heisman Trophy finalist in 2023 during his first season starting for the Tide. He finished that season with over 65% completion, 2800 yards passing, 23 touchdowns, and another 500+ yards rushing. Milroe is a well-built QB with dense limbs and outstanding strength throughout his frame. The definition of a dual-threat QB is that Milroe is a dynamic athlete with big-play potential as a runner, both on designed and broken-down plays. Lower body strength and contact balance are impressive as a runner, routinely shrugging off uncommitted tacklers and picking up additional yardage. He has excellent open-field vision and shiftiness to create for himself in space. As a passer, Milroe has experience playing in a pro-style NFL offense. He has the arm strength to test defenses at all levels horizontally and vertically. Can throw with velocity at different trajectories and off-platform in tight windows. Utilizes a large variety of ball skills to create spacing for his QBs, whether it's play-fakes or eye manipulation to look off-targets. Trusts his receivers in difficult situations to make plays down the field. Routinely turns negative yardage or limited plays into big plays with his feet and arm. Played his best in the brightest moments of games and the biggest games. He's a tough-as-nails kid with some early difficulties, but he showed his competitive drive to win the starting spot back. Puts his body on the line repeatedly, showing fearlessness to pick up the 1st down while taking big hits.

Weaknesses: Milroe is a better athlete now than a pure QB. He's very raw as a thrower, routinely utilizing poor mechanics in the pocket with his footwork. Throws with a very low trajectory, getting a lot of balls knocked down at the line of scrimmage. Very reliant on ditching the pocket and winning off-platform while he's on the move. His accuracy on intermediate to deep balls is erratic, frequently requiring his receivers to adjust to the ball down the field. Mostly played in a simple one-read offense where he locked his eyes onto his first target. His biggest issue is his inability to get rid of the football in ample time, failing to make throws unless he has clean looks and wide-open targets. Overall, pocket presence and awareness within the framework are underdeveloped at best.

Best Fit: Developmental QB

Player Ranking (1-100): 81.8 - Milroe is one of the biggest boom or bust prospects ever seen. His evaluation is going to be greatly varied among evaluators. Due to his ceiling, I could see some of them having him very high on their boards. Please make no mistake: his upside is HUGE. But he's still incredibly raw right now, and you'd be drafting him based on intangibles and physical characteristics. He has a lot of things to overcome. I wouldn't take him until the 2nd round.

5. Quinn Ewers - Texas - 6'3 206 lbs

Strengths: The former top-ranked high school recruit, Ewers, initially went to Ohio State before transferring to Texas and starting for three straight seasons. Exploded during his sophomore season with nearly 3500 yards, 22 touchdowns, and only six interceptions. A large ceiling prospect, Ewers has become more confident during each subsequent season as a starter. Looking the part, Ewers always maintains confidence and poise, especially during high-stakes football games. He's an impressive thrower of the football when he can stay on the platform, setting his feet and looking effortless, releasing the ball to all areas of the field. Ewers alters his arm motion to throw from different trajectories and angles, allowing him to make improbable completions. A rhythm-based thrower that plays with good tempo and proper urgency. Shows patience behind the pocket, allowing plays to develop and quickly release the football. He puts the ball on a platter for his receivers when he has ample time in the pocket, showing good anticipation and placement. Advanced understanding of the game with an impressive internal clock, rarely getting rattled or taking unnecessary sacks. Unique sidearm mechanics allow him to generate rare velocity in tight windows. While not a great athlete, Ewers displays the functional abilities to extend and buy additional time inside the pocket.

Weaknesses: He missed two games in his final season with Texas after suffering from an abdominal sprain. He also suffered from a high ankle sprain at the end of the season as well. He is a smaller-built quarterback who lacks ideal body armor on his frame to sustain NFL hits. He is a one-trick pony as far as threatening a defense, as Ewers rarely threatens a defense with his feet. The majority of his offense was check-downs and simple one-read progressions. Struggles when forced to move off-platform, as his accuracy is erratic outside of the pocket. Late to respond to adjustments made, rarely seeing 2nd or 3rd looks down the field. He has major accuracy concerns outside of the shorter areas of the field, constantly making his receivers adjust to his balls.

Best Fit: Developmental QB

Player Ranking (1-100): 78.4 - Ewers is a high-ceiling QB prospect who continues to get better and gain more and more confidence from the coaching staff. I wish he had an opportunity to air out the ball more downfield so we could have seen him in different circumstances. Undoubtedly, he has a chance to continue developing as he has the natural skillset. My worry is he's not an overly accurate QB, and coupling that with his lack of ideal NFL size makes me concerned he won't be able to be a consistent NFL starter. 3rd round player.

6. Kyle McCord - Syracuse - 6'3 220 lbs

Strengths: McCord started his career at Ohio State for three seasons, during which he served as the backup to CJ Stroud during his first two seasons before taking over as the starter in 2023. While McCord looked good at times, he ultimately had struggles, causing him to leave Ohio State and transfer to Syracuse. McCord has looked refreshed since transferring, improving many of his previous weaknesses. McCord is a prototypically built NFL quarterback with pro-style offense experience with excellent overall size and body armor. A good thrower of the football that is capable of making all of the throws, showing both the velocity and the deep ball strength to challenge at all levels. McCord has proven to be a good decision-maker who wins mostly inside the framework and is a reliable pocket passer. Upon receipt of the ball, McCord scans the field, never unnecessarily committing to his 1st read. Has shown impressive ball placement and touch when working the intermediate parts of the field. While he doesn't get into flight mode often, when he does, he showcases impressive touch and accuracy while off-platform. A smart kid who recognizes things pre-snap has proven to be a reliable signal caller who adjusts and alters plays. McCord utilizes a quick release to get rid of the ball when pressure weighs down.

Weaknesses: While McCord has improved in many facets, he's had some awful turnovers for Syracuse, throwing the ball into unnecessary situations. He can be a little trigger-shy, wanting to see his targets be completely open before releasing the ball. His internal clock could use some additional seasoning and refinement. A true pocket passer that lacks any significant threat as a runner. When he has significant green in front of him to run for the 1st down, he still hesitates to take advantage. With pressure weighing down, his footwork can get all over the place, frequently getting jittery and antsy in the pocket.

Best Fit: Developmental QB

Player Ranking (1-100): 75.4 - McCord is one of the best of the rest regarding QBs in this draft class. He has some impressive physical tools, but he still needs refinement. His success and experience with a big-time program bodes well for his development, and he has starter potential, but he's not quite there yet. 3rd round player.

7. Will Howard - Ohio State - 6'4 235 lbs

Strengths: Howard played four seasons for Kansas State, starting in 34 games before transferring to Ohio State to play his final season and winning the National Championship with the Buckeyes. Howard has played in several big-game moments for Kansas State and Ohio State, showing the ability to succeed in big moments against top-tier college opponents. The first thing that stands out with Howard is his frame, showing incredible size dimensions and girth, possessing the prototypical NFL frame. Excelling within the framework of the pocket, Howard scans the entire field while not being reliant on his 1st read. Shows good pocket presence and poise, willing to stand in the pocket and take a hit. Has more than enough arm strength to challenge vertically and across all areas of the field. Can adjust and create with his feet, showing the ability to make plays off-platform. He is comfortable throwing on the run and regularly throws darts when throwing across his body to the left or on designed roll-outs to his right. Has anticipatory abilities and places some beautiful throws where only his receiver can make a play on the field. While naturally a fairly safe QB, Howard isn't afraid of taking risks in some situations. Excellent ball skills when working out of play-action, allowing his receivers to generate some separation down the field. Has dual-threat potential, moves surprisingly well for a man of his size, and will pick up yards with his feet. His toughness and body make it difficult for the 1st defender to fight for additional yardage through contact.

Weaknesses: An older prospect who will be 24 years old as a rookie. Howard's offense was often predicated on making simple one-reads and often short to intermediate-based routes designed to get his receivers in space. He relied on his arm strength, failing always to have the proper mechanics through his lower body when setting up. Can get erratic with his accuracy at moments, even in simple out routes and running back option routes. Fails to drive the football with velocity down the field when needing to make tough window throws. Can be late with recognizing things and forcing the ball into double coverage. Despite good athleticism, he isn't great at buying additional seconds in the pocket, often taking poor sacks.

Best Fit: Developmental QB

Player Ranking (1-100): 73.9—Howard has had a very impressive college career and finished it strong winning the National Championship with the Buckeyes. Due to his size and physical attributes, it won't surprise me if a team takes him earlier. I don't think Howard is bad, and it wouldn't surprise me if he gets a chance to start at some point. He is a fourth-round player.

8. Kurtis Rourke - Indiana - 6'5 223 lbs

Strengths: A rare 6th-year senior, Rourke has extensive college experience, starting in each of the last 4 seasons. He began his career with the MAC-Conference program in Ohio before transferring over to Indiana for his final season. Rourke has prototypical QB size for the next level, far exceeding requisite size dimensions. A highly experienced and adept pocket passer, Rourke shows impressive seasoning and mental acuity to transition to the next level. Rarely rattled, Rourke stands tall in the pocket, displaying patience as he goes through his progressions. A full-field reader, Rourke keeps his eyes moving at all times, making quick but patient decisions. He's shown the ability to challenge all field levels, opting to choose safety instead of risk. A cerebral signal caller who doesn't panic when plays break down, navigating the pocket well while being capable of escaping and extending plays if needed. A tough kid who bounces back quickly after a big hit, always showing fearlessness and toughness. Displays nice touch and placement on balls, throwing very friendly balls to his receivers. He trusts his receivers to make plays on the ball, giving them and only them an opportunity to make a play. Rourke is very good regarding timing-based routes, showing impressive anticipation and timing when releasing the ball.

Weaknesses: Rourke will be 25 years old when his rookie season begins. Rourke lacks the excitable arm talent that others possess in this class, having just an OK overall arm. He's limited when it comes to truly testing the back halves of defenses. He also has velocity concerns that limit his ability to win in tight windows against defensive backs. Has played in mostly very simple offenses, often predicated on the first read. He has a bad habit of throwing off his back foot when pressure is weighing down. Tends to get caught locked in on his first read, as opposed to looking them off.

Best Fit: Backup QB

Player Ranking (1-100): 69.1—Rourke is a very smart and cerebral quarterback with backup NFL traits. He could have a long career at the next level as a backup, proving his worth in moments. Unfortunately, his ceiling for growth is limited, impairing his overall outlook. He is a fifth-round player.

9. Dillon Gabriel - Oregon - 6'0 200 lbs

Strengths: A rare 6th-year senior, Gabriel has had a long and storied college career, starting at UCF before transferring to Oklahoma and finishing at Oregon. He's started for all three programs, consistently succeeding during each campaign and inside three different conferences. Gabriel is a gunslinging lefty who has proven to win at the highest level, showing NFL traits. First and foremost, Gabriel is a good decision-maker, as evidenced by his low interception numbers in every campaign. He's predominantly a pocket passer who does most of his damage when working between the tackles, showing a terrific internal clock and pocket poise. He always keeps his eyes downfield while climbing and sliding within the framework. If needed, he is excellent at buying himself additional time with his quick feet. If he needs to get off-platform, Gabriel has the mobility to do so, showing good accuracy on the move. He is a capable dual-threat option who can create big chunks on broken-down plays or designed plays with his feet. Gabriel has terrific anticipation and touch to all levels of the field, showing the ability to lead receivers and throw them open. A whole field reader that scans the entire field before making a decision. His football IQ is a major plus, as he quickly recognizes pre- and post-snap things. Remains in control and disciplined with pressure weighing down, rarely making a poor decision.

Weaknesses: Gabriel lacks ideal physical measurables and height and body armor requisites for the next level. Lack of girth could cause durability concerns. He's also an older prospect who will be 25 years old during his rookie NFL season. His tools are subpar, as he lacks the necessary zip to fight the ball consistently in tight windows against man coverage and appears to lack the confidence to do it consistently. A little bit of a dink-and-dunk QB that relies on simple shallow routes and RB outs often. He tends to be an overly cautious decision-maker, tending only to make the throw when there's significant certainty.

Best Fit: Backup QB

Player Ranking (1-100): 68.9—Gabriel looked terrific at times throughout his career, especially during his final campaign at Oregon. His problem is that he lacks ideal physical tools, and there will be concerns over why he transferred multiple times. I think Gabriel could be a solid backup quarterback with a minimal ceiling for significant growth. He is a fifth-round player.

10. Max Brosmer - Minnesota - 6'2 225 lbs

Strengths: A 6th-year QB, Brosmer began his career at New Hampshire for five seasons before transferring to Minnesota for his final campaign. Brosmer stepped up to greater competition this year in the Big Ten and had a solid season, finishing with 2800 yards and a 66% completion percentage. Brosmer is an advanced and cerebral student of the game, showing experience playing in a pro-style NFL system. Brosmer stays composed pre-snap, recognizing defensive looks while being trusted to alter at the line of scrimmage. He doesn't lock onto his first target, scanning the field, and can adjust on the fly. Brosmer gets rid of the ball quickly, providing a quick and accurate release. He puts the ball on the numbers when working in the shallow areas of the field and isn't afraid to attack the middle of the field in congested traffic. Brosmer has the arm strength to challenge vertically, showing impressive touch and ball placement down the field. He steps up tall in the pocket when there's pressure on either side of him, sensing his surroundings well. While he wins mostly within the framework, Brosmer isn't afraid to create, with his legs showing more than enough functional athleticism. He's known to be a natural-born leader who demands the locker room's respect.

Weaknesses: Brosmer is an older prospect who will be 24 years old on draft day. He's had injuries to both of his knees, including ACL and LCL tears. His medical at the combine will be vital for his status at the next level. He's struggled with significant ball security problems throughout his college career, including extensive fumble issues. Brosmer struggles when facing interior pressure and tends to drift far backward. When he does this, he often throws off his back foot, unnecessarily allowing the ball to flutter in the air, leading to chances for the defense. His decision-making has been a major question mark as he frequently fails to adjust or recognize additional defenders in the box. While he has a good arm, it falls short of being an elite arm.

Best Fit: Backup QB

Player Ranking (1-100): 68.1 - Brosmer is one of this draft class's most underrated players. While he lacks elite tools, he's a solid football player. His intelligence and accuracy within the pocket are major strong points for a weak QB class. Brosmer could have a long NFL career, likely as a backup. 5th round player.

11. Tyler Shough - Louisville - 6'5 225 lbs

Strengths: Shough has had a long and storied 7-year college career, initially being recruited to Oregon. He played with the Ducks for three seasons before transferring to Texas Tech for another three seasons and finally to Louisville for his final year in 2024. Shough saved his best season for last, improving in every statistical metric showing his NFL readiness. Shough is built with prototypical next-level size, displaying ideal proportions, height, and body armor. He wins mostly inside the pocket, showing good poise and pocket presence. A smart and cerebral QB who stands tall while scanning the field, never getting stuck on his first read. Shough has abundant physical tools, showing the arm strength and flexibility to make difficult throws at different trajectories to all levels. Shough throws with good velocity and ball placement when working the shallow and middle parts of the field. He shows fearlessness when attacking the deeper parts of the field, throwing an impressive deep ball to give his receivers a chance to make a play on the ball. Shough can extend and create with his feet when asked to move off the platform. A natural athlete, Shogun is impressive in space, catching defenders off guard, and can both break tackles and evade.

Weaknesses: Shough's main issue throughout college is his inability to stay on the field. He's only played in 1 full season despite all his years and with three different programs. He's struggled with various injury issues; his medical will be important. The other major concern with Shough is that he will be 26 years old during his rookie season, which will cause questions about his overall ceiling for significant growth. Shough lacks great pre-snap awareness and appears not to see pressure packages. He often panics when pressure weighs down and throws fluttery balls in the air or takes unnecessary sacks. He's late to see things, causing his receivers to adjust as he allows defensive backs to recover constantly. His overall accuracy and completion percentage throughout college have been subpar, failing to throw with precision for long durations. He throws lofted balls behind receivers and needs to know when/where to utilize additional velocity on intermediate to deeper balls. His footwork mechanics inside the pocket can get sloppy, frequently dropping to improbable depths.

Best Fit: Backup QB

Player Ranking (1-100): 66.2—Shough is a low-ceiling, high-floor prospect who will likely earn backup status at the next level. His age, sporadic accuracy, and injury history will likely limit teams from drafting him early despite his nice traits. He is a fifth-round player.

12. Riley Leonard - Notre Dame - 6'4 205 lbs

Strengths: Leonard was initially recruited to Duke, where he started for two seasons before transferring to Notre Dame before his senior season in 2024. Leonard had arguably his best season for the Fighting Irish, throwing over 66% completion percentage. Leonard is a former track athlete in high school, showing two dual-threat capabilities. He is a threat to take it and run on every snap of the ball, as evidenced by his 700+ rushing yards in two seasons in college. A tall and lanky-built QB, Leonard has an ideal frame with room for substantially more mass on his frame. Leonard learned his craft after working with former Duke coach David Cutcliffe and received his important endorsement. Leonard is an impressive arm talent capable of making all of the throws to all field levels. Leonard possesses a quick release and can alter trajectories to make throws from various mesh points, enabling him to adjust on the fly constantly. High IQ prospect that recognizes pre-snap looks and frequently adjusts and audibles before the snap. He is a competitive kid with full command of the offense and willing to sacrifice his body on important plays. Footwork and nimble feet enable him to buy additional time within the pocket. He generally remains composed under pressure and can stand tall and climb the pocket with pressure weighing down. Has the velocity in his arm to make tight-window throws in the middle of the field or anticipate openings along the boundaries down the field. He utilizes good touch and placement on vertical throws, giving his receivers a chance to make a play on the ball.

Weaknesses: Leonard had an ankle issue at Duke, requiring multiple surgeries. He's a streaky passer who can get off for long game durations. He's had questionable ball security concerns, with multiple fumbles during each campaign at Duke. While Leonard has a good arm, he lacks top-end arm strength. He racked up a high completion percentage this year in Notre Dame's offense with a mostly 1-read system predicated on getting rid of the ball fast. His accuracy off-platform is a major work in progress, as he constantly forced receivers to adjust to the ball. He takes a lot of unnecessary hits in the pocket as he fails to feel the pressure around him. Not a full field reader, appears to have tunnel vision, and gets locked onto one target. He lacks patience in the pocket when there's no rush, always appearing to want to get in 'flight mode' and get on the move.

Best Fit: Backup QB

Player Ranking (1-100): 65.4—Leonard has traits that show room for continued growth. But watching the tape of him, he just lacks the 'IT' factor for me. He falls into the gunslinger mentality, but he just doesn't make enough plays consistently. He tends to be a safer quarterback who relies on his athleticism more than his true pocket ability. He is a fifth-round player.

13. DJ Uiagalelei - Florida State - 6'4 252 lbs

Strengths: A former five-star high school QB, Uiagalelei has had a long and varied college career. After starting 2+ seasons for Clemson, Uiagalelei moved to Oregon State and started for the Beavers for one season. Then, finally, Uiagalelei transferred to Florida State for his final season, playing in only 5 games before an injury in his throwing hand. Uiagalelei is a massive physical talent, possessing rare size and girth for the QB position. He also has one of the biggest arms we've seen in a long time, capable of throwing the ball 80+ yards down the field. Uiagalelei has played in multiple offensive systems, showing adaptability and a high-functioning football IQ. Uiagalelei is a solid, functional athlete who is dangerous to run due to his frame and ability to absorb blows. He's at his best in red-zone situations with his ability to plow it in, as evidenced by his 21 rushing touchdowns. As a passer, Uiagalelei shows good pre-snap awareness and can adjust and audible depending on his read. He stands tall in the pocket, remaining calm and composed. He is patient as he throws his progressions, showing fearlessness in throwing the ball through tight windows. Uiagalelei is at his best when throwing the ball to the intermediate and deeper parts of the field, showing outstanding touch and placement to all levels. He can alter his trajectory and velocity on different types of throws.

Weaknesses: After requiring surgery on his throwing hand, Uiagalelei's medical will be important. He's also an older prospect who will be 24 years old on draft day. His completion percentage average throughout his career was about 58% and even lower in his last two seasons, causing significant accuracy concerns. Uiagalelei has a long and elongated release that leads to timing issues on shorter routes, constantly forcing his receivers to adjust to the ball. He's a streaky passer that is very rhythm-based, and when he's on, he's great, and when he's off, it isn't good. He's not always the best decision-maker, as he throws the ball into impossible windows unnecessarily, putting the ball in harm's way. He can sometimes appear overconfident, leading to poor fundamentals and mechanics. Despite plus athleticism, Uiagalelei is stagnant in the pocket and fails to climb the pocket or buy additional time when pressure is weighing down. He doesn't appear to make full-field reads and is often late in recognizing and seeing things.

Best Fit: Developmental QB

Player Ranking (1-100): 64.8 - Uiagalelei is the type of prospect that could be a big BOOM. He's worth a gamble, as his talent level is insane. However, he will need to improve in the fundamentals of playing football, particularly the mental side. The fact that he's seemingly regressed in the last year is a bit worrisome. He's worth the risk somepoint on Day 3. Low risk and HUGE reward potential. 6th round player.

14. Will Rogers - Washington - 6'2 216 lbs

Strengths: A 5th-year, highly experienced, and acclaimed senior, having started in over 50 games throughout his college career. Rogers played 4 seasons for Mississippi State before transferring to Washington during his final season. He's switched offenses multiple times in college, showing the ability to adapt quickly while playing in a pro-style system during his final year at Washington. Rogers is a cerebral QB who wins mostly within the pocket framework, showing veteran-like poise and composure. He stands tall in the pocket without panicking, showing good footwork to sidestep defenders and buy additional time. He has enough athletic ability to create and run on designed and broken-down plays when nothing is open. He has an excellent feel for defenses pre-snap, proving to recognize blitzes and defensive looks quickly. He makes his living on the shorter to intermediate parts of the field, showing good placement and accuracy when working there. He's proven a reliable decision-maker who takes care of the football, rarely making foolish mistakes, especially in the red zone. Rogers displays good eye discipline and recognition of zone looks, quickly finding and recognizing opportunities down the field. He works well with his teammates, showing good anticipation on timing-based throws.

Weaknesses: Rogers lacks great physical characteristics in terms of athleticism and size. While he has slightly above-average athleticism, he's not a guy who will scare defenses consistently with his feet. His subpar arm makes life difficult, especially with his poor mechanics. He frequently throws off his backfoot, limiting his velocity and trajectory outside the numbers throws. He fails to have the arm necessary to scare back halves of defenses, frequently putting balls behind his receivers on deeper routes and making them constantly have to adjust. He's also tended his career to hold onto the football for far too long, failing to make decisive decisions in ample time. His accuracy can be erratic at best, especially since he's off-platform. He will miss some very simple throws at times.

> **Best Fit: Backup QB**

Player Ranking (1-100): 62.4—Make no mistake, Rogers has had a nice college career. He's limited at the next level and will likely have to earn his keep as a backup. His experience and football IQ will serve him well as a backup. He is a sixth-round player.

15. Cam Miller - North Dakota State - 6'1 212 lbs

Strengths: A 4-year starter for FCS-level North Dakota State, Miller broke the team's single-season passing record in 2024 (previously held by Carson Wentz), finishing with 3251 yards and 33 touchdowns. Miller is a highly experienced NFL prospect who has seen it all at the FCS level, winning two national championships while not missing a game during the last four seasons. While Miller lacks the elite physical components, he makes up for it smartly. Miller is a cerebral quarterback who plays on a pro-style offense and shows composure and poise at all times. Miller is capable of winning both within the pocket and on the run; Miller is a terrific athlete who has run for over 500 yards in the last three seasons. When playing under center, Miller patiently scans his reads while going through each progression, never unnecessarily rushing. A smart decision-maker, Miller rarely puts the ball in harm's way and has never eclipsed the five-interception number in any of his seasons starting. Rarely panicking, Miller maintains composure despite duress. Miller wins mostly at the shorter and intermediate areas of the field, showing good accuracy and ball placement when working between the hashes. He throws with terrific anticipation and touch to all levels, throwing a catchable ball for his receivers. He is comfortable behind center, utilizing ball manipulation play fakes to create spacing opportunities down the field for his teammates. Highly accurate, as evidenced by his 68% and above completion percentage each campaign.

Weaknesses: Miller lacks prototypical size and bulk thresholds for NFL QBs, lacking the desired build many evaluators have. There will be concerns over his level of competition, as he rarely plays Division I programs. Miller isn't a guy who will challenge the back halves of defenses, lacking the desired arm strength and velocity to threaten vertically or in extremely tight windows. He played in a very safe offense predicated on open looks and 1st reads.

> **Best Fit: Backup QB**

Player Ranking (1-100): 57.8 - Miller is a good all-around QB that lacks top-end developmental traits. He has the smarts, athleticism, and decision-making ability to be a reliable backup QB at the next level. A high floor/low ceiling prospect. 7th round player.

16. Alan Bowman - Oklahoma State - 6'3 220 lbs

Strengths: Bowman has had a 7-year college career, bouncing around from three different programs. He was initially recruited to Texas Tech, transferred to Michigan, and finally ended up at Oklahoma State his last two seasons. To say Bowman is experienced is an understatement; he's seen it all and has played in multiple offensive systems. Bowman had his best season in 2023, finishing with nearly 3500 yards passing and 15 touchdowns. Bowman is NFL-level in size and possesses the ideal framework for a next-level quarterback. Bowman also possesses an NFL arm, capable of testing and throwing the ball to all field levels. Bowman plays with a backyard gunslinger mentality, always trying to create something out of nothing. He utilizes various ball skills, such as play-fakes, to create openings for his receivers when coverage is tight. Bowman displays terrific touch and anticipation on down-the-field throws, allowing his receivers the chance to catch the ball in stride. Bowman has a good pocket presence and can stand tall in the pocket, climb the ladder, and make difficult throws with pressure weighing down. During fairly limited running, Bowman will run on needed occasions to pick up 1st downs or touchdowns in the red zone.

Weaknesses: Bowman is an older prospect who will be 25 years old on draft day. Bowman has had a long string of injury issues throughout his career, including breaking his collar bone, suffering a partially collapsed lung, and an ankle injury. He's only played in one full season. Bowman is a fairly limited quarterback who lacks significant threat with his feet and only runs on a need basis. While his touch and placement are impressive when working the deeper parts of the field, his accuracy is sporadic when working the intermediate parts of the field. He repeatedly makes his receivers adjust, leading to interceptions and dropped balls. He's thrown double-digit interceptions in each of the last two seasons. His footwork within the pocket leaves something to be desired, frequently throwing off his back foot and not getting set before delivering the ball, leading to clunky and slow velocity balls. His internal clock lacks sophistication, and his timing and rhythm inside the pocket always appear unnecessarily rushed. He doesn't appear to see the full field, frequently missing shaded defenders and putting the ball in harm's way.

Best Fit: Backup QB

Player Ranking (1-100): 54.2 - Bowman likely will be an undrafted free agent due to his age and limited ceiling for growth. While he has experience, he lacks significant areas for improvement. His best chance will come as a backup quarterback if he proves himself in camp. Undrafted free agent.

17. Hunter Dekkers - Iowa Western Community College - 6'3 235 lbs

Strengths: A former four-star high school prospect, the lefty gunslinger Dekkers was part of the Iowa State program for three seasons. The last season he started for them was in 2022, finishing with over 3000 yards passing and 19 touchdowns. Just before the start of the 2023 campaign, Dekkers was charged with placing bets on Iowa State sports. He then transferred to Iowa Western Community College and threw for over 3800 yards and 32 touchdowns, putting him back on the NFL Draft map. A dual-threat QB, Dekkers is effective both behind the line of scrimmage and on designed runs. He can buy additional yardage in the pocket or run for significant yardage if plays break down. A big-bodied QB, Dekkers has good density and size on his frame, with tree trunk-sized legs. Dekkers, a smart and cerebral QB, displays good pre-snap awareness to adjust and signal call. His frame enables him to play the game aggressively without fear. A capable thrower of the ball, Dekkers has the arm strength to challenge all three levels of a defense. Dekkers remains patient and in control behind the line of scrimmage, rarely panicking under duress. He doesn't get dead-set on throwing to his 1st option and keeps his eyes scanning continually. Dekkers throws a catchable ball for his receivers, utilizing nice touch when working the shallow areas of the field.

Weaknesses: The biggest concern for scouts and evaluators will be the gambling probe that Dekkers was at the center of and the negative publicity. Dekkers is going to be 24 years old shortly after the draft. Dekkers played mostly in a simple one-read system at Iowa State, failing to make many complicated reads. He has a bad habit of unnecessarily throwing the ball into double coverage, taking on needless interceptions. On other occasions, Dekkers proves to be gun-shy in delivering the ball, taking too long to channel through his reads while taking unnecessary sacks. Dekkers has had major accuracy concerns when throwing the ball past 10 yards, lacking ideal anticipation and placement. His receivers have to adjust frequently to the ball down the field. He fails to adjust his velocity and trajectory on different routes, lacking the needed velocity in tight windows.

Best Fit: Developmental QB

Player Ranking (1-100): 53.6 - Dekkers has the frame and the arm strength to succeed, but his lack of accuracy and questionable decision-making limit his overall upside. He could be a developmental prospect for a team.

Top-10 QB's:

1. Cameron Ward
2. Jaxson Dart
3. Shedeur Sanders
4. Jalen Milroe
5. Quinn Ewers
6. Kyle McCord
7. Will Howard
8. Kurtis Rourke
9. Dillon Gabriel
10. Max Brosmer

Chapter 3

RB's

1. Ashton Jeanty - Boise State - 5'9 215 lbs

Strengths: Jeanty began his career as a true freshman for Boise State, where he played mostly as a part-time player before exploding as a sophomore in 2023 with over 1300 yards of rushing. Jeanty improved on his sophomore campaign with an even better 2024 season, finishing with nearly 2500 yards rushing and finishing 2nd in the Heisman race. Jeanty is a compact and densely built runner who utilizes his natural leverage advantage and thick limbs to succeed. Jeanty runs behind his pads, staying on his feet through multiple tackle attempts on almost every run, rarely going down to first contact. His contact balance is amongst the best we've seen since Marshawn Lynch. Plays with a relentless motor and urgency, taking every snap like it's his last, and fights for each additional yard as he keeps his legs churning through impact. Explosive in short bursts, Jeanty immediately gets to top gear upon receipt of the ball. He displays the right amount of patience as he waits for lanes to open while also displaying the anticipation and vision to pick the best expiring lane. In space, Jeanty displays a nasty stiff arm to prevent defenders from reaching his frame. He also shows good open-field vision and change of directional abilities to create spacing for himself. Flexibility through his hips enables him to cross the field, showcasing impressive lateral movement skills and suddenness as a runner. Sustains speed well on big runs, rarely getting caught from behind or running out of gas, showing 'take it to the house' abilities for the next level. Has an impressive receiving resume, used both in the slot and out of the backfield to run simple routes. Despite being undersized, Jeanty's wingspan and soft hands allow him to make plays as a receiver extended from his body.

Weaknesses: Jeanty has taken a lot of big hits in the last couple of years and has quite a bit of mileage on his frame, causing some concern over the longevity of his career. He tries to do too much on every carry, causing him to take some poor negative plays due to overaggressive makeup. Jeanty is a 1-speed runner who lacks the secondary burst to explode or to leave defenders in his shadows once he takes a pathway. Has had some poor fumbles due to ball security concerns when fighting for additional yardage. He could benefit by diversifying his route tree as a receiver, as he ran mostly safe and underneath routes in his offense. Shows upside as a pass protector but could use some additional seasoning and recognition work.

Best Fit: Starting RB

Player Ranking (1-100): 90.5 - Jeanty is a rare running back that should go in the 1st round. His combination of explosiveness and contact balance is rare! He's the definition of a bellcow that should immediately be a 1,000+ yard rusher at the next level. One of the best players in this draft class.

2. Omarion Hampton - North Carolina - 6'0 220 lbs

Strengths: A 2-year starter for the Tar Heels, Hampton has led the ACC in the last two seasons in rushing, finishing with over 1500 yards during the last two campaigns. Hampton is built NFL-ready, showing impressive density with a muscled-up physique to handle the rigors of NFL life. Hampton is a downhill, between-the-tacklings runner who gets to top gear quickly. He's a quick processor who wastes little time in the backfield, showing the right amount of patience and decisiveness as a runner. Generates impressive pop-on contact against defenders, putting his head down and continuing to keep his legs churning through contact. He has good overall power and contact balance to stay on his feet through contact, showing impressive ability in short-yardage situations. Has a good feel for working through blocks, only needing the tiniest creases to rattle off a big chunk play. If his initial lane offers little upside, Hampton has the redirect ability and change of directional skills to alter course without gearing down. Difficult to bring down in the open field, Hampton requires full commitment from tacklers. As a receiver, Hampton has shown an ability to be used effectively on 3rd downs with soft mitts. In pass protection, Hampton shows toughness and the ability to stay square while having the anchorage strength through his lower body to absorb.

Weaknesses: Hampton is a very upright runner that leaves defenders significant surface area to work into when working between the tackles. While he's got a good burst, he lacks the dynamic home-run ability to consistently challenge defensive backs at the 2nd level, getting caught from behind at times. Not an overly creative runner in space, failing to make defenders miss, lacking ideal elusive traits. Hampton must widen out his route arsenal as a receiver other than running simple routes. His pass protection technique isn't bad, but he must refine and improve his hand usage and technique.

Best Fit: Starting RB

Player Ranking (1-100): 83.9 - Hampton has been among college football's best running backs for the last two seasons. His durability, toughness, and size bode well for the next level. He has a very good skillset that should warrant him a starting role on the sooner side. 2nd round player.

3. TreVeyon Henderson - Ohio State - 5'10 208 lbs

Strengths: A former five-star high school prospect and the number one ranked running back in the country, Henderson has been the bellcow back for the Buckeyes since his freshman campaign, in which he compiled over 1200 yards rushing and 300 yards receiving. Henderson is the ideal package of explosiveness and big-play potential, showcasing elite talent both in the running and receiving games. As a receiver, Henderson shows natural route-running abilities to create on-wheel or swing routes, in which he always maximizes his opportunities with the ball. Natural soft hands allow him to pluck away the ball effortlessly. As a runner, Henderson follows his blockers while displaying top-end acceleration, getting to 6th gear instantly. He understands how to utilize his natural low center of gravity to run low and hard, staying on his feet through contact. He is very good in space with shifty hips, capable of making the first guy miss routinely, rarely allowing defenders to get two hands on him. He is comfortable and able to win north/south or east/west due to his top-end speed and agility to shift his frame without losing any built-up momentum. Very good vision lets him see expiring lanes, wasting little motion in the backfield. He can create for himself when nothing is available, taking losses into positives. A strong lower half allows him to generate impressive leg drive in congested lanes, constantly pushing his lanes and picking up additional yardage through contact.

Weaknesses: He has not quite lived up to his freshman season regarding production. He has had to deal with injury concerns in multiple seasons in college, including breaking a bone in his foot and a knee issue. A very direct runner who sometimes fails to wait for openings and runs into blind alleys on occasion. While he's tougher and stronger than his size indicates, Henderson isn't a power back who consistently breaks tackles against defensive tackles or ends. Could benefit by continuing to refine his pass-blocking technique, as it's not a strong suit of his game.

Best Fit: Starting RB

Player Ranking (1-100): 83.0 - Henderson is one of my favorite running backs of the last several years. While I have some minor concerns about his injury history, they result from luck more than a continuous problem. His big-play record is unreal, proving to be a true home-run hitter for any offense. He will make an offense significantly better, and I'm confident. This kid is the real deal. 2nd round pick.

4. Kaleb Johnson - Iowa - 6'0 225 lbs

Strengths: Johnson began setting freshman rookie rushing records for Iowa as the secondary back. But he had his best season in 2024, finishing with over 1500 yards rushing and 21 rushing touchdowns, leading the Big Ten. Johnson proved this past season that he can be a bellcow back at the next level, showcasing outstanding size and body armor. A young kid with a huge future that will only be 21 years old on draft night. Johnson is a decisive north/south ball carrier who does most of his damage when working between the tackles. He wastes little time in the backfield, finding expiring lanes and exploding through with good initial bursts and acceleration. Despite playing slightly upright, Johnson stays on his feet through narrow creases and shows impressive overall contact balance to escape improbable situations. When he sees a hole, he hits the hole with power and makes powerful collisions with tacklers, always grinding and almost always falling forward. Upon receipt of the ball, Johnson remains patient, pressing the line of scrimmage while waiting for his blocks to open up things. He sets up his runs well at the 2nd level, understanding how to create openings in space. As a pass protector, Johnson shows good upside, instincts, and awareness. Despite minimal snaps as a receiver, Johnson has shown upside with smooth footwork and soft hands.

Weaknesses: Johnson struggled with some injury concerns during his sophomore season 2023, causing him to miss a few games. He was also suspended for the first half of the season opener in 2024 for violating team rules. Johnson is quicker in short bursts than fast, as he tends to run out of juice on bigger runs and can get caught from behind. Not an overly loose-hipped back in space and tends to be a straight-ahead runner who always fails to take advantage of cutback opportunities. In space, Johnson fails to have elusive traits that make defenders miss. He shows upside in pass protection but fails to anchor down and stay square against oncoming rushers. He frequently gets blown off the ball and allows pressure. His route tree as a receiver is limited, and he will need additional experience if he wants to be a three-down back.

Best Fit: Starting RB

Player Ranking (1-100): 81.4 - Johnson was fantastic this season for the Hawkeyes. He's got a great NFL frame and good juice as a runner. He should compete to be a starter fairly quickly and work great in a split carry offensive system with a change of pace back working alongside him. 2nd round player.

5. Quinshon Judkins - Ohio State - 6'0 219 lbs

Strengths: A 2-year starter for Ole Miss, Judkins transferred following the 2023 season to Ohio State. Judkins was the bellcow with the Rebels before playing more of a rotational role for the Buckeyes. As a freshman, Judkins immediately exploded with nearly 1600 yards rushing and 16 touchdowns, leading the SEC. Built with a sizeable frame and good density, Judkins has the body armor to handle NFL rigors. Judkins displays a good blend of quickness, power, and contact balance as a runner. Upon receipt of the ball, he remains patient as he waits for blockers to open up 1st level options. Judkins immediately explodes once he sees the best opening, showing an excellent burst. Maintains a good pad level when working between the tackles, keeping a low center of gravity, allowing him to bounce off tackle attempts without losing any built-up momentum. Judkins keeps his legs churning through impact when running in short-yardage situations to grind out additional yards. Loose limbs and flexibility through his lower body allow him to make sharp cuts, showing good elusiveness and shifty qualities as a runner. Makes the most out of every opportunity, constantly turning small creases into big plays. Displays good 1st and 2nd level vision to pick out the right rush lane. Judkins has been impressed in the screen game and running routes out of the backfield as a receiver. He displays soft hands and can create separation against linebackers.

Weaknesses: Judkins was a rotational player in his final season, failing to have the same volume of success or attempts as he had in his two previous seasons. A good athlete with an impressive burst but isn't a top-tier athlete who will offer true home-run potential every time he touches the ball. Most of his big plays were on outside-zone runs, failing to have great production when working between the tackles consistently. He is still developing in pass protection, failing always to recognize pre-snap looks to understand where he needs to be. Has had some ball security concerns throughout college. Can be indecisive in moments when receiving the ball, causing some hesitations to allow defenders to make plays on him behind the backfield. Showcases upside as a receiver but still works with a minimal route tree and is prone to poor concentration drops.

Best Fit: Potential Starting RB

Player Ranking (1-100): 79.3 - Judkins is a good all-round runner who needs to increase his value as a 3rd down back. While he shows upside as a receiver and has had nice moments, he's not great in the receiving game or pass protection. With continued development, Judkins could develop into a nice starter at the next level. 3rd round player.

6. Dylan Sampson - Tennessee - 5'11 201 lbs

Strengths: Sampson is a 1-year starter with the Vols who has excelled during his opportunity, leading the SEC in both yards and touchdowns. Before 2024, Sampson played in a RB committee where he took advantage of opportunities given to him. Sampson is a former high school track athlete, which is apparent with his explosive touch upon receiving the ball. He's an angle killer who utilizes altered run tempo to explode when he hits his secondary gear once he sees an ounce of daylight. Despite being a smaller back, Sampson runs far bigger than his listed size. He does most of his work between the tackles, showing excellent patience while following his blockers to find the best expiring lane. He presses the line of scrimmage while keeping his eyes fixated on any cutback opportunities to maximize every chance. His contact balance and lower body strength are exceptional for his size, staying on his feet through impact and regularly churning his legs through impact. His explosive lower body enables him to make explosive cuts and change directions easily without slowing down. He is a big-play threat every time he touches the ball, showing outstanding open-field abilities. He has had a clean health bill throughout his college career and had minimal wear and tear before 2024. Shows upside as a receiver with impressive route running upside and natural hands.

Weaknesses: Sampson is an undersized running back who lacks elite compactness and density in his frame. There will be questions about whether he can be a consistent bellcow at the next level. He tends to play very upright when working between the tackles, enabling defenders to get clean looks at his frame. While he shows upside as a receiver, he hasn't been used extensively yet. He has had some poor fumble concerns due to doing too much in every place, leading to some ball security concerns. At this point, he's a major liability in pass protection, lacking pre-snap recognition awareness and the lower body anchorage ability to stay square and sustain blocks.

Best Fit: Potential Starting RB

Player Ranking (1-100): 77.8 - Sampson could be a heavy contributor at the next level. His ability to have success against defenses like Alabama and Georgia this season bodes well for his future. While he would best fit in a running back committee, Sampson could handle significant touches at the next level. 3rd round player.

7. Jarquez Hunter - Auburn - 5'10 202 lbs

Strengths: Hunter has been a mainstay of the Tigers' offense for the last four seasons, proving to be a reliable and consistent performer in a shared backfield. Hunter is a small, low center-of-gravity runner that maximizes available openings. When running between the tackles, Hunter shows the decisiveness and vision to pick the best option immediately. He wastes little time and explodes through narrowing gaps, showing terrific quickness and burst out of the blocks. If he reaches the second level or needs to capture the edge, Hunter shows the secondary burst to distance himself from pursuers. Incredible agility and looseness through his lower half limit the opportunity for defenders to get two hands on him in space, showing true escapability and lateral explosiveness. He doesn't need much space, and there are many instances of Hunter creating something out of potential negative yardage plays. Makes the most out of every opportunity, as evidenced by his 6+ yards per carry average throughout college. Has the long speed to be a take-it-to-the-house runner on every instance. Despite being small, Hunter runs tough and falls forward through impact. He maintains excellent leverage when working between the tackles, staying on his feet and displaying impressive contact balance. Shows upside as a receiver, taking what the defense gives him while showing reliability as a hands catcher. Has experience on special teams and was the kickoff return specialist for the Tigers.

Weaknesses: Despite being a starter, Hunter has often been part of a shared backfield where he's been able to stay fresh throughout games and hasn't been relied upon to be the bellcow. Hunter is slightly undersized to handle short-yardage, and 20+ carries a game at the next level. Lacks ideal point-of-attack power and the ability to stay square as a pass protector, which limits him on 3rd down, and he will have to improve substantially to stay on the field at the next level. While he shows receiving prowess and upside, his overall experience is limited, and he will need further advancement and experience in running a more complex offensive system. Has had some minor ball concern issues and can be a little loose with it down the field.

Best Fit: Potential Starting RB

Player Ranking (1-100): 77.4 - I love Hunter as a football player, perhaps more than most. He's explosive, creative, maximizes every opportunity, and is durable. The guy hasn't been hurt through college and has played four valuable seasons for Auburn. While he'd ideally be used in a shared backfield, there's no reason he can't play 15-20 carries a game. 3rd round player.

8. Kalel Mullings - Michigan - 6'2 233 lbs

Strengths: As a 5th-year senior for the Wolverines, Mullings was a former college linebacker before transitioning into a running back. Featuring a stacked physique, Mullings has the body armor and the head-to-toe density to hold up at the next level. An iron man that has played in almost every game of his Michigan career. Mullings was a change of pace back during the Wolverines championship season in 2023 before transitioning to the main bellcow for the Wolverines in 2024. Mullings has the frame and the POP to be able to have success in pass protection, showing good physicality and willingness. A true north/south runner who does the bulk of his damage working between the tackles. He will stay on his feet through contact, showing good contact balance. He churns his legs through impact, fighting for each additional yard, showing impressive short-yardage and red-zone upside for the next level. Wastes little movement in the backfield and is a direct 1-plant runner who gets downhill in a flash, showing a good initial burst. He has far quicker feet than you'd expect for a runner of his size, showing the ability to make the first defender miss. He is a physical thumper who regularly showcases his former linebacker tendencies, showing fearlessness and power. While he's direct, Mulligans is smart and measured in the backfield, running behind his blocks while waiting for available lanes. His excellent vision causes him to pick the right available opening. A very good special teams contributor and will immediately be a key cog for a special teams unit.

Weaknesses: He hasn't been used in the receiving game much since transitioning to running back, and he lacks ideal numbers of reps. Only a 1-year starter as a running back, lacking the experience for the position. While willing in pass protection, Mullings can benefit from more recognition work pre-snap. An upright runner could reduce his surface error by dropping his pads when working between the ball carriers. While he moves very well for his size, he's not a dynamic home-run threat capable of threatening the back half of a defense at the next level. Appears to struggle to reset his frame and change directions when needing to get off the north/south route.

Best Fit: Potential Starting RB

Player Ranking (1-100): 77.0 - Mullings has earned his keep this year for the Wolverines, showing his bellcow upside. He's a true downhill physical back who is VERY hard to bring down the ball carrier. The way he shrugs off tackle attempts is impressive. He's a smart kid who seamlessly transitioned from LB to RB. I think he will have a great role immediately in the NFL. 3rd round player.

9. Jo'quavious Marks - USC - 5'10 210 lbs

Strengths: A 4-year back for Mississippi State before transferring to USC and playing his final year for the Trojans. He played mostly rotationally for the Bulldogs before finally getting his chance to be the bellcow for the Trojans this season. Saved his best season for last as he exploded for the Trojans, showcasing his true upside as a solid starter. Marks is the definition of a dual-threat runner, setting school records at Mississippi State with 214 receptions. Marks can line up in the slot and run routes like a receiver, showing true 3-down potential, not just a simple out-route emergency receiver. He has excellent hands and reliability in contested situations to snatch the ball away from his frame. Marks even has upside as a special teams contributor, having some kickoff return experience at Mississippi State and as a gunner on the coverage teams. As a runner, Marks is dynamic, showing incredible elusiveness and lateral twitch to set up his runs. He makes it difficult for defenders to get two hands on him as he sets up his runs to perfection. Explosive in short bursts, getting to top gear quickly. He is a decisive runner who follows his blockers and wastes little time in the backfield, finding a narrow hole and immediately exploding through it. Keeps his legs churning through contact to grind out additional yards. Can win north/south or outside the hashes as a runner. Impressive as a pass protector, showing tremendous upside despite limited reps. Processes blitz quickly post-snap and get in an excellent position to square up and anchor down.

Weaknesses: For some, Marks might be a little undersized to be a true bellcow at the next level, lacking ideal girth and body armor on his frame. He does not love contact, tending to shy away from it rather than exploding through it. Doesn't have ideal contact balance and can often go down at the first tackle attempt, failing to stay on his feet through traffic. Quicker than fast, he isn't a true home-run threat to take plays to the house, lacking the ideal amount of long speed.

Best Fit: Potential Starting RB

Player Ranking (1-100): 76.7 - Marks showed this season that he can be a bellcow runner. His upside as a pass protector and tremendous receiving characteristics are rare for college runners. While he's not a dynamic home-run hitter, he's a very good back that will maximize opportunities. He could be part of a terrific running back committee as a change-of-pace runner. 3rd round pick.

10. RJ Harvey - Central Florida - 5'8 195 lbs

Strengths: A 5th year senior for the Knights, Harvey has been outstanding the last two seasons, finishing atop the Big 12 in many statistical categories. Built with a compact and low center of gravity frame, Harvey maximizes the most out of every opportunity. As a runner, Harvey is explosive at every turn. He utilizes his rare lateral agility to make dynamic cuts, starting and stopping on a dime and making it incredibly difficult for defenders to get two hands on him. He reads things quickly while remaining patient upon receipt of the ball, finding the best available opening before committing. If initially picking wrong, Harvey's ability to redirect his frame and change course is second to none, showing rare suddenness and change of directional abilities. Harvey understands how to minimize his surface area when running between the tackles, maintaining leverage while showing outstanding contact balance. All he needs is a tiny little crease to create a big play. If there's daylight in front of Harvey, he shows the secondary gear to explode and take it to the house. Harvey is once again dynamic in the open field, understanding how to make guys miss in space while showing open-field vision. He is tougher to bring down than his size would indicate in 1v1 settings for defenders, staying on his feet through ankle swipers and uncommitted tackle attempts. Receiving production and upside has been evident. He is a reliable hands catcher who can extend and make plays outside of his frame. Can run various routes when used as a 3rd down receiver, offering a threat down the field on wheel routes. Shows good recognition skills and willingness as a blocker, staying square and facing up to oncoming blitzers. Has extensive experience as a return specialist throughout college.

Weaknesses: Tore his ACL in preseason camp, causing him to miss the 2021 campaign. Harvey hasn't had to compete against many top-tier defenses throughout college. His patience, while generally a strength, can sometimes become a weakness. He sometimes spends too much time dancing in the backfield, always looking for a big play, causing him to take on a lot of negative yardage plays in the backfield. He's a little smaller than ideal for an NFL bellcow, and whether he can handle a full NFL workload will be asked. He lacks the power and forward driving abilities to offer much consistently in short-yardage situations. While willing in pass protection, his lack of anchorage strength and point-of-attack power will likely take him off the field at the next level.

Best Fit: Change of pace back and return specialist

Player Ranking (1-100): 76.5—Harvey is a fun and dynamic gadget player who absolutely deserves 15-20 touches a game for an NFL offense. He maximizes his opportunities and shows incredible explosiveness at every turn. His upside as a receiver and on special teams adds to his value. He is a third-round player.

11. Brashard Smith - SMU - 5'10 196 lbs

Strengths: A former four-star wide receiver prospect, Smith was originally recruited to Miami, where he started his career as a wide receiver for three seasons in college. After transferring to SMU before the 2024 campaign, Smith transitioned to playing as a running back. He immediately impressed, rushing for over 1300 yards and 14 touchdowns while also contributing another 327 yards and four touchdowns receiving. Smith is a smaller, low center-of-gravity-built runner with electric athleticism and rare explosive characteristics. The definition of a dual-threat runner is that Smith utilizes his receiving experience to be a dynamic 3rd down back. Not just limited to simple routes, Smith is capable of attacking all areas of the field as a receiver. He possesses natural hands while showcasing an impressive ability to separate against linebackers and defensive backs. His flexible body control allows him to adjust and make plays in contested settings. Smith also holds additional value as a return specialist, proving to be a dynamic kickoff returner, running one back for Miami in 2023. As a runner, Smith has picked up a new position in record timing despite never having played the position. He's capable of winning between the tackles or winning along the perimeter. He gets to top gear quickly, showing rare acceleration and bursts. He displays good vision and knows cutback opportunities when pressing the line of scrimmage. Smith minimizes his surface area when working through traffic, staying low and square, and bouncing off tackle attempts. Smith truly excels in getting to top gear quickly in the open field while showing outstanding open-field vision. Smith can make guys miss in a phone booth, showing the exceptional change of directional abilities, shiftiness, and open-field moves.

Weaknesses: Smith is still a 1-year runner and is still raw when it comes to winning between the tackles. He must refine his footwork and timing when taking the ball under center. Smith is undersized and lacks ideal body armor on his frame to be a bellcow at the next level and will likely be more of a 'change of pace' back at the next level. Regarding pass protection, Smith shows upside but lacks ideal recognition abilities and anchorage ability to absorb contact consistently. Smith can be a little reckless with the ball in his hands, holding the ball a bit loose, making him susceptible to swipers. When outside the framework, Smith lacks a power profile to break tackles consistently and often goes down to first contact in the open field.

Best Fit: Change of pace back and return specialist

Player Ranking (1-100): 76.3 - Smith was electric this year, and he shows a ridiculous upside with further development. While he's likely not a guy that can handle 20+ carries a game, there's no reason to think he can't handle 10-15 carries and additional snaps as a receiver. Smith is so fun to watch, and he will make an offense better and more explosive. 3rd round player.

12. Devin Neal - Kansas - 5'11 215 lbs

Strengths: A 4-year starter for the Jayhawks, Neal has been a steady performer for their offense during each campaign while showing steady production improvements each year. A compact and low center of gravity runner, Neal utilizes his size and build to his advantage. Neal runs behind his blockers as a runner, showing good patience while pressing the line of scrimmage before exploding through openings. Excellent vision allows him to sense his surroundings well in space. Dynamic in the open field, showing both the 2nd level vision and the slippery running style that makes him very difficult to bring down when there are lots of greens. Neal does a nice job of minimizing his contact area when running north/south and staying on his feet through contact. A decisive runner who wastes little time in the backfield, showing quick feet and reliable decision-making. Flexibility through the lower half allows him to be a true game-changing back that can turn something out of nothing, showing rare agility and change of directional abilities. Constantly makes defenders miss at all levels. Understands how to alter his speed at different areas of the field to buy himself additional spacing down the field. An excellent receiver that shows naturalness as a pass catcher, used in various ways. He's dynamic on wheel routes and screens when he can utilize his athleticism to be a nightmare mismatch in space against inferior athletes. Possesses upside in pass protection, displaying good awareness and willingness to stay square through impact.

Weaknesses: Neal is a lean runner who lacks ideal body armor on his frame to handle 20+ carries a back and could be viewed strictly as a 3rd down runner or change of pace back. Not a power back and struggles in short-yardage or when defenses put eight defenders in the box, failing to win consistently with power. Stops his legs upon impact, failing to push piles forward or pick up additional yardage through contact. Quicker than he is, he lacks the elite home-run speed to take the top off defenses. Shows upside as a pass protector but lacks the necessary POP and point of attack power and could benefit from more experience and technique work. Runs a limited route tree as a pass catcher and could benefit by continuing to add additional tools to his route-running arsenal.

Best Fit: Change of pace back

Player Ranking (1-100): 76.0 - Neal is an explosive and fun back for an offense that deserves 15-20 touches a game as both a runner and receiving back. If he continues to add good weight and strength onto his frame, there's no reason he can't contribute immediately as a rookie, possibly even start games. 3rd round player.

13. DJ Giddens - Kansas State - 6'1 212 lbs

Strengths: A 2-year starter and 3-year contributor to the Wildcats offense, Giddens has been incredibly productive in the Big 12 for three straight seasons. He's rushed for over 1200 yards in the last two seasons. A well-built runner with good size and density on his frame has room for additional growth. He is a durable runner who hasn't missed a game during his 3 years at Kansas State, showing reliability and toughness. Giddens is a late riser with a massive ceiling, and he didn't start playing high school until his sophomore season in high school. Giddens is a north-south runner who maximizes opportunities when working between the tackles. He shows outstanding vision and patience as he sets up his runs, pressing the line of scrimmage. His outstanding shiftiness and agility enable him to adjust quickly and choose a new cutback opportunity if it arrives. He can make guys miss in a phone booth, regularly breaking the ankles of safeties and linebackers who attempt to take him on head-on. He does a terrific job absorbing contact and staying on his feet through contact. He has excellent 0-10 yard quickness, showing good burst and core strength to fit through narrowly expiring windows. He has a nose for the end zone, as evidenced by his 13 touchdowns in 2023. A natural receiver who shows impressive route running upside to create spacing and separation against linebackers. He routinely extends and snatches the ball away from his frame, showing soft and reliable hands.

Weaknesses: Giddens is far quicker in short spaces than truly dynamic. He often creates for himself in the open field and then gets tracked down from behind by defensive backs, showing subpar long speed. He tends to run very upright when working between the tackles, playing with high pads and allowing himself to absorb unnecessary contact frequently. He's not a power back, and he cannot consistently push piles or win in short-yardage situations. He's still growing into his frame and gaining experience and will likely need more time in an NFL-style offensive system. Giddens is limited right now as a pass protector and will likely need more recognition work.

Best Fit: Potential Starting RB

Player Ranking (1-100): 74.7 - I like Giddens quite a bit. He's probably the most shifty runner in this draft class and offers true creative abilities as a runner. His upside is massive as he gains more experience. He will need some time and likely split carries early on before he proves he can be a true bellcow. 4th round player.

14. Cameron Skattebo - Arizona State - 5'9 225 lbs

Strengths: Skattebo was a 2-year starter for FCS-level Sacramento State before transferring to Arizona State to play his final two seasons. Skattebo has had a stellar college career, showcasing outstanding production for two programs in three conferences. A short but compactly built runner, Skattebo utilizes his size and natural leverage to his advantage. When working between the tackles, Skattebo maintains low pads and minimizes his surface area to bounce off tackle attempts and stay on his feet. Requires committed tackle attempts to bring him down, as he has terrific contact balance. Has some suddenness to the way he runs, showing the ability to shift between tackles and change directions with impressive lateral mobility. A patient runner who waits for holes to develop before picking, showing impressive vision to pick right generally. At the 2nd level, Skattebo's physicality and toughness are on display as he looks for contact, staying on his feet through ankle swipers. Has been used in a variety of wildcat-style offensive plays throughout college, showing his versatility to be used as a gadget player. Has shown impressive ability as a receiver to pick up considerable yardage after the catch when used on screens and swing passes. As a pass protector, Skattebo shows good competitive toughness and physicality to stay square and sustain blocks well.

Weaknesses: Skattebo is not built like a true running back and has almost a FB frame. His overall athleticism and movement skills are average, as he lacks any burst on receipt of the ball. He's not a guy who will threaten to take plays to the house at the next level, as he lacks great long speed or home-running ability. He struggles to make defenders miss, and he routinely takes on a lot of contact. As a receiver, he will need to continue to widen out his route arsenal to be used on more than simple routes.

Best Fit: Change of pace back and short-yardage

Player Ranking (1-100): 74.2 - Skattebo is an intriguing player who has been dominant at the college level. His skill set makes me wonder how translatable it'll be at the next level, but at the same time, he's got some impressive traits, and he's a hardworking blue-chip kid who will earn his place. He will likely have to prove his worth in camp and win on special teams reps. He is a fourth-round player.

15. Ollie Gordon II - Oklahoma State - 6'2 225 lbs

Strengths: A 2-year starter for the Cowboys and former Heisman Trophy contender in 2023, Gordon rose to prominence during that campaign, rushing for over 1700 yards and 21 touchdowns. Gordon possesses an NFL frame, showing good density and power throughout. As a runner, Gordon is incredibly patient, following his blocks and choosing the right option. He sees things quickly behind the line of scrimmage, showing good pre-snap and post-snap vision. Gordon is a downhill thumping back who loves to lower his shoulder and deliver pop-on impact against tacklers. He's proven to have reliable ball security, with very few fumbles on his resume despite the amount of carries he's received. A strong and powerful lower body enables him to stay on his feet through impact, providing impressive contact balance. He is a build-up speed athlete who possesses secondary gear once he sees daylight. Has been impressive when utilized as a receiving back, showing the ability to run various routes while having naturally soft hands. A willing pass protector shows good pre-snap instincts and awareness to pick up blitzers and stay square through impact while absorbing.

Weaknesses: Gordon can sometimes be overly patient, waiting too long in moments before he picks a lane. Due to this, he gets caught in the backfield for many negative plays. Following his stellar sophomore season, Gordon's final campaign was disappointing, with significantly decreased production in every metric. Gordon isn't a very explosive back, as he lacks the top-end acceleration upon receipt of the ball. This limits him in short-yardage situations as he fails to have the decisive quickness needed to get the yardage needed. His high-hipped frame limits him when changing directions, as he often needs to gear down when changing course, allowing defenders to reach his frame.

Best Fit: Potential Starting RB and special teams

Player Ranking (1-100): 73.2 - Unfortunately, Gordon's draft stock fell quite a bit this year. His weaknesses were highlighted far more. Gordon is a good back that lacks the elite traits to be a bellcow immediately for a team. His size and toughness as a runner will likely offer him a chance to earn a role for his team quickly. 4th round player.

16. Damien Martinez - Miami - 5'11 241 lbs

Strengths: Martinez was a 2-year starter for Oregon State, rushing for nearly 2200 yards during his two campaigns. Following his sophomore season, Martinez transferred to Miami, where he was immediately the star bellcow back for the Hurricanes, impressing immediately. One of the youngest players in this draft class, Martinez, just turned 21 years old. Martinez has a completely stacked physique, with minimal unnecessary weight, showing outstanding proportional density. Martinez shows surprising burst and acceleration in the backfield for being as large as he is. He's patient upon receipt of the ball, looking and scanning the 1st level before making any decision. If he notices cutback opportunities, Martinez displays the agility and change of direction to reverse course. A creative runner who can win with both finesse and power. Martinez shows the ability to consistently make the 1st defender miss in the backfield, rarely going down upon first contact. He is a tenacious back that runs like a hammer in search of a nail in the open field, inviting contact and lowering his shoulder. He finishes his runs and fights with competitive toughness for every possible inch. He sees things well at the 2nd level, showing good open-field vision and instincts in space. Martinez is terrific in short-yardage situations and the red zone, showing decisiveness and nonstop leg drive to push piles and win necessary yardage. While Martinez was fairly limited as a receiver, he's improved in each subsequent campaign. He has the frame to be a reliable pass protector with additional experience and technique.

Weaknesses: Martinez's size causes some challenges regarding the explosive arenas of playing running back. While he has a good burst, considering his size, he lacks the top-end burst and long speed to consistently threaten as a home-run hitter. He tends to be too patient sometimes in the backfield, allowing defenders to reach his frame before he makes up his mind. When working between the tackles, Martinez can expose too much of his frame, failing always to minimize surface area and drop his pads. A limited receiver that has been mostly used on screens and simple out-routes. Despite being the size to be an effective pass protector, Martinez plays upright far too often and allows defenders to bounce off him. He fails to latch on, stay square, and sustain blocks consistently when used in protection.

Best Fit: Potential Starting RB with ideally a change of pace back working alongside him

Player Ranking (1-100): 73.1 - Martinez is a physical and downhill thumper who ideally would work in a split-carry running back committee. He can certainly handle the rigors of NFL life, and his ability to stay on the field for the last three seasons is proof of that. 4th round player.

17. Donovan Edwards - Michigan - 6'0 210 lbs

Strengths: A former five-star recruit who has significantly contributed to the Wolverines backfield in the last four seasons. Edwards had his best season as a sophomore in 2022, in which he finished just under 1000 yards rushing at 7.1 yards per attempt and added another 200 yards receiving. Edwards is built with a solid frame, showing adequate room for additional muscle and girth. Edwards is the definition of a dual-threat, showing outstanding versatility as a receiver. He shows nuance as a receiver, running routes as a receiver in the slot and showing true reliability other than an emergency option. He is an excellent hand catcher who can easily extend and snatch the ball from his frame. A big-play back, Edwards has take-it-to-the-house speed and explosiveness. Dynamic when used on manufactured plays, showing dynamism on screens and option-style plays. Has the cutback ability and lateral explosiveness to win between the tackles and outside the hashes. Loose limbs and agility allow him to change direction and alter his course without losing build-up speed. Runs behind his pads and shrugs off ankle swipers. Runs with good tempo and patience, timing his burst to perfection. Comfortable playing in different running systems, showing comfort with zone and gap concepts. A willing blocker that shows toughness and willingness to be used in clear passing settings.

Weaknesses: Edwards has been part of a running back committee most of his career, failing to be a true bellcow consistently. Hasn't quite lived up to the production of his sophomore campaign, appearing to regress the last couple of seasons. Has battled nagging injuries throughout college, albeit he showed toughness by playing through injuries. While he's explosive and has agility throughout his frame, he's mostly a 'take what the defense gives' kind of back that lacks true creativity. He can sometimes be too patient, missing expiring lanes or taking the wrong opening. Lacks ideal contact balance and will go down to solo tacklers far too often, failing to stay on his feet consistently through tough windows. As a pass protector, he's raw and lacks the recognition skills to position himself properly. Doesn't sustain his speed well and appears to tire out on long runs, allowing defenders to catch him from behind.

Best Fit: Change of pace back

Player Ranking (1-100): 72.9 - Edwards is a good north/south runner who offers exceptional upside as a receiver. He's been a steady contributor while not being consistently dominant. He should have a real shot to compete as a #2 back for a team immediately. 4th round player.

18. Bhayshul Tuten - Virginia Tech - 5'11 209 lbs

Strengths: Tuten started his career with North Carolina A&T before transferring to Virginia Tech for the 2023 campaign. Tuten dominated the ACC this season, especially before his ankle injury, finishing at nearly 1200 yards rushing and 15 rushing touchdowns. Tuten is built with a low center of gravity frame, featuring good density through his lower body. He does most of his damage between the tackles, showing decisiveness and outstanding burst. A former track athlete, Tuten has blazing speed when he sees a glimmer of daylight, and he sustains his speed very well on longer runs. Tuten follows his blocks while running behind his pads, utilizing his natural leverage advantage to minimize surface area. He has very good contact balance when working between the tackles, exploiting narrow gaps and staying on his feet through contact. He falls forward through impact, grinding and fighting for additional yards through contact. He is a multi-speed runner with a 5th gear that he maximizes when hitting holes. Terrific open-field vision and shiftiness in the open field enable him to change directions and flip his hips with relative ease. Has proven to be a dynamic return specialist with two kickoff returns for touchdowns in 2023. Tuten flashes upside in the passing game, showing soft hands and a natural route-running upside. He routinely separated from linebackers down the field, showing naturalness and 3-down upside. He is a dynamic screenback who can maximize opportunities, given that he has the ball in his hands.

Weaknesses: While Tuten has good overall strength through his frame, he lacks punch and power as a bellcow runner. He suffered a bad ankle injury this season that he played through, but it appeared to have a noticeable effect on his explosiveness as a runner. Tuten is a better creator in the open field than in the backfield, as he lacks elite agility and creative attributes to make guys miss behind the line. He struggles to find cutback opportunities, lacking top-end vision in the backfield. Offers little as an east/west runner and tends to keep all his runs between the tackles. Tuten has had some ball security concerns, as he can be a little reckless and loose at moments. Tuten is a major liability in pass protection at this moment in time, lacking both power and recognition abilities to be relied upon. While he flashes upside as a receiver, he has been used sparingly and lacks a diversified route tree.

Best Fit: Change of pace back

Player Ranking (1-100): 71.7 - Tuten impressed me on tape. As long as his ankle injury concerns don't appear to be a reoccurring issue, I think Tuten will immediately be a dynamic return specialist and change of pace back. He is a fun player to watch. He is a fourth-round player.

19. Jordan James - Oregon- 5'10 210 lbs

Strengths: James was a change of pace back for the Ducks during his first two years on campus before finally taking over as the bellcow in 2024, finishing with over 1200 yards of rushing and an additional 200+ yards of receiving. James is a compact and low center of gravity runner that runs between his pads. While he lacks typical NFL measurables for a bellcow, James runs with surprising amounts of physicality and toughness. James is a patient north/south runner who reads what's available while scanning other possibilities. James utilizes his natural leverage advantage to minimize surface area and stay on his feet through contact. He runs downhill and requires committed tackle attempts, as he will easily shrug off ankle swipers. James is willing to drop his shoulders in the open field and deliver punishing blows to tacklers. James has quick feet and can destroy angles from linebackers and safeties in the open field. He runs the ball with urgency and intensity on every snap, leans forward, and fights for every additional yard. He has a knack for picking up yards in short-yardage and the red zone, showing good competitive toughness. James has proven to be a valuable three-down weapon in the receiving games, running various routes for the Ducks offense. He shows soft hands while proving to be a good last-minute option for his QB on broken-down plays.

Weaknesses: James lacks significant experience as a bellcow and is only a 1-year starter. He's mostly been used in the passing game when he's on the field for 3rd down, lacking significant experience as a pass protector. When he's used to protect, he's looked a bit lost and needs recognition work. He frequently loses sustain when he makes initial contact. James fails to have the ideal vision and can miss cutback opportunities at the 1st level. While James has some big plays on his resume, he fails to ideal top-end burst and speed to offer significant home-run abilities at the next level.

Best Fit: Potential starter

Player Ranking (1-100): 71.0 - James is a good back who is likely best suited in a split-carry running back committee. His lack of pass protection experience and his lack of explosiveness as a runner means he will likely have to earn himself a spot as a backup initially. 4th round player.

20. LeQuint Allen Jr - Syracuse - 6'0 201 lbs

Strengths: As a 2-year starter for Orange, Allen rushed for over 1000 yards during each campaign. Allen had a tremendous season in 2024, finishing with over 1500 yards from scrimmage, including 500+ as a receiver. Allen is a lean and twitched-up back that offers 3-down ability at the next level. As a runner, Allen excels in working north/south. He wastes little time in the backfield, getting downhill quickly while immediately getting to top gear. His vision and loose lower body enable him to cut back and redirect his frame if there are better pathways. His burst and acceleration enable him to run away from defenders when working outside the hashes. He navigates well in tight spaces, showing the ability to minimize surface area. Allen has a knack for big plays in the open field, showing tremendous open-field agility. He plays far bigger than his listed size and repeatedly puts his shoulders down to roll over defenders and break tackles in space. He is excellent in the red zone and repeatedly sacrifices his body to extend and jump over defenders. Allen will only be 20 years old on draft day and 21 shortly before the start of his rookie season. He plays every snap with urgency and intent, utilizing a HOT motor. He's shown iron-man reliability throughout his 3-year career, not missing one game. Allen excels most in the receiving game, proving his ability to alter games out wide or in the backfield. He's a dynamic screenback who disguises them well while also showing the ability to maximize his available openings consistently. He frequently lines up in the slot on the outside in empty formations, showing impressive receiver-like route running and precision. His soft hands enable him to extend and make plays outside his frame.

Weaknesses: Allen dominated in the ACC but didn't consistently compete against top-tier defenses during his two years. He also lacks an ideal running back physique and could benefit by continuing to maximize his frame with additional girth and muscle. He will likely be limited to playing in a split-back role due to his frame, notwithstanding the rigors of a bellcow. Allen can play a bit too upright when working in space, enabling defenders to knock him off balance easily. He's a 1-speed runner, quicker in short spurts than he is truly dynamic in the open field. His lack of pass protection experience is a concern, as he generally was used as an additional receiver in passing situations.

Best Fit: Change of pace back

Player Ranking (1-100): 70.8 - Allen is a terrific option for a team wanting a guy who can get 10-15 touches a game. He maximizes every chance, and his ability to be used as an additional receiver makes him incredibly versatile. 4th round player.

21. Tahj Brooks - Texas Tech - 5'10 220 lbs

Strengths: A significant contributor to the Texas Tech offense for five straight seasons, Brooks has been atop Big 12 rushing categories in each of the last two seasons, finishing with over 1500 yards in both seasons. Brooks is a low center-of-gravity runner with a dense frame and outstanding strength. Brooks is a between-the-tackle north/south bulldozer who runs behind his pads, minimizing his surface area and staying on his feet through contact. Upon receipt of the ball, Brooks scans his available openings and remains patient while waiting for the best option. He does his best work in crowded boxes, showing extreme effectiveness in short-yardage situations, keeping his legs churning through impact. Has proven consistency and sturdiness throughout the last four seasons, proving the ability to carry the load in a high-volume system. Brooks is an effective blocker with good recognition skills and good pop behind his hands. He anchors down well, showing the ability to stay square and absorb. Despite a lack of significant pass volume, Brooks has shown upside when handling the role. He has soft hands and is effective with the ball post-catch.

Weaknesses: Brooks has significant wear and tear on his frame in college, having carried the ball around 600 times in the last two seasons alone. Brooks is a 1-speed runner that lacks noticeable short-area burst and acceleration. His home-run threat is limited, as he also lacks top-end speed. He's frequently tracked down from behind with daylight in front of him, proving his big-play potential at the next level is limited. He's not a creator with the ball, and he struggles to make defenders miss both at the 1st level and in space. He can occasionally be too indecisive behind the line, causing gaps to close and get caught in the backfield. As a pass catcher, Brooks is limited and needs significant volume and route work before being relied upon.

Best Fit: Power back in a 2-back system

Player Ranking (1-100): 70.4 - Brooks could be an ideal fit for a team with a better niche/change of pace back. Brooks would be the short-yardage, red-zone back, and someone else to fit in elsewhere. He's a good runner who has repeatedly proven it for the last several seasons. He's a tough kid who runs with power! 4th round player.

22. Raheim Sanders - South Carolina - 6'0 230 lbs

Strengths: A 3-year workhorse back for the Razorbacks before transferring to the Gamecocks for his final season. Sanders rose to stardom following his 2022 season, in which he ran for over 1400 yards and received nearly another 300 yards. Sanders is built with a power-packed frame for a workhorse back and has more than enough body armor. A dual threat, Sanders is impressive as a receiving back, showing naturalness and soft hands when splitting wide or running routes out of the backfield. As a runner, Sanders impresses with his vision, showing the propensity to locate and find the narrowest of creases while exploding through them. Sanders can win both between the hashes and to the outside, showing good acceleration and having the long speed to take plays to the house. Dangerous in space, Sanders can run over guys or make them miss. He has terrific contact balance when running between the tackles, easily bouncing off uncommitted tacklers.

Weaknesses: After his 2022 campaign, Sanders lost some of his explosiveness. He hasn't looked the same player following his injury that ended his 2023 campaign at Arkansas. Sanders can waste steps in the backfield at times, doing a little bit too much dancing. Has had ball security issues multiple years in college and can be a little reckless with the ball. While Sanders is a natural hands' catcher, he isn't a guy who will successfully split out wide and threaten defensive backs in space. He has very limited experience in pass protection, as he was often used as a receiver in clear passing situations. While he has the frame to succeed, he will need additional technique and recognition work.

Best Fit: Potential Starting RB

Player Ranking (1-100): 70.1 - Sanders is an intriguing prospect due to his frame and explosiveness. It's rare to see guys with his combination of burst and power. Unfortunately, he's been a bit disappointing since his injury. Hopefully, he can regain his explosiveness because he has a bright ceiling. He's a fourth-round player.

23. Jaydn Ott - California - 5'10 205 lbs

Strengths: A 3-year contributor to the Golden Bears offense, Ott exploded in 2023, finishing with over 1300 yards rushing and 12 rushing touchdowns. Ott is a versatile play-making machine who has also proven his worth as a return specialist, returning a kick in 2023. An explosive home-run hitter, Ott wastes little time or motion in the backfield before planting and exploding downhill. He is a decisive runner who appears to see things quickly in the backfield, generally picking right. He gets to top gear quickly, showing a rare initial burst and acceleration. While he plays in a mostly north-south system, Ott can bounce runs to the perimeter, showcasing elastic-like flexibility through his lower body to change directions and stop/go with ease once he is in space. He is an angle killer who outruns even the most acute angle pursuers due to his long sustained speed down the field. Dynamic in space, Ott can make guys miss in a phone booth with his agility and open-field moves. Ott has shown flashes of brilliance as a receiver at Cal, especially during his freshman campaign, showing the ability to run his routes with urgency and intent. He is dynamic on swings and wheel routes, showing the ability to separate from linebackers up the field while showing reliable hands. As a pass blocker, Ott shows good instincts and a willingness to step up and stay square to rushers.

Weaknesses: Ott had a disappointing final season at Cal, struggling with a lower-body injury all season, causing him to be somewhat limited and lacking that burst he had in 2023. He's a lean, slim runner who lacks the ideal body armor and density on his frame to be a bellcow. He's an upright runner running vertically, exposing his entire frame when working between the tackles. He has a bit of a high-cut frame that causes him to struggle to redirect his frame in congested traffic at the 1st level, as he often takes what's available at his first read. Lack of pop and strength in his frame causes him to struggle in short-yardage situations, failing to generate much movement, not for lack of trying. He occasionally gets tripped up and ankle-swiped when he's in space, easily getting brought down by halfhearted tackle attempts.

Best Fit: Change of pace runner

Player Ranking (1-100): 69.9 - I love Ott's film from 2023. If he can somehow get back to that, he can be a game-changer on offense for a team. His intensity, urgency, and explosiveness are so fun to watch. With his injury-plagued 2024 season, I worry that he might have a hard time getting back to that. 5th round player.

24. Phil Mafah - Clemson - 6'1 230 lbs

Strengths: Mafah had a niche role for the Clemson offense during his first three years on campus before finally taking over in 2024 as the main every-down back. He did not disappoint in his only year starting, finishing with over 1100 yards rushing and eight touchdowns. Mafah has ideal running back measurables, featuring a thick and stout frame capable of handling the rigors of NFL life. He is a grinder who wears defenses out throughout games, getting better as games go on. Mafah is a patient runner in the backfield who scans available openings while looking for cutback opportunities. Upon receipt of the ball, Mafah quickly gets downhill and gets his legs churning. Despite his size, Mafah's good looseness and fleet feet enable him to cross directions and switch gaps. He's difficult to bring down to the ground in 1v1 situations, regularly churning out additional yardage after contact. He's particularly effective in short-yardage and red-zone settings, regularly setting up his runs and showing the competitive toughness to win. Mafah is equally adept in zone and gap concepts, showing versatility for different NFL offenses. Despite not having significant stats as a receiving back, Mafah has shown upside when used. He has a natural feel as a screenback, showing good open-field vision to create big plays.

Weaknesses: Mafah has had an ongoing shoulder issue that will likely need monitoring and evaluation pre-draft. Mafah is a long strider that takes a bit to get going, lacking elite burst and home-run abilities. He isn't a creator in the open field or the backfield, and he tends to 'take what the defense' gives the type of back. He rarely makes defenders miss in space, lacking ideal finesse as a runner. Very reliant on overpowering and winning with physicality and power. He shows upside as a pass protector but lacks ideal recognition and technique.

Best Fit: Change of pace back

Player Ranking (1-100): 69.5 - Mafah is a solid physical specimen who ideally would fit in a running back committee where he can take on the bulk of the carries while partnering with a more explosive number 2 back. 5th round player.

25. Tre Stewart - Jacksonville State - 5'10 192 lbs

Strengths: Stewart began his career with the Division II program Limestone before entering the transfer portal before the 2024 campaign. He transferred to Jacksonville State, where he finished atop Conference USA running back production, finishing with over 1600 yards rushing and 25 touchdowns. Stewart is a smaller but explosively built runner who excels when working between the tackles. He utilizes good patience as he waits for the best expiring lane, always following his blockers. Once he sees daylight, Stewart utilizes his outstanding burst to explode through lanes. His secondary burst and long speed enable him to break off big chunk plays, destroying advantageous angles from both linebackers and safeties. Stewart shows looseness throughout his frame, allowing him to alter and redirect his frame if he finds a better opportunity when pressing the line of scrimmage. As a smaller back, Stewart maximizes his frame with toughness and competitive drive. He keeps his legs churning through impact, grinding additional yardage after contact. In the open field, Stewart displays good shiftiness and change of directional skills to alter course without gearing down. Stewart has been used in various roles as a receiver, including lining up in the slot or being used out of the backfield. He has soft hands and can be a reliable last option for a quarterback.

Weaknesses: The biggest concern for Stewart will be his lack of competition against top-tier opposition, racking up yards against Division II programs and lesser Conference USA programs this past season. He's a slight runner lacking bulk and ideal density through his frame. He's taken significant carries over the last few seasons, building up a lot of wear and tear on his smaller frame. As a pass protector, Stewart shows willingness but lacks the point-of-attack strength to consistently hold up and sustain blocks.

Best Fit: Change of pace back

Player Ranking (1-100): 68.9 - Stewart is an intriguing running back prospect who deserves more love and attention. He's slight, but he's a dynamic runner who should 100% have a chance to compete for a role next season as a rookie. His explosive twitch, creativity as a runner, and better-than-expected toughness are impressive! You can't ignore the production he had this season, as it's been elite. I like this kid and take him in the 5th round.

26. Nate Noel - Missouri - 5'10 190 lbs

Strengths: A 4-year contributor to Sun Belt school Appalachian State, Noel transferred to Missouri for his final season in 2024. Noel played in a split-backfield with the Tigers this year, but he still maximized his opportunities rushing for over 5 yards per carry and 800 yards. Noel is a short and athletically built runner with terrific athleticism and twitch. Before receipt of the ball, Noel scans the defense and quickly identifies looks. He utilizes his anticipation and vision to find the best opportunity and explodes. Noel is a creator in the backfield, capable of making something out of nothing with subtle footwork and shiftiness to make defenders miss. He is a decisive runner who wastes little time in the backfield, and his redirect ability enables him to cut back if another opportunity arrives. He is a former high school track athlete, which shows in his ability to go from 0 to 60 in a flash. When he sees an ounce of daylight, Noel turns on the jets and gets to top speed quickly. In the open field, Noel's loose-limbed frame and change of directional skills enable him to re-route his frame and alter his course. Noel maximizes his frame with good contact balance and competitive toughness. He keeps his feet churning upon impact and can grind out additional yards, particularly in short yardage. Noel has proven reliable ball security with no fumbles in the last two seasons. Noel keeps a solid base in pass protection and quickly identifies blitz pickup. He's generally a sound blocker who takes his assignment seriously, showing good toughness and instincts.

Weaknesses: Noel has obvious size limitations and lacks the ideal bulk and body armor on his frame to be a bellcow runner. Noel possesses limited receiving experience, and when he's used it, it's been mostly as a last-case check-down option. He must widen out his route tree to be a 3-down player at the next level. Noel has had a string of lower body injuries the last few seasons, including a foot and a leg injury that caused him to miss some game time. Noel isn't a physical back, and he's likely not a guy who will handle 15+ carries a game at the next level. He will need to be in a complementary system. While willing to pass protection, he struggles when asked to handle bigger blitzers at the point of attack.

Best Fit: Change of pace back

Player Ranking (1-100): 68.4 - Noel is an explosive back who could develop nicely into a change-of-pace runner at the next level. His twitch, vision, and explosive characteristics could be a valuable commodity for an offense. He proved his ability to have success against better defenses this year, playing in the SEC. He is a fifth-round player.

27. Trevor Etienne - Georgia - 5'9 205 lbs

Strengths: The younger brother of former Clemson RB Travis Etienne, Trevor, began his career at Florida for two seasons before transferring to the Bulldogs for his final season in 2024. Etienne has played in mostly a split-backfield throughout his college career, proving to be a dynamic complementary back. Etienne is incredibly explosive in short spurts, showing both lateral twitch and a good initial burst. Etienne has outstanding vision and can press the line of scrimmage while scanning potential other openings. He utilizes explosive jump cuts to reverse and alter course if a better opening presents itself. Once he reaches daylight, he senses his surroundings well, anticipating both 1st and 2nd level blocks. His natural leverage advantage enables him to minimize his surface area when working between the line of scrimmage, making space for himself when little is presenting. Etienne is a creator with the ball in the backfield, utilizing rare start/stop ability and wiggle to make the 1st defender miss. He can manipulate angles from defenders in the open field, altering speed and setting up his runs. In the passing game, Etienne has shown to be a versatile weapon. He effectively runs wheel routes and other simple shallow routes, showing good route-running ability and soft hands. He's proven to be a safe ball carrier with minimal fumbles on his resume. He's comfortable in congested windows and can extend and snatch it with his hands. Etienne has significant experience as a return specialist.

Weaknesses: Etienne is slight and lacks the ideal power profile for a bellcow at the next level. His production throughout the school has been marginal, never rushing for more than 753 years in a season. Etienne can be too reliant on bouncing his runs to the perimeter, often doing too much in the backfield. His contact balance is below average, and he's frequently tripped up by ankle swipers in space. He's quicker than he is and lacks the top-end speed to be a true home-run hitter. He's had some character concerns that will need to be looked into. He's struggled with minor injury wiggles, including a rib issue in 2024. As a receiver, Etienne needs to diversify and add to his route tree, as he only has a few simple routes he runs. At this point, Etienne is a liability in pass protection, failing to absorb and sustain as a blocker.

Best Fit: Change of pace back

Player Ranking (1-100): 67.5 - Etienne is the definition of a finesse runner who cannot be a bellcow. He could be a terrific #2 option for a team that wants a RB committee. I like his traits as long as his off-the-field concerns check out OK during the interview process. 5th round player.

28. Corey Kiner - Cincinnati - 5'10 213 lbs

Strengths: Kiner was recruited first to LSU, where he shared a part of a multiback committee as a freshman before transferring to Cincinnati and playing the last three seasons for them. Kiner has had back-to-back outstanding seasons, rushing for over 1,000 yards in each campaign. Kiner has a bowling ball build with a low center of gravity and thick limbs. He plays in a pistol offense that relies mostly on outside-zone concepts and makes the most of his opportunities. Kiner is quick in short spurts, getting to top gear quickly. He has the change of directional abilities and good vision to cut back and alter his course at the 1st level. His contact balance is his best attribute, frequently bouncing off tackle attempts to stay on his feet. He utilizes his natural leverage advantage to minimize surface area between tackles. He runs behind his pads and will deliver pop upon impact to defenders, churning his legs to grind out additional yards. In the open field, Kiner shows good, elusive traits and can make guys miss in space. He has proven excellent ball security with only four fumbles the last two seasons despite nearly 400 carries. A willing pass protector that shows the ability to recognize pre-snap looks. He stays square and proves to absorb well. A durable iron-man that has not missed hardly any game time with no injury concerns during the last four seasons.

Weaknesses: Kiner lacks an ideal running back frame and lacks the frame of a bellcow at the next level. Kiner is much more explosive in short spaces than he is truly explosive. His long speed is a major hurdle as he's frequently chased down from behind, lacking the home-run hitting abilities. He's not a creator with the ball in his hands and tends to be a 'take what is available' runner. Kiner has been used sparingly as a receiver and has a minimal route tree. Kiner has taken a major beating in the last couple of years and has major wear and tear on his frame.

Best Fit: Power back in a RB committee

Player Ranking (1-100): 65.8 - It's hard to ignore Kiner's production playing for a Power-5 program in the last two seasons. He lacks elite physical characteristics, but he's a darn good runner between the tackles. He should have a significant chance to be part of a RB committee and immediately warrant some preseason snaps. 5th round player.

29. Nate Carter - Michigan State - 5'10 202 lbs

Strengths: Carter began his career at Connecticut for two seasons, starting games as a redshirt freshman. After his third season on campus, Carter transferred to Michigan State and played for the Spartans the last two seasons. Carter displays a compact and low center of gravity of frame capable of handling the rigors of NFL life. He's mostly a 1-cut runner who shows decisiveness and vision when hitting the hole. Carter remains open to alternative routes, keeping his eyes fixated on cutback opportunities. He's capable of making guys miss in the backfield or the open field, showing good shiftiness and change of direction. Carter can win between the tackles or on the outside, showing good burst and acceleration to work the field's boundaries. Carter runs more physically than expected, with a downhill and aggressive style capable of fighting for additional yards through contact. He churns his legs through contact, allowing him to fall forward effectively on short yardage. As a receiver, Carter has taken advantage of opportunities despite lacking opportunities. He's a reliable hands catcher who can successfully run elementary routes while showing the potential for expanded opportunities. A reliable pass protector with good toughness and recognition skills to pick up free rushers. He generally stays square and can absorb well.

Weaknesses: He suffered a shoulder injury in his redshirt freshman season in 2022, causing him to miss most of the season. Carter has been mostly in a running back committee throughout his college career, failing to have more than 800 yards rushing in any season. His production and yards per carry numbers during his final season showed regression. Carter is quicker than he is truly explosive and repeatedly gets chased down from behind when he sees daylight. His limited experience and expanded route tree leave his receiving upside somewhat in question. He lacks any dynamism as a runner, lacking elite physical or athletic qualities. While his vision is mostly good, there are glimpses of significant missed opportunities in the backfield.

Best Fit: Change of pace back

Player Ranking (1-100): 64.2 - Carter is a quick and versatile runner who is mostly adept at everything. He lacks defining qualities or attributes, but his ability to be useful everywhere is certainly enticing. He is a sixth-round player.

30. Ja'Quinden Jackson - Arkansas - 6'2 230 lbs

Strengths: Jackson is a former high school quarterback who began his career in Utah. Following his freshman season, he transitioned into being a full-time runner, and he played there for an additional two seasons before transferring to Arkansas for his final campaign. Jackson is a dense and thickly-built runner far exceeding the size thresholds for NFL backs. Jackson is a physical and downhill runner, and he does most of his damage when working between the tackles. Jackson looks for contact and drops his shoulders, forcing committed tackle attempts. For a bigger runner, Jackson does a good job of minimizing his surface area and getting skinny through expiring lanes. He runs behind his bands and maintains excellent contact balance to stay on his feet through traffic. A decisive runner who utilizes good footwork and little wasted movement in the backfield. At the 1st level, Jackson does a good job remaining patient as he presses the line of scrimmage, conscious of cutback opportunities. Jackson keeps his legs churning through contact, capable of consistently winning in short-yardage situations. Jackson shows some shiftiness upon receipt of the ball, capable of making the 1st guy miss behind the line of scrimmage. He's best utilized in a zone-style system as he has terrific 1st and 2nd level vision and can alter his course. Jackson is a willing pass protector with the size and physicality to continue growing into it.

Weaknesses: Jackson is still growing into the position and learning the finer nuances of playing the position. Jackson missed two games during his final season for an ankle concern. He's never been a top-end production guy throughout college and has mostly been part of a split-carry committee. Jackson lacks elite physical explosiveness; his burst and overall long speed are average. He can sometimes be a little reckless with the ball on his carries, leading to some poor fumbles. As a runner, Jackson is upright, leaving his frame exposed to take unnecessary hits. As a pass protector, Jackson is willing and able but cannot adjust on the fly and can be late to recognize things. He's been used sparingly in the receiving game, with only about 200 career yards throughout college.

Best Fit: Short-yardage and occasional power back

Player Ranking (1-100): 61.9 - Jackson has a big and bruising frame and is certainly physically capable of playing at the next level. However, he lacks any overly exciting physical attributes to have consistent success at the next level. His best chance is to be on special teams and consistently take advantage of short-yardage carries. He could eventually be part of an RB committee, in which he is used as the physical bruiser. He is a sixth-round player.

31. Marcus Yarns - Delaware - 5'11 190 lbs

Strengths: Yarns is a 2-year starter for FCS-level Delaware who has rushed for nearly 1800 yards and an additional 600 yards receiving in the last two seasons combined. Yarns is a lean and athletically built runner with outstanding burst and speed. He takes advantage of the tiniest creases to break off big runs, showing elite 0-10 quickness and long speed to threaten to take it to the house with every touch. Yarns best operates in zone runs, enabling him to press the line of scrimmage while utilizing his patience to re-route or change course if needed. His frame allows him to minimize his surface area while showing agility and quickness in tight spaces. He plays the game more physically than expected, showing the ability to shrug off arm tackles and ankle swipers. He's proven extremely reliable with the football, with only two career fumbles on his resume. Yarns proves to be a reliable receiving back that can run effective routes from various alignments. He's a mismatch against linebackers, and he can find space repeatedly.

Weaknesses: Yarns hasn't competed against top-tier competition, and the jump up in levels will be a major hurdle for Yarns. Considering the competition he went up against, he didn't have elite production and had a bit of a down final campaign. Yarns is slight and will likely be limited to a niche role at the next level. As a pass protector, Yarns is willing, but he's overstaffed repeatedly. He struggles consistently anchoring and staying square to blitzers, often getting bowed over. As a runner, Yarns lacks ideal creativity. He frequently takes advantage of his available openings while relying on his speed in the open field. He doesn't consistently make defenders miss and often needs to gear down when attempting to change course.

Best Fit: Change of pace back

Player Ranking (1-100): 58.4 - Yarns is an explosive back who should have a chance to earn a role as a change of pace back and possibly a return specialist. 7th round player.

32. Jaydon Blue - Texas - 6'0 200 lbs

Strengths: Blue has been a major contributor to the Lornhorns backfield in the last two seasons. He finished his final season in 2024 with over 730 yards rushing and another 360 yards receiving. Blue is a former four-star athlete who excelled at both football and track in high school. Blue is a dynamic, game-changing, explosive threat who takes it to the house with every touch he has. Capable of running between the tackles or bouncing his runs to the outside, Blue has easy acceleration and stop/go explosiveness. His lateral mobility enables him to easily change directions and re-route his frame without needing to gear down. While Blue isn't a powerback, he has enough toughness and competitive drive to break tackles and stay on his feet through impact. He does a terrific job of maximizing his frame with urgency and leg drive, churning his legs through contact. Once Blue reaches space, he showcases his open-field vision and shiftiness. He can make defenders miss in a phone booth, showing impressive creativity in space. Even when safeties and linebackers take good angles to the ball, he is an angle destroyer. His receiving upside and naturalness will be an enticing factor for teams. He can line up in the slot or the backfield and find space. He shows outstanding hands and above-average route-running ability.

Weaknesses: Blue's overall production throughout college has been marginal at best. He's never been tasked with carrying the load completely. He's struggled with nagging lower body issues that have caused him some games. He had repeated knee issues in high school. He's had significant issues in the last two seasons due to his ball security concerns, causing him to get benched. Blue lacks elite contact balance and strength when defenders can reach his frame, failing to stay on his feet through impact consistently. He's not a runner you'll want to be tasked with pass protection responsibilities, as he lacks the anchorage ability and point-of-attack strength to sustain blitzers.

Best Fit: Change of pace back

Player Ranking (1-100): 56.0 - Blue is an athlete first and a football player second. He needs to improve on so many aspects of playing the game. His explosiveness and ability to be an effective receiver out of the backfield will enable him to get drafted. He did perform his best under the biggest lights. He should compete as a #3 back as a rookie. 7th round player.

33. Roman Hemby - Maryland - 6'0 208 lbs

Strengths: Hemby was a 3-year starter for the Terrapins, and he had his best season as a sophomore in 2022, finishing with nearly 1000 yards rushing and 300 yards receiving. A dual-threat runner who can assist both in the running and passing games. Hemby is built like an athlete, proving to be a big-play runner capable of taking plays to the house every chance. Hemby is a 1-speed runner who gets to top gear instantly and sustains his speed well on big plays. As a runner, Hemby is decisive, wasting little movement in the backfield. Sees things developing quickly, proving to have good vision and patience. For being smaller, he does a good job of playing through contact and staying on his feet. His 1-cut ability and shifty hips allow him to make often the first defender miss. With minimal wear and tear, Hemby doesn't have significant carries on his frame. Doesn't go down easily and will shrug off ankle swipers when working between the tackles. Maximizes his frame by running efficiently, keeping his legs churning through contact. As a receiver, Hemby shows naturalness with soft hands and reliability as both a check-down target and a screen threat.

Weaknesses: Hemby is an undersized runner who will likely have to play a niche role or change of pace situation. His production throughout college has been mostly modest, lacking top-end production in the Big Ten. Lack of size and functional power limits him in short-yardage situations, failing to have the ideal push to generate movement. He isn't a guy who is creative as a runner, tending to take what the defense gives him as opposed to creating something out of nothing. He is not elusive or great in the open field, in which he can make 2nd-level defenders consistently miss. As a pass protector, Hemby is limited both in technique and power. He fails to recognize things quickly and lacks the anchorage power to sustain blocks. Has had ball security concerns throughout college, leaving the ball a little loose.

Best Fit: Change of pace back

Player Ranking (1-100): 55.7 - Hemby offers upside as a change of pace back that offers explosiveness and receiving ability. He's not a dynamic runner, but he's certainly got impressive long speed that will maximize what the defense gives him on the opportunities given. 7th round player.

34. Peny Boone - Central Florida - 6'1 232 lbs

Strengths: Boone has played for three different programs in college, beginning with Maryland for his two seasons. Then he transferred to Toledo in the MAC-Confenrece for two seasons before eventually ending up in the Big-12 with UCF. Boone came into NFL discussions following his junior season with Toledo, in which he led the MAC Conference with 1400 yards rushing and added another 200+ yards receiving. Boone is a dense and physical runner with outstanding power and strength through his frame. He's a decisive runner with a good initial burst to press the line of scrimmage. He runs with impressive wiggle for a man of his size, capable of missing the 1st defender miss in space. He stays on his feet when working through traffic, with a powerful lower half that can absorb and stay on his feet through impact. He's a physical tone setter that runs downhill, inviting contact from defenders. A difficult guy to bring down to the ground in 1v1 situations, Boone requires full commitment from tacklers. He runs with urgency and intent on every snap, playing each snap like it's his last. His toughness and physicality are particularly evident in his ability in the red zone and in short-yardage spots. Boone is a natural receiver that offers 3-down abilities. He is comfortable extending and making plays outside of his frame look routine. His route-running abilities are harnessed by his ability to run various routes for his quarterback.

Weaknesses: Boone has had one great season of college production. In all of his other seasons, he's struggled with injuries or was a role player that lacked significant exposure. His injury history is a bit troublesome as he's missed games due to a variety of different niggling injuries, and he required shoulder surgery. Boone hasn't consistently competed against top-tier opposition and took advantage of lesser opposition in the MAC Conference. Boone is an upright rusher who plays with high pads when working between the tackles. He lacks any explosive burst or home-run abilities, and he's frequently caught from behind in open space. While he has the frame and the toughness to be a good pass protector, he has struggled when called upon in college. He lacks the recognition abilities and the proper technique to sustain blocks.

Best Fit: Short-yardage back and special teams

Player Ranking (1-100): 54.3 - Boone likely would have been drafted if he entered the draft following the 2023 season with Toledo. But a disappointing campaign in 2024 will likely cause him to get undrafted. Undrafted free agent.

Top-10 RB's:

1. Ashton Jeanty
2. Omarion Hampton
3. TreVeyon Henderson
4. Kaleb Johnson
5. Quinshon Judkins
6. Dylan Sampson
7. Jarquez Hunter
8. Kalel Mullings

9. Jo'quavious Marks
10. RJ Harvey

Chapter 4

WR's

1. Tetairoa McMillan - Arizona - 6'5 212 lbs

Strengths: A dominant force for the Wildcats offense, McMillan has been amongst the top statistical receivers in college football in the last two seasons, showing outstanding production. A former dominant high school football player who was a five-star recruit and the former highest-ranked signee in Wildcats history. The first thing that stands out about McMillan is his size, displaying both rare height and wingspan. A versatile receiving threat that aligns all over the offensive front, including on the outside and in the slot. A mismatch wherever he is lined up, McMillan is a nightmare defensively that frequently requires double teams. A bad-ball catcher, McMillan utilizes his flexible body control and reliability in contested situations to come up with the ball in the most improbable scenarios. He is comfortable extending and making plays away from his frame, utilizing his catch radius to present a QB-friendly target. A red-zone nightmare that can get vertical with the best of them, winning repeatedly in jump ball scenarios showing rare high-point abilities. He is an excellent ball tracker who makes plays with his back to the ball, showing incredible ball skills. A nuanced route-runner that has quicker-than-expected feet at the top of routes to create separation. He runs his routes with tempo and altering speeds, understanding how always to keep defensive backs guessing. Understands how to find space against the zone, showing an advanced understanding of defenses. Works tirelessly on broken-down plays to find space and openings. Fights hard for additional yardage after the catch, showing good open-field elusiveness and competitive toughness to stay on his feet.

Weaknesses: McMillan's frame could use additional functional strength to better dominate the more physical press corners at the next level. He appears to struggle against guys that can challenge him at the line of scrimmage and re-route him. Comes out of his stance very upright, allowing himself to be disrupted easily. He's a bit long and lanky and could go down too easily by ankle swipers. Not an overly dynamic athlete that will create separation on shorter to intermediate routes, tending to be more of a build-up speed runner. He relies on winning with his size advantage over college defensive backs and could struggle when the size discrepancies aren't as noticeable. McMillan cannot sustain blocks as a blocker, so they are regularly allowed to shed.

Best Fit: Starting 'X' Receiver

Player Ranking (1-100): 89.2 - It's hard not to get excited about McMillan at the next level. Defenses game planned for him week after week, and he still dominated. Even on plays where it was obvious the ball was going to him, he still somehow would come down with it. He has rare physical traits that will only improve with additional seasoning and muscle. He has Pro Bowl potential. 1st round player.

2. Tre Harris - Ole Miss - 6'3 210 lbs

Strengths: A 2-year starter for Louisiana Tech before transferring over to play his final two seasons for Ole Miss. Harris has improved throughout his career, saving his best season for his final season in 2024 for the Rebels. Harris has proven huge success with two programs and different QBs throughout college. With a long-levered and high torso cut build, Harris utilizes his size and length to his advantage on every ball snap. A physical specimen, Harris utilizes body positioning, strength, and physicality to bully defensive backs. Excels against press coverage, Harris utilizes his hand strength and quick feet to beat jams with relative ease. Frequently wins in tight windows, Harris will catch the ball in the most improbable situations and the tiniest margins. One of the best sets of hands I've ever seen in years of evaluating, Harris shows rare comfort in snatching the ball out of the air with one hand. His length, hands, and vertical leaping ability make him a nightmare for defenders in red-zone settings. He is perfectly comfortable extending and making plays far away from his frame. Comfortable and experience playing both inside and outside. Natural ball tracking abilities allow him to quickly locate and track down the ball, even with his back to the ball. His high football IQ allows him to find cushions and space against zone coverage, regularly finding pockets and sitting in for QBs. He has noticeable vertical speed with a secondary gear that allows him to be effectively used on double moves, showing his ability to change his speeds.

Weaknesses: An older prospect who will be 23 years old on draft day. While Harris is good in vertical lines, he's not a guy who will consistently separate vertically and be 'wide open' for quarterbacks who prefer more spacing from their receivers. A long-levered frame causes him issues when working laterally against smaller corners that can mirror him easily on in-breaking routes. It can be a little too handsy and physical at the top of routes and will lead to some PI calls at the next level. While he's OK with the ball in his hands, he's not overly dynamic or a major fear to break significant amounts of tackles. Could still benefit from some finesse and refinement through his routes, as he lacks ideal nuance through his stems.

Best Fit: Starting 'X' Receiver

Player Ranking (1-100): 86.7 - I'm usually not a big fan of receivers who can't consistently separate, but not so with Tre Harris. This kid's ball skills and catch ability are RARE. I don't think QB needs to have any fears about throwing to him in the tiniest of windows because he always somehow catches it. He's an absolute nightmare to deal with on 3rd downs or in red-zone situations. The true definition is an 'X' receiver with NFL readiness immediately. 1st round player.

3. Savion Williams - TCU - 6'5 225 lbs

Strengths: As a 5th-year senior for the Horned Frogs, Williams has shown increased success and production during each subsequent campaign. A long and athletically built specimen, Williams is a versatile playmaker who is a threat whenever he touches the ball. Has a large frame that can continue to add refinement and muscle. Williams can be used on several gadget plays, including in some RPOs and as a wildcat QB. Williams, a former high school QB, is still raw as a receiver but displays a massive ceiling with continued refinement. Williams is at his best when attacking the middle of the field, utilizing his toughness and body to shield and dominate at the catch point. Trustworthy in highly contested settings, Williams wins most 50/50 balls. Dynamic with the ball in his hands, Williams shrugs off uncommitted tackle attempts and fights for every additional yard. Good contact balance through tight windows while falling forward through impact. Slippery in the open field, Williams displays the vision and creates the ability to turn small plays into chunk plays. Terrific body control and ball skills allow him to be a red-zone dynamo, showing the ability to high point and make incredible circus catches against double coverage. Can track the ball comfortably with his back towards the ball, showing anticipation and timing to attack the football at precisely the right moment. A true 'take it to the house' vertical threat, Williams displays the long speed to threaten the back halves of defenses.

Weaknesses: Williams is still raw as a receiver and could use additional refinement regarding the nuances of playing the position. His route tree at this moment in time is slow and is most predicated on deep and intermediate routes. While he has good hands and makes some unbelievable grabs, he's prone to poor concentration drops. For as big a skill set as Williams, his production has been mostly modest, failing to be a dominant college receiver. Has minimal experience in competing against press looks in college and will likely need to work on his release packages. He's not a guy who is going to create significant spacing at the top of his routes due to his frame, winning mostly in very compact windows. Lacks the technique and the competitive toughness to be a dynamic run blocker and will need sizeable improvements to assist at the next level.

Best Fit: Boundary 'X' Receiver

Player Ranking (1-100): 85.9 - I love Williams as a receiver. The kid has an incredibly high ceiling, and while he's still raw, he has insane physical tools. He's a guy that will consistently make plays wherever he's used. If he continues to refine as a route runner while furthering his route tree, he could be a terrific 'X' receiver. 1st round player.

4. Luther Burden III - Missouri - 5'11 205 lbs

Strengths: A 3-year contributor to the Tigers offense and former five-star recruit, Burden had his coming out party as a sophomore in 2023, finishing with over 1200 yards receiving and nine touchdowns. He's also been used as a punt returner, showing tremendous upside as a return specialist with multiple return touchdowns. Burden is a smaller but compactly-built receiver with muscular density throughout his frame, most notably in his lower half. While comfortable playing inside and outside, Burden is dynamic when used as a gadget player or out of the slot. Exploding out of his stance, Buren has rare 1st step quickness. He also displays the speed to threaten vertically. He is an instinctual athlete who is dynamic with the ball in his hands, proving to take runs or short passes to the house, maximizing available yardage on every play. He runs his routes with altered tempo and urgency, consistently finding pockets of space against zone. Against man coverage, Burden shows the change of directional abilities and the fluidity through his frame to turn on a dime while creating moments of separation. Capable of winning both in the shorter/intermediate areas of the field or on deep plays, Burden has both the burst and the long speed to threaten all levels. Don't let his size fool you; Burden is incredibly tough to bring down, regularly bouncing off uncommitted tackles. His dynamism is apparent with the ball in his hands, showing outstanding elusive characteristics while keeping his frame low and compact. His strong hands and concentration allow him to win against bigger defensive backs in the middle of the field, and he shows excellent tracking skills and ball awareness. Shows willingness and competitive toughness as a blocker, regularly sustaining blocks through the whistle in the run game.

Weaknesses: Burden's production has significantly waned as a junior after a dominant sophomore campaign. Although he's willing and has experience playing outside, Burden's size might limit him to slot-only duties at the next level. He hasn't handled many assignments against press coverage and will struggle to keep his frame clean through longer defensive backs. Lack of size and catch radius will likely be difficult in tight windows or contested settings. Quicker than he is fast, Burden has good but not great long speed to challenge NFL athletes consistently. Most of Burden's big plays were manufactured plays designed to get him in space, including many screens. He lacks the refinement and experience as a route runner and will likely need substantial improvements at the next level to consistently win reps against good coverage corners.

Best Fit: Slot receiver

Player Ranking (1-100): 85.4 - Burden is a dynamic, game-changing slot receiver that maximizes every single rep as a player. His ability to gain additional yardage when there's nothing available is incredible. His lower body is built like a running back. He will immediately be a return specialist while winning reps on offense fairly quickly. 1st round player.

5. Emeka Egbuka - Ohio State - 6'1 203 lbs

Strengths: Egbuka is a 4-year significant contributor to the Buckeyes offense after initially being a former top five-star recruit. He was an excellent kick returner immediately as a true freshman before winning the starting job as a sophomore, exploding with over 1100 yards receiving. He is a well-built athlete with dense limbs and a strong lower body, allowing him to be effective with the ball in his hands. A truly versatile player who is often used to carrying the ball as a runner and playing both inside and outside as a receiver. An explosive athlete is known to have 4.3 speed, showing upside for continued usage as a serious threat at the next level. A smart and highly knowledgeable footballer who understands how to find creases and spaces against defenses, frequently taking advantage of soft coverages and zone cushions. Works tirelessly on broken-down plays to always create a QB-friendly target even when he's not open initially. He does most of his damage in the middle of the field and on short/intermediate-based routes showing veteran-like savvy and nuance in the way he runs his routes. He is fearless when attacking the middle of the field, constantly putting his body in harm's way, and isn't afraid to take a big hit. Has had some of his better games in college against better defenses, proving to be a big-game player. An experienced return specialist that showcases the ability to do damage with the ball in his hands, showing good open-field vision and shiftiness. A willing blocker that shows toughness and a fiery demeanor to sustain blocks along the perimeter.

Weaknesses: While Egbuka had a tremendous sophomore campaign, he hasn't quite lived up to his billing in the last two campaigns with the Buckeyes. Has battled through some minor injury concerns in the last couple of seasons, causing some durability concerns. As great of an athlete as he is on paper, I don't see it frequently popping off on tape. He doesn't consistently generate any separation laterally or vertically and hasn't produced many big plays in college. He is a body catcher who struggles to play outside his frame, dropping many catchable balls when extending. Not a guy who has overly strong hands that will win consistently in contested situations.

Best Fit: Slot receiver and Special Teams

Player Ranking (1-100): 84.3 - Egbuka is a highly intelligent and experienced receiver who has regularly been on the field for the Buckeyes since his freshman campaign. He projects best for me as an oversized slot receiver. I'm not as high on him as others are, although I think he can be a very effective NFL slot. 2nd round player.

6. Tez Johnson - Oregon - 5'10 165 lbs

Strengths: Johnson started his career with Troy for three seasons, impressing with them before transferring over and playing his final two campaigns with Oregon. Johnson is a versatile chess piece that has succeeded wherever he's used, proving to be a dynamic return specialist with multiple return touchdowns. Playing with several different starting QBs throughout college, Johnson has had success with each. Johnson is a high-volume receiver who makes his living on short and underneath routes, showcasing his yards-after-catch ability. He does a nice job of utilizing his frame and short-area quickness to win in short spaces. Footwork and route running in both the short and intermediate of the field are very good, showcasing the finesse and transitional quickness to win at the top of routes. High IQ with a knack for finding space against zone looks, showing impressive spatial instincts and awareness. Dynamic in space, Johnson's shiftiness and work in space enable him to turn small chunk plays into game-changing big plays. Quickly out of the blocks, Johnson gets into top gear. Routinely makes circus catches, showcasing his flexible body control and ball-tracking abilities at all levels of the field.

Weaknesses: Johnson is slight and lacks the body armor and durability that teams will covet. Although playing on the outside at the next level, he's likely going to be limited to slot duties and a return specialist at the next level. Johnson gets bullied and easily redirected when handling more physical corners, failing to have the upper body strength and physicality to beat jams. While he's good in space, he struggles to break out of any tackle attempts as he goes down easily. A body catcher who waits for the ball to reach his chest instead of attacking the ball at the catch point. Has had some ball security concerns and can be a little reckless with the ball. Quicker in short spaces than he is fast; he's not a guy who consistently creates separation in straight lines or vertically.

Best Fit: Slot receiver and return specialist

Player Ranking (1-100): 82.5 - Johnson is a very good football player who catches a TON of balls. He's a hardworking kid who has shown multiple coaching staffs his reliability. Despite being small, he plays the game fearlessly. He could be a solid slot receiver and special teams contributor immediately for a team. 2nd round player.

7. Isaiah Bond - Texas - 5'11 180 lbs

Strengths: A former Alabama receiver, Bond transferred to Texas following his sophomore season with the Tide in 2023, in which he finished with nearly 700 yards receiving and four touchdowns. Bond has proven to be the big-time home-run threat for two different programs against top-tier competition. A dynamic down-the-field threat, Bond has track-level explosiveness and speed. Bond has played all over the offensive formation, from the backfield to the slot to the outside, showing rare versatility. Incredibly explosive in short bursts, Bond utilizes his quick hands and sudden-release ability to beat jams at the line of scrimmage. He understands how to vary his route tempo to beat defensive backs at varying points of his stems. Incredibly sudden at the release point, Bond shows the ability to separate on shorter to intermediate routes. A chess piece that is used on runs and screens to rattle off a big play every time he touches the ball. Has the speed to cause concerns for corners, as he frequently draws penalties on vertical routes. Despite being smaller, Bond is fearless in the middle of the field, showing the ability to stay on his feet through contact. Good overall reliability as a hands' catcher, rarely dropping the ball. Dynamic in the open field, showing good field vision and suddenness as a runner to create spacing for himself. Impressive ball skills and flexible body control allow him to adjust to the ball down the field. He does a nice job of staying on his feet through impact, especially when he sees the contact coming. He is a willing stalk blocker who shows good competitive toughness and willingness for his teammates. He has upside as a return specialist, even though he has only done minimally in college.

Weaknesses: Bond hasn't had any statistical seasons that you'd expect for a guy of his skillset, not showing true #1 receiving production in either program. Bond is very small and wiry and can be disrupted at the line of scrimmage and throughout his routes. He gets bullied at the catch point, lacking the strength to be a reliable QB target in contested situations. A lack of size and catch radius might limit him to slot duties at the next level. While he's mostly a reliable catcher of the football, he, at times, can be too reliant on utilizing his body to corral the ball into his frame.

Best Fit: Slot receiver and gadget player

Player Ranking (1-100): 80.9 - Bond is a fun player who can make big plays whenever he touches the ball. He will likely be a gadget player for a team that can play inside initially. The game's physicality might be difficult for him, but his explosiveness should immediately grant him significant opportunities. 2nd round player.

8. Elic Ayomanor - Stanford - 6'2 210 lbs

Strengths: Ayomanor has been a steady offensive weapon in the ever-changing Stanford offense in the last two seasons, showing solid production during each campaign. Ayomanor is built with a terrific frame, showcasing an impressive blend of height, length, and muscularity. A former high school track athlete, Ayomanor has the speed to threaten and take the top off of a defense. Ayomanor is not just fast; he is a fluid athlete with excellent start/stop quickness when exploding into his stem. This makes him a nightmare on stop/start routes, creating consistent separation on double moves. Highly comfortable winning at all field levels, Ayomanor is a catch magnet that displays big mitts to snatch the ball away from defensive backs. He can take a small play and break off a big chunk with his ability in space to create additional yards and make defenders miss. Had to deal with inept QB play for much of his career, still showing the ability to adjust and make plays despite it. Has a good understanding of how to find space against zone coverage, showing good sideline awareness. He has an innate feel for playing the ball down the field, showing impressive ball skills to adjust and high point down the field. He has a highly advanced understanding of altering his releases, creating unpredictability for defensive backs at all levels. He knows how to utilize his frame to box out at the catch point against smaller defensive backs, winning in 50/50 settings. He is a willing and highly competitive blocker who consistently shows physicality when working along the edges for his teammates.

Weaknesses: Ayomanor missed the entire 2022 season with a bad knee injury. As fast and explosive as he is, he appears to struggle when asked to change directions, lacking ideal lateral quickness and agility. He is not a consistent separator that will grant a QB steady separation, often relying on his physicality to outmuscle at the catch point. He must widen out his route arsenal, as he only has a few relied-upon routes. Fires out of his stance very upright, allowing more discerning defensive backs to disrupt and reach his chest plate to re-route him at the line of scrimmage. Ayomanor will make tremendous circus catches but sometimes make the simple focus drop.

Best Fit: 'X' Receiver

Player Ranking (1-100): 80.5 - I like Ayomanor and his unique and intriguing skillset. He has the frame, ball skills, and speed to be a starter in this league. If he can continue to refine his route-running prowess, he has a chance to be a valuable contributor. 2nd round player.

9. Xavier Restrepo - Miami - 5'10 195 lbs

Strengths: As a full-time starter for the Hurricanes in each of the last two seasons, Restrepo became the focal point for their offense, showing incredible reliability. Jumped into the NFL discussion following his 2023 campaign, in which he finished with 85 catches, nearly 1100 yards receiving, and six touchdowns. A small but mighty receiver is a dynamic reception machine that makes the most of every opportunity. Don't let his size fool you; Restrepo plays far bigger in all aspects, showing toughness with the ball in his hands. He will routinely break tackles in the open field, requiring committed tackles. He dominates in the shorter to medium areas of the field, willing in the tiniest of windows. Can win contested catches against the corner, showing strong hands and ball-tracking abilities. He is a sudden route runner with impressive foot quickness and precision through his routes. Flexibility and loose limbs allow him to change direction on a dime, showing separation ability through his transitions. Understands how to find openings against zone coverage. He is a tireless worker who makes a living on broken-down plays, never giving up on plays and allowing his QB to find him for big plays. Shows willingness in the blocking areas of the game, with impressive competitive toughness and willingness. Has experience in the return game.

Weaknesses: He battled some injury concerns early in his career for the Hurricanes, causing him not to get his full chance until the 2023 campaign. While he handled both slot and outside duties in college, his size limitations will strictly cause him to be an inside player at the next level. Will get overwhelmed against longer press corners that can get physical with him inside contact windows. While he's a terrific catcher, he waits for the ball to arrive in his chest rather than attacking it. Quicker than he is fast, he isn't a game-changing athlete who will threaten vertically at the next level.

Best Fit: Slot receiver and return specialist

Player Ranking (1-100): 79.1 - Restrepo is a dynamic high-volume receiver that will make an offense better with his ability to win in tough windows. He's a reliable contested ball catcher who adds value as a return specialist. 3rd round player.

10. Jalen Royals - Utah State - 6'0 205 lbs

Strengths: Royals began his career at Georgia Military College before transferring to Utah State and starting his final two seasons in the Mountain West Conference. Royals became prolific in his 1.5 years of starting, posting terrific production and big plays, including 15 touchdowns and nearly 1100 yards receiving in 2023. Royals was a former all-state high jumper, showcasing his outstanding athleticism and explosive power. Capable of playing any of the receiver spots, Royals shows versatility and a high football IQ. Royals is used in many manufactured plays, including on screens, constantly showing his dynamism to create with the ball in his hands. His electric speed can destroy pursuit angles from defenders, shrugging off uncommitted tackle attempts. As a nuanced route runner, Royals understands how to utilize leverage and sharp footwork to create separation at various points of his stem. Has the short-area quickness, fluidity, and long speed to threaten at all three levels of a defense. He is the definition of a big-play receiver, with several 50+ yard touchdowns on his resume. A natural hands' catcher, Royals frequently extends and easily makes plays outside his frame. He shows impressive body control and ball-tracking abilities down the field, making over-the-shoulder grabs look routine. Has the start/stop quickness to be dynamic on double moves and play-action plays. Against zone looks, the Royals show impressive instincts to find soft spacing, sit in, and present a QB-friendly target. Has true vertical abilities to high-point and be dynamic in red-zone scenarios.

Weaknesses: Royals missed the final half of his final season after dealing with a foot injury. Many of his touches were on manufactured plays. Did not have to compete against many NFL corners in the Mountain West and could struggle against athletes on his level. Had some struggles against more physical defensive backs that would disrupt him at the line of scrimmage. Royals must develop a larger route tree and a more varied release package at the next level. Has a slimmer frame and had some struggles against longer defensive backs at the catch point, allowing them to get inside his frame and knock the ball away. More of a power runner with the ball in his hands than a true creator, lacking the finesse and the shiftiness to create or make guys miss.

Best Fit: Developmental receiver

Player Ranking (1-100): 78.4 - Royals is one of this draft class's best smaller school receivers. His ability to consistently dominate the competition level he played at was impressive. The skies are the limit for Royals as he continues to refine his football attributes. I wouldn't be surprised if he wins a significant role. 3rd round player.

11. Matthew Golden - Texas - 6'0 195 lbs

Strengths: Golden was initially recruited to Houston, where he spent two seasons with the Cougars before transferring to Texas for his final campaign. While impressing in moments for Houston, it wasn't until he transferred to the Longhorns that he had his breakout season in 2024. Golden is a versatile receiving threat used both outside and in the slot. He also has proven to be a dynamic return specialist, returning two kickoffs for touchdowns for the Cougars in 2023. As a receiver, Golden is smooth as ice. He utilizes a varied release package to keep defensive backs second-guessing at all times, creating unpredictability as a route-runner. His lightning-quick feet and route salesmanship enable him to create spacing at all levels of the field. His start/stop quickness enables him to be dynamic on double moves. Golden displays impressive competitive toughness at the top of routes, winning the majority of 50/50 balls. He can adjust and extend down the field, proving to be a dynamic red-zone option. He also shows outstanding focus and concentration on over-the-shoulder grabs to make them look routine. He recognizes zone looks and is quick to find and locate spacing opportunities. Golden isn't just quick in small spaces; he showcases his long speed when there's daylight in front of him. He displays good open-field vision and can find tiny creases of space. A natural hands' catcher that can extend and snatch the ball away from his frame. A willing run blocker that shows fearlessness along the perimeter to take on defenders.

Weaknesses: During his two years at Houston, he struggled with multiple injuries, causing him to miss games during both seasons. Golden lacks a prototypical frame to play the outside or the inside at the next level. His lack of top-end length and bulk will cause him some difficulties against larger defenders who can get their hands on him. This is evident when he's lined up on the LOS, failing to disengage and easily allowing defenders to disrupt him quickly. His lack of size and strength limits him with the ball in his hands, frequently getting ankle-swiped and going down to first contact. Despite good speed, he's not a vertical separator and often relies on circus catches to win up the field. Many of his touches during his college career have been on schemed touches, enabling him to pick up significant yards on manufactured plays. Despite being a willing blocker, Golden fails to have the upper-body strength to sustain blocks, frequently enabling defenders to disengage and make plays in the run game. Golden will make the circus catches, but he's prone to poor concentration drops throughout his career.

Best Fit: 'Z' receiver that can kick inside

Player Ranking (1-100): 78.3 - Golden is a dynamic route-runner with the finesse and the speed to scare defenses. If he can continue to gain functional strength and mass, he can be an outstanding number-two receiver for a team. His ability to find space and creases in the defense is rare. His plus upside as a return specialist gives him additional excitement for a team. 3rd round player.

12. Jack Bech - TCU - 6'2 207 lbs

Strengths: Bech, a former LSU recruit, began his career with the Tigers in the first two seasons before transferring to TCU. Bech played mostly as a role player for the Tigers but still offered impressive production, finishing with nearly 500 yards as a true freshman. In his final season in 2024 with TCU, Bech showed his true upside, finishing with over 1000 yards receiving and nine touchdowns. Built with an impressive physique, Bech shows the ideal proportions to play at the next level. While he plays mostly from the inside, Bech can also play on the outside. Bech is a hard-nosed and tough character who loves the physical aspects of playing football, where he shines most. Capable of winning at all three levels of the field, Bech shows smooth-moving athleticism and a large variety of routes. Bech is a hands-magnet that catches everything in his vicinity, showing outstanding strength and comfort in contested settings in the middle of the field. Bech isn't afraid of taking big hits, regularly sacrificing his body to make a big play. Bech, a crafty and nuanced route-runner, sells his routes at all stem levels, utilizing varied tempos and transitional quickness. He regularly finds space against zone coverage, showing good spatial awareness, nonstop urgency, and motor on every snap. Utilizes his frame at the top of his routes to box out at the catch point, showing reliability in 50/50 situations. A high-volume chains mover that shows rare competitive toughness after the catch. He fights for every inch and regularly stays on his feet through multiple tackler attempts.

Weaknesses: Bech isn't going to thrive on timed running metrics, as he lacks top-end explosiveness and speed. He can sometimes struggle to separate against defensive backs in man coverage consistently. He hasn't competed against many press corners in college, as he frequently played in the slot or as the flanking wide receiver who played off the line. He sometimes struggles against corners that match him with physicality that can outmuscle or win hand positioning inside his frame.

> **Best Fit: Oversized slot receiver that can play on the outside as well**

Player Ranking (1-100): 78.0 - Bech is one of my favorite plays in this draft class. While he lacks elite timed metrics, his football speed and acceleration are more than sufficient. He regularly finds space and creates separation at every level of the field. He has even proven over and over again that he can separate vertically with his ability to sell double moves. I love Bech, and he immediately makes an offense better. He is a third-round player.

13. Tai Felton - Maryland - 6'2 186 lbs

Strengths: A significant 3-year contributor to the Terrapins offense that had his breakout season in 2023, where he finished with over 700 yards and six touchdowns. He improved even more in 2024, offering steady improvements during each subsequent campaign. Felton is a versatile receiving threat that offers the flexibility to play all over the offensive front, both inside and outside. Felton is a nuanced route runner who excels as a technician at all route levels. Possessing a wide array of releases, Felton excels when fighting through jams and keeping his frame clean through contact windows. Smooth and quick feet allow him to display sharpness and separation quickness when working at the top of his routes. Displays flexible body control while adjusting to the ball, showing impressive ball-tracking skills. Can regularly adjust to poorly thrown balls and win in heavily congested windows in the middle of the field. Has an excellent sense of his surroundings, especially when playing against zone coverage. He knows exactly how to find space while displaying excellent spatial awareness. A tough kid who, despite being thinner, shows outstanding competitive toughness to win against bigger defensive backs at the catch point. After the catch, Felton shows good open-field vision and physicality to fight for additional yardage. Had some of his best games against the best competition and in the biggest games, proving to up his levels against the best.

Weaknesses: Felton is a long, lean prospect with a frame lacking top-end body armor and girth. He is a good athlete but lacks top-end vertical speed and burst that will consistently allow him to win up vertical seams against NFL competition. Felton could benefit from additional technique and awareness work in the blocking department, as he cannot sustain blocks along the perimeters.

> **Best Fit: #2 receiver for a team**

Player Ranking (1-100): 77.9 - Felton is a great player who has shown considerable improvement each season. He's essentially good at everything while not being an elite athlete. If he continues to maximize his frame, he could be a starter on the sooner side for an NFL offense. He is highly refined and NFL-ready to contribute. He is a 3rd round player.

14. Pat Bryant - Illinois - 6'3 200 lbs

Strengths: Bryant has been a mainstay of the Fighting Illini offense for the past 4 seasons but finally had his breakout campaign in 2024, stopping many of the Big Ten statistical categories. A long and rangy-built receiver, Bryant plays far more physically than you'd think with his size dimensions. Bryant plays mostly on the perimeter but has some experience playing inside. A nuanced and savvy route-runner, Bryant understands how to sell his routes with precision and salesmanship. He utilizes a steady blend of finesse and physicality through his stems and head/body fakes to create spacing for himself. A build-up runner, Bryant has shown the field-stretching abilities to challenge on vertical planes. He's a smart football player used in various gadgets and trick plays, including playing out of the backfield. A natural hands' catcher, Bryant utilizes his strong mitts and physicality at the catch point to dominate most 50/50 battles. He tracks the ball excellently down the field, showing instincts and timing to secure at the right moment. He does a nice job of selling play-action and double moves, creating separation for himself. He is a physical player with a ball, inviting and absorbing contact well. He fights for every additional yard with the ball in his hands, showing impressive competitive toughness. Dynamic in the red zone, Bryant can high point and go vertical over defensive backs to make plays. One of the better run blockers in college football, Bryant shows willingness and toughness to dominate his assignment.

Weaknesses: Bryant has played with a fairly limited route tree and could benefit by continuing to widen his arsenal. His release package throughout college has been predictable, lacking varied releases through his stems. He lacks elite speed and acceleration, causing him to struggle to consistently separate against better man-cover corners on vertical and linear planes. He has struggled in separation and handling press corners that get in his face, and he will need to refine his press technique.

Best Fit: Possession 'X' Receiver

Player Ranking (1-100): 77.0 - Bryant is a good all-around football player who excels in all the physical aspects of football. Coaches will love this kid, and his willingness and toughness are outstanding. He will likely win significant reps in training camp with his football IQ and physicality. 3rd round player.

15. Ricky White III - UNLV - 6'1 190 lbs

Strengths: He came onto the scene for Michigan State in 2020, where he impressed in moments before transferring over to Nevada in the Mountain West, where he started for the last three seasons. White exploded in 2023, finishing atop the CFB statistics charts with nearly 1500 yards receiving and eight touchdowns. White is a long and lean build with a high-cut frame. He is an explosive athlete who threatens all levels of the field with his ability to stretch the field vertically. White has experience playing at all the receiver positions and is frequently moved inside to create mismatches against defenses. A highly intelligent receiver who works tirelessly in finding openings showing spatial awareness against zone looks. Despite being a thinner-built receiver, White plays incredibly tough. He's willing to take big hits in the middle of the field while being a reliable 50/50 catcher in congested windows. He's also impressive post-catch, routinely making the first guy miss while fighting for additional yards. He attacks the football with his hands, showing an impressive catch radius with soft hands to pluck it outside his frame. Tracks the ball impressively down the field, showing good ball tracking and high-point abilities. He runs his routes with nuance and complexity, selling his routes with a large variety of releases. Excellent on broken-down plays, always working hard to find space while showing tremendous sideline awareness to make fantastic sideline grabs. A physical blocker who takes the run game seriously, showing the 'want' with good competitive toughness.

Weaknesses: White didn't compete routinely against top-tier competition in the Mountain West. His high-cut frame segments his routes, failing to have an ideal change of direction and agility when working through his breaks. This makes it easy for more athletic defensive backs to jump their routes and get their hands on the ball. More straight-line fast than quick, failing to get separation on a horizontal plane. While he does a nice job of running his routes with savvy, he lacks foot sharpness at the top and tends to round off his breaks. Lack of physicality and upper-body strength is prevalent when handling press-man looks, struggling to disengage inside contact windows.

Best Fit: 'Z' Receiver

Player Ranking (1-100): 77.4 - It's hard to knock White's production the last few seasons, dominating game after game with tremendous production. He's an explosive speedster who can consistently challenge NFL defensive backs up the field from any position. His willingness to do the dirty work and win in the middle parts of the field is incredibly enticing as well. I like him playing the Z position, where he doesn't have to handle press-man coverage consistently. 3rd round player.

16. Tory Horton - Colorado State - 6'2 175 lbs

Strengths: A 5th year senior for the Rams, Horton started his college career for Nevada for two seasons before transferring to Colorado State and playing his final three seasons for the Rams. A versatile, dynamic production machine, proving to be a big-play game in multiple facets, including the return game. He's had punt return touchdowns in each of the last three seasons. As a receiver, Horton can be used in various ways, both inside and outside. Yards after catch ability is prevalent, showing dynamism in the open field. Can make defenders miss in a phone booth, with terrific quickness in bursts and fluidity to stop/go quickly. Has the necessary long speed to win at the next level, showing very good north/south speed. Excellent ball skills allow him to track the ball and constantly adjust to poorly thrown balls. Horton can go vertical in red-zone settings, showing the high-point ability to win in a jump ball scenario. Trustworthy in highly congested spots, coming up with the football against double and even triple teams sometimes. Despite a lean physique, Horton shows fearlessness in short-yardage situations in the middle of the field and is willing to take big hits. Has an understanding of how to find spaces against zone coverage, frequently finding soft creases.

Weaknesses: Horton has a high-cut frame with little body armor to withstand the rigors of NFL life, appearing to have little additional room for muscle. Relied on very simple routes throughout college against inferior athletes and will have to broaden his routes and refineness in running his routes. Not an overly physical receiver who will win hand battles or fights against NFL corners at the catch point. Shows passiveness when it comes to the blocking areas of the game, failing to have adequate toughness and strength. He is too hesitant to extend and snatch the ball away from his frame, looking too content to wait until the ball reaches his frame.

Best Fit: #2 or 3 receivers for a team as well as return specialist

Player Ranking (1-100): 76.2 - Horton has been a production machine for several seasons, proving to be anything but a 1-trick pony. He's a versatile weapon that will make his mark wherever he is used. The problem with Horton is he isn't great at any one thing. He's a good athlete, not great, and has a slighter build. And he still needs additional refinement as a route runner. He can be a solid #2 or 3 receiver for a team, but not a guaranteed starter. 3rd round player.

17. Kyren Lacy - LSU - 6'2 213 lbs

Strengths: A 5th year senior for the Tigers, Lacy began his career for Louisiana Lafayette in the Sun Belt, where he started for two seasons before transferring over to LSU. Lacy has been a steady performer, showing durability season after season, saving his best season for last. Built with a stacked physique, showing NFL size and length dimensions. Lacy has the positional flexibility and the football IQ to be used anywhere across the offensive front, showing experience playing both outside and in the slot. Lacy is a 1st down machine, doing the bulk of his work in the intermediate parts of the field. A reliable hands' catcher, Lacy is trustworthy in heavily congested situations. Lacy is excellent in the red zone, showcasing impressive body control while maximizing his catch radius to extend and high-point the ball. Impressive ball skills and tracking ability to locate down the field and adjust to underthrown or poorly thrown balls. Not passive at the catch point, Lacy attacks the football with physicality and strong hands. He is savvy and nuanced in his routes, utilizing both head and body fakes to create separation through his stems. He has good balance and hand usage when fighting through jams, showing the ability to keep his frame clean through contact. He plays with excellent sideline awareness, living on the perimeters while keeping his feet in bounds. A hardworking target when plays break down, Lacy keeps his motor going while looking for openings down the field. Has some yards' catch ability with toughness and physicality, possessing a nasty stiff arm to disarm potential tacklers.

Weaknesses: While Lacy has had a nice college career, he hasn't had a top-tier production season and mostly has finished with modest numbers. He is not a dynamic athlete who can win consistently with quickness or long speed, as he is generally relied upon to win in narrow windows. While he's adept at running routes, he could use some additional refinement and sharpening at the top as he frequently rounds off his routes, allowing defensive backs to jump the route. He is not a great stalk blocker as he doesn't want to dominate defenders at the point of attack, allowing them to consistently get off in the running game.

Best Fit: Versatile receiver that can battle for a #2 or #3 receiver role

Player Ranking (1-100): 75.7 - Lacy is an intelligent and hardworking receiver who wins consistently both inside and outside. While he's not an athletic specimen, he's a good all-around receiver who runs good routes and has outstanding size and reliability catching the football. 3rd round player.

18. Arian Smith - Georgia - 6'0 185 lbs

Strengths: Smith is a 5th year senior for the Bulldogs who has had an up-and-down college career before his senior season in 2024. In 2024, he finally showed his upside as a big-time offensive threat, finishing with, by far, his best college production. A former top track athlete, Smith is a long, lean speedster with true home-run-hitting potential. Exploding out of his stance, Smith gets to top gear in a flash, proving to be dynamic in both vertical settings and on intermediate routes, consistently separating against defensive backs. His explosiveness has carried over into his route running, understanding how to alter his speeds and tempo through his stems to create unpredictability throughout his routes. Smith has showcased continued development and improvement in all phases. Smith is at his best down the field with his ability to track the football and adjust to the ball. Impressive ball skills and contested ball abilities, showing strength at the top of routes to win in contested settings. Comfortable winning both inside and outside, Smith is respected by defensive backs who know he can get behind easily. Smith has extensive special teams experience being used on several of the coverage teams and in the return game. A willing contributor in the running game, Smith takes blocking personally and regularly showcases his ability to be a reliable stalk blocker along the perimeter.

Weaknesses: Smith has had injury concerns throughout college, causing him to miss a lot of game time early in his career. His overall production before his senior season was minimal, failing to stay on the field consistently. His runner's physique is small, failing to have ideal body armor and strength on his frame. While Smith has improved his route arsenal this past season, he's still a bit of a 1-trick pony that relies on winning deep, failing to offer significant tools at his disposal. The main concern with Smith is his drops. His hands are amongst the worst in this draft class, and he is beyond frustrating with his ability to separate, be wide open, and routinely make terrible drops. He lacks confidence in his hands and prefers to wait for the ball to arrive at his chest to secure it.

Best Fit: #3 receiver for a team

Player Ranking (1-100): 74.9 - Smith finally showcased his ability this past season, impressing greatly. While his college career has been disappointing, he has enough physical tools to be an enticing NFL prospect. If he can clean up his drops, he can be a significant contributor to an offense. 4th round player.

19. Jaylin Noel - Iowa State - 5'11 200 lbs

Strengths: Noel has been a versatile playmaker for the Cyclones in the last four seasons, showing reliability on both offense and special teams. Noel is a smaller but athletically built receiver with experience handling outside and inside receiving duties. Noel has improved every campaign, finishing his final season with well over 1000 yards receiving. Excelling in short spaces, Noel shows outstanding twitch to win in the shorter to intermediate parts of the field. Despite being a smaller target, Noel maximizes his frame with aggression and a fearless mentality to win in contested settings in the middle parts of the field. Exploding out of his stance with great 0-10 acceleration, Noel can utilize various release packages to keep defensive backs guessing. A nuanced and savvy route runner, Noel understands how to utilize body/head salesmanship to win leverage and set up defenders through various parts of his stem. His separation quickness and sharp feet allow him to win separation at the top of his routes consistently. He understands how to utilize body positioning and strong mitts to win at the catch point. He maximizes his entire frame in the air, showing good body control and high-point abilities to adjust and track the ball in the air. He works hard on broken-down plays, regularly finding soft spots in zone coverage to sit in and present a QB-friendly target. He maintains excellent sideline awareness and routinely drags his feet in bounds with toe-dragging abilities.

Weaknesses: While Noel has played both inside and outside, he unfortunately lacks a frame to play within the boundaries and might be limited to slot duties only at the next level. Noel is quicker than he is fast and lacks the straight vertical speed to be a threat down the field. Noel struggled When he had to go against more physical press corners and was re-routed and disrupted frequently. He mostly has reliable hands, but he will occasionally have some bad concentration drops in the middle of the field. Not a tackle breaker; Noel mostly goes down to the first contact. Noel shows willingness as a blocker but lacks the upper-body strength and grip strength to sustain blocks along the edges.

Best Fit: Slot receiver

Player Ranking (1-100): 74.5 - Noel proved this year he can be a nice weapon for an offense. He immediately offers upside as a return specialist while getting on the field in clear passing situations. He could be a stellar slot option at the next level. His savvy, quickness, and route-running abilities are going to be loved by a QB. 4th round player.

20. Kyle Williams - Washington State - 6'0 185 lbs

Strengths: A 5th year senior for the Cougars, Williams exploded during his final season at Washington State with nearly 1200 yards receiving and 14 touchdowns. Williams is a long and rangy receiver who plays with outstanding versatility. Williams has been used to handling outside and inside duties as a high-volume target who took advantage of the spread offenses that he's been in. A smooth and quick accelerator, Williams gets to top gear quickly. He's silky in how he works in and out of transitions, showing good separation quickness and loose hips. A varied route runner who runs his routes with salesmanship, utilizing head and body movements to sell his routes at various points of the stem. He can win at all three levels of the field, running a diverse route tree. Williams is fearless when working in the middle parts of the field, sacrificing his body in tight windows. He alters his tempo through his routes, understanding how to create spacing. He is a smart and instinctive athlete who knows how to set up his subsequent routes, selling his double moves well. He's a QB-friendly target who works tirelessly on broken-down plays, regularly finding openings and sitting in. He has a natural feel for zone looks and an understanding of how to find pockets of space. Williams is a good ball tracker down the field, regularly making over-the-shoulder grabs look routine. He utilizes flexible body control and good competitive toughness to win along the sidelines and in the red zone.

Weaknesses: Williams took advantage of his volume passing offenses to rack up a lot of production. He's a smaller receiver with a lankier build that could benefit by adding density and muscle to his frame. While Williams is an above-average athlete, he lacks elite long speed and doesn't appear to generate separation on up-the-field routes. Williams is a body catcher who prefers to wait for the ball to corral into his frame rather than consistently attacking it in the air. He has a lot of double catches and simple drops on his resume. He has limited experience handling tight press coverage and will struggle to beat jams at the next level. A limited danger with the ball in his hands, as he often goes down to the first tackle attempt.

Best Fit: 'Z' or slot receiver

Player Ranking (1-100): 74.3 - Williams is a slighter receiver, lacking the ideal physicality and toughness for the next level. I love his ability to consistently separate, especially in the shallow and intermediate parts of the field. I'd like to see him get stronger and gain more mass in an NFL strength and conditioning program, but I could see him being a solid contributor by his 2nd year at the next level. 4th round player.

21. Nick Nash - San Jose State - 6'2 184 lbs

Strengths: Nash has had a long and storied 6th-year college career, beginning his college career at both QB and RB before eventually transitioning to a full-time wide receiver in 2022. Nash has picked it up quickly despite being new to the position, proving to have a tremendous ceiling with additional experience. Nash exploded in 2024, leading the Mountain West Conference in receptions, yards, and touchdowns. A long and rangy-built receiver, Nash has enough room in his frame for continued development and mass. A dynamic mismatch, Nash does most of his damage as an oversized slot receiver. A plus athlete, Nash shows the ability to win at all three levels of the field with field-stretching components. A reception machine that racks up significant yardage on underneath routes and critical 3rd downs. Strong hands and physicality throughout his stems allow him to win at the catch point, frequently extending and securing. A natural route-runner that understands how to sell and set up subsequent routes with varying tempo and timing. He understands leverage, often putting defenders on their heels as he wins inside leverage on inbreaking routes. Has a natural feel for space and zone coverage, regularly finding and locating soft spaces in coverage and sitting in and presenting a QB-friendly target. Nash has impressive ball skills down the field, showing ball-tracking capabilities and body control to contort and adjust to the ball.

Weaknesses: Nash hasn't consistently competed against top-tier opposition throughout school. He lacks ideal body armor and density through his frame, causing him to sometimes get manhandled in the physical components of the position, such as run blocking and defeating physical corners. He is still new to the position and will need time and patience. He lacks versatility and the ability to play on the outside, as he is strictly a slot receiver. He's not a guy who consistently separates against man coverage, tending to rely on adjusting and ball skills to win in constantly contested situations.

Best Fit: Developmental receiver

Player Ranking (1-100): 73.5 - Nash had a tremendous final season at San Jose State. His size and explosiveness cause him to be a mismatch against more slot corners, constantly finding openings at all different levels. He is a true reception machine that will be a constant 1st down machine at the next level. 4th round player.

22. Jayden Higgins - Iowa State - 6'4 210 lbs

Strengths: A 2-year starter for Eastern Kentucky before transferring to Iowa State and playing his final two seasons. Higgins has been impressive in the Big-12 the last two seasons, showing the ability to win against stellar opposition. Comfortable playing both outside and inside, Higgins has his most success when he's used as an oversized slot. Higgins is built with outstanding size and length, utilizing his frame to win in contested situations constantly. Not an oversized slouch as a mover, Higgins eases out of his stance with good quickness and burst. Fearless when working the underneath and middle parts of the field, proving to be a reception machine that repeatedly dominates on 3rd downs. Strong mitts at the catch point, winning and capable of snatching the ball through traffic with ease. A savvy route-runner who runs with precision and salesmanship, showing the ability to utilize route tempo to win on short and intermediate routes. Understands how to utilize his massive frame to win leverage to position his body so only he can win in 50/50 settings. A dynamic red-zone target shows the flexible body control and body contorting ability to high point and pluck the ball out of the air. Highly intelligent and with good spatial instincts, Higgins can find soft zones and present a QB-friendly target when handling zone looks. Shows impressive post-catch ability to create for himself and fall forward through impact.

Weaknesses: Higgins is a long and wiry-built target that could benefit from adding strength and weight to his frame. He struggles against more physical press-man corners that can jam him at the line of scrimmage, failing to have an ideal jam technique. He needs to add more release packages to his arsenal to better hold up against NFL corners inside contact windows. He can occasionally be too passive at the catch point, waiting for the ball to arrive in his chest. Quicker than he is fast, Higgins fails to challenge or offer vertical abilities, lacking the straight-line speed to threaten defensive backs. Struggles mightily as a run blocker, failing to sustain blocks and repeatedly allowing defenders to disengage.

Best Fit: Oversized slot receiver

Player Ranking (1-100): 73.0 - Higgins is best used as an oversized slot receiver that can offer upside as a 3rd or 4th receiver for a team. He's a reliable target in the middle of the field that can repeatedly win on 3rd downs. He's not a big-play threat, nor is he a dynamic speedster that will consistently separate, but there are certainly roles for a player like Higgins. 4th round player.

23. Will Sheppard - Colorado - 6'3 198 lbs

Strengths: A 4-year contributor to Vanderbilt before transferring to Colorado for his final campaign. Sheppard has been an incredibly consistent performer for four straight seasons for different teams and with multiple different QBs, showing reliability. Sheppard has experience playing all over the offensive front, playing in each alignment while showing inside and outside comfort. A nuanced route-runner, Sheppard runs his routes with precision and tempo, altering his route speeds at various points of his stem. Quick feet at the top of his routes allow him to sell his routes while creating spacing opportunities. He is a chain mover who does most of his damage on shorter to intermediate routes, winning inside leverage and positioning on routes. Runs each route with urgency, playing with a relentless motor. Understands how to routinely win against zone coverage, finding soft spaces while proving to be a QB-friendly target. He has a large catch radius that can routinely extend and make plays outside his hands. Highly trustworthy in contested situations, proving to have good soft hands. Understands how to win in the red zone, utilizing good competitive toughness at the catch point while boxing out and high-pointing against smaller defensive backs. Has some post-catch ability to fight off uncommitted tackle attempts while falling forward through impact. Has had success in the SEC against top-tier competition. Good stalk blocker that understands how to sustain blocks and open up perimeter rush lanes for his teammates.

Weaknesses: He didn't have to consistently compete against press coverage, winning the bulk of his yardage against softer off-man coverage. When handling press, Sheppard needs to understand how to better utilize his hands to disengage without getting slowed up within contact windows. Lacks top-end physical traits, both in terms of physicality and athleticism. Not a guy that is going to consistently separate, lacking elite speed or short-area quickness. Generally has good hands but is prone to some poor concentration drops at inopportune times of games. He has worked hard to maximize his frame the last few seasons but could use additional muscle and bulk to improve his play strength.

Best Fit: 'Z' Reciever

Player Ranking (1-100): 72.2 - Sheppard is a good all-around receiver who plays his best when he can get free releases off the line of scrimmage. He's a savvy all-around receiver who could fight for a team's #2 or #3 receiver spot. 4th round player.

24. Antwane Wells Jr - Ole Miss - 6'1 208 lbs

Strengths: A former FCS receiver for James Maddison, Wells has had quite a varied college career. After transferring to South Carolina, Wells immediately found success, finishing with over 900 yards receiving and 6 touchdowns. After two seasons with the Gamecocks, Wells transferred to play his final season with Ole Miss. Wells has an NFL frame and a good combination of compactness through his frame and athleticism. Wells is a physical specimen, playing best with a defender on his back. Capable of winning along the perimeters or when lined up as a slot. Strong hands allow him to win in contested situations. Excellent body control and tracking abilities allow him to make plays down the field. A good athlete in short areas, Wells showcases impressive short-area quickness and foot quickness to separate on short to intermediate routes. High IQ and awareness allow him to eat up zone cushions, regularly find spacing in the middle of the field, and routinely eat up large chunks of yards. He is a limbed athlete who shows shiftiness in space, rarely allowing defenders to get two hands on him in space, showing an impressive change of directional abilities. Dynamic when used on screens, turning small gains into first downs routinely.

Weaknesses: They had an injury-plagued second season with the Gamecocks, causing him to miss most of the season. Went from dominating for a few seasons, both at James Maddison and then at South Carolina, to underperforming for a couple of seasons. Quicker than he is fast, Wells isn't a separator on vertical routes, and corners don't struggle to stay in phase with him vertically. Has had some really poor concentration drops on his record throughout college. Could use continued refining of his route tree, as he has a bad habit of rounding off some of his more direct routes.

Best Fit: Backup WR

Player Ranking (1-100): 71.9 - Wells is an intriguing prospect who plays the receiver like a smaller receiver despite having a sizeable frame. That isn't a knock, as Wells moves quickly in short spaces and can release and separate against defensive backs. While he's had a unique college career, the talent is there. He can be a real steal on Day 3 of the draft. I'd take him in the 4th round.

25. Ja'Corey Brooks - Louisville - 6'2 190 lbs

Strengths: Brooks was a 5-star recruit for Alabama who had some inconsistencies but showed upside moments before transferring to Louisville before the 2024 campaign. Brooks finally showed his true upside with Louisville, having a career season and embarking on outstanding production amongst the top ACC receiving charts. Brooks is a long and rangy receiver who plays along the boundaries, showcasing mostly as an 'X' receiver. A true speedster, Brooks was a former track and field athlete with rare explosiveness and top-end speed. Brooks is not just fast; he is a fluid athlete who shows smoothness in and out of his breaks and how he runs routes. He understands how to win inside leverage on underneath routes, regularly dominating the field's middle parts. Utilizes route savvy when running his routes, showing subtle head and body fakes to make his routes unpredictable for corners. Brooks shows upside after the catch, impressive open-field vision, and change of directional abilities to cut back and reverse course. A large catch radius is a weapon that Brooks utilizes to win in contested settings, extending and making plays outside of his frame. Excellent in the red zone, showing flexible body control and high-point abilities to extend and snatch the ball over defensive backs. A dynamic special teams player who is effective as a return specialist and a blocker.

Weaknesses: Brooks had major inconsistencies during his three years at Alabama, taking him on and off the field. He had injury concerns during his last season at Alabama with his shoulder, and his medical will be very important. As explosive as Brooks is, he doesn't always show it on tape. He fails to consistently separate on vertical and lateral routes, needing to win in contested situations. His route tree is still a work in progress, and he could benefit from adding more tools to his toolbelt. Brooks has struggled against physical corners throughout college, both at the line of scrimmage and the catch point. Brooks can be passive and hesitant as a run blocker, failing to have the necessary physicality and competitive toughness.

Best Fit: 'X' Receiver that can compete as the 3rd or 4th option

Player Ranking (1-100): 70.9 - It was nice to see Brooks finally showcase some of the upside he had in high school in his final season at Louisville. He is still raw in many ways, but there is a fantastic athlete in here who can continue to get better. He's a bit of a boom-or-bust prospect with a major ceiling, but there are also concerns. 4th round player.

26. Kaden Prather - Maryland - 6'3 210 lbs

Strengths: Prather was initially recruited to West Virginia, where he played for two seasons before transferring to Maryland for his final two campaigns. Prather has had solid production in the three seasons, showing remarkable consistency and iron-man reliability, finishing with over 500 yards receiving in each campaign. Prather is a big, long receiver with enough room on his frame for additional mass. Prather is a highly intelligent and nuanced receiver who operates well both in the slot and on the outside. Prather does the bulk of his work in the shorter and intermediate parts of the field, utilizing his length to consistently dominate in contested settings. His massive catch radius enables him to extend and make plays outside of his frame look routine. He has terrific hands and consistently wins in 50/50 settings, making remarkable acrobatic catches. Prather has impressive body control and can contort and high-point the ball down the field, showing impressive red-zone upside. For being a larger target, Prather shows fluidity and ease of movement skills, showing effortless hips as he moves in and out of his routes. Prather displays good urgency and tempo throughout his routes to find openings on broken-down plays. He has a good sense of his surroundings in zone coverage and understands where the softer spots are located. Despite not playing against top-tier competition consistently, Prather played some of his best games against his better opponents. A physical and willing blocker in the run game who looks for contact and isn't afraid to get physical.

Weaknesses: Despite Prather's size and physical prowess, he doesn't consistently win with physicality. He can sometimes struggle to get off the line of scrimmage against physical corners that get in his face and disrupt him. He also lacks physicality with the ball in his hands, frequently going down to the first contact. While Prather is a smooth mover, there is still some stiffness and rigid movements when asked to play laterally or change directions quickly. He tends to telegraph his slants and inside routes, allowing defensive backs to jump his route at the top. His overall production has been good through college, but he's never shown the #1 production for a receiver of his skillset. Prather doesn't consistently separate against man coverage as he lacks top-end transitional quickness and long speed to threaten.

Best Fit: 'X' Receiver

Player Ranking (1-100): 70.5 - Prather is a good receiver with excellent size and easy movement skills. He has a skill set that should translate well to the next level. I don't think he's ever going to be a #1 receiver for a team, but he could develop into a nice #2 or 3 option. 4th round player.

27. Kobe Hudson - Central Florida - 6'1 200 lbs

Strengths: As a 5th-year senior for the Knights, Hudson began his career at Auburn, where he spent his first three seasons in the SEC. Hudson had a stellar first season with the Knights, finishing with 900 yards receiving and eight touchdowns, finally showcasing his upside. A well-built kid that has the frame for additional mass. A highly nuanced and seasoned college receiver who has seen it all at the college level. Highly adept and comfortable playing from any alignment, including the slot, the X, and the Z receiver. Hudson plays with excellent intangibles and football intelligence, which allows him to win before the snap. A savvy and nuanced route-runner, Hudson understands how to utilize many releases while altering his tempo through his routes. He does the bulk of his damage on a shorter to intermediate route, where he is fearless about sacrificing his body to make difficult contested grabs. He has the flexible body control and the strong mitts to routinely win in contested settings while adjusting to poorly thrown balls. A smooth athlete that works seamlessly in and out of his breaks, showing good initial quickness and transitional separation skills. He understands how to find soft spaces in coverage against the zone, recognize defensive looks, and find space down the field. Has shown the ability to pick up additional yardage after contact with good open-field skills and shiftiness to make defenders miss in space.

Weaknesses: Hudson has never been a top-tier producer for any offense he's been on and has mostly been a role player. He lacks the top-tier athletic traits to be a consistent separator at the next level, lacking both the upper echelon of speed and explosiveness. While he's got reliable hands, he possesses more of an adequate catch radius that limits him in extending and consistently winning away from his frame. His lack of twitch and length limits him when going up against more physical press corners that can disrupt his route timing at the line of scrimmage. As a run blocker, Hudson looks passive and uninterested at moments.

Best Fit: #3 or 4 receivers for a team

Player Ranking (1-100): 69.4 - Hudson is a good, all-around, experienced football player who lacks any overwhelmingly enticing characteristics for a team. He can be a #3 or 4 receiver with a good training camp. He's been solid the last 4 seasons for two different programs and has the football IQ to be used anywhere. 5th round player.

28. Jaylin Lane - Virginia Tech - 5'9 174 lbs

Strengths: A 5th year senior for the Hokies, Lane began his career with Middle Tennessee State in the Conference USA for three seasons before transferring to the Hokies for his final two campaigns. Lane is a versatile weapon that has been used on offense and special teams, proving to be one of the best return specialists in the country in the last few years with multiple returned touchdowns. Lane had his best season in 2022 with Middle Tennessee State, finishing with nearly 1000 yards receiving. Lane is a smaller receiver that operates primarily from the slot but is used by the coaching staff in various ways. A smooth and initial burst enables Lane to get into his routes quickly, showing good lateral mobility and changing directional skills. Despite his size, Lane is far more physical than one would suggest with his ability to play through contested windows and win many 50/50 balls. He is excellent and fearless when working in the middle of the field, sacrificing his body in crucial settings. He's excellent with the ball in his hands, as he was frequently used on short outs and screens to take short receptions into big-chunk plays. He has terrific open-field vision and moves, showing elusiveness and shiftiness in space. He plays through contact well and shows a good balance to win additional yardage after contact. He is a natural hands catcher who maximizes his frame, adjusting to the ball and coming up with difficult grabs. Lane is a reliable and sturdy receiver who has played virtually every game of his college career with no injury concerns.

Weaknesses: Lane has clear size, weight, and density limitations at the next level. Lane's frame makes it difficult to play anything at the next level other than inside. He requires precise throws due to his limited catch radius and size. While Lane is quick and accelerates well, he lacks the top-end speed to be a vertical separator at the next level. His overall production has been modest at best, failing to have #1 receiver most of his college career. A lot of his touches and yards come as a result of manufactured play designs that were predicated on allowing him to play in space. He lacks a diversified route profile, running mostly simple interior routes.

Best Fit: Slot receiver and return specialist

Player Ranking (1-100): 66.1 - Lane is a versatile chess piece that can be used on special teams and in the receiving game. He has some good traits, and he can earn a role for a team at the next level with an impressive training camp. 5th round player.

29. Elijah Badger - Florida - 6'1 185 lbs

Strengths: Badger began his career at Arizona State for four seasons before transferring to Florida before his senior campaign. Badger has had three solid seasons of production the last three seasons, averaging about 800 yards receiving during each campaign for two different programs. Badger also has kickoff return experience at Arizona State. Badger is a versatile receiving threat who has played outside and in the slot. Built with a long and lean frame, Badger has outstanding length with room on his frame for additional bulk. Badger is a savvy and nuanced route runner who utilizes route manipulation and altering tempo to create separation at various points of a route. He is a natural hand catcher who utilizes his entire catch radius to extend and snatch balls outside his frame. He uses these long arms to be a red-zone nightmare, attacking at the high point and proving to be a red-zone threat. Impressive body control enables Badger to adjust to the ball and make difficult catches look routine. Very comfortable in congested traffic, Badgers plays far bigger than his size. He's a reliable and physical stalk blocker who takes his assignments seriously. Post-catch, Badger proves to have good open-field vision and shiftiness to create additional yardage with daylight. He often evades first tackle attempts or showcases the ability to break tackles, showcasing good contact balance. He has good sideline awareness to toe-drag while finding available openings against different coverage schemes.

Weaknesses: Badger is more of a shorter to intermediate-route receiver that lacks the home-run threat as a big-play threat on vertical routes. His lack of size and strength limits him when taking on more physical defenders that challenge him at the line of scrimmage. He's not a consistent separator against better-man coverage corners and relies on his length and body contortion abilities to win in tight windows. While he has some impressive route details, he lacks the sharpness at the top, and he can telegraph his routes, enabling corners to jump his routes. He needs to vary his releases to defeat jams at the line effectively. He racked up the bulk of his yards against lesser opposition and failed to impress against the better defenses on the schedule.

Best Fit: #3 receiver that can play inside or outside

Player Ranking (1-100): 64.8 - Badger is a good receiver that lacks elite athleticism and explosiveness. His length, hands, and football IQ give him an edge over his opponents. But I'm not sure he can consistently separate and win against better NFL corners. 6th round player.

30. Bru McCoy - Tennessee - 6'3 230 lbs

Strengths: McCoy was a 5-star recruit who began his career with USC, where he spent his freshman season before transferring to Tennessee, playing his final three seasons with the Volunteers. McCoy possesses a massive frame with thick limbs and muscularity throughout. A difficult matchup for defensive backs, McCoy utilizes his large frame to dominate at all levels of the field. Capable of playing both inside and outside, McCoy does the bulk of his damage when working as the 'X' receiver. A long strider that can eat cushions quickly, showing good overall athleticism and straight-line speed. McCoy is a bully at the catch point, frequently dominating the physical battles while showing vacuum-like hands to extend and snatch the ball away from his frame. McCoy is a bad ball catcher, and he adjusts on the fly while giving his quarterback comfort when throwing in contested windows. McCoy runs his routes with salesmanship, utilizing tempo changes throughout his stems and head fakes to create separation at various points. McCoy's size and high-point abilities make him a difficult red-zone challenge, showing flexible body control to adjust to the ball. Once again, McCoy plays like a bully with the ball in his hands, showing outstanding toughness and contact balance to fight for additional yards after contact, proving to be a difficult guy to bring down. A physical and aggressive run blocker that shows good competitive toughness and 'want' when sustaining blocks along the edges.

Weaknesses: McCoy is an older prospect who will be 25 years old shortly after the NFL Draft. His production throughout college has been modest at best, never proving to be a dynamic #1 any season. McCoy struggles to separate due to a lack of acceleration and burst off the line of scrimmage. A laborer who struggles when changing directions or attempting to separate on in-breaking routes. Has had a number of injury concerns throughout college, including requiring ankle surgery. While he can pick up additional yardage after contact, he's not overly elusive or shifty in space and tends to take on a lot of contact. McCoy dominates matchups against smaller defensive backs but struggles against guys who can challenge him with length and physicality. Longer corners can re-route him or cause him issues when securing contested balls.

Best Fit: 'X' Receiver

Player Ranking (1-100): 63.2 - McCoy is a physical kid with great size who shows promise, but overall, he lacks the athletic components to be a consistent separator at the next level. His injury concerns, being an older prospect, and lack of top-end production will cause him to drop slightly. 6th round player.

31. Dominic Lovett - Georgia - 5'10 187 lbs

Strengths: He was a 2-year player for Missouri before transferring to Georgia and playing his final two seasons with the Bulldogs. Lovett played a major role in two programs, showing the ability to win in various ways. Despite being small, Lovett can play both inside and outside. A terrific athlete, Lovett shows both the short-area quickness and the long speed to challenge at all field levels. A reliable catcher of the football that repeatedly shows the ability to make plays outside of his frame with soft mitts. Fearless when working through the middle of the field, Lovett is a tough and hard-nosed kid who consistently makes tough catches in contested settings. Runs his routes with precision and sharpness, showing the ability to consistently create openings in the shorter to intermediate parts of the field. Sees the field really well with good spatial awareness, understanding how to find openings against softer zone looks. Flexible body control and ball skills allow him to adjust to poorly thrown balls regularly. Toughness after the catch manifests as he stays on his feet through impact and shows good open-field vision to take short plays long distances.

Weaknesses: Lovett has major size concerns and could be limited in playing in the slot at the next level. His production throughout college has been OK, but he's mostly been used as a secondary or third option. He will need to consistently vary his releases at the line of scrimmage to get off-press coverage consistently inside contact windows. Lack of physicality and size can cause him to struggle against longer corners, reaching him at the catch point. Lacks the ability to high-point and consistently win in red-zone or jump-ball scenarios. Would like to see Lovett be a more consistent stalk blocker, failing to always have the physicality and competitive toughness.

Best Fit: Slot Receiver

Player Ranking (1-100): 62.8 - Lovett is a good slot receiver with athleticism and the route running prowess to carve himself out a niche role for a team playing inside and creating separation. 6th round player.

32. Theo Wease Jr - Missouri - 6'2 210 lbs

Strengths: A former five-star recruit for the Sooners, Wease transferred to Missouri following the 2022 campaign with Oklahoma. Started finally living up to his potential for the Tigers during the 2023 campaign, where he finished with nearly 700 yards receiving and 6 touchdowns. Wease has a prototypical 'X' receiver size and a long-levered and lean physique. Has the catch radius to make plays far outside of his frame. Has experience and comfort playing both inside and outside. Wease is a varied and efficient route-runner who wins at all three levels of the field. His college coaches trusted him and threw to him in must-win situations on 3rd and 4th downs, showing incredible confidence and trustworthiness. Sells his routes with precision and nuance, utilizing a combination of head and body fakes to create separation through his stems. Sets up subsequent routes, varying his tempo and timing to create unpredictability as a route-runner. Shows outstanding awareness of zone spacing and cushioning to find soft zones and create a QB-friendly target down the field. He had some early struggles with reliability with his hands but has improved to being a tremendous football catcher. Excellent sideline awareness allows him to make routine 3rd down grabs while dragging his feet in-bounds. Has had great success and experience against top-tier college competition. Can win in vertical settings and is a great red-zone target, showing his ability to high-point and utilize his entire wing span. Has some toughness to stay on his feet with the ball in his hands, showing good post-catch ability.

Weaknesses: Will be 24 years old before his rookie season due to playing 6 years in college. Wease isn't a true separator due to not having ideal amounts of short-area athleticism. The straight-line speed is good but isn't elite, and it relies on consistently winning at the catch point rather than separating. Has some stiffness when asked to change directions or flip his hips, needing to gear down and losing his built-up speed. Will get re-routed and jammed easily at the line of scrimmage against the more physical press corners. Lacked the necessary physicality in the running game, looking hesitant and limited at the point of attack.

Best Fit: Battle for backup receiver spot

Player Ranking (1-100): 61.9 - Not many receivers are as nuanced of a route-runner as he is coming out of college, showing an impressive route tree and good precision throughout his stems. He's a limited athlete who will fail to separate consistently. Still, his combination of QB-friendly reliability in contested situations and route-running should allow him to compete for a backup receiver role. 6th round player.

33. Jimmy Horn Jr - Colorado - 5'10 170 lbs

Strengths: The son of former NFL great Jimmy Jr has proven to be an electric playmaker at the college level. Starting his career with South Florida for two seasons, Jimmy proved his dynamism as a return specialist and a secondary receiving option. Jimmy transferred to Colorado for his final two campaigns, proving an important offensive weapon. Horn does the bulk of his damage as a receiver on shallow and intermediate-based routes. He's a reception machine that takes short receptions and maximizes them with explosive post-reception production. Once he hits the open field, Horn utilizes his vision and sudden change of direction to make defenders miss easily. Buffaloe's coaches maximized this with screens, which he proved highly adept. Horn is an explosive big-play threat that can stretch all three levels of a defense. He's quick and shifty off the line of scrimmage, making it difficult for defenders to reach his frame within contact windows. He plays fearless in the middle of the field and often takes big hits. He sells his routes with salesmanship and alters route tempo to lull defenders at the top of routes. Down the field, Horn is a natural in his ability to track and adjust to the ball. He appears to have good spatial recognition and finds pockets of space in the middle of the field on broken-down plays.

Weaknesses: Horn is extremely slight, and his lack of play strength is exposed if he's tasked to play outside. He's almost entirely been a slot receiver at the college level, and his frame likely only suits that at the next level. Most of Horn's touches have been manufactured to get him in space. If Horn has to take on physical corners, he struggles at the catch point getting outmuscled. He's frequently disrupted and re-routed at the line of scrimmage if defenders can get a hold of his frame. While he normally has good hands, he has struggled with some concentration drop issues.

Best Fit: Slot receiver and return specialist

Player Ranking (1-100): 60.4 - Horn is a dynamic return specialist who should add some value to an offense as an explosive weapon. He's not as refined as you'd like to see on offense, but he has the athleticism and the traits to continue to excel. 6th round player.

34. Chimere Dike - Florida - 6'1 200 lbs

Strengths: Dike was a 4-year contributor to the Badgers before transferring to Florida for his final year in 2024. He saved his best season for last against SEC competition, finishing with nearly 800 yards receiving. Dike is a long and lean receiver that has vines for arms and additional room on his frame for continued development. A track athlete who brings a vertical element to a passing offense, showing the speed to burn. Dike has experience lining up all over the offensive formation for Florida and Wisconsin, but he does his best work out of the slot. While capable of threatening at all levels, Dike is a significant threat when working in the middle parts of the field. He shows fearlessness across the middle and reliability to consistently win in heavily contested settings. Dike's flexible body control and catch radius on down-the-field routes enable him to win in jump ball settings and along the perimeter. He excels when matched up against zone looks and appears to show good recognition abilities to find available openings. A smart and instinctual athlete who recognizes looks works tirelessly on broken-down plays and presents a QB-friendly target when nothing is available. He plays bigger than his listed size and shows good competitive toughness and physicality with the ball in his hands. He regularly stays on his feet through contact, showing good balance and vision when working in space. His upside as a return specialist will give him additional versatility at the next level.

Weaknesses: Although he's worked hard to gain muscle in the last few years, he still has a bit of a long and wiry frame that could use additional seasoning. Dike has mostly been a secondary or third option for a passing offense throughout his career, not showing the ability to be a #1 option. While he has great speed, he lacks the transitional quickness and change of directional abilities against man coverage. He lacks finesse and precision in his route-running, often telegraphing his routes for defensive backs to jump. Despite his speed, he's not a separator and often relies on acrobatics and his length to win outside of his frame.

Best Fit: Developmental receiver

Player Ranking (1-100): 58.4 - Dike is a speedster who doesn't quite know how to utilize it to his benefit yet. If he can refine his route-running while continuing to gain functional strength and size, he could compete for snaps down the road. There are definitely traits here; they need to be harnessed. 7th round player.

35. Zakhari Franklin - Illinois - 6'1 185 lbs

Strengths: Franklin has a 6-year college career bouncing between UTSA, Ole Miss, and Illinois. In his last two years at UTSA, he had over 1,000 yards during each campaign, leading the conference in touchdowns with 15 in 2022 as well. Franklin is a long and athletically built corner with excessive experience for the next level. Comfortably playing inside and outside, Franklin does most of his work in the middle of the field. A smooth mover in space, Franklin gets to top gear quickly, easing in and out of his breaks. He's excellent in contested situations, utilizing his frame to box out defenders. Despite being thinner, Franklin understands how to beat jams at the line of scrimmage with good quickness and active hands. He's fearless in the middle of the field, willing to take big hits to make crucial 3rd down plays. A nuanced route runner that sells his routes well, allowing himself to maintain leverage on underneath routes. He utilizes his flexible body control to adjust to the ball, possessing good reliability in contested settings. Franklin is a good ball tracker with high-point ability and dynamic in red-zone scenarios. He is a reliable hands catcher who can extend and make plays outside his frame, utilizing his catch radius. A willing and competitive blocker who plays with good toughness and physicality.

Weaknesses: Franklin is an older prospect who will be 25 years old early in his rookie season. Franklin possesses a long and wiry frame with less-than-ideal body armor throughout his frame. When challenged against bigger defensive backs, Franklin struggles consistently to win throughout his stems. He lacks ideal speed, bursting in and out of his breaks, and the home-run ability to challenge NFL athletes on vertical routes. He consistently struggles to separate against man coverage and must rely on accurate passes or adjust to the ball. He's not a threat with the ball in his hands and often goes down to the first contact.

Best Fit: Developmental receiver

Player Ranking (1-100): 56.3 - Franklin had a bounceback year this year for Illinois after dealing with an injury-plagued season at Ole Miss. While his ceiling isn't massive for growth, he could develop into a potential 3rd or 4th option for a team. 7th round player.

Top-10 WR's:

1. Tetairoa McMillan
2. Tre Harris

3. Savion Williams
4. Luther Burden III
5. Emeka Egbuka
6. Tez Johnson
7. Isaiah Bond
8. Elic Ayomanor
9. Xavier Restrepo
10. Jalen Royals

Chapter 5

TE's

1. Tyler Warren - Penn State - 6'6 249 lbs

Strengths: A 2-year starter for the Nittany Lions, Warren had a breakout year in 2023 as a junior, finishing with over 400 yards receiving and seven touchdowns. He finished his college career with an even more impressive production in 2024, improving greatly on his junior campaign. The definition of a warrior, Warren is a tough-as-nails kid who has outstanding strength and toughness throughout his frame. A former QB, Warren understands defenses and has an instinct for space and presenting a QB-friendly target at all levels of the field. A noteworthy athlete, Warren eases out of his stance, getting to top gear quickly. Comfortably playing inline, as an H-back, or even playing out wide, Warren shows incredible versatility, even being used to carry the ball on important 3rd downs. A volume machine that wears down defenses with additional touches. Plays the position like a bully, almost Gronk-like, showing incredible contact balance to stay on his feet through impact. He looks to deliver impact to tacklers, dropping his shoulder and pushing forward through contact. As a route runner, Warren shows sharp footwork at all levels of his stem while displaying the transitional quickness to separate at the top. A trustworthy target in the middle of the field, Warren dominates smaller targets at the catch point, utilizing his big mitts to win. A bad ball catcher, Warren shows flexible body control to adjust and make plays down the field on the ball. A terrific red-zone target, Warren has a knack for getting into the end zone, whether high-pointing vertically or utilizing his competitive drive to break tackles and will his way. A physical and nasty run blocker that often serves as the H-back on outside-zone runs, showing the ability to open up exterior lanes. Possesses the anchorage power and strength to sit on blocks when used in max protect passing situations.

Weaknesses: A former high school quarterback, Warren is new to the tight end position before college, having never previously played the position. Penn State played in a unique gimmicky offense that allowed Warren to get the ball in various manufactured plays. He is still developing into his frame as he has continued room for development and growth. While he shows toughness and willingness in pass protection, he will sometimes get overaggressive and play over his toes, getting caught off-balanced.

Best Fit: Starting TE

Player Ranking (1-100): 89.5 - I love Warren as a prospect. His upside is through the roof with his athleticism, toughness, and football IQ. Considering he's new to the position, the amount of success he's had in college is huge, especially during his final season. Coaches are going to love this kid, and he plays like an old-school TE but has the athleticism of a new-school TE. 1st round player.

2. Harold Fannin Jr - Bowling Green - 6'4 230 lbs

Strengths: Fannin has been a mainstay of the Bowling Green offense for the last three seasons, but he exploded in his final season in 2024 with over 1200 yards receiving, completely dominating the MAC

Conference. Fannin is a dynamic chess piece that can be used in any number of alignments, including playing in the backfield, in the slot, as a stand-alone receiver, or inline. A plus athlete, Fannin gets to top gear in a flash, showing easy movement skills out of his stance. A highly-nuanced route runner who utilizes impressive route salesmanship at all levels, creating unpredictability through his stems. Has good lateral twitch and flexion to work in and out of his breaks to create separation. A good ball tracker that utilizes flexible body control to adjust to the ball down the field. Fannin is a tough-nosed kid who dominates in the game's physical components, playing far bigger than his size indicates. He excels when working in the middle of the field, showing strong mitts to win routinely in contested settings. Plays with an alpha mentality with the ball in his hands, regularly requiring at least two tacklers to bring down and constantly falling forward through impact reliably. Capable of taking small routine plays and turning them into large chunk plays. Fannin is dynamic on screens and manufactured-style plays designed to get the ball in his hands. Despite playing against MAC-Conference programs, Fannin has excelled in his matchups against Power 5 competition. Mentality is also shown in the run game, showing impressive physicality and technique when attacking along the perimeter. Fearless when handling linebackers and defensive ends, capable of opening and clearing rush lanes. Has stayed healthy and on the field for three seasons in a row, rarely missing a snap, showing steady durability.

Weaknesses: Fannin's biggest concern will be his lack of consistently competing against top-tier competition. He lacks the ideal prototypical frame for a tight end, lacking both the wingspan and the height. Many of Fannin's touches have been manufactured over the years, failing to have excessive experience against man coverage. At times, he can be disrupted against press defensive backs at the line of scrimmage, limiting his ability to get free releases. He is far better as a run blocker than in pass protection. Fannin's lack of size and anchorage power have been exposed against bigger edge defenders when handling inline duties.

Best Fit: Starting TE

Player Ranking (1-100): 86.4 - Fannin is one of the most dynamic receiving tight ends we've seen in years. His ability to consistently dominate the physical components of the game is incredible. He's a true weapon, and he LOVES playing football. This kid will immediately make an offense better and more fun. 1st round player.

3. Colston Loveland - Michigan - 6'5 245 lbs

Strengths: Loveland has been a dominant offensive force for the Wolverines' last two seasons, showing outstanding production during each campaign. Loveland is a complete size mismatch for both linebackers and safeties, featuring a long-levered frame with good height and length. Comfortable playing all over the offensive formation, Wolverines' coaches trusted him with various uses. Loveland possesses outstanding athleticism and has easy movement skills and transitional quickness to escape against linebackers easily. Against defensive backs, Loveland's catch radius proves to be overwhelming, showing his ability to high-point and extend away from his frame to box out at the catch point. A rare tight end that can separate consistently on vertical seams, constantly attacking all levels of the defense. Wins laterally, showing fluidity in his movement skills, capable of flipping his hips and selling underneath routes. A nuanced route-runner who showcases quick and precise feet to sell his routes at varying points of his stems. Comfortable making contested catches in the red zone or the middle of the field. Very good ball tracking skills enable him to utilize his flexible body control to adjust to the ball. The rare post-catch ability looks like a receiver who can create for himself and pick up additional yardage after receipt. Has a knack for finding soft cushions against zone coverage, regularly sitting in and presenting a

QB-friendly target. A willing blocker that shows good effort to be used along the perimeter to win with positioning and angles.

Weaknesses: Loveland is still growing into his frame and a little lightweight through his lower body, as he struggles to anchor when in max protect pass protection situations. Lacks hand strength as a blocker, failing to sustain and control blockers for any duration. Will need to continue to improve as a run blocker, especially if asked to play inline. A very good athlete but not quite elite. Struggles when playing out wide or in bunch formations when defensive backs can rough up him at the line of scrimmage, failing to have a nuanced jam technique. He is normally a reliable hands' catcher, but he has had poor concentration drops over the last couple of seasons.

Best Fit: Starting TE

Player Ranking (1-100): 85.2 - Loveland is one exciting prospect! He's a mismatch wherever he's lined up and can repeatedly win and find space against linebackers and safeties. His production in the Big Ten has been fantastic, and he should have had an easier transition than most. 1st round player.

4. Jake Briningstool - Clemson - 6'6 240 lbs

Strengths: Briningstool is a 2-year starter for the Tigers, who began receiving significant snaps as a sophomore in 2022. Briningstool has been a production machine in the last two seasons, proving to be a high-volume-reliable target in their offense with three different offensive coordinators. Briningstool possesses a long and lean physique with a massive frame, allowing him to be a constant mismatch for defensive backs and linebackers. A reliable safety blanket for QBs on underneath routes, Briningstool utilizes his wide frame and length to shield against defenders. Briningstool can threaten the seams vertically, not just a safety blanket, showing impressive long speed. He is a smooth operator who eases out of his stance, showing good initial quickness off the blocks. He is dynamic in the red zone and jump-ball situations, where he can consistently utilize his body control and high-point ability to win. Understands how to run routes with altering tempo, showing the ability to sell his routes at various points through the stem. He has long arms and reliable hands that are perfectly comfortable extending and snatching the ball away from his frame. A high football IQ enables Briningstool to recognize zone looks and is quick to find soft spaces to present a QB-friendly target at all times. Despite lacking great size, Briningstool plays the game tough and looks for contact, showing good fight and competitive drive to fight for additional yardage after the catch. Has upside as a blocker, showing good awareness and recognition skills. He is frequently used to seal off when playing inline, understanding how to utilize his frame to win positioning.

Weaknesses: While Briningstool has done a nice job adding good weight to his frame, he's still very slender and would benefit from adding more 'good weight.' Despite good toughness and competitiveness after the catch, his long-levered frame limits him as he's an easy target for defenders to trip him up and get him to the ground. Lacks any shiiftiness or threat with the ball in his hands other than speed. Despite having good hands, he can be too reliant on waiting for the ball to arrive into his chest rather than consistently attacking it. Briningstool will need additional power through his lower body to hold up as an inline blocker at the next level.

Best Fit: Starting TE

Player Ranking (1-100): 84.1 - Briningstool is a refined receiving TE that can consistently win against defenders. His athleticism, route-running, and physical toughness are all impressive. His blocking skills aren't bad, but they aren't a strength, and with his slender physique, he will likely need additional power and girth through his lower body to hold up the line. 2nd round player.

5. Oronde Gadsden II - Syracuse - 6'5 236 lbs

Strengths: A former receiver for the Orange, Gadsden switched to playing as a full-time TE before the 2022 campaign. Gadsden exploded in his first season, starting for the Orange and finishing with nearly 1000 yards of receiving and 6 touchdowns. Showed no ill effects from his foot injury, having a tremendous bounceback season in 2024. Gadsden possesses a long and lean physique with room for additional growth. Former receiver qualities are evident in how he plays the position, showing rare athleticism and movement skills for a TE. Eases out of his stance, showing a good initial burst and explosiveness. A nightmare mismatch that is too explosive and speedy for linebackers and too big and long for safeties. Dynamic playing above the rim, showing outstanding high point and vertical leaping abilities to snatch the ball. Attacks the football in contested situations; Gadsden can adjust to poorly thrown balls and make 50/50 catches. He can be a red-zone nightmare for defenders. Has extensive experience playing outside, in the slot, or inline. A savvy route-runner who understands how to utilize tempo and leverage to win on shorter to intermediate routes. Fluidity through his lower body allows him to change directions and cross the field without looking clunky or being too predictable as a receiver. High levels of awareness and football IQ allow him to frequently find space against zone coverage, making plays at all levels. A true yards' after catch specimen that can peel off large runs and break tackles in the open field, showing impressive toughness and vision in space.

Weaknesses: He suffered a season-ending foot injury requiring multiple surgeries in 2023, causing him to miss most of the season. Still possesses a tweener frame that looks more like a wide receiver than it does TE at this point. Can come out of his stance very upright down the field, slowing him down through transitions. Can be too physical at the top of his routes, getting away with noticeable push-offs in college. Lack of size and functional power will limit him in inline situations where he must hold up at the point of attack in pass protection. Limited variance in his route tree, and he will need to widen out his options for the next level. He lacks the sustain in his upper body and hands to latch on in the run game, allowing defenders to stack/shed in pursuit easily.

Best Fit: Starting TE

Player Ranking (1-100): 82.5 - He was very happy to see that Gadsden had a bounceback season in 2024, showing his 2022 season was an anomaly and that he's fully recovered from his injury. Gadsden is a dynamic receiving mismatch with true versatility as an oversized slot or a receiving TE. His production is rare for the TE position, and he has an incredible ceiling if he can continue to add quality mass and muscle to his frame without losing his explosiveness. 2nd round player.

6. Terrance Ferguson - Oregon - 6'5 255 lbs

Strengths: A significant contributor to the Ducks offense since his freshman campaign, Ferguson has been a mainstay with impressive consistency and production during each campaign. Ferguson is built with ideal measurables for the next level, showcasing impressive height, density, and wingspan. An all-around TE prospect who brings upside both as a receiver and a blocker. Ferguson lines all over the offensive formation, including as an H-back, in the slot, and outside. He gets out of his stance with a good initial burst off the line, getting to top gear quickly. Has some savvy in the way he runs his routes, showing sharpness in and out of his breaks. Utilizes his frame to dominate at the catch point, boxing smaller defenders out and utilizing his massive wingspan to secure contested balls comfortably. A bad ball catcher who can adjust and make plays outside his frame routinely. Physicality is present against press coverage, showcasing good upper-body strength and toughness to quickly blow through jams and release. Has an understanding of how to win against zone looks, showing good spatial recognition and instincts to find space. Impressive body control and red-zone abilities give offenses an additional target in the end zone. An effort blocker that shows impressive toughness and aggressiveness in the running game.

Weaknesses: He was often schemed open in Oregon's offense, creating many big plays. Overall athleticism is average, lacking the separation quickness or vertical speed to threaten defensive backs. He's not much of a threat with the ball in his hands, frequently going down to first contact in the open field. Will benefit by continuing to refine his pass protection technique in addition to continuing to increase anchorage strength. Shows willingness and toughness as a run blocker, but he lacks the hand strength to sustain blocks, frequently allowing defenders to disengage.

Best Fit: All-around TE

Player Ranking (1-100): 75.1 - Ferguson has had an impressive college career and is a do-everything tight end. His ceiling is low, and his floor is high. He'll never be a dynamic receiver, but he'll be a contributory player in every facet, and he has the potential to be a good blocker. 3rd round player.

7. Gunnar Helm - Texas - 6'5 250 lbs

Strengths: Helm was mostly a blocking tight end his first few seasons on campus with Texas before transitioning into a starting role during his senior campaign. He greatly impressed in 2024, finishing with his best numbers and showing true NFL potential. Helm has a well-developed, long, lean physique, showing prototypical NFL traits. Helm is a highly intelligent tight end that is used in a variety of different alignments and looks. Can win out of the slot, inline, or even as a receiver out wide. A hard worker who commits himself to winning on broken-down plays. Has a real feel for spacing, finding space in zone looks while showing the aptitude to create a QB-friendly target in available space. A terrific football catcher, Helm is completely trustworthy in 50/50 balls and highly contested situations. Snatches the ball away from his frame, showing good aggression and reliance at the catch point. Shows some flexible body control and ball skills to track the ball down the field and adjust to poorly thrown balls. His large catch radius and high point ability make him a mismatch in red-zone opportunities. A savvy and nuanced route-runner that can create separation at various levels of the field. Has the athleticism and speed to attack the seams, showing the rare ability to separate against safeties and linebackers in vertical settings. Can create additional yardage after the catch, showing competitive toughness and the ability to make guys miss. Highly experienced blocker who utilizes good fundamentals and technique to maintain positioning, showing good awareness and recognition skills.

Weaknesses: Helm has been used modestly before his senior season, lacking production in earlier seasons, and is a 1-year wonder. While experienced in blocking, he lacks top-notch strength and point-of-attack prowess against guys with whom he can't win the size battles. Could add some additional muscle in his lower body to better hold up in the run game, failing to get an ideal push when run blocking. Lacks any elite characteristics and isn't a guy that will consistently separate against NFL athletes, lacking top-end speed and athleticism.

Best Fit: All-around TE

Player Ranking (1-100): 73.9 - Helm has had a fantastic senior season, showing he has NFL traits. He's a good mix of size, athleticism and toughness. He's not great at any one thing, nor does he have any clearly defined weaknesses. His ability to be an effective receiver and blocker is impressive. 4th round player.

8. Mason Taylor - LSU - 6'5 255 lbs

Strengths: The son of NFL Hall of Famer Jason, Taylor took over as a starter on the Tigers' offense during his true freshman season. He has been a reliable starter for the last three seasons, showing impressive consistent production. He's finished each campaign with over 300 yards receiving and finished his final season with over 500 yards. Taylor is an intelligent and savvy football player with extensive experience in the offensive formation, including in the slot, in the backfield, out wide, and as an inline blocker. Possessing a good frame with a large catch radius, Taylor is a developed prospect with NFL readiness. Taylor is a big-game football player frequently relied upon in the biggest moments and on key 3rd downs. He's a smooth mover out of his set, showing easy acceleration. He works well in and out of his breaks, utilizing good urgency and route tempo to create deception. His football intelligence and spatial awareness enable him to find soft spaces against zone coverage, sitting in and presenting a QB-friendly target. He utilizes his large frame well to box out, frequently winning in the middle parts of the field. His strong mitts and physicality at the catch point allow him to dominate when playing through contact frequently. He is a natural hands catcher who can extend and utilize his entire wingspan to make plays outside his frame, adjusting to badly thrown balls. Taylor is a physical tone-setter with the ball in his hands, showing the ability to fight for additional yards while always falling forward through contact. In the blocking department, Taylor understands how to utilize his arms to frame his blocks. He shows good competitive toughness and works hard to sustain and maintain positioning in both phases.

Weaknesses: Taylor's ceiling for growth is limited and appears to be mostly maxed out as far as a prospect. His overall athleticism is good, but it falls short of being top-end. He consistently fails to offer much of a vertical passing option and tends to offer a shorter to intermediate route option. He's a bit of a laborer who runs very upright out of his stance, causing him to hesitate when changing directions. This enables him to be an easy cover for defensive backs, as he fails to separate against man coverage. His footwork at the top of his routes leaves something to be desired, as he frequently rounds off his routes, failing to have sharp footwork or transitional quickness. He has to continue to develop his nuance as a receiver while widening out his route tree. He's failed to offer much as a red-zone receiving target. As a blocker, Taylor shows willingness, but his lack of great anchorage strength causes him to struggle to absorb and sustain blocks.

Best Fit: All-around TE

Player Ranking (1-100): 73.5 - Taylor is an all-around tight end who lacks fantastic attributes but does everything reasonably well. The concern is he doesn't appear to have significant room for growth. I think Taylor will fight for a starting spot, but at the very least, be a high-floor number 2 tight end at the next level. 4th round player.

9. Oscar Delp - Georgia - 6'5 245 lbs

Strengths: Part of a split reps tight end committee at Georgia, Delp has proved to be a valuable cog in the wheel for the offensive coaches in the last two seasons. Capable of lining up all over the offensive formation from the backfield, to the slot, to the outside, or as an inline option. Delp is a versatile threat that enables coaches to utilize him in various ways, showing high football intelligence to be successful at each. A fluid and smooth mover, Delp has a speed that can easily separate it from linebackers. With excellent lateral mobility and change of directional explosiveness, Delp sinks in his hips and creates multiple gateways to separation through his stems. Utilizes good salesmanship on his routes, showing transitional quickness and sharp footwork at the top. A seam stretcher that can open up the vertical game for a defense but is also content doing the dirty work on the inside. Veteran-like savvy allows him to succeed and find spacing against soft zone looks, sitting in and presenting a QB-friendly target. Understands how to box out and utilize his frame to win against smaller defensive backs in contested situations. Maximizes his frame with toughness and blue-chip characteristics in the running game, playing with urgency and intensity. He makes first contact, showing good sustain and competitive toughness. A core special teams contributor who has played on all of the units for Georgia.

Weaknesses: He has been part of a tight-end committee during his time at Georgia and never posted stellar production during his time. This raises questions about his viability as a true #1 tight-end option at the next level. Still developing his frame, and he's a little light through the lower body, limiting his ability to hold up in pass protection. He lacks the point-of-attack strength and the anchorage ability to sit on blocks without allowing the pocket to collapse when handling inline duties. As a receiver, Delp lacks a physical profile with the ball in his hands and tends to often go down to first contact.

Best Fit: Receiving TE

Player Ranking (1-100): 72.8 - Delp has been a reliable contributor for the last two seasons, albeit not blowing anyone away. His athletic profile shows an upside as he gets to the next level. His blue-chip characteristics, special teams experience, and versatility should enable him to carve out a role for a team at the next level. 4th round player.

10. Bryson Nesbit - North Carolina - 6'5 235 lbs

Strengths: Nesbit has been a noteworthy contributor to the Tar Heels since his freshman season in 2021. He's been a steady and high-volume receiving tight end during the last three seasons while playing with different QBs, showing impressive production each campaign. He was a former high school basketball player before beginning to play football during his junior campaign, where he rose to be a four-star prospect. Nesbit is a long and rangy-built TE who almost looks like a power forward in how he plays the position. Lining up all over the offensive front, including inline, in the slot, and out wide as a receiver, Nesbit is a receiving mismatch for defenses. Easing out of his stance and into his routes, showing easy movement skills and acceleration. It is far too athletic for linebackers, and it has been proven to create separation both laterally and up the seams as a vertical option. Tracks the ball excellently down the field, adjusting and contorting his body. Length and catch radius make him a dynamic red-zone option, proving high-point abilities and flexible body control to adjust his body to make plays in the air. He is a reliable hands catcher who utilizes his entire catch radius to extend and attack the football. Shows fearlessness when running routes in the middle of the field, willing to take big hits while making tough contested catches. When manned up against safeties, Nesbit knows how to box out and utilize his frame to win positioning at the catch point. He is an impressive route-runner who runs his routes with good pacing and transitional quickness. A nightmare in the open field, Nesbit has 'take it to the house' athleticism, speed, and vision to turn short receptions into big plays. Keeps his legs churning through impact, picking up additional yardage through contact.

Weaknesses: Missed the end of the 2023 campaign due to a lower-body injury. Will be 24 years old at the beginning of his rookie season. His long and narrow high-cut frame limits potential growth, with minimal room for substantially more mass. Can be re-routed and disrupted inside contact windows due to his upright nature when coming out of his stance. Has some hip tightness due to his frame, allowing his in-breaking routes to be televised at the top as he creates separation. As a blocker, he's very limited at this point, lacking the power to be used at the point of attack. Will fire out of his stance upright in passing sets, getting overwhelmed against better-leveraged defenders.

Best Fit: Receiving TE

Player Ranking (1-100): 71.9 - I like Nesbit as a receiving option. While he's limited as a blocker, he's a solid receiver who offers the flexibility to be successfully lined up all over the offense. His size, hands, and terrific athleticism make for a very difficult coverage assignment for defenses. 4th round player.

11. Elijah Arroyo - Miami - 6'4 245 lbs

Strengths: Arroyo was a highly regarded four-star college recruit but was mostly a utility player during his first three seasons on campus in Miami. He finally took his chance in 2024, showing impressive production with over 500 yards receiving. Arroyo has an athletic frame with impressive proportional length and little unnecessary body fat; he also has sufficient room for additional development and mass. Arroyo is a flexible move tight end who spends his time split all over the offensive formation from H-back to inline to outside to slot. An athletic weapon, Arroyo proves to be a seam stretcher that can attack linebackers up the field. He is an impressive athlete who eases out of his stance with good initial quickness and smooth acceleration skills. Arroyo makes a living finding space against zone looks, showing impressive zonal instincts and awareness to find space. A former track athlete who competed in the long jump, proving upside as a true red-zone threat. He is willing to go vertical in contested situations in the middle of the field, showing impressive high-point abilities and concentration in traffic. He regularly extends and makes plays outside his frame, utilizing his entire catch radius with reliable hands. Physical and competitive with the ball in his hands, Arroyo shows good competitive toughness and contact balance to pick up additional yardage through contact. He's worked hard the previous few years to improve as a blocker, which was evident this season. He's frequently used to lead the way on screens and running plays, showing good point-of-attack strength and rolling power through his lower body to generate displacement at the 1st level.

Weaknesses: Arroyo has only played in one full season throughout college, which was his final season. He's been a 1-year wonder with virtually little to no production before his senior season. He's struggled with various injury concerns throughout college, and his medical condition will be very important. He's a much better run blocker than a pass blocker, as he lacks ideal inline size, although he has improved in the last couple of years. His 2nd level of blocking can improve, as he frequently whiffs in space and fails to sustain for long durations. His production this season can be a lot from broken-down plays and simple routes out of the backfield. He will need to diversify his route tree while gaining additional experience as a route runner.

Best Fit: Receiving TE

Player Ranking (1-100): 70.1 - Arroyo has impressed this year, finally showing his upside. He added strength and bulk before the start of the season, which assisted him in the blocking department. His athleticism, catch radius, and competitive toughness are impressive. As long as his medical looks good, he should go in the 4th round.

12. Caden Prieskorn - Ole Miss - 6'6 255 lbs

Strengths: Prieskorn has had a long and extensive college career, starting his career at Memphis for three seasons before transferring over to Ole Miss for his final two campaigns. In his last three seasons, he's had excellent production, proving successful both at Memphis and in the SEC. His best season was in 2022 with Memphis, where he finished with over 600 yards receiving and seven touchdowns. Prieskorn has an ideal frame with the length, and the body armor teams covet an inline tight end. A versatile prospect who has played extensively all over the offensive formation, including as an H-back, in the slot, and out wide. Prieskorn utilizes his big frame and massive catch radius to bully smaller defenders, knowing how to box out at the catch point and win in contested situations. Excellent sideline awareness to make toe-touching grabs along the perimeter. He is an excellent hands catcher who routinely makes plays outside his frame, including some terrific 1-handed grabs. Makes his living in the intermediate parts of the field, finding soft spaces against zone cushions and presenting a reliable target. Has some body control and tracking abilities to make plays down the field. Shows enough athleticism and long speed to separate against linebackers in the shallow areas of the field. A difficult guy to bring down to the ground, bouncing off uncommitted tacklers and always falling forward. He is a hardworking teammate that is always hustling and working his butt off to block downfield for his teammates. A willing and able blocker with the size and point of attack power can handle some inline blocking assignments. Has played extensively on special teams with a plus upside for the next level.

Weaknesses: An older prospect who will be 26 years old at the beginning of his rookie season. Had an injury-plagued 2023 campaign after undergoing surgery to break the metatarsal in his foot. He was penalized throughout college for getting a bit of a grabby in protection and frequent push-offs at the top of his routes. Not a guy who will consistently separate against better NFL athletes, lacking the explosiveness and the refinement as a route runner. He is limited after the catch as a runner as he lacks any elusiveness or change of directional abilities with the ball. Can be careless with the ball, leaving the ball completely exposed. Plays too upright when in line as a blocker. Will need to continue to strengthen his lower body to better anchor in pass protection. Hand usage and footwork when attempting to sustain blocks needs refinement.

Best Fit: All-around TE

Player Ranking (1-100): 69.5 - While I don't love that he will be 26, it's hard to ignore his production the last few years, especially when competing against SEC competition. The kid is tough as nails and a reliable all-around TE with the size, dimensions, and toughness to develop into a nice inline TE. He's limited athletically, but he can be a solid #2 TE for a team. 5th round player.

13. Benjamin Yurosek - Georgia - 6'3 245 lbs

Strengths: He was a 4-year Stanford Cardinals player before transferring to Georgia before his final season in 2024. Yurosek had some impressive moments with the Cardinals, including as a sophomore when he finished with 658 yards and three touchdowns. Yurosek is a 'jack of all trades' TE with experience playing out wide, in the slot, and inline. He is a smooth mover who shows subtleness and balance off the line of scrimmage to allow his frame to build up speed. He is a very reliable hands' catcher who shows trustworthiness in tight situations, showing comfort and strong hands to make plays outside of his frame. Flexible body control and ball-tracking abilities down the field. Utilizes his frame to box out at the catch point. Has a high-point ability to snatch the ball out of the air and win against defensive backs in the red zone. A smart and savvy football player with good instincts and play recognition skills to recognize zone looks, paying close attention to soft zones. Makes the most of his physical abilities as a route runner, selling his routes with head fakes and altering route tempos to create separation at the top. A tough kid who plays fearless in the middle of the field, showing 0 hesitancy when he knows he's going to take a big hit. Will fight for additional yards post-catch, paying attention to 1st downs and showing good competitive toughness. He is a willing blocker who maximizes his size limitations with good angles and positioning.

Weaknesses: He missed half of his 2023 season with Stanford after dealing with a shoulder injury. Didn't have much of an impact at Georgia, failing to get used anywhere near as much as he did at Stanford. An undersized TE that lacks ideal measurables, both in height and weight, must be a steady inline TE. Not a true field stretcher who can attack the seams consistently and is mostly a contested ball catcher and a shorter-to-intermediate guy. Has some tightness in his lower half when asked to change directions, losing built-up speed and allowing defensive backs to jump his routes. He is not a poor blocker, but he will get overwhelmed at the point of attack against bigger defenders that can overwhelm him at the point of attack. Struggles to sustain blocks and generate any movement in the run game.

Best Fit: Backup TE

Player Ranking (1-100): 68.9 - Yurosek likely would have been a Day 2 consideration if he continued off of his success at Georgia, but unfortunately, he had a down year. While he's a good football player, he lacks any enticing characteristics of a starting TE at the next level. I think he could be a solid number 2 TE for a team with continued development to his frame. 5th round player.

14. Luke Lachey - Iowa - 6'6 248lbs

Strengths: Lachey is next in the line of long and successful TEs from the Iowa lineage. Lachey has been a 4-year contributor to the Hawkeyes offense, having his best year as a sophomore in 2022 with nearly 400 yards receiving and four touchdowns. Lachey possesses a prototypical NFL frame with good height and length, allowing for additional bulk at the next level. A versatile offensive threat, Lachey has experience playing as an H-back, an inline TE, and split out wide. Lachey is a smooth operator who gets to top gear quickly, showing easy movement skills. His average long speed allows him to be a seam stretcher, showing enough vertical capabilities to separate against linebackers. Capable of threatening with the ball in his hands, Lachey will bounce off uncommitted tacklers, showing terrific competitiveness and toughness post-catch. Physicality at the catch point allows him to win in the middle of the field with safeties and linebackers draped on his back. Comfortable playing away from his frame, Lachey will easily make outstretched catches. Can win in jump ball situations and down the field against undersized corners. Understands how to find spacing when competing against zone looks, regularly finding soft cushions and sitting in for his QB. A natural route runner, Lachey is impressive in the way he utilizes his footwork at the top of routes, showing sharpness to separate.

Weaknesses: An older prospect who will be a 24-year-old rookie. Missed most of the 2023 season after requiring ankle surgery. Other than his sophomore campaign, Lachey has had subpar production for the position. Could use continued development through his lower half, will get completely overwhelmed at the point of attack in the running game. As a pass blocker, Lachey frequently gets caught lunging and getting caught off-balanced. Not a game-changing athlete and will struggle to separate against NFL-level athletes.

Best Fit: Backup TE

Player Ranking (1-100): 67.9 - I like Lachey, and although he isn't a great athlete, he knows how to play the position. His lack of production resulted from playing on some poor Iowa football teams. Lachey certainly has toughness and upside, and I think he could develop into a nice number-two TE for a team. 5th round player.

15. Eli Stowers - Vanderbilt - 6'4 234 lbs

Strengths: A former 4-star QB prospect, Stowers was initially recruited by the Aggies, where he spent two seasons before transferring to New Mexico State for 1 season and then finally to Vanderbilt. Stowers transitioned into a TE towards the end of his time with the Aggies, and he proved his upside at New Mexico State by playing in a dual role. He exploded his final season at Vanderbilt, finishing with nearly 600 yards receiving and four touchdowns. Stowers operates best in a detached receiving role, lining up in the slot, the outside, or as an H-back. Stowers is a high-upside athlete who eases out of his stance and shows fluid movement skills. His success and quick transition to a new position while succeeding in the SEC bodes well for Stowers's future. Stowers plays the position with technical nuance and finesse and is likely helped by his former QB days. In the receiving game, Stowers does the most damage on underneath and intermediate routes, proving to be a reliable 50/50 catcher in the middle of traffic. A comfortable hands catcher, Stowers extends and makes plays outside his frame look routine. He's a savvy and nuanced route runner who utilizes good salesmanship throughout his route stems. At the top of routes, Stowers shows good precision and sharpness to create separation. In zone coverage, Stowers has good spatial awareness, enabling him to find softer spots in coverage and find space easily. He does a terrific job utilizing the sidelines and keeping his feet in bounds on boundary passes. Stowers has the vertical speed to threaten the seams and separate against linebackers. Stowers is a tough runner with the ball in his hands, showing good competitive toughness and shiftiness.

Weaknesses: Stowers has only played the tight end position for a few seasons and is still getting better and smoothing the edges. He lacks an ideal frame and likely won't be able to assist as an inline blocker early on. When blocking, Stowers gets overwhelmed at the point. He fails to consistently sustain blocks and win positioning, lacking anchorage power and iron-grip strength in his hands. While a good athlete, Stowers isn't an elite athlete who will challenge NFL defensive backs. His lack of physicality causes him to struggle when matched up against more physical cover assignments that can challenge him through his stems or at the catch point.

Best Fit: Receiving TE

Player Ranking (1-100): 67.5 - Stowers is an intriguing tight-end prospect who is improving. He lacks the frame or the functional power to win in physical battles, but he can separate and present a fun gadget offensive player that can be utilized as a chess piece on offense. His getting significantly better each season brings confidence that he has a bright future and a large ceiling. 5th round player.

16. Jackson Hawes - Georgia Tech - 6'5 260 lbs

Strengths: As a 6th-year senior for the Yellow Jackets, Hawes spent his first five seasons with Yale before transferring to Georgia Tech for his final season. Hawes has a prototypical NFL frame, showing outstanding density and durability. Hawes is a versatile offensive role player who excels in handling the dirty work. Hawes can line up all over the offensive formation, including inline and outside, as an H-back, split-flow FB, and more! He's an incredibly high-IQ football player who understands his team role, showing outstanding physicality and toughness. In the passing game, Hawes has the power in his hands to disrupt and ease pass rushers. He can drop his anchor and sit on rushers, including bigger edge defenders, without sacrificing much ground. In the running game, Hawes plays with ferocity, rolling his hips forward and generating good leverage through his lower body. He has the core strength and upper-body power through his frame to uproot linebackers in space. He has terrific body control and anticipation while on the move, consistently showing a good batting average in space. Hawes utilizes his former high-school basketball background in the passing game to win against undersized defenders with his frame and high-point abilities. He has a good spatial awareness and can find soft spaces in the middle of the field.

Weaknesses: Hawes' overall receiving production has been inconsequential at best, with very few catches throughout his college career. Most of his receptions came from being a last resort when playing out of the backfield on swing routes. He lacks a significant route tree and will likely serve little upside at the next level in the receiving game. He struggles to separate when running routes, lacking twitch or flexibility through his lower body to change directions easily. When he's contested at the catch point, Hawes struggles to win through contact.

Best Fit: Versatile blocking TE

Player Ranking (1-100): 66.5 - Coaches love kids like Hawes. He will no doubt play a vital role on special teams while also being a versatile chess piece on offense. He doesn't want the glory; he wants to do his job. He will likely be a team's #2 or #3 tight end, but he will always serve a role in a game. 5th round player.

17. Gavin Bartholomew - Pittsburgh - 6'4 260 lbs

Strengths: Bartholomew has been the definition of steady and reliable for four straight seasons, almost with the same production during each campaign. Bartholomew is a versatile offensive weapon used all over the offensive formation, including on the outside, in the slot, as an H-back, and, of course, inline. Bartholomew is a blue-chip competitor that excels in the physical components of playing football. With a smooth accelerator and long strides, Bartholomew gets to top gear quickly, showing the ability to stretch the field against linebackers. Willing to get in dog fights at the catch point, Bartholomew brings competitive fights and physicality at the top of routes. He shows good body control and ball tracking abilities to adjust and contort his body to snatch the ball, adjusting to badly thrown balls. A tireless worker who plays with a hot motor on every snap of the ball, working hard to find space on broken-down plays. Shows good zonal instincts and awareness to find soft spaces in coverage. Brings competitive toughness and a downhill mentality with the ball in his hands, fighting for every additional yard. Bartholomew packs a punch as a run blocker, rolling his hips forward through impact and generating impressive displacement power. He utilizes good hand placement and wins leverage and positioning along the perimeter. A highly experienced special teams contributor, Bartholomew has played on all the units.

Weaknesses: Bartholomew lacks elite size and catch radius, failing to make plays away from his frame consistently. He prefers corralling the body inside his frame and is a bit of a catcher. He has a lot of examples of bobbling balls on his resume, lacking top-end hands. His high-cut frame causes him limitations when playing laterally, appearing to struggle when asked to play on a linear axis. He is not a smooth or sharp route-runner and tends to round off his routes at the top, failing to have the necessary precision and transitional quickness. Needs to win consistently in tight windows as he fails to offer consistent separation against safeties or linebackers. Plays very upright through his route stems, allowing defensive backs to jump his routes. His 2nd level of run blocking is inconsistent. He flashes at times, but other times, he completely whiffs and lunges in space. Bartholomew plays over his toes as a pass blocker and struggles to stay square and mirror.

Best Fit: Versatile TE

Player Ranking (1-100): 64.7 - Bartholomew is an all-around tight end who lacks elite athletic traits but packs a punch as a physical football player. He will get better and better as a blocker, as he certainly has the mentality and the physical toughness to do so. He's not a bad receiver but lacks the tools to win against NFL athletes consistently. 6th round player.

18. Gee Scott Jr - Ohio State - 6'3 243 lbs

Strengths: A former four-star wide receiver prospect, Scott transitioned into a tight end after his freshman season on campus. Scott finally proved some of his upside during his senior season, finishing with 253 yards and two touchdowns. Scott is an athletically built tight end who shows versatility when used all over the offensive front, playing inline, in the backfield, or split out wide. Scott has impressive all-around athleticism, showing the speed and the burst to threaten linebackers at all levels of the field. Scott does most of his damage on underneath and intermediate routes, showing good smoothness and fluidity. A reliable target in the middle of the field, Scott utilizes his frame to box out at the catch point and win in contested settings. He possesses savvy route-running prowess, selling his routes at the top with salesmanship while altering route tempo. His flexible body control allows him to adjust and contort his body to poorly thrown balls. Scott shows excellent hands and comfort in utilizing his entire catch radius to extend and snatch the ball out of the air. Scott is good with the ball in his hands post-catch, showing good competitive toughness and contact balance to bounce off tackle attempts. He also has shiftiness through his lower body that enables him to make the 1st defender miss often. A locker room veteran beloved on campus for his work ethic and leadership intangibles. Scott is a willing run blocker who shows good timing and physicality when opening up things for his teammates.

Weaknesses: Scott's production throughout school has been underwhelming, with only one season of receiving more than 100 yards. He's only had four career touchdowns throughout college. Despite his natural athleticism and speed, he's never been given a chance to be a down-the-field separator. He has mostly gotten his production with underneath manufactured touches designed to get him in space. He's not a separator and will continuously force his quarterback to throw to him in tight windows. As a pass blocker, Scott is entirely unproven. He lacks the upper-body power and the lower-body anchor to sustain when lined up.

Best Fit: Receiving TE

Player Ranking (1-100): 63.8 - Scott is a very good athlete for the TE position, but he's still incredibly raw as a prospect. He can be 100% better as an NFL TE than he was in college. He wasn't given enough chances. The talent is certainly there, but he will likely be initially limited to a receiving role. 6th round player.

19. Moliki Matavao - UCLA - 6'6 263 lbs

Strengths: Initially recruited to play for Oregon, Matavao stayed with the Ducks for two seasons before transferring to UCLA for his final campaign. Matavao had a breakout campaign with UCLA, finishing with over 500 yards receiving in his final season. Matavao is a big and physically tight end with outstanding density and size. Comfortable playing inline, in the slot, or the backfield, Matavao shows versatility when used in a hybrid TE role at the next level. Matavao does the bulk of his damage when working underneath, showing fearlessness and toughness in the middle of the field. He utilizes his body and frame to box out at the catch point, winning most 50/50 situations. He has the size and the high-point ability to be a red-zone threat at the next level. He is hardworking in his routes and has good spatial awareness when finding openings against zone looks. Matavao, a physical specimen bulldozer with the ball in his hands, brushes off contact and generally requires full commitment to bring him down. Matavao flashes upside as a blocker in both the running and passing games. He utilizes his frame to engage quickly in the running game, showing good sustain and power in his hands. While he wasn't used often as a pass blocker, Matavao showed good competitive toughness and anchorage power through his lower body to stay square to targets and minimize push.

Weaknesses: Matavao is a laborer in space, lacking both the acceleration and the speed to threaten consistently at any level. He lacks the lateral twitch and fluidity to separate against man coverage. Matavao is a body catcher who prefers securing the ball into his frame as opposed to attacking the ball. He doesn't always secure the ball as well as you'd think, as he has frequent bobbles and double catches. He racked up a sizeable amount of his yards on manufactured plays and screens designed to get him the ball in space. His route tree has been fairly minimal throughout college, running mostly simple in/out shallow routes.

Best Fit: Versatile TE

Player Ranking (1-100): 63.0 - Despite Matavao's great season, I don't think he has the tools to start TE at the next level. With additional development in the blocking side of his game, he could eventually become a #2 or 3 TE at the next level, which will have to earn him a place on special teams. 6th round player.

20. CJ Dippre - Alabama - 6'5 250 lbs

Strengths: Dippre began his career at Maryland for two seasons before transferring to Alabama following his sophomore campaign. Dipper immediately became an important player for the Tide's offense, assisting both in the receiving and the blocking department. Possessing a power-packed frame, Dippre has a good proportional size and length for the next level. He has more than enough room on his frame for continued development. Dipper has played all over the offensive formation, including inline, as an H-back, and on the outside. Dipper shows good burst and acceleration off the line in the receiving game. He works tirelessly on broken-down plays, always working and trying to find space in the middle of the field. Good movement skills in the open field, showing easy movement and speed. He has a good sense of his surroundings in zone coverage, finding soft creases and sitting in. He is a reliable contested ball catcher and wins with his big, strong mitts. With the ball in his hands, Dippre shows his physicality and toughness, regularly fighting through contact and staying on his feet. He looks for contact, showing good competitive toughness. Dipper is at his best in the blocking department, proving reliable as both a run blocker and in pass sets. Dipper has held his own against defensive ends in the passing game, showing good hand strength and the anchorage power to absorb. He is a physical run blocker who places his hands well in the run game at the 1st level, rolling his hips through contact. He does a nice job of consistent 2nd-level contact in space. He's had minimal injury concerns and has been reliable for four seasons.

Weaknesses: Dippre has had ball security concerns throughout college, with multiple bad fumbles. Dipper has underrated athleticism as a receiver but fails significantly short of being a top athlete at the tight end. His route tree has been limited to a few simple routes, and he will need to diversify his route offerings. Dipper needs to do a better job of utilizing finesse through his stems as a route runner. At the top of his routes, he frequently rounds them off, failing to separate against defensive backs. Most of his receptions were on broken-down or manufactured plays while at Alabama. As a blocker, Dippre shows significant upside, but he still has areas for improvement. He frequently leans in and gets caught off-balance. He needs to do a better job placing his hands, stifling, and slowing down pass rushers. Not a people mover in the run game, more of a positionally sound blocker that wins with angles and leverage.

Best Fit: Blocking TE

Player Ranking (1-100): 61.4 - Dippre shows the mentality and the urgency to be a good blocking TE. He's not a slouch as an athlete, but he's not a guy who will create consistent separation at the next level. There are traits to work with here. He could be a good sleeper pick on Day 3. I'd take him in the 6th round.

21. Mitchell Evans - Notre Dame - 6'5 248 lbs

Strengths: A 4-year contributor to the Fighting Irish offense, Evans showed his potential as a junior in 2023, finishing with over 400 yards receiving. Evans is a well-built TE prospect with ideal amounts of power and length on his frame, showing NFL readiness and body armor. Evans utilizes his size and catch radius to dominate against smaller linebackers and defensive backs, winning in the tight areas of the field. Very good hands catcher who shows complete trust to extend and win at the catch point, making some difficult grabs look easy. He can be used as a red-zone target with his reliability in tough windows and length. Decent 1st step quickness allows him to reach full speed in a few steps, easing into his routes. Can track the ball down the field, showing flexible body control and high-point skills. A smart kid who excels at finding spaces against softer zone looks, frequently sitting in and presenting a QB-friendly target in the middle of the field. Has the power in his frame to handle inline responsibilities. As a run blocker, Evans maintains good positioning and angles to open up outside runs.

Weaknesses: Evans has had very modest production throughout college besides his junior campaign. Has had his fair share of minor injury concerns, causing him to miss some game time. A limited athlete who is not exactly a seam stretcher who can be counted on to stretch the field against NFL linebackers and safeties. Runs very upright after making the catch, causing him to go down very easily, showcasing very little yards' after catch ability. Runs a very limited route tree. While he certainly has improvement in blocking, he will struggle to handle 1 v 1 pass-blocking opportunities due to poor hand usage and overaggression.

Best Fit: Backup TE

Player Ranking (1-100): 60.9 - Evans had a great junior season, and if he followed it up with another great senior year, he could have likely pushed himself in the Day 2 discussion, but unfortunately, he didn't. He's a tough kid with terrific hands, but unfortunately, he is a very limited athlete and isn't a refined blocker at this point. 6th round pick.

Top-10 TE's

1. Tyler Warren

85

2. Harold Fannin Jr
3. Colston Loveland
4. Jake Briningstool
5. Oronde Gadsden II
6. Terrance Ferguson
7. Gunnar Helm
8. Mason Taylor
9. Oscap Delp
10. Bryson Nesbit

Chapter 6

OT's

1. Will Campbell - LSU - 6'6 324 lbs

Strengths: A 3-year starter for LSU at left tackle, Campbell won the blindside job almost immediately upon arriving on campus, starting from Day 1 as a true freshman. Campbell has an NFL-ready frame, proving both the experience and the readiness to transition to the next level. Easing off the snap of the ball, Campbell displays good fundamentals and technique with bent knees and width. If initially beaten or given any ground in pass sets, Campbell quickly resets, proving to have the core strength and recovery quickness to regain control of reps. Excellent power at the point of attack allows him to win most hand fights and gain control of defenders with his vice-like grips. Maintains control throughout reps, rarely letting defenders out of his grasp on counter moves. Impressive footwork to mirror in space, showing lateral mobility and change of direction to maintain spacing. Has the power throughout his frame to succeed against bigger defenders, dropping his anchor quickly against bull rushers and absorbing with minimal movement. In the running game, Campbell fires out of his stance with good anticipation and quickness. Has the upper body power to displace defenders out of 1st level rush lanes. Can also generate powerful torque through his lower body to drive in short-yardage situations. Shows an upside when used in zone-blocking looks, proving the ability to be used effectively in space. Plays with a violent and nasty demeanor, playing each snap like it's his last.

Weaknesses: Campbell lacks elite-level arm length, and some believe he might be forced to kick inside. While Campbell is a good overall athlete, he isn't elite and will sometimes be challenged vertically. Due to a lack of confidence against the more explosive rushers, Campbell can sometimes overset on his kick slide, leaving interior rush lanes exposed. When getting rushed head-on, Campbell often fires first and has had some strike accuracy concerns. Has some reps where he fires out of his stance too upright in passing sets, causing him to give up some initial movement. He can have some reps where he plays a little out of control in the running game, causing him to play off his toes and get caught off-balance and lunging in space.

Best Fit: Starting Left Tackle

Player Ranking (1-100): 87.8 - Campbell is the definition of a smooth operator with very, very few bad reps on his resume. His success and domination in the SEC lead me to believe he will transition to the next level well. I don't believe there's any reason to transition him to playing guard, but I think he can succeed as a tackle at the next level. 1st round player.

2. Kelvin Banks Jr - Texas - 6'4 320 lbs

Strengths: A 3-year starter and former top 5-star Longhorn recruit who immediately won the starting left tackle gig as a true freshman. Banks is one of the youngest players in the draft class, having just turned 21. Banks is a mountain of a man with incredible size, dimensions, and thickness throughout his frame, most notably in his lower half. A physical specimen, Banks displays the tools to be a franchise LT at the next level with his combination of athleticism and power. Banks displays the initial quickness and movement skills as a pass blocker to gain depth quickly. He couples that with smooth lateral agility and change of directional skills to mirror in space easily. Maintains good technique throughout reps and keeps his weight evenly distributed while remaining under control. He was a technician with his hands, understanding how to strike with accuracy and timing, proving to have heavy and powerful hands. Keeps his pads low and leveraged against bull rushers, displaying excellent anchorage strength to absorb. Recognizes blitzes and stunts quickly, adjusting while keeping his head on a swivel. Comfortable playing in zone and power-blocking run schemes, Banks has the schematic versatility to play in any offense. An easy mover that displays good awareness to seal off backside runs while proving effective when used on pulls at the 2nd level. Displays the acceleration to beat defenders to the spot, winning positioning and leverage. He is excellent when working with his teammates on combination blocks and double teams, arriving with good timing and displacement power to open up both first and second-level lanes. He generates movement through his lower body to create a powerful push at the 1st level, frequently used to run behind in short-yardage situations.

Weaknesses: Bank's main issues come from his overaggressive nature in both passing and running sets. Banks tend to play over his toes in the passing game, giving up his base and chest far too easily. When he overextends, he gets caught off-balanced and struggles resetting. His overall recovery abilities, when initially beaten, aren't great; he sometimes fails to regain control of reps. Lacks elite hip mobility, as he shows some stiffness when mirroring against better quick-twitch rushers. In the running game, he fails to strike accurately with his hands and fails to control throughout reps. He allows defenders to disengage, failing to have ideal grip strength in his hands to control. He gets caught off-balanced in the running game when he plays over his toes, whiffing in space in moments.

Best Fit: Starting Left Tackle

Player Ranking (1-100): 86.9 - Banks is a terrific and experienced prospect with the athleticism of a franchise LT. While he needs to be more patient at times in passing sets and play more under control in the running game, he has an incredible ceiling with additional development. The skies are the limit for Banks as a prospect, as he already is good. But he could get significantly better. 1st round player.

3. Josh Conerly Jr - Oregon - 6'4 315 lbs

Strengths: A former consensus five-star recruit, Conerly took over as a starter during his sophomore campaign, starting in each of the last two seasons. A former high school running back, Conerly has worked hard to completely transition his frame and maximize his physical tools while showing prototypical length to play on the outside. A natural athlete, Conerly shows incredible ease of motion in all areas of the game. In passing sets, Conerly shows fluidity and foot quickness to get vertical in passing sets while maintaining spacing with defenders. His change of directional abilities and his agility let him have complete comfort handling rushers in space, showing impressive mirroring skills. If initially beaten, Conerly easily resets and recovers. He wins both with natural leverage advantages and utilizing good knee bend out of his sets. Highly aware of sensing things, quickly adjusting and recovering against loops and late blitzes. Showcases heavy hands while displaying a good understanding of strike timing and accuracy. Conerly is frequently used as the move blocker in the running game, showing repeated success when handling screens and pulls. His excellent balance and anticipation of the move allowed him to succeed in reaching 2nd and 3rd-level defenders. Understands how to utilize positioning and leverage along the perimeter to open up outside-zone runs. Works well with his teammates in handling combo blocks, showing good urgency and intensity on every snap. Possesses a constant work ethic with a tireless motor on every snap.

Weaknesses: Conerly is an undersized tackle that lacks ideal size dimensions despite having good length. He could benefit by adding strength to his frame, notably his lower body. He will get bullied by speed-to-power rushers who can get underneath and challenge his leverage advantage. Anchorage power overall is OK but isn't top-tier. He doesn't appear to have great grip strength, as he will fail to sustain blocks through the duration fully. Has significant penalty issues during his sophomore campaign. Understands how to utilize his hands, but his accuracy can be wide, completely missing at times. He's not a people mover in the run game, failing to generate POP in his hands or rollback power through his lower body. Lacks a fit in a power or gap-heavy run offense.

> **Best Fit: Starting LT**

Player Ranking (1-100): 86.4 - Based on his 2023 tape, Conerly would likely be a Day-3 player, but he's shown incredible growth in his final season. His ceiling is through the roof as he continues to gain functional strength. At only 21 years old and with a high floor, Conerly is worth a 1st round pick.

4. Josh Simmons - Ohio State - 6'5 310 lbs

Strengths: Simmons spent two seasons at San Diego State before transferring to Ohio State before beginning his junior campaign. Simmons has extensive experience playing on both sides of the line of scrimmage, playing right and left tackles at different points. Before the injury, Simmons was having his best campaign to date, not giving up one sack on the blindside for the Buckeyes. A well-proportioned tackle, Simmons has zero unnecessary body fat and carries his frame well, with noteworthy length. Simmons is a natural athlete who eases out of his kick-slide with fluidity and foot quickness. He regularly beats defenders to spots, winning positioning and leverage. He arrives to contact with good pop in his hands, showing impressive upper and lower body strength. Commits himself to playing with good pad level and technique, maintaining knee bend and patience in his pass sets. Has enough lateral mobility and speed to take on the quick-twitch rushers at the next level, rarely getting beat along the edges. If he initially gets beat, his reset and recovery allow him to regain control of reps. As a run blocker, Simmons is equally as powerful and physically imposing. He works out of his stance with urgency and a good understanding of spatial awareness. His length and body control allow him to have success as a move blocker, frequently being used at the 2nd level. In short-yardage situations, Simmons churns his legs through contact, continuing to generate movement. Simmons has competed against top-tier competition the last two seasons at Ohio State, more than holding his own.

Weaknesses: He suffered a left knee injury, causing him to miss half the season in his final campaign. Simmons can sometimes be caught lunging, getting caught off-balanced by push/pull techniques by rushers. He struggled with significant penalties during his first few seasons, starting at San Diego State and Ohio State. His overall hand usage in both phases can be inconsistent, often striking too wide of the mark. Lacks top-end hand strength, which would allow him to sustain blocks better.

> **Best Fit: Left Tackle in any scheme**

Player Ranking (1-100): 85.9 - As long as Simmons medical checks out OK, he should be a 1st round player. He had no durability issues whatsoever before this season. He's a rare combination of athlete and natural power. He fails to have a true weakness and could be a terrific franchise LT for years. 1st round player.

5. Aireontae Ersery - Minnesota - 6'6 330 lbs

Strengths: A 3-year starter for the Gophers at left tackle, Ersery played a little bit of right tackle for the Gophers during his first few seasons. Only beginning to play football as a junior in high school, Ersery's talent and ceiling are through the roof. Ersery has a massive frame with long arms and thickness throughout his frame, showing the ability to impose his frame on defenders. A competitive finisher, Ersery loves the physical sides of the game, dominating until the echoes of the whistle on every snap. Power at the point of attack and core strength allows him to redirect his frame and adjust. Heavy hands cause him to knock defenders off the ball, greatly slowing down their rushes. Length and lower body anchorage power make him an impossible guy to move for rushers attempting to drive him on the ball. He is an above-average athlete who shows impressive initial quickness in his kick slide, causing very difficult angles for rushers to attempt to win along the edges. Ersery dominates in the run game, frequently creating momentum through his lower half, driving defenders off the ball. A true people mover, Ersery can create massive lanes at the 1st level, excelling when in a phone booth against defenders. When Ersery latches on to defenders in the running game, he never lets them out of his grasp, showing iron-grip strength throughout his hands. He is at his best in a power-blocking system.

Weaknesses: Ersery is still raw and needs refinement on some of the game's mental aspects. He can react slowly, especially when defenses through unique looks or blitzes in his direction. While he is a good athlete, he isn't elite, and he can overset to the outside, leaving interior rush lanes wide open. Strike accuracy and placement get too high on occasion in passing sets. He needs to do a better job of remaining leveraged through snaps, allowing his pads to rise and smaller defenders to get under his pads. A bit of a waist bender that fails to use knee bend to stay square with defenders properly. He is not a guy who will excel in zone-style running looks, as he lacks the experience and athleticism to play with range.

Best Fit: Starting Tackle in a Power-Blocking System

Player Ranking (1-100): 84.8 - Ersery has a massive ceiling! He will have frustrations if he's expected to do too much too soon, as he still needs to iron out his passing game sets. But when it comes to the running game, Ersery is truly dominant and is a joy to watch. He can single-handedly open up rush lanes. 2nd round player.

6. Ajani Cornelius - Oregon - 6'5 315 lbs

Strengths: Cornelius started his collegiate career at FCS-level Rhode Island, where he started two years at right tackle before transferring over to the Ducks and starting for them two years. He's the definition of reliable and sturdy, having started for four straight seasons. Cornelius possesses an impressive frame, showcasing the length for continued refinement and additional muscle. Had a relatively smooth transition to playing for a big-time college program from FCS, showing impressive traits. Cornelius is a smooth-moving athlete and impressive as a pass protector. Easing into his kick-slide, he shows smooth footwork and easily transitions laterally to mirror in space. Cornelius is not just an athlete but has the lower body power and strength to absorb bull rushes against quick-twitch rushers, showcasing impressive anchorage ability. Smart and high football IQ to recognize pre-snap defensive looks, regularly picking up blitzes and stunts. Can quickly reset his feet if he's initially beaten, showing good recovery ability. Has gotten better and better in the run game the last couple of seasons, showing the schematic versatility to play with both power blocking and zone blocking concepts. Can climb to the second level on zone-style runs, showing impressive body control, balance, and strike accuracy when working in space. A violent finisher, Cornelius shows the toughness and mean streak to maintain sustain throughout plays. The rapid improvement shows Cornelius' massive ceiling as he continues to develop.

Weaknesses: Despite Cornelius' length, he can play a little too belly up, allowing defenders into his chest plate too easily. Has played RT throughout his career, lacking the experience to play on the blindside. He still is growing into his frame and is a little too thin through his upper body. He will struggle against the more powerful defenders that can match his length. Has a bad habit of allowing his pads to rise mid-play, allowing defenders to get underneath him. He is still working on consistent hand placement, as he will often get too high with his strikes.

Best Fit: Starting Tackle in Either System

Player Ranking (1-100): 83.3 - I'm impressed with Cornelius, as he has the demeanor, athleticism, and lower body strength to succeed. I'd like to see him continue to maximize his frame while gaining additional upper-body mass and strength. He has the skill set to exceed on both the right and left sides and in any offensive system. 2nd round player.

7. Armand Membou - Missouri - 6'3 314 lbs

Strengths: A 2-year starter for the Tigers, Membou has extensive experience at right tackle but has played some inside during his first season of starting in 2023. An athletically built specimen, Membou has ideal measurables and length to play along the perimeter at the next level. He has enough room in his frame to continue adding quality mass. Membou excels at the athletic sides of the game, proving to have a terrific twitch throughout his frame. Membou eases out his stance in passing sets with good initial quickness and burst, getting to good depths to maintain spacing. He showcases excellent patience and discipline, rarely playing over his skis. His powerful upper body allows him to deliver devastating punches at impact and control rushers with his hands. His iron-grip strength in his hands allows him to control reps. A fluid mover throughout his lower body, Membou can mirror and match up against most edge rushers. He appears to process things quickly, recognizing stunts and blitzes and adjusting. Membou utilizes his power and explosive lower body twitch in the running game to displace and uproot defenders off their spots. He can clear out 1st level rush lanes while pushing back piles in short-yardage spots. A highly intelligent blocker who plays with urgency and anticipation. He recognizes things quickly, cutting off and sealing gaps against backside defenders. When on the move, Membou maintains good balance and recognition, regularly making good 2nd level contact in space.

Weaknesses: Membou is still refining his frame and could benefit by adding weight and mass to his frame, most notably in his lower body. Lack of top anchorage strength causes him to lose his anchor against bigger bull rushers. Membou has a high-cut frame that causes him sometimes to struggle to change directions. This limits him when handling against top-tier speed athletes that will challenge him at the top of the arc. He tends to be too patient sometimes, allowing defenders into his frame. He's often too quick to drop to depths in vertical passing sets, allowing power rushers more direct pathways to the QB. Lacks the aggressive mean streak and finishers' mentality in the running game.

Best Fit: Right Tackle or can kick inside

Player Ranking (1-100): 83.0 - Armand has a massive future with continued development. Most of his weaknesses are coaching-related, and he can improve on them. He has the athleticism and upper-body strength to succeed at the next level, not to mention the positional versatility. 2nd round player.

8. Cameron Williams - Texas - 6'5 335 lbs

Strengths: While Williams saw some reps as a freshman and sophomore, it wasn't until his junior season that he became the regular starter at right tackle for the Longhorns. Williams is a massive man with vines for arms, possessing the size and frame to play both outside and inside. Williams has plenty of natural athleticism as a pass protector, easing out of his kick-slide with quick initial movement skills. He utilizes his long arms and vertical sets, making it incredibly difficult for defenders to flatten the arc against his outside shoulder. Impressive power at the point of attack allows him to absorb power rushers that attempt to rush him head-on. The iron grip in his hands enables him to sustain blocks once he reaches the chest pads of blockers. Williams is dominant in the running game when working in a phone booth. Fully capable of uprooting defenders with point-of-attack power, Williams generates significant pop in his hands while utilizing lower body torque to displace. Impressive when used on the move, showing good initial quickness while having the balance and body control to reach 2nd level blockers. Williams plays with a nasty mean streak, finishing every rep with urgency. Williams is incredibly toolsy, and being a 1-year starter, the skies are the limit for Williams.

Weaknesses: Williams is still incredibly raw and needs to learn to utilize his hands fully. He frequently misses late and too wide, enabling quicker-twitch rushers to have free access to the QB. He appears to have mental lapses, not always knowing his assignment and allowing free rushers on blitzes and stunts. Can get too aggressive in passing sets, oversetting, and lunging at defenders. He is not a great pass protector when left on an island, appearing to struggle with some tightness in his lower half. He flashes as a 2nd level move blocker, but he's hot and cold, sometimes playing far too upright and whiffing in space.

Best Fit: RT

Player Ranking (1-100): 82.5 - Williams has the physical tools to be a starting tackle in this league. But he's going to have major growth curves initially. He can sometimes be a liability in the passing game, and he will certainly give up some poor sacks. But his raw physical traits, including his movement skills, length, and point-of-attack power, are incredibly enticing for the future. Not many have Williams' physical traits. 2nd round player.

9. Emery Jones Jr - LSU - 6'6 322 lbs

Strengths: Jones is a 3-year starter on the right side of the Tigers' offensive line, which immediately won the RT spot as a true freshman. A big-bodied tackle displaying the power-packed profile with the length to match. Jones has shown consistency against top-tier competition for the last three seasons, showing NFL readiness. Power and nastiness are the name of the game for Jones, playing with a violent, mean streak and finishers mentality on every snap of the ball. In passing sets, Jones maintains patience, rarely playing over his skis. He utilizes his powerful hands to jolt and deliver blows to oncoming rushers. Has the iron-grip strength in his hands to latch on while staying square to his target. When he's left without an assignment, he looks for work. Keeps his head on a swivel at all times, adjusting and responding to stunts and late blitzes. He controls the chest place of rushers by his length. Has outstanding lower body strength to drop his anchor and minimize movement against bull rushers. In the running game, Jones truly excels due to his point-of-attack power. Showing impressive quickness out of his stance, Jones rolls his hips forward while showing displacement power to uproot at the 1st and 2nd levels. He is effective in zone-style runs, regularly getting out in space and showing good balance and anticipation when he's on the move.

Weaknesses: There are some suggestions that Jones could be forced to kick inside due to his lack of ideal foot speed and movement skills. He struggles to play on an island in space, failing to mirror against quick-twitch rushers while repeatedly giving up the outside rush lane. He comes out of his stance upright, losing his base early and allowing leveraged defenders to get underneath his pads. Overall, weight distribution isn't ideal as he's very bottom-heavy, which minimizes his athletic upside. Has a bad habit of stopping his feet upon impact in the run game, minimizing his overall movement skills.

Best Fit: RT or kick inside to guard

Player Ranking (1-100): 81.9 - Jones can be a really good RT at the next level or a potential Pro-Bowl interior guard. His massive frame and power are rare, and he's no slouch as an athlete; he just isn't elite. I'd be fine with how a team uses him, and I think he'd succeed. 2nd round player.

10. Anthony Belton - North Carolina State - 6'6 336 lbs

Strengths: A 3-year starter at left tackle for the Wolfpack, Belton also has two additional years playing at Georgia Military Academy before transferring to North Carolina State. Belton is a massive man with the ideal measurables to play outside the offensive line for years to come. His length and size cause him to be a real problem for rushers, as Belton understands how to force improbable angles for rushers to win the corner. Despite his height, Belton does a good job utilizing width with a strong base to absorb against bull rushers, limiting movement significantly. Lower body strength is prevalent, showing excellent absorption ability. Utilizes good hand fundamentals in the passing game, showcasing good strike accuracy and hand placement to control for the duration of plays. If initially beaten, Belton has noticeable athleticism to reset his feet and regain control of reps. Highly intelligent blocker that recognizes things pre-snap and understands when there are additional rushers. His awareness allows him to react and pick up against stunts and blitzes. He is a durable starter who has been on the field almost every snap of his college career. In the running game, Belton shows upside in zone runs, understanding how to get in space with good strike accuracy while on the move. Showcases his displacement power in short-yardage runs, as Belton will generate impressive momentum through his lower body at the point of attack.

Weaknesses: Despite his starting experience, Belton is still raw and has many highs and lows. He's a bit of an erratic player who looks like a surefire 1st round pick on some games, and on others, he looks like a Day 3 player. Belton's overall athleticism is good, but his massive frame limits him when he attempts to play laterally. If he misses with his hands, he will be highly susceptible to speed rushes on the outside or inside swim moves against quick-twitch rushers. Lack of finishing ability and nastiness can be frustrating at Belton, who doesn't always finish plays, allowing defenders off consistently on counter moves.

Best Fit: Potential Starting LT or RT

Player Ranking (1-100): 81.4 - Belton certainly has traits, but expecting too much too soon with Belton can be a recipe for disaster. Scouts like to say that if you see it once, you can do it again, but Belton will frustrate at times. There's no denying there's a player here, as he can be a real dominant force at times, even against the better defenses in college football. I'd take him in the 2nd round. There aren't too many people with Belton's size and athleticism measurables.

11. Earnest Green III - Georgia - 6'4 320 lbs

Strengths: Green is a 2-year starter for the Bulldogs, who have played on the blindside in the last two seasons. Green is a well-built prospect with prototypical size proportions and good muscularity and length. Green has seamlessly transitioned to the role, with a nice blend of athleticism and power through his frame. Green eases out of his stance with good lateral agility in passing sets, proving his ability to mirror in space. His powerful upper body enables him to deliver violent blows to defenders to disrupt and alter their rush plan. He generally places his hands well, controlling rushers for the duration of the rep. Green keeps his head on a swivel, effortless and smoothly picking up stunts and blitzes. Against power, Green shows his ability to drop his anchor timely and absorb speed-to-power rushers with minimal damage being done. Green is a finisher who battles until after the whistle, repeatedly putting guys on their backs. Green has positional versatility as he has played some guard earlier in his career. In the running game, Green excels when playing in space. He displays good quickness out of his stance to reach set points before defenders to take them out of plays. He's fully capable of being used on outside-zone style runs, including pulling and reaching in space. He is a physical blocker who makes first contact, commits to winning inside hands, and utilizes good positional and angle blocks to open up running lanes.

Weaknesses: Green is still raw and needs additional development. He tends to overset in passing sets to his outside, leaving the 'B' gap exposed at times against power rushers. He fails to always play with patience, playing over his skis and losing leverage due to his aggressive nature. He needs to do a better job utilizing leverage and bending from the knees, as he is frequently caught lunging while bending at the waist. He's a good athlete but not a top-tier one, as he will struggle against the quicker twitch rushers that can consistently threaten to arc the corner. His hand timing can sometimes be a tad late, as he allows defenders into his chest plate too easily. While Green is a powerful man with a strong upper body, he lacks the torque and the lower body driving power to be a people mover in the run game.

Best Fit: Zone-blocking tackle or kick inside to guard

Player Ranking (1-100): 80.0 - I like Green quite a bit as an overall prospect. While he's not as refined as others in the draft class, he's got terrific upside. The Georgia offensive line lineage has also been quite successful in transitioning to the NFL. I like that Green has the experience against SEC competition, and he's both an athlete and incredibly powerful. 2nd round player.

12. Jack Nelson - Wisconsin - 6'7 304 lbs

Strengths: A 3-year starter for the Badgers, Nelson started his career as a right guard before transitioning to the left tackle for the last two seasons. Possessing a wide and large frame, Nelson far exceeds NFL measurables to play on the outside. Looking capable and comfortable playing both outside and inside, Nelson is a positionally versatile next-level line prospect. Has experience playing in both power and zone-blocking concepts, proving to be adept at any offensive system. He has incredible durability, as he's started every game in the last three seasons. As a pass blocker, Nelson understands how to utilize his wide base and positional sensibility to minimize opportunities for rushers. Lower body strength is prevalent as he can quickly recover and reset his anchor if he initially grants any movement. Rarely gets overwhelmed with power. Outstanding latch on strength in his hands, rarely letting defenders out of his grasp. In the running game, Nelson is a space-clearing bulldozer. Generating terrific rolling power through his lower body, Nelson will clear 1st level rush lanes. He can also be used as a fundamentally sound reach blocker, winning with positioning and angles along the perimeter. A finisher that plays until the echoes of the whistle, constantly bringing defenders to the ground.

Weaknesses: He still needs to develop and get better with his hand technique, as he frequently places his hands too low in pass sets, allowing defenders to disengage easily on counters. He will struggle against rushers that can match or reach him, as he is quick to give up his chest plate. Foot quickness is average to below average for an offensive tackle. Due to that, he lacks confidence against quicker twitch rushers as he frequently oversets with short and choppy steps, leaving the inside counter completely vulnerable. While he does a good job of winning positioning, he occasionally gives up the outside rush lane, failing to mirror in too much space. Doesn't always process things quickly post-snap, as he can be late to react to blitzes and stunts, leaving free rushers. Hand placement on rushes can get too far outside and will get a bit grabby, leading to some holding calls at the next level.

Best Fit: Right Tackle or Guard

Player Ranking (1-100): 77.4 - I like Nelson, and he could be a good RT or guard. He's got the power and the toughness to excel at either position. While he isn't a great athlete, he isn't BAD per se. He lacks the ideal elite foot quickness to handle NFL athletes consistently. 3rd round player. This kid is tough and will make your offensive line nastier.

13. Marcus Mbow - Purdue - 6'5 305 lbs

Strengths: A 3rd-year starter for the Boilermakers, Mbow has shown the ability to be a versatile piece for their offensive line, playing at both tackle and guard during his time. Mbow is built with an athletic lean frame capable of handling tackle responsibilities. A terrific and free-moving athlete, Mbow utilizes fluid and a fleet of feet to drop in his vertical passing sets, maintaining good depth to the mirror. Easily moves laterally, showing impressive fluidity throughout his lower body. Fully capable of handling quick-twitch rushers on an island, matching them for quickness. If he initially grants any movement, Mbow has the core strength and the power to reset and recover. He is a technician in the way he fits his hands, showcasing a wide variety of different hand tactics to control defenders. Mbow explodes out of his stance in the running game, utilizing built-up momentum to generate displacement power. Impressive when used on the move, showing body control, anticipation, and twitch to reach 2nd level blockers and overwhelm with power. Not content simply winning his assignment, Mbow plays with a nasty edge and a finishers' mentality to play until after the whistle.

Weaknesses: Mbow lacks the ideal frame for a tackle or guard and doesn't appear to have significant room for additional growth. Likely only a fit in a zone-style offensive running system. He plays with an overaggressive mindset in both phases of the game, getting caught playing over his toes and losing his balance. His hand strength doesn't appear to be his strength, as he frequently loses sustain and lets defenders disengage on counter moves. He missed most of the 2023 season with a leg injury. His anchorage strength and his upright pads limit him against powerful bull rushers. It causes him to frequently lose ground upon the snap of the ball, always in make-up mode attempting to recover. Pre-snap awareness isn't ideal, as he sometimes misses his assignments on blitzes and stunts.

Best Fit: Developmental Tackle

Player Ranking (1-100): 76.4 - I like Mbow. His ceiling is through the roof. He's a natural, smooth-moving athlete who looks the part in passing sets. In some games, he gets it; in others, he looks like an undrafted free agent who is completely overwhelmed. He has a massive ceiling with continued development but will need time. 3rd round player.

14. Brandon Crenshaw-Dickson - Florida - 6'7 322 lbs

Strengths: Crenshaw-Dickson was a 3-year starter for San Diego State before transferring to the Gators for his final campaign in 2024. Crenshaw-Dickson has played as both a blindside and strong-side tackle, showing the ability and comfort to play both. As a Gator, Crenshaw-Dickson played on the right side of the line of scrimmage, proving he could be successful against elite competition. Crenshaw-Dickson has prototypical size and length, displaying the density and the length to hold up on the outside. Crenshaw-Dickson has seen it all and had experience in spades, and that's clear both pre and post-snap. Quickly recognizing defensive looks, Crenshaw-Dickson shows zero hesitancy against stunts and blitzes. He knows exactly who to pick up and who to pass. Crenshaw-Dickson is an above-average overall athlete with quick feet and a smooth kick-slide, enabling him to widen the pocket. His strong upper body lets him displace and slow defenders, knocking them back. Lower body strength is prevalent against bull rushers, Crenshaw-Dickson can drop his anchor while absorbing. In the running game, Crenshaw-Dickson quickly fires out of his stance. He generates good momentum through his lower body to deliver big blocks while moving. He's often used to lead the way for screens, showing impressive straight-line speed. A bully in short-yardage and red-zone situations, Crenshaw-Dickson showcases good point-of-attack displacement power to open up rush lanes. He is a beast who proves to be a finisher in how he plays the position, seemingly effortlessly bringing defenders to the ground.

Weaknesses: Crenshaw-Dickson will be 24 years old on draft night. He can sometimes be too patient in pass sets, enabling rushers to get too big a runway into his frame. Crenshaw-Dickson has some balance issues in the running game due to his aggressive playstyle, leading to him playing over his toes. A good athlete, but Crenshaw-Dickson struggles when asked to mirror against the quicker twitched rushers. He lacks elite agility and change of direction and will get put in recovery mode against nuanced and explosive rushers. While Crenshaw-Dickson displays terrific hand power, he sometimes can get out of sync between his upper and lower body. This causes him to frequently whiff with his hands, incorrectly timing and placing his punches.

Best Fit: RT in either scheme

Player Ranking (1-100): 75.1 - I like what I see from Crenshaw-Dickson. His experience will serve him well at the next level. While I don't think he's an elite NFL starter with a massive ceiling, he could be a solid starter with a high floor and low ceiling. He's seen it all and is 100% NFL-ready. 3rd round player.

15. Charles Grant - William & Mary - 6'4 300 lbs

Strengths: As a 5th-year senior for the FCS program William & Mary, Grant has been a dominant starter at left tackle in the last three seasons. Grant is built with a long and lean physique, showcasing an athletic profile to transition to the next level. A fluid and easy mover, Grant works out of his kick-slide with smooth movement skills and quick feet. Grant remains patient and has good width and knee bend when working through his pass sets. Lateral mobility and change of directional abilities allow him to mirror in space, rarely getting beat by speed. Grant utilizes all of his length to win with positioning and angles, forcing defenders to take wide pursuit lanes to the QB. Once Grant gets his hands on defenders, he can generally control them by dropping his anchor while allowing minimal movement. Grant has extensive experience handling zone-style runs while playing in a zone-based offensive system. Has a good understanding and feel for working blocks in space, showing impressive timing and anticipation on cut-off and reach blocks. Capable of making 2nd level contact in space and being used as the lead puller on outside-zone runs. Not content simply making contact, Grant is a finisher who takes his assignment seriously.

Weaknesses: Grant needs to continue to develop his frame, as he lacks a significant power profile. His lack of anchorage strength limits him when handling bigger defenders in passing sets. Grant has had several penalty concerns in the past couple of seasons. His patience can sometimes be a detriment as he allows longer defenders to reach his frame upon contact. While he has fluid athleticism, his footwork can sometimes be choppy when working to gain depth, especially when challenged by quicker twitch rushers. Tends to overset to his outside shoulder, leaving the 'B' gap completely exposed to counter rushes. Grant hasn't competed against top-tier edge defenders and will likely have significant growth challenges initially playing at the next level.

Best Fit: Developmental Tackle

Player Ranking (1-100): 74.3 - Few guys have Grant's size and movement skills, which will enable him to get drafted potentially higher. Grant is a talented kid who must live in an NFL strength & conditioning program to maximize his physical tools. He isn't a Day 1 starter, but in a year or two, he 100% could be. 4th round player.

16. Ozzy Trapilo - Boston College - 6'8 309 lbs

Strengths: After redshirting his first season on campus and starting in just two games during his redshirt freshman campaign, Trapilo has started in almost every game in the last three seasons. He has experience playing at guard and left tackle, but he has played predominantly right tackle the last two seasons. Displaying a massive frame, Trapilo has both the size and frame for continued development. Trapilo excels in passing sets, utilizing his monster frame to force improbable angles for defenders. He's given up hardly anything in the passing game in three straight seasons, completely dominating mostly. Despite his massive leverage disadvantage, Trapilo can easily absorb against speed-to-power rushers, rarely giving them an inch. He repeatedly stones walls defenders and then fails to let them off on counter attempts with his iron-grip strength in his hands. He quickly adjusts and recognizes things pre and post-snap, passing off blitzes and stunts easily. In the running game, Trapilo excels most when utilizing a vertical plane power-blocking scheme. He can open up rush lanes with his massive frame, utilizing leverage and angles to his advantage. He can generate movement at the 1st level with his point of attack power, generating impressive rolling torque through his lower body.

Weaknesses: Trapilo is much further behind in the running game. He repeatedly has balance issues playing in space, getting caught on the ground when attempting to make 2nd level contact. He doesn't consistently utilize his hands well in the run game, missing with timing and placement. A laborer in space that likely isn't suited for a zone-style system. In the passing game, Trapilo gets by with his size but lacks smooth and natural movement skills on an island. His lack of fluidity and change of directional skills in his lower half isn't exposed due to his wide blocking radius. He can be very slow with his hands and overly patient, allowing defenders to get big jumps on him in passing sets.

Best Fit: Right Tackle in Power/Gap system

Player Ranking (1-100): 73.8 - I like Trapilo and think he has a shot to be a starter in this league. While he needs additional refinement in the running game, his ability to consistently hold up in the passing game is outstanding. Even when he makes mistakes, he's able to recover and reset. His anchorage strength and size are a complete impairment for pass rushers. It was rare to see him even allow a pressure on tape. 4th round player.

17. Logan Brown - Kansas - 6'6 315 lbs

Strengths: A 6th-year senior and former five-star high school prospect, Brown initially began his career at Wisconsin for four seasons before transferring over to play his final two seasons with the Jayhawks. Brown was used sparingly for the Badgers before arriving at Kansas but finally got his chance in 2024 to be an every-down starter at right tackle for the Jayhawks. Brown has outstanding proportional size and length, exceeding prototypical NFL standards to play on the outside. Brown is a noteworthy athlete who easily matches the feet of edge rushers in passing sets, easing between bent knees and maintaining good leverage throughout. He utilizes his length to control edge rushes, utilizing full extension and lockout, not allowing defenders to reach his pads. He locates and places his hands well, showing impressive strike accuracy and timing. He does a nice job of playing leveraged to maximize his frames' power, utilizing knee bend and width to absorb. Brown shows schematic versatility in the running game when playing in any offensive system. He's a road grader in gap schemes, showing the ability to uproot and generate rollback power through his lower body. A violent mauler, when engaged at the 1st level, Brown takes his assignments seriously and often brings defenders to the ground.

Weaknesses: Brown missed the end of the 2023 season for Kansas after dealing with a season-ending leg injury. Brown is a person with type-1 diabetes who will need to stay diligent in monitoring his blood sugar. Brown struggles when asked to play in too much space in the run game, lacking the anticipation and decisiveness required to reach moving targets consistently. Brown will often overset to his outside shoulder, leaving his inside shoulder open for inside counter moves. Despite Brown's terrific strength and size, he tends to lose sustain and enable defenders to disengage, failing always to finish plays. Brown has played in a unique college offense throughout his career and will need some adjustments in a pro-style scheme.

Best Fit: Right Tackle in either scheme

Player Ranking (1-100): 72.1 - Brown has a massive ceiling, as evidenced by his former five-star pedigree. Considering he's only played football since high school, there is still developmental upside with Brown. It wouldn't surprise me if Brown takes over as a starter on the sooner side. 4th round player.

18. Jalen Travis - Iowa State - 6'7 340 lbs

Strengths: A former four-year starter for Princeton, Travis took advantage of his additional year of eligibility to transfer to the Hawkeyes to start for a Power-5 program. With five years of starting experience, Travis has moved and played at both tackle positions, providing an extensive resume. Travis has a massive frame and ideal amounts of bulk and length. Despite his size, Travis is no slouch regarding his movement skills. A smooth operator who has refined his footwork over the years, Travis displays good lateral range in his kick slide to maintain spacing. He does a terrific job of mirroring while utilizing his length to force improbable rush lanes in passing sets. He's quick to engage defenders, utilizing his length to keep them off his frame. He keeps his head on a swivel and maintains good post-snap awareness to adjust to late-onset blitzes and stunts. Travis is a powerful force in the running game, particularly when working in gap runs. He displays good initial quickness and core flexibility to be effective on down blocks, latching on and sustaining blocks throughout. His size can engulf defenders along the perimeter, showing the ability to seal the edges and open up rush lanes. He utilizes his strong hands and rolling lower body power to generate good movement at the 1st level.

Weaknesses: Travis has a high-cut frame that can cause him some struggles when attempting to change direction or re-route his frame. His frame lacks natural bend and flexibility, causing him to play very upright. He's a classic waist bender who still doesn't know how to play leveraged and consistent pad level consistently. While he does well on outside rushes, he struggles when rushers challenge him on the inside shoulder. Despite his massive frame, he lacks ideal anchorage power. He will struggle to control the point of attack against better-leveraged speed-to-power rushers. In the running game, Travis lacks synchronization between his upper and lower body. He gets out of sync, causing him to get caught leaning and playing off-balanced. I'd like to see Travis play with more of a violent finisher mentality, failing to have the mean streak.

Best Fit: Developmental tackle

Player Ranking (1-100): 71.5 - Travis has noticeable skills and traits for development. While he's not the finished package yet, his size and athleticism are incredibly enticing. I wouldn't be surprised if he could immediately win a job as a swing tackle for a team while eventually getting a chance to start. 4th round player.

19. Hollin Pierce - Rutgers - 6'8 354 lbs

Strengths: Piece is a 4-year starter for the Scarlet Knights, starting his first two seasons at right tackle and then kicking over and starting at left tackle his final two seasons. The definition of durable: Pierce hasn't missed a game since arriving on campus after redshirting. Pierce is a massive man who weighed over 400 pounds upon arriving on campus and slimming down. His frame and length cause him challenges for defenders in both passing and running sets. Pierce utilizes his size and length in the passing game to control the point of attack. He rarely grants any movement against power, dropping his anchor and controlling reps. If he is initially beaten, he can quickly reset and recover. He's got powerful hands and delivers upper-body blows to defenders, slowing them in their tracks. His sheer size causes rushers to take incredibly wide angles in their pursuit of winning at the top of arcs. He's quick to recognize things pre-snap, adjusting for stunts and twists. In the running game, Pierce plays with aggression and urgency. He's a road grader at the 1st level, generating impressive displacement power to open up lanes and create serious pushback in short yardage. He works well with his teammates in combo blocks and double teams, regularly opening up lanes in the running game. His frame allows him to create massive angles and wall-off backside defenders. He's a mauler who plays until the whistle on every snap.

Weaknesses: While Pierce's physical components are sometimes a strength, they are sometimes a detriment. He struggles in passing sets against quicker-twitch rushers, which can cause him to play laterally. When asked to play on an island, he's a laborer who lacks the twitch in his kick slide. He tends to get too aggressive sometimes, causing him to play over his toes and lean in, losing his balance. He loses a lot of leverage battles due to his size and failing to play with adequate bend. He lacks the range in the running game to play in a zone-style run scheme, as his lateral mobility is modest at best.

> **Best Fit: Developmental Tackle in Gap/Power Scheme**

Player Ranking (1-100): 69.7 - Not many have Pierce physical attributes in the entire world. His ceiling is massive with additional development. The concern is that he isn't quite ready to play a meaningful role despite starting 4 years in college. Pierce has a chance, but he needs to hone his fundamentals while continuing to refine his frame. 5th round player.

20. Xavier Truss - Georgia - 6'7 320 lbs

Strengths: A 6th-year senior for the Bulldogs, Truss has extensive experience in the SEC playing with the Bulldogs. Has been a regular starter at right tackle for the Bulldogs in the last three seasons. Has experience playing both tackle and guard spots, showing positional flexibility. A natural athlete who has played against top-tier competition while playing in a pro-style system, Truss possesses fluid footwork and balance out of his stance. He is quick-footed and has good lateral agility, which allows him to mirror effectively in space. Good awareness and recognition skills enable him to make quick decisions to adjust and pick up blitzes and stunts. Always looks for an assignment when he doesn't have one. Has the upper body strength to sustain his blocks, showing impressive grip strength in his hands. Has the athleticism and twitch to be effective when used in zone-style runs, showing above-average upside in a zone scheme. Gets his lower body firing quickly, allowing him to seal blocks on traps and outside runs while also displaying the fluidity to cross the face of blockers to reach in space. Impressive change of direction and anticipation when handling 2nd level blocks, showing the range to succeed at the next level. Plays the game in both the running and passing games with tenacity and a mean streak, often battling and finishing defenders on the ground.

Weaknesses: An older prospect who will be 24 years old during his rookie season. He is a good athlete, but he isn't an elite one, and he struggles against top-tier bendy athletes who can challenge him vertically along the edges. Might be forced to kick inside at the next level. Has significant power concerns through his lower half, in which he gets overwhelmed at the point of attack. He couples a lack of lower body power with poor leverage in pass sets to consistently allow the pocket to collapse against more powerful edge defenders. Needs some hand technique work, as his strikes can be wide and inaccurate, leading to many holding calls. Not a space mover in the running game and is likely only a fit for a zone-style system.

Best Fit: Developmental tackle or possibly kick inside to guard

Player Ranking (1-100): 68.9 - Truss is a highly experienced and durable tackle prospect with some athleticism to develop. His frame makes it difficult for him to win consistently at the point of attack, but there are some traits to develop if he can improve his leverage and lower body strength. 5th round player.

21. Chase Lundt - UConn - 6'8 305 lbs

Strengths: A rare 4-year starter at right tackle for the Huskies, Lundt has extensive experience and reliability. Lundt is a long and rangy-built tackle with enough room on his frame for continued development and mass. A smooth operator, Lundt eases out of his stance with bent knees and quick feet. Lundt maximizes his ability to sink his hips and play with leverage and balance despite his frame. Capable of mirroring in vertical passing sets, Lundt reaches set points quickly while winning positioning. A rangy athlete that has good agility and change of directional abilities to mirror and match. Lower body strength is prevalent as Lundt does a nice job dropping his anchor in ample time to set his feet and absorb against bull rushers. He maintains hyper-awareness of blitzes and stunts post-snap, pointing things out and quickly adjusting. In the running game, Lundt shows good quickness out of his stance. In short-yardage situations, Lundt drops his pads while maintaining leverage and keeps his legs churning through impact to generate movement. Has flashed good upside in zone-style runs, showing good balance and anticipation while on the move to reach moving targets.

Weaknesses: Lundt is still lean for the position and lacks an ideal power profile. He needs to continue maximizing his frame with clean weight. While his quickness is apparent, the depth of his kick-slide can be all over the place. He often oversets to his outside, leaving the 'B' gap completely vulnerable to power and good counter rushers. He tends to be very late with his hands, missing accuracy and timing. Lundt has a bad habit of dropping his head upon impact in the running game.

Best Fit: Right Tackle in any scheme

Player Ranking (1-100): 67.2 - Lundt is a highly experienced tackle prospect with more than enough developmental upside to be given a chance. While he lacks any top-tier traits, he lacks any significant deficiencies either. Lundt should be given a chance to swing a swing tackle spot as a rookie. 5th round player.

22. Josh Fryar - Ohio State - 6'5 320 lbs

Strengths: A 5th year senior for the Buckeyes, Fryar has started in the last two seasons at right tackle. Fryar has a good overall build to play on the outside, with long limbs and good density through his frame. He has sufficient room on his frame for continued development and mass. Fryar is at his best in the passing game, showing good initial movement and smoothness out of his kick-slide. He displays quickness and agility when mirroring in space, maintaining good spacing between him and his assignment. He eases off the snap of the ball with good knee bend and leverage, maintaining a good pad level. His anchorage strength is above average, and he does a good job of dropping his anchor quickly and sustaining bull rushers well. Fryar does a nice job of fitting his hands against blockers, showing good strike accuracy and hand placement. He's quick to recognize things post-snap, keeping his head on a swivel, and is quick to recognize blitzes and stunts. In the running game, Fryar is positionally sound and understands how to utilize angles and leverage to open up the 'B' and 'C' gaps. He does a good job of beating defenders to the spot when working in space, showing ease of movement in space. A hardworking kid who plays with terrific intelligence while working hard to improve each campaign.

Weaknesses: Fryar tore his ACL during his sophomore campaign. Fryar lacks elite qualities in any respect and is mostly average to slightly above average in all respects. He was exposed against quicker-twitch rushers this past season, lacking the ideal footwork to handle rushers that can bend, dip, and threaten the apex. While he sets his hands well, he struggles to sustain blocks, allowing defenders to disengage on counter moves frequently. He struggles when asked to consistently play in space, frequently missing whiffing targets and struggling with balance. In the running game, Fryar is more of a positional blocker than a move blocker. He fails to churn his legs through impact, limiting his effectiveness in short-yardage and red-zone opportunities.

Best Fit: Developmental tackle or might kick inside

Player Ranking (1-100): 65.8 - Fryar isn't a bad football player. He had some struggles at times, but he displays the football IQ and the blue-chip characteristics to continue to improve. I wouldn't be surprised if he earned a spot as a swing tackle early in his career. 5th round player.

23. John Campbell Jr - Tennessee - 6'6 330 lbs

Strengths: A rare 7th-year senior who started his career with Miami for five seasons before transferring to Tennessee and playing his final two campaigns with the Vols. Campbell is a positionally flexible prospect who has had significant game time at both tackle spots, kicking inside and playing guard at times. Despite missing game time, Campbell has played in many major college football games, starting games for 6 seasons throughout college. A fluid mover, Campbell eases off the snap of the ball with good initial quickness out of his kick-slide. Campbell is built with a powerful lower half, understanding how to reset and re-anchor quickly if initially beaten. He won't hesitate to drop his anchor and control the point of attack on passing sets, allowing him to limit any movement against bull rushers. Campbell showcases good initial movement skills in the running game, winning leverage and positioning on outside zone runs. It can be used effectively on outside zone runs as well as second-level blocks, showing good balance and strike accuracy while on the move. Plays with a nasty and fiery demeanor, finishing plays in the running game.

Weaknesses: An older prospect who will be 25 years old before his rookie season. Has had some lower body injuries throughout college, including breaking his leg that sidelined him for most of one season. Campbell is overaggressive on pass sets, playing over his toes and getting caught reaching. He has difficulties with leverage, consistently playing with high pads and allowing them to continue to rise throughout plays. Struggled to play at left tackle due to a lack of elite athleticism and movement skills and might still be forced to kick inside. Lacks ideal prototypical proportions to play on the outside and will get outreached by longer defenders. Could benefit from additional mass and strength, most notably in his upper body. Struggles to control pass reps, lacking the sustain, mirror ability, and iron-grip strength in his hands. Lacks ideal lateral mobility to win positioning against quicker twitch rushers when rushers take the corners, oversetting his feet to the outside and leaving his inside shoulder wide open.

Best Fit: Developmental RT or kick inside to guard

Player Ranking (1-100): 61.1 - Campbell is a developmental tackle who will likely have to earn a spot on the team in camp. He's got some athleticism in his frame and impressive lower-body strength. His big-game experience will likely suit him well as he transitions to the next level. 6th round player.

24. Carson Vinson - Alabama A&M - 6'6 305 lbs

Strengths: A 4-year starter for FCS-program Alabama A&M, Vinson is a highly touted and experienced tackle prospect who has been strong these last few years. Vinson has an NFL frame featuring good size, density, and wingspan, enabling him to maintain playing on the outside at the next level. Despite not playing against top-tier competition, Vinson made the most of every opportunity, dominating his level of competition. When he did compete against better competition, such as Auburn this year, Vinson didn't shy away and showed impressive results as he gained more and more experience throughout the game. A natural athlete, Vinson shows fluid and active feet to reach his spot and win positioning quickly. His lateral mobility enables him to mirror in space, maintaining good spacing while showing lateral agility to change directions. Powerful upper body and heavy hands enable Vinson to ease up rushers. Latch-on strength is prevalent; Vinson rarely lets defenders out of his grasp once he reaches their pads. A finisher who plays with a nasty demeanor and finishers' mentality on every snap of the ball. Vinson eases out of his stance in the running game with good initial quickness. He has the movement skills to be used on reach and pulls, showing excellent 2nd-level ease of motion.

Weaknesses: The biggest transition for Vinson is going to be the massive hurdle between competing against FCS edge rushers and NFL edge rushers. Vinson can sometimes be too patient in passing sets, allowing defenders to utilize built-up speed to collapse the pocket on him with their bull rush. He quickly gives up leverage and hand placement, failing to always fire his hands with proper timing and placement. His upper body is further developed than his lower body, and power rushers can sometimes threaten his anchorage power. He tends to play over his toes when he's playing in space, frequently looking off-balanced and struggling to hit moving targets consistently.

Best Fit: Developmental tackle

Player Ranking (1-100): 60.8 - Vinson has a good combination of size, athleticism and mentality. But he's not quite ready for the NFL yet. He has traits that give evidence of a clear upside, but he will have to continue to get better and stronger to compete at the next level. 6th round player.

25. Gerald Mincey - Kentucky - 6'6 335 lbs

Strengths: Mincey has had a long road to the next level, starting his career in Florida before transferring to Tennessee and finally to Kentucky. Mincey started his career playing left tackle, but during his last two seasons, he played on the right side of the line. Mincey is built with a massive frame, displaying density and thick limbs. Mincey shows a smooth and efficient kick slide as a pass blocker, displaying the necessary depth and foot quickness. He maintains good width and utilizes his long arms to force improbable rush lanes. His heavy hands allow him to show good initial displacement, easing past rushers' initial moves. When he's left without work, he looks for it, proving to be a reliable help blocker. He's quick to react to stunts and blitzes, adjusting if needed. In the running game, Mincey proves to be a capable people mover who can clear rush lanes. He utilizes momentum and rollback power through his lower body to generate push. He's particularly effective in red-zone and short-yardage situations. Has shown an ability to be successful when working in space, showing good acceleration and anticipation on the move. A nasty and violent tone-setter who appreciates the physicality, always looking to finish plays.

Weaknesses: Mincey frequently leans in pass sets, making him susceptible to push/pull techniques. A waist bender that struggles with balance, frequently ending up on the ground. His hand placement is generally wide of the mark, exposing his chest plate far too easily. When he makes good initial contact, he lacks the iron-grip strength in his hands to sustain, frequently allowing defenders to disengage. He tends to overset to his outside shoulder, leaving the 'B' gap completely exposed to counter moves. Has some noticeable stiffness concerns when playing laterally and struggles against quick-twitch rushers that can capture the edge.

Best Fit: Developmental tackle

Player Ranking (1-100): 54.3 - Mincey has struggled in the passing game, failing always to hold up and be reliable. He's a road grader in the run game with the necessary power and pop to succeed immediately. I worry his lack of top-tier strength or athleticism will hinder teams from drafting him. Undrafted free agent.

Top-10 OT's:

1. Will Campbell
2. Kelvin Banks
3. Josh Conerly Jr
4. Josh Simmons
5. Aireontae Ersery
6. Ajani Cornelius
7. Armand Membou
8. Cameron Williams
9. Emery Jones
10. Anthony Belton

Chapter 7

Interior Offensive Lineman (Guards or Centers)

1. Donovan Jackson - Ohio State - 6'4 320 lbs

Strengths: A 3-year starter at Left guard for the Buckeyes, Jackson was a former five-star recruit and the consensus number 1 high school prospect from Texas. Jackson moved to left tackle in week 10 of his final season, dominating at the end of the season and throughout the playoffs and National Championship. He wasted little time showing that immediately getting on campus, winning the starting job as a true freshman. Jackson is built exactly in the mold of a player of a football player you want, with thick and long limbs. His length is a true weapon on the interior of a line, as Jackson shows the ability to play with extension and lockout, keeping defenders off of his frame. A high-IQ football player who shows systematic versatility and is a game-changing starter in NFL offensive lines, who plays in both man-blocking looks and zone-style runs. Quickly recognizes defensive looks pre- and post-snap, enabling him to adjust to interior blitzes or stunts. Jackson is the rare offensive lineman who is an athlete and a bully. Terrific mobility and lateral movement skills enable him to mirror in pass protection easily. When rushers attempt to rush Jackson head-on, his powerful lower half and natural leverage advantage cause him to win out on almost every rep. Heavy hands and power at the point of attack cause him to overwhelm rushers off the snap. In the running game, Jackson is explosive off the snap of the ball, moving out of his stance with ease. Finishes blocks, controlling defenders until the final whistle. Very good in space and is frequently used on pulls and traps, showing good body control and strike accuracy while on the move.

Weaknesses: Jackson's overaggressive nature can occasionally cause him to get lungy in pass sets, playing over his toes. Would like to see Jackson do a better job of keeping his pads down when in space, as he can play a bit too upright when working in space. Jackson can have some leverage concerns in moments, and would like to see him more consistently use knee bend in his pass sets. While he's got powerful hands, his strike accuracy and hand placement can occasionally get too high.

Best Fit: Starting Guard but could move to tackle too

Player Ranking (1-100): 85.8 - Jackson is an immediate Pro-Bowl level guard at the next level. He could kick outside at the next level, but it's a position he hasn't played consistently much and will need further development. He has the rare combination of being both incredibly athletic and powerful. Coupling those two things with an incredibly high IQ makes for a VERY good NFL football player. 1st round pick.

2. Tyler Booker - Alabama - 6'5 352 lbs

Strengths: A 2-year starter and former five-star recruit for the Tide, Booker has started in every game for the Tide at left guard the last two seasons. A massively built man, Booker has incredible size, length, and density throughout his frame, allowing him to dominate in small spaces. Despite Booker's massive frame, he still has the systematic versatility to make him appear in both power/gap systems and heavy zone offenses. Comfortable and experienced playing both right and left guard, Booker has experience against top-tier opposition. In the passing game, Booker shows the powerful anchorage strength that allows him to stifle bull rushers. If he grants any movement, he quickly regains control and resets and recovers. Heavy hands allow him to deliver body blows to rushers, finishing defenders off until the whistle echoes. Above-average awareness allows him to adjust and pick up blitzes and stunts. He is highly adept in the run game with his ability to overwhelm at the point of attack with power inside phone booths. Booker quickly looks for initial contact while pushing his hips and lower body forward through impact. Has enough movement skills to be able to work angles in zone-style runs. Comfortable as a lead blocker, showing the ability to stay square and displace defenders at 1st and 2nd level lanes.

Weaknesses: Booker is still developing his frame, and while he's done a great job cleaning up some of his weight, he still carries some sloppy weight. Allows his pads to rise progressively throughout plays, limiting his ability to play with leverage. His squattier build causes him to have some struggles when it comes to redirecting his frame and changing directions. His overaggressive nature in pass sets causes him to bend at the waist, losing his balance on counter moves. He lacks ideal levels of foot quickness, causing him to struggle when isolated on an island against better athletes. If initially beaten, he can struggle to regain control and reset. While dominating against power rushers, Booker struggles more against smaller and quicker rushers.

Best Fit: Starting Guard

Player Ranking (1-100): 84.5 - Booker is a powerful interior blocker that excels in small spaces. He's likely better suited to a heavy gap/power-blocking system, although he could play in a zone setup. He's a better run blocker than in the passing game, but he's no slouch in either. This kid should be a Day 1 starter. 2nd round player.

3. Tate Ratledge - Georgia - 6'6 320lbs

Strengths: A 3-year starter at RG for the Bulldogs, Ratledge has NFL readiness and experience to contribute immediately. Featuring a road grader physique, Ratledge has strength in spades throughout his physique. Physicality is the name of the game for Ratledge, as he displays a violent demeanor, finishing every play until after the whistle. As a run blocker, Ratledge showcased the power and zone-blocking instincts, which gave him schematic versatility. Regularly used as the 'move' blocker for the Bulldogs' offensive line, Ratledge showed impressive body control and strike accuracy when used to reach and trap blocks in space. In short-yardage situations, Ratledge's lower body displacement power allowed him to open up 1st level lanes to control blockers, constantly rolling his hips forward through impact. Routinely brought guys to the ground as he controlled them with his powerful hands and finishing power. In the passing game, Ratledge's awareness was always on display, keeping his head on a swivel at all times. He's a terrific help blocker who would recognize things pre-snap quickly, understanding who to pass and who to pick up. Tremendous power at the point of attack through his lower body allows him to quickly reset and regain control of reps, sustaining against bull rushers. Has an advanced understanding of how to set his hands and win placement through the chest plate of defenders, quickly resetting if his strike misses.

Weaknesses: An older prospect who will be 24 years old on draft weekend. Has only played one position throughout his time at Georgia, limiting his versatility at the next level. Sprained his left ankle and MCL during his final season, causing him to miss a few games. His overaggressiveness will cause him to overset and extend too quickly, allowing guys to disengage on counter moves. He must maintain his leverage throughout the plays, as he sometimes allows his pads to rise. The lack of elite length causes him to struggle against longer rushers who can win against his outside shoulder.

Best Fit: Starting Guard

Player Ranking (1-100): 84.0 - Ratledge is a terrific NFL prospect who should immediately win a starting role at the next level. He's a great mix of athleticism and strength but excels in the game's physical areas. He helped Georgia's running game to be amongst the best in college football the last several seasons, and there's no reason to think he won't do the same for an NFL team. 2nd round player.

4. Wyatt Milum - West Virginia - 6'6 317 lbs

Strengths: A 4-year starter for the Mountaineers who took over a few games into his freshman campaign, starting every game since. While initially starting at RT, he was quickly moved to LT during his sophomore campaign. A highly experienced prospect with the frame thresholds to play on the outside or the inside. Milum is a hard-nosed, tough kid who excels in the physical areas of the game, proving to be a true road grader in the run game. Has the lower body power to generate some displacement power at the 1st level. Schematically-versatile is present in Milum as he shows the capability to play in a power-blocking setup and a zone-style offensive system. The way he moves in space is impressive, regularly used as the move blocker to get along the edges and locate and lock. Terrific body control and anticipation give him a good batting average when reaching moving targets. Understands how to utilize angles and body positioning to win in the run game. Milum has also impressed in the passing game, allowing very few pressures throughout his last couple of seasons of starting. He is an impressive athlete who shows fluidity in his ability to play on an island in a 1v1 situation. If he's initially beaten, he has the recovery quickness to reset and recover. Maintains a good base throughout, dropping his anchor and allowing little movement against bull rushes. Plays with an edge, finishing every play and battling until after the whistle.

Weaknesses: While Milum has impressed throughout college, he's had minimal chances to compete against top-tier edge rushers through college. It's likely that Milum will have to move to guard at the next level due to lack of elite length. When he does struggle, it's due to poor leverage, giving up his chest plate far too easily. He can continue to refine his hand usage and whiffing with his strike timing and placement. A good athlete, but I'm not sure he's elite, as he can look a bit stiff when challenged by quicker-twitch rushers that can get him moving sideways. Highly susceptible to outside rushers that will challenge the arc.

Best Fit: Guard or RT

Player Ranking (1-100): 82.9 - Milum is a smart, experienced tackle prospect with few downsides. While his ceiling perhaps isn't as great as others in this draft class, he's a refined and high-floor prospect who should immediately be a starter in this league. I worry he will get exposed more in the passing game against better rushers, even though he wasn't in college. Milum is the case of a guy who has no obvious weaknesses. 2nd round player.

5. Jonah Savaiinaea - Arizona - 6'5 330 lbs

Strengths: A 3-year starter for the Wildcats, Savaiinaea has played almost entirely as the teams' RT but has also been used at times on the interior. Possessing a wide frame with massive limbs, Savaiinaea has vines for arms and outstanding overall strength. Has the positional versatility to be used both as a tackle or kick inside. Has handled zone and gap-blocking concepts in school and can be effective in either offensive scheme. As a pass protector, Savaiinaea eases off the snap with good initial quickness out of his stance to react setpoints. He utilizes his wide body to wall off the right side of the line, forcing rushers to take incredibly wide arcs or attack his inside shoulder. Keeps his head on a swivel and shows good awareness to pick up stunts and blitzes. He understands which blocker to man and which blocker to pass, showing impressive overall football IQ. Has impressive power throughout his lower body, allowing him to absorb speed-to-power rushers, rarely giving up considerable ground against bull rushers. Savaiinaea does a nice job of making 1st contact as a run blocker. His strong core and hands allow him to control the 1st and 2nd levels to open up rush lanes. While not a great athlete, Savaiinaea shows savvy and body control when pulling in space to reach 2nd-level contacts. Understands how to utilize his body positioning to win leverage and angles on outside runs.

Weaknesses: Savaiinaea's overall athleticism is subpar and could benefit by kicking inside to guard. If he's initially beaten, he struggles badly trying to regain control. Overall lateral mobility and range are average, causing him to struggle mirroring against quick-twitch rushers. Lack of foot quickness causes him to overset to his outside shoulder, frequently leaving his inside shoulder completely exposed to rushes. His hands are powerful but overzealous and inaccurate, frequently bending at the waist and striking high. His overall pad level is inconsistent, firing too upright while allowing his pads to rise even more mid-play.

Best Fit: Guard in any scheme and can kick outside as RT if needed

Player Ranking (1-100): 81.5 - While I love Savaiinaea's overwhelming size and frame, his lack of ideal movement skills should likely kick him inside. He struggled mightily at times as a pass protector, and I think in shorter spaces as a guard with his size and power combination, he can be very good. 2nd round player.

6. Grey Zabel - North Dakota State - 6'6 304 lbs

Strengths: Zabel is another one on the long list of successful FCS-level offensive line prospects that have come out in the last several years. Zabel is a 2.5-year starter who has played 4 out of 5 positions along the offensive line, showing rare versatility and experience. Zabel is likely the best project inside at the next level. Zabel is a smooth operator built with a good proportional size and frame. He eases out of his stance with bent knees and smooth agility as he works laterally. Zabel maintains leverage and spacing against blockers despite his long frame, rarely letting them into his frame. He stays square and shows terrific athleticism and hip fluidity to mirror, especially when playing inside. He handles power well, showing good core and anchorage power to absorb. He quickly reacts and redirects to reach loopers and blitzers. Zabel plays in a heavy run-first system, and he has excessive experience in the running game, and that's where he truly shines. A mauler that stays engaged with defenders, Zabel rolls his hips forward and generates impressive displacement power. Successful working both in a vertical plane and laterally, Zabel has the schematic versatility to be successful in both gap and zone systems. He successfully works in tandem with his teammates on combo blocks, generating strong movement at the first level. He shows comfort and balance when climbing to the second level to reach linebackers in space. Zabel has played nearly 60 games throughout college, a sturdy contributor, showing his reliability.

Weaknesses: The main concern with Zabel will be the transition to the NFL game, as it's a whole new ball game in the FCS competition. Zabel has good athleticism when playing on the inside but lacks top-tier movement skills when playing on the outside. He struggled oversetting to the outside and completely exposing the 'B' gap. He struggled against elite quick twitch rushers that can consistently beat him to set points. Zabel lacks ideal length and consistently gives up first contact. He's had significant issues with penalties early in his career due to getting too wide with his hand placement.

Best Fit: Zone-blocking guard or center

Player Ranking (1-100): 80.7 - Zabel impressed me this season on tape. He is incredibly smooth in his movement skills. And although he's exceptional in the run game, he's also very good in passing sets. He understands how to play the game and looks like a technician. When playing against Colorado this year, he showed he can more than hold his own against better competition. 2nd round player.

7. Luke Kandra - Cincinnati - 6'4 323 lbs

Strengths: Kandra began his career with Louisville, where he appeared in 21 games during his final two seasons before transferring to Cincinnati. Kandra has played almost entirely at Right Guard, showing outstanding consistency and reliability over the last three seasons. A shorter and low center of gravity blocker, Kandra utilizes his natural leverage advantage over blockers in the passing game. Bending at the knees and winning with low pads, Kandra drops his anchor and rarely gets moved off his spot. Terrific football intelligence and post-snap awareness allow Kandra to see blitzes and stunts, easily adjusting and picking them up. Strong punch and grip strength allow Kanra to sustain blocks, rarely allowing rushers to succeed on counter moves. Kandra is a dominant run blocker, consistently road grading and paving lanes for his runners. Not just content clear lanes, Kandra finishes plays, frequently bringing defenders to the ground. In short-yardage situations, Kandra churns his legs through impact to get a significant push. Works with his teammates to work combo blocks to spring forth 1st-level rush lanes. As a move blocker, Kandra shows impressive 1st step quickness out of his stance, balance, and anticipation on the move to succeed in reaching moving targets. A very disciplined blocker that had zero penalties in 2023.

Weaknesses: Kandra is undersized and will likely only be a schematic fit for teams with a heavy zone-style offensive system. He is still learning to utilize his hands in pass protection, as his strike accuracy can be a little high as he gets caught playing over his toes. Overall, point of attack power and strength are good but aren't in the upper-tier category. Kandra can struggle in pass sets against better athletes who can reach his pads, but he lacks the high-end lateral mobility and athleticism to play on an island.

Best Fit: Zone-blocking guard

Player Ranking (1-100): 79.0 - I greatly like Kandra. He's a technician the way he plays the game, showing impressive skills as a run blocker. Despite being undersized, he understands how to maximize every pound of his body and plays a LOT bigger than his size indicates. He's a tough kid who is incredibly smart and loves football. No reason to believe he can't be a starter at the next level. 3rd round player.

8. Dylan Fairchild - Georgia - 6'5 315 lbs

Strengths: A 2-year starter for the Bulldogs at left guard, Fairchild has proven to be a stable force for the Georgia offensive line. A former state champion wrestler, Fairchild has the physical components to excel at the next level. Possessing an ideal frame, Fairchild has a well-developed frame with minimal unnecessary fat. Fairchild shows schematic versatility in both zone and power/gap fronts. His former wrestling prowess is displayed in his playing with outstanding leverage and technique. Fairchild drops his pads in passing sets while playing with a wide base. His powerful upper body and strong hands allow him to deliver powerful punches to slow down and erase rushers. He maintains control with iron-grip strength in his hand. Fairchild works hard to regain control with his hands while dropping his anchor when he grants any initial movement. He quickly recognizes pre and post-snap looks, adjusting quickly for blitzes and stunts. Fairchild shows good explosion and quickness out of his stance in the running game. He has more than enough movement skills to be utilized on reach and pulls, regularly making 2nd level contact in space. He works hard to fit his hands inside against defenders. A tireless worker who looks for work when he doesn't have any. Fairchild plays with a mean streak and a violent demeanor on the field.

Weaknesses: Fairchild has struggled against longer defenders that can reach his chest despite playing with good technique. He fails to control rushers that gain access to his frame, lacking top-end anchorage strength. When he's left on an island, his lack of change of direction abilities and lateral mobility are apparent. While he flashes patience in passing sets, he's sometimes not immune to playing over his toes and getting caught off balance due to his aggressive makeup. He sometimes gets wide with his hands, leading to several holding calls.

Best Fit: Guard in any scheme

Player Ranking (1-100): 78.3 - Fairchild is a 2-year starter who has played against elite competition for the last two years. He's had some struggles in passing sets, but he will get better with more playtime. I'd like him to continue strengthening his anchor and adding quality mass to his large frame. 3rd round player.

9. Jared Wilson - Georgia - 6'3 310 lbs

Strengths: A 2-year starter for the Bulldogs at center, Wilson has proven to be one of the better centers in this draft class. Wilson is a smaller, low center-of-gravity center that excels in the technical and athletic aspects of playing center. Wilson is one of the best athletes for an interior offensive lineman in this draft class, and it is abundant in how he plays the position. In the passing game, Wilson utilizes his natural leverage advantage and hand technique to control the duration of a snap. He has advanced hand technique, perfecting his timing and strike accuracy to ease rushers. This makes it nearly impossible for defenders to win inside hand leverage against him despite being outreached. He maximizes his pad level with good knee bend to absorb and minimize movement against bull rushers. He easily mirrors against 3-techniques, showing impressive change of direction and looseness through his hips. Wilson's explosive 1st step quickness in the running game enables him to beat defenders to landmarks to control the rep. Wilson flashes his balance and body control when working in space. He's frequently used to lead the way on pulls and screens. Once he makes contact, he showcases vice-like strength in his hands, rarely enabling defenders out of his grasp once he initially fits them.

Weaknesses: Wilson missed two games this season due to a lower leg injury. Wilson has zero positional flexibility at the next level and will be limited to playing in a zone-style system as a center only. His lack of length can sometimes cause him to struggle against longer-levered interior rushers. Lack of functional strength and point of attack power can stifle his ability to dominate in gap schemes, failing to be a people clearer. While he shows upside at the 2nd level, he needs to anticipate linebackers and safeties in space better, frequently whiffing. He can be late to identify and adjust for stunts and blitzes pre-snap.

Best Fit: Zone-blocking center

Player Ranking (1-100): 77.4 - Wilson is an athletic specimen with abundant physical tools. While his frame is mostly maximized, he understands how to utilize it. He should be an immediate starter for a heavy zone system team. 3rd round player.

10. Clay Webb - Jacksonville State - 6'3 310 lbs

Strengths: A former five-star recruit for Georgia, where he started his career with the Bulldogs for three seasons before transferring over and starting for FCS-level Jacksonville State the last three seasons. He played mostly as a left guard throughout college but has some experience playing center and right guard. Webb's former high school credentials are displayed in every game tape, completely dominating against lesser competition. Webb is an elite pass protector, showcasing incredible movement skills and mirror ability. He hardly gave up any pressure throughout his time, showing loose limbs and light feet. Commits himself to playing with good leverage, utilizing good knee bend, and always staying square. A durable guy who has hardly missed a snap in the last three seasons. His former high school wrestling prowess is evident in his ability to win with positioning and angles. He has a strong upper body and wins most hand battles with his ability to win inside placement. Smart recognizes things pre- and post-snap, allowing him to adjust easily. In the running game, Webb shows the athleticism to win at both the 1st and 2nd levels. Generates power through his lower body to create movement and push, opening up lanes and winning ground in short yardage.

Weaknesses: There will be questions about why Webb didn't get more of a chance with the Bulldogs. Playing for Jacksonville State, he didn't compete against top-tier competition. Webb isn't the biggest guy and is a little slight, most noticeably in the lower half. Lack of elite anchorage power and strength limits him when sitting down against larger defensive tackles that can reach his pads. He is likely only a fit for a zone-style running scheme as he lacks the power and drive-blocking ability to fit in a power-blocking scheme.

Best Fit: Zone-blocking guard or center

Player Ranking (1-100): 76.3 - Webb has dominated the FCS level the last three seasons. While there will be questions as to why it didn't work out at Georgia, there's no denying his talent, as he was a former top high school recruit in the nation. If he can continue to add lower body girth and functional strength, he can be a solid starter for a long time at the next level. 3rd round player.

11. Jonah Monheim - USC - 6'5 310 lbs

Strengths: A 4-year starter for the Trojans who has played games at right tackle, left tackle, and right guard and finished his final season as a center. The definition of versatility is that Monheim has looked good and is willing to play any position along the offensive front, never looking out of position at any one spot. A highly intelligent football player who plays the game with impressive technical ability and awareness. In the passing game, where Monheim excels, he understands how to win with hand usage, showcasing impressive strike accuracy and timing. Quick to set his feet while maintaining good width and leverage, Monheim remains patient and in control during each rep. A good athlete who can play laterally, showing impressive overall agility to mirror in space. High levels of awareness allow him to be effective on combo blocks and, when unassigned, to pick up additional rushers. Can win against interior rushers due to his fundamentals, staying square and leveraged while absorbing power. In the running game, Monheim understands how to win with angles and positioning, walling off blockers, and utilizing his frame to win positioning. Looks comfortable on zone-style runs, getting ahead of runners while showing impressive anticipation while on the move. He can open up 1st level rush lanes on both traps and reach blocks. A finisher who shows toughness on every play plays until the whistle echoes.

Weaknesses: A jack of all trades, master of none, who has consistently moved around without stamping his mark on any position. Lacks the ideal length to play on the outside at the next level. Not an overly powerful run blocker who will be an effective driver blocker or someone who can clear rush lanes in a power-blocking setup. His footwork can get choppy when dealing with better athletes, showing susceptibility against quick-twitch rushers.

Best Fit: Zone-Blocking Guard or Center

Player Ranking (1-100): 74.9 - I like Monheim as an excellent role player for a team that can be a guy who can contribute anywhere along the interior of an offensive line. While he's not a top-end athlete or a dynamic drive blocker, he's a smart and highly intelligent blocker who offers positional versatility while never looking out of position. 4th round player.

12. Miles Frazier - LSU - 6'5 325 lbs

Strengths: He started his career at Florida International for two years, starting one season before transferring to LSU. A 3-year starter for the Tigers, playing at both guard spots and even some time at tackle. While he's likely best suited to play inside at the next level, Frazier has the length and the powerfully built frame to be positionally versatile for teams. Power is the name of the game for Frazier, and it is overwhelming at the point of attack in both the running and passing games. As a pass protector, Frazier maintains good width while playing with full extension to keep defenders off his frame. Utilizes good knee bend and sits in his stance while he anchors down against the most powerful interior defenders. He shows good awareness while keeping his head on a swivel to pick up blitzers and adjust to stunts and twists quickly. Heavy hands and a good upper-body strike allow him to deliver powerful punches to unsuspecting defenders. Iron-grip strength in his hands and good placement allow him to lock on and latch against defenders, minimizing their ability to shed. He is a mauler in the run game, rolls his hips forward, and generates impressive driveability. Effective when used to trap and reach block at the 1st level, showing good strike accuracy and initial quickness to get off the ball. A finisher who commits himself to bringing defenders down to the ground, playing every snap like it's his last. Durable and reliable, playing almost every snap for LSU for the last three seasons.

Weaknesses: Frazier is likely only a fit at the next level for teams that run heavy power-blocking looks, failing to have ideal success playing in acres of space as a run blocker. Struggles when handling zone-style runs, lacking the range as a 'move blocker' outside the 1st level. Can allow his pads to rise mid-play when playing on the move, limiting his ability to change direction and play in space. A little heavy-footed and lacks the change of directional abilities and elite mirroring skills to handle the most athletic interior blockers on an island. Despite positional flexibility, he will likely only have appeal to teams when playing on the inside.

Best Fit: Power-blocking Guard

Player Ranking (1-100): 72.3 - Frazier is a good player who can consistently maul at the 1st level. He's equally adept in both the running and passing games. While he isn't great in space and isn't a top-notch athlete, he's a powerful guy who consistently won at the point of attack against SEC defenders. He should immediately improve a running game for defense and could compete immediately for a starting gig. 4th round player.

13. Jalen Rivers - Miami - 6'5 325 lbs

Strengths: Rivers began starting games for the Hurricanes as a freshman and has started every season since, showing exceptional experience and reliability. Rivers is the definition of positionally versatile, having started his career at guard before moving to left tackle in his final two seasons. Rivers has a physically imposing frame, displaying thick and wide limbs. He maintains patience and balance out of his stance, rarely playing over his skis or caught leaning. Rivers has exceptional lower body strength, enabling him to drop his anchor upon contact, absorbing and rarely granting any movement. He maintains leverage throughout snaps, allowing him to sustain his blocks and clamp on. His hyper-awareness lets him quickly identify and see things pre and post-snap, identifying stunts and twists. In the running game, Rivers excels when playing on a vertical plane. He generates good rolling power through his hips and lower body to create displacement at the first level. Works well with his teammates in combination blocks and double teams, timing them to perfection and opening up lanes. Rivers is a physical imposer who battles until the whistle, proving to be a tone-setter.

Weaknesses: Rivers has had minor injury concerns, missing five games during his final season with an undisclosed injury. He also missed the end of the 2022 season. While he can create some displacement, he's not entirely a people mover in the run game. Rivers lacks an ideal wing span and feet to play on the outside, and he was consistently exposed against quick-twitch rushers. He appears to have lower body tightness, limiting his ability to play laterally and handle playing on an island in passing sets. He has a bad habit of stopping his lower half upon contact in the running game, failing to utilize his built-up momentum to generate movement. His hand tactics in both phases must improve, as he frequently misses late and wide. When handling 2nd level assignments, Rivers's lack of range and fluidity are exposed in space, frequently missing moving targets.

Best Fit: Guard but can kick outside in an emergency

Player Ranking (1-100): 68.7 - Rivers is a versatile blocker who is best suited inside at the next level. His experience, football IQ, and power bode well for him to be a successful, versatile piece for an offensive line. 5th round player.

14. Weston Franklin - Georgia Tech - 6'4 310 lbs

Strengths: Franklin is a 3-year starter for the Yellow Jackets, proving to be a reliable presence for them in the middle of their offense. Franklin has a good build for a center, displaying above-average functional length and a wide base. Franklin has proven iron-man durability, playing every game for the last three seasons. Franklin operates heavily out of a zone-style running system, and his skill set best fits it. Franklin is a technician in how he operates, utilizing his natural leverage advantage to control the point of attack. He understands how to use angles and positioning to open up lanes at 1st and 2nd levels. He has very quickness out of his stance when working on the move, showing good balance and anticipation. He plays with nasty intentions until far after the whistle, showing good toughness and a finishers' mentality. As a pass blocker, Franklin is smooth and efficient. He moves easily between bent knees, showing good lateral agility and natural movement skills. He effectively mirrors in space, keeping a good distance between him and his assignment. He's a good communicator and shows the ability to adjust protection assignments. Franklin keeps his head on a swivel post-snap, always adjusting and quickly recognizing stunts and blitzes. He looks for an assignment when he's left without one.

Weaknesses: Franklin hasn't competed against many top-tier defensive lines in college. His hands can often be late and high, and he needs to do a better job of consistently locating them. While his size is good for a center, it's still small for interior lineman thresholds, and he will struggle to sustain bigger dominant nose tackles. When fighting against guys who can reach and out-muscle him, Franklin will grant movement and give up torque when attempting to sustain. His anchor strength overall is adequate, but it isn't elite, and he needs to utilize his leverage to maximize it consistently.

Best Fit: Zone-blocking center

Player Ranking (1-100): 68.5 - Franklin knows what he is and that is worth something. He isn't a dominant mauler or people mover in the run game, but he's a reliable pass protector who generally plays well in the run game, especially on the move. He will best suit a zone-style system. 5th round player.

15. Marcus Wehr - Montana State - 6'4 300 lbs

Strengths: A 6th-year senior, Wehr initially began his career at Montana State at defensive end before transitioning to playing on the offensive side of the ball. Wehr has played guard and tackle, starting in the last three seasons. He's been a First Team FCS All-American during his time at Montana State, dominating his level of competition. Wehr best projects the next level at guard. Wehr is a good combination of athlete and strength. Despite not being the biggest guy, Wehr has impressive power and strength through his frame. In the passing game, Wehr shows a strong lower half to sustain and anchor against bull rushers. His natural leverage advantage allows him to stay underneath the pads of bigger defenders. He stays square and maintains control with his strong hands, rarely losing sustain. Wehr is at his best in the running game, particularly in zone-style runs. He eases off the snap of the ball with good lateral quickness and explosiveness. His burst enables him to reach landmarks, beating defenders to the spot. Good core strength enables Wehr to sustain blocks in space, driving forward with his legs to clear rush lanes. A natural mover in space that shows good balance and body control when climbing to the 2nd level. A tough kid who finishes plays, battling until the end.

Weaknesses: He's played far more at tackle throughout his career than guard and will need more experience playing on the inside. He hasn't consistently competed against top-tier competition at the FCS level. Wehr still needs to work on his footwork in the passing game, struggling at times to mirror against quicker-twitch rushers. He often gets either too narrow or too wide. If he's initially beaten off the snap, he lacks the recovery quickness to regain control of a rep. He has some slight mental lapses that cause him to be late to react to blitzes and stunts. In the running game, he's frequently caught leaning and off-balance. This causes him to miss secondary targets in space, overextending and whiffing too often.

Best Fit: Zone-blocking guard

Player Ranking (1-100): 67.2 - Wehr has shown impressive abilities in the last few years in the FCS. Considering he's new to the position, he will need some time to continue ironing out his kinks, but he's proven to adapt quickly. 5th round player.

16. Jake Majors - Texas - 6'3 315 lbs

Strengths: A 4-year starter at center for the Longhorns, Majors has proven to be a durable and reliable interior presence. A highly experienced football player who has seen it all at the college level, playing in big moments and shining on the biggest stages. Majors is equally adept in both phases of the game. Major has proven to be incredibly consistent in the passing game, rarely allowing even a pressure. He eases off the snap of the ball with good initial quickness and lateral mobility. He maintains good leverage and width, maximizing his frame. If he initially grants any movement against power, Majors generally do a good job of resetting and recovering. His powerful upper body enables him to control reps, showing violent hands and a powerful punch. He's a high IQ football player who recognizes defensive looks pre-snap, proving to be a reliable signal caller. He will quickly adjust pickup against stunts and blitzes. In the running game, Majors show experience and comfort when playing in zone and power schemes. He plays with a nasty demeanor and a finisher mentality. Capable of displacing runners at the 1st level, Majors utilizes his leverage and lower body torque to generate power. His latch-on strength is mostly reliable, showing the ability to sustain blockers in space. A good move player that shows good balance and anticipation when working 2nd level blocks.

Weaknesses: Majors lacks ideal size dimensions to play for some NFL offenses, lacking both the girth and the length. His anchor strength will sometimes be challenging against longer and more powerful interior defenders who can reach his pads. This causes him to get put in recovery mode quite frequently. Major sometimes lacks patience and can get caught leaning in and caught off-balanced. In the running game, Majors lacks great POP in his hands and consistently fails to dominate at the point of attack. Stubby limbs can sometimes cause him issues locating and reaching in space.

Best Fit: Center in any scheme

Player Ranking (1-100): 66.2 - Major is a consistent, solid player in all phases. He lacks the elite mobility or the point-of-attack strength to be a high-ceiling blocker. His frame will likely cause some scouts to be concerned about translating at the next level. 5th round player.

17. Garrett Dellinger - LSU - 6'5 333 lbs

Strengths: Dellinger is a 2.5-year starter for the Tigers who has shown impressive versatility when used at guard, center, and tackle. A stoutly built prospect with good thickness and density through both upper and lower halves. Dellinger excels most in the passing game, playing with good natural width and a strong anchor. He can absorb against speed-to-power rushers, showing good points of attack, lower body power, and iron-grip clasp strength to latch and lock. He always keeps his head on a swivel, maintaining hyper-awareness of additional rushers and stunts. In the running game, Dellinger plays with good effort and power. He excels in most vertical run sets, as in a gap/power scheme, showing the ability to create displacement power through his lower body. He can seal both inside and outside runs with body positioning and angles. His upper body strength and heavy hands deliver power punches to unsuspecting defenders, creating pushback power. He's generally very good at creating engagement with linebackers at the 2nd level, maintaining sustain throughout. Dellinger has improved throughout his time at LSU, showing consistent improvement.

Weaknesses: Underwent Tightrope surgery in his final campaign to help his high ankle sprain heal, causing him to miss several games during his final season. Miss some game time in 2022 with a broken hand that required surgery and an MCL strain in his right knee. Dellinger lacks elite length and is too quick to allow defenders to enter his frame. Once they arrive in his chest, he struggles to regain control of a rep and will get bullied backward. He's frequently battling leverage issues in both run and pass sets, playing off his toes and getting caught off balanced and leaning. He's on the ground far too much for my liking. His overall mobility laterally is suspect, and he allows defenders to cross his face, consistently win his inside shoulder, and attack the 'A' gap.

Best Fit: Developmental guard/center, ideally in a gap/power scheme

Player Ranking (1-100): 62.4 - Dellinger has experience playing against top-tier competition, and his versatility more than helped LSU coaches. While he doesn't have any awful blunders on tape, he lacks the top-end skillset of a starter at the next level. His versatility can earn him a role as a swing player who can play both guard and center. 6th round player.

18. Seth McLaughlin - Ohio State - 6'4 304 lbs

Strengths: A 3-year starter with the Tide before transferring to Ohio State for his final season of eligibility. A highly seasoned and experienced interior line prospect who has consistently played against top-tier competition in two different programs. McLaughlin is a low center-of-gravity blocker built with squatty legs and impressive power through his frame. He is a technician in how he plays the position, showcasing excellent technique and fundamentals. High IQ and relied on making signal calls for both programs, recognizing pre-snap looks, and adjusting the offense. He always keeps his head on a swivel, always looking for an assignment when left without one. He communicates well with his teammates, recognizing blitzes and stunts immediately and showing adaptability and reactionary instincts. A smooth mover that shows the lateral mobility to mirror in space. If he initially misses with his hands, he displays the recovery quickness to adjust and recover. Shows schematic versatility and has played in different offensive line systems. Adept in the run game, showing the acceleration and body control to excel in zone concepts. Works hard to maintain leverage, showing good sustain through his blocks. He is a finisher with space-moving power through his frame, clearing out 1st-level rush lanes.

Weaknesses: He has played virtually every snap of his college career at center, failing to have ideal positional experience to play guard. McLaughlin tore his Achilles towards the end odf the season, and will likely miss some time in 2025. A smaller interior prospect that lacks the frame for much additional growth. Lacks confidence in pass sets when attempting to block head-on against bigger interior prospects, as he had noticeable concerns with erratic snaps. Can get too aggressive at moments, lacking the necessary patience, and will lunge to attempt to make first contact. Hand placement can be high due to poor pad level, giving up his chest against bull rushers. Lacks top-end anchor and core strength and will grant movement against speed-to-power rushers.

Best Fit: Center in any scheme

Player Ranking (1-100): 61.9 - McLaughlin has had a stellar college career with two different programs. He struggled at times at Alabama, most noticeably during his final season. But there's no denying he's a reliable and highly experienced big-game player. If he can show his ability at guard, he can be a nice dual-flex player on your gameday roster. 6th round player.

19. Jackson Slater - Sacramento State - 6'4 316 lbs

Strengths: A 4-year starter at guard for the Hornets, Slater has been a dominant presence for Sacramento State each season. While he's played mostly at left guard during his career, he also started two games at left tackle. In high school, he had experience playing in every position along the front. Slater is a compact and densely built blocker with good proportional length and size. A workout warrior, Slater has impressed greatly, power cleaning over 400 pounds and squatting well over 600 pounds. Slater isn't just a workout warrior but proves his strength and power on the field. Slater is an easy mover in passing sets, showcasing loose hips to transition and slide to mirror easily. His powerful lower body lets him sit on blocks, dropping his anchor quickly and rarely allowing much movement. Slater's core strength and recovery abilities allow him to quickly reset and regain control if he initially loses any ground. He keeps his eyes on a swivel and quickly adjusts and recognizes blitzes and stunts. Slater is at his best in the running game, specifically in zone-style runs. He explodes out of his stance and is frequently used to lead the way on runs, showing terrific balance and anticipation on the move. His large mitts enable him to quickly gain control of linebackers and safeties, showing iron-grip strength in his hands.

Weaknesses: Despite Slater's experience at the FCS level, the clear concern will be the transition to competing against NFL talent. Slater lacks ideal measurables for the guard position and might have to kick to center. In the passing game, Slater will sometimes be challenged against quicker-twitch rushers that can get underneath his pads. He doesn't always play with ideal pad level and will occasionally succumb to allowing them to rise mid-play. Can get grabby when defenders stress his outside shoulder. He needs to do a better job of finishing plays and sustaining through the whistle, oftentimes allowing defenders off on counter moves to make the play.

Best Fit: Zone-blocking center or guard

Player Ranking (1-100): 61.5 - Slater is a great athlete with impressive physicality. He plays with a nasty mean streak and will be a real asset in the run game. He will likely struggle to transition to competing against NFL athletes, but he's got a chance to make an NFL roster. 6th round player.

20. Connor Colby - Iowa - 6'6 298 lbs

Strengths: A 4-year starter with the Hawkeyes, playing at both guard spots and some right tackle. A highly experienced guy who has virtually missed no snaps for the last four seasons, showing reliability, dependability, and durability. Colby is a proportioned athlete with noteworthy size and length to play on the inside at the next level. Easing off the snap of the ball, Colby is a good athlete with the quickness and agility to mirror in space in passing sets. A highly aware blocker who keeps his head on a swivel while looking for an assignment when left without one. Adjust well to blitzes, twists, and stunts in pass protection. He has good hands and strike accuracy that commits him to win inside positioning at proper depths. He is at his best in zone-style runs, showing a terrific understanding of positioning and leverage to open up opportunities at both the 1st and the 2nd level. Change of directional abilities are above average when working in space. Stays balanced and leveraged while on the move, possessing a good batting average to reach defenders in space. A tough kid that works hard to battle until after the whistle. He works well and communicates well with his teammates when handling combination and double-team blocks.

Weaknesses: Colby is a tall interior prospect who will struggle with pad level and leverage. Lacks the ideal hand strength in his hands to sustain blocks. Can play over his skis and get caught bending at the waist. If initially beaten, Colby lacks elite core strength and athleticism to reset and regain control with reps. His lower half is modest and could utilize additional strength and anchorage power. Has a bad habit of dropping his head upon impact in passing sets. He is likely limited to a zone-style system as he lacks the power profile to handle a power-blocking system. Not a space clearer or a people mover in the run game, but generally a positionally sound and angle blocker. While he has good lateral movement skills, he will be challenged against better rushers, which can significantly challenge his lack of elite agility.

Best Fit: Zone-blocking guard

Player Ranking (1-100): 60.9 - Colby is a highly experienced prospect who has shown consistent success for four straight seasons. While he lacks exciting physical traits, he's a smart and disciplined blocker that showcases reliability and positional versatility. He could be a guy that competes for a backup role. 6th round player.

21. Willie Lampkin - North Carolina - 5'11 290 lbs

Strengths: A 3-year starter at Coastal Carolina who played practically every position for their offensive line during his time there before transferring over to North Carolina. His size constraints will likely push him to center at the next level, and he's already shown he can succeed playing there. Lampkin makes up for his lack of size with outstanding technique and athleticism. Lampkin is a smooth operator in pass sets, easily moving back and forth between bent knees while maintaining positioning. His quick feet and lower body fluidity enable him to mirror with ease against quicker twitch rushers. His heavy hands cause him to disrupt rushers, slowing them down. He maintains control throughout snaps, showing outstanding hand strength to latch on and lock. His natural leverage advantage enables him to control the point of attack despite being outmatched in size and length. He quickly recognizes and adjusts to blitzes and stunts. In the running game, Lampkin shows road-grader toughness and mentality. He plays with a wrestler's mentality, grappling with defenders while keeping his legs churning to bring defenders to the ground. He has light feet working at the 2nd level, showing good balance and anticipation while working in space. He's got iron-man reliability, starting 5 years of college with hardly any missed time until the end of his final season.

Weaknesses: Lampkin's biggest concern will be his undersized frame and lack of length. While he was able to make do at the college level, there will be major concerns at the next level. His arm constraints can cause him to struggle against longer-levered interior blockers that can utilize push/pull techniques on him and control the point of attack. Lampkin isn't suited to play in a gap system and will likely only appeal to teams with heavy zone schemes. While he generally can reset and recover if initially giving up ground, Lampkin's lack of anchorage power and size can sometimes put him on skates.

Best Fit: Zone-blocking center

Player Ranking (1-100): 60.5 - Lampkin is the type of guy you take on Day 3. He would be the perfect center if he were a few inches taller and had slightly longer arms. He's a master technician with how he plays the position. He does an impressive job maximizing his physical tools. He should have a chance to impress in the right scheme. I'm rooting for him; I really think he has a shot. 6th round player.

22. Joshua Gray - Oregon State - 6'4 310 lbs

Strengths: A rare 5th year starter for the Beavers, Gray has been the starter on the blindside of the Oregon State offense in each of those seasons. Extensive experience and durability at the college level and competing against top-tier edge rushers enable Gray to be NFL-ready. Gray is a terrific athlete with the athleticism and the footwork to excel in space. Lateral mobility is present as Gray can mirror edge rushers in space. His strong upper body and hands allow him to stun defenders when he can get his hands on them. A high football IQ and post-snap awareness allow Gray to recognize stunts and late-onset blitzes, frequently picking them up seamlessly. Gray is at his best in the running game, specifically zone-style runs. He is seamless when playing in space, climbing to the second level, showing anticipation and body control to reach moving targets. He is a downhill run blocker who churns his legs and generates power through his lower body as he clears both 1st and 2nd level rush lanes.

Weaknesses: Gray has serious size limitations, failing to have necessary measurables at height, weight, or length. He will likely have to transition to guard or center, where he has zero experience. Lack of power and functional strength at the point of attack causes him to get completely engulfed. He is likely only a fit for a zone-based running team as he lacks the experience or the point-of-attack strength to play in a power-blocking system. Frequently caught lunging into his pass sets, getting caught off-balanced. Oversets his feet to the outside, leaving interior gaps wide open for counter opportunities. Has a bad habit of dropping his head and ducking upon contact. Lacks the necessary anchor to recover if granting any movement, failing to sit on speed-to-power rushers. Allows his pads to rise mid-play, allowing defenders to consistently get under his pads and capture the edge against him.

Best Fit: Developmental Guard or Center

Player Ranking (1-100): 59.7 - Despite Gray's experience and athleticism, he's still a big question mark. He will have to transition to playing inside at the next giant unknown level. Savvy coaches and evaluators will be intrigued by his athleticism and upside. But he needs considerable strength to be a starter at the next level. 7th round player.

23. Drew Kendall - Boston College - 6'4 300 lbs

Strengths: A 3-year starter for the Eagles at center, Kendall is a highly experienced and decorated center. While lacking ideal size and bulk, Kendall makes up for it with technique and football intelligence. A smooth operator, Kendall plays with good initial burst and quickness off the snap. He remains patient, rarely playing over his skis, showcasing bent knees and leveraged pads. He utilizes powerful hands perfectly, showing good timing and placement. The strength of his iron grip allows him to control and maintain his position in the passing game. A cerebral blocker that recognizes pre-snap looks, proving the ability to signal call and adjust protection schemes. When left without an assignment, Kendall looks to help his teammates. He has a knack for being the move blocker on screens and pulls, regularly timing them to perfection while disguising them well. Despite being repeatedly outmatched in the size and strength department, Kendall shows good recovery abilities to regain control of reps if initially beaten. In the running game, Kendall understands how to utilize body positioning and leverage to seal runs. He plays with a relentless motor and urgency on every snap, maximizing his physical tools with toughness and physicality. Kendall has iron-man reliability, starting every game with a clean bill of health throughout his career.

Weaknesses: Kendall is a technician in how he plays the position but lacks the physical tools for continued development. He's maxed out likely in terms of his frame and athleticism. His size dimensions mean he has no position flex to play at guard and is likely only a fit at center. He's frequently in recovery mode against bigger interior defenders who can quickly reach his pads. His lack of length causes him to struggle when plays go outside his frame, frequently allowing defenders to get outside his frame on counter attempts. While he's a good athlete, he lacks top-end athleticism for a center. In the running game, Kendall lacks the point-of-attack power to displace defenders. In short-yardage situations, Kendall struggles to get any movement or push, often allowing the interior of the pocket to collapse.

Best Fit: Zone-blocking center

Player Ranking (1-100): 54.8 - Kendall has had a really good career, but in terms of starter potential, he will likely be a developmental center only. He will struggle in a gap scheme and is likely much better suited to play in a zone-style system. Undrafted free agent.

24. Cooper Mays - Tennessee - 6'4 310 lbs

Strengths: Mays is a 5th year senior for the Vols and began starting games at center as a true freshman in 2020. A highly experienced prospect with extensive experience against some of the best defensive lines in football for five straight seasons. Incredibly smart kid who has been responsible for signal calling for Tennessee's high-tempo offense. Keeps his head on a swivel for every play and always looks for an assignment when left without one. Remains in good positions in pass sets, easing off the snap of the ball with terrific initial quickness out of his stance. Can mirror against more athletic defensive tackles, showing looseness and lateral mobility to stay square throughout the duration. Understands how to win with positioning and angles, maintaining his natural leverage throughout the snap. He is a tough kid who maximizes his physical tools with tenacity and toughness, finishing at every opportunity he can. Shows the movement skills and the anticipation to win in a zone-style system, getting out in space effortlessly.

Weaknesses: Missed the start of the 2023 season due to requiring hernia surgery during camp. He also missed a few games during his sophomore campaign in 2021 due to injury. Mays has serious size limitations, lacking in both length and size. While he's done a nice job maximizing his frame, there is limited additional room for growth. Lacks the positional versatility and experience to move to a different spot, including guard. Mays lacks the power through his frame to control blockers and appears to be hanging on for dear life in moments. Not a space mover in the run game that will generate any movement at the first level. Lack of length limits him from sustaining blocks, often allowing defenders off on counter moves that can shed. While he has the athleticism to excel in space, his lack of length and body control limits him in reaching blocks.

> **Best Fit: Zone-blocking center**

Player Ranking (1-100): 54.3 - Mays is a limited prospect who, unfortunately, doesn't have size, power, or length. While he's vastly experienced and deserves a shot in a zone-style system, he lacks the positional versatility to be a guy that teams can carry to gameday, unfortunately. Undrafted free agent.

25. Jacob Gideon - Western Michigan - 6'2 290 lbs

Strengths: Gideon is a 4-year starter who has bounced between guard and center, showing positional experience and versatility. Gideon lacks in size and length because he makes up it in technical nuance and football smarts. Gideon is a smaller and lower center-of-gravity blocker who utilizes his natural leverage advantage to win the pad-level battle at the snap of the ball. Gideon has been responsible for helping Western Michigan lead the way in the MAC Conference in rushing for multiple seasons. A smart and cerebral blocker, Gideon works the best out-of-zone-style running system. He has an excellent feel for spacing and works well with his teammates on combo blocks and double teams to open up 1st level rush lanes. He utilizes angles, body positioning, and leverage to win the running game. He keeps his legs churning through impact to push piles forward in short-yardage and red-zone settings. He's smooth and effortless when climbing to the 2nd level, showing good anticipation and balance. In the passing game, Gideon eases off the snap of the ball with good quickness and change of directional skills. He mirrors well and stays square to his assignment, maintaining width and good knee bend.

Weaknesses: Gideon hasn't competed against many top-tier interior defensive linemen. Gideon has obvious size concerns for the next level. While he maximizes his frame out with technique, he lacks the length and the size to win against larger interior defenders continuously. He struggles to control for long durations, allowing defenders to shed on counter moves consistently. He needs to better place his hands in passing sets, frequently whiffing high and to the outside. He lacks a power profile and struggles to sustain his anchor against speed-to-power rushers that can get underneath his pads. He had a season-ending injury in 2022.

> **Best Fit: Developmental center**

Player Ranking (1-100): 54.0 - Gideon is a developmental center that needs to grow and gain functional strength through his frame. His ceiling is limited, but he could compete for a roster spot with NFL coaching and strength & development coaches.

Top-10 Interior Offensive Lineman:

1. Donovan Jackson

2. Tyler Booker
3. Tate Ratledge
4. Wyatt Milum
5. Jonah Savaiinaea
6. Grey Zabel
7. Luke Kandra
8. Dylan Fairchild
9. Jared Wilson
10. Clay Webb

Chapter 8

Edge Players
(4-3 DE's and 3-4 OLB's)

1. Abdul Carter - Penn State - 6'3 252 lbs

Strengths: Carter immediately began starting games as a true freshman, playing his first two seasons as an off-ball linebacker. He transitioned to playing on the edge in 2024, proving his upside as a pass rusher. Built with a long-levered frame, showcasing good length and overall size. Carter has proven himself to be one of the most effective pass rushers in the country in the last three years, even when playing off the ball his first two seasons. Used in various ways, including effectively as a QB shy against running QBs, showing impressive athleticism and closing ability. A dynamic athlete, Carter utilizes incredible first-step quickness coupled with snap anticipation to explode upon the snap immediately. His speed and secondary quickness make it hard for offensive tackles to get two hands on him. Excellent bend and ankle flexion allow him to dip his shoulder and win outside rush lanes. Sets up subsequent rushes well with a large arsenal at his disposal. Wins his rush reps both inside as an 'A' gap blitzer or on the outside. His relentless urgency and motor skills allow him to effectively use counter moves even when initially blocked. He makes several plays in pursuit when working back toward the ball. He shows comfort in rushing both in a 2-point stance and with his hands in the dirt. Frequently, I had to take on double teams with shading linebackers or running backs. In coverage, Carter shows upside, fluidly changing directions and flipping his hips with minimal gear down. He was used in both zones, and man looks to cover receivers and running backs in the shorter areas of the field. A violent and downhill football player who reacts quickly, exploding upon impact with ball carriers.

Weaknesses: Carter was arrested for a misdemeanor assault in April 2024. Carter was sometimes undisciplined as a linebacker, taking poor pursuit angles and constantly overrunning plays. He doesn't appear to have the greatest play recognition abilities, always in catch-up mode and chasing plays instead of sniffing them out prior. Commits a lot of penalties for a defensive player. Needs to learn how to utilize his hands better when pass rushing, far too frequently playing belly to belly and leaving his chest plate exposed. He is still developing his frame and could use more of a power profile as both a rusher and in the running game. In the run game, he will get easily stymied by double teams and combo blocks due to failing to play leveraged and with ideal anchorage strength. Struggles stacking and shedding in pursuit, frequently running right into blockers and failing to utilize his length and upper-body power to disengage. He relies on winning as a tackler with his initial jolt, failing to always utilize good wrap-up fundamentals due to leverage and poor technique. He missed a lot of tackles throughout college.

Best Fit: Edge rusher in either scheme

Player Ranking (1-100): 91.7 - Carter is one of this draft class's best pure pass rushers. His ability to get into the backfield with speed, bend, and closing speed is outstanding. He's effective wherever he rushes. Initially, he needs a lot of work in the running game, although he certainly has the frame for it. If he is checked out OK for off-the-field concerns, he should be a high 1st round player. He will immediately be a great pass rusher in clear passing settings for a team.

2. Mykel Williams - Georgia - 6'5 265 lbs

Strengths: A former five-star recruit and significant contributor to the Bulldog's defense in the last three seasons, Williams has been used in various ways for their defensive front. Capable of playing both inside and outside, Williams has the prototypical power-packed profile that allows him to have success in different schemes and alignments. Williams shows up the most in the biggest games and is a big-game performer. Has rare physical tools with explosive twitch in his frame, tremendous power, and the length to overwhelm blockers consistently. As a rusher, Williams utilizes a large assault of attacks, showing quick and active hands to swipe away blockers quickly. Generates forceful POP through his hands to displace blockers. Understands how to maximize speed-to-power to consistently win inside hand placement and keep his legs churning through impact to put unsuspecting blockers on skates. He's used devastatingly on stunts as the looper, showing impeccable timing and burst to close on the QB quickly. His long legs and stride lengths allow him to close cushions in pursuit as both a rusher and in the running game. Shows the power to be effective when kicked inside, beating interior blockers with power and length. When he can't get home, Williams understands how to disrupt the QB's vision by getting his hands up. Plays with a relentless motor, showing terrific urgency and intensity on counter moves. Williams shows good ball awareness and anchorage power to handle combination blocks in the running game. He is a mostly reliable open-field tackler who utilizes his entire wingspan to close down rush lanes.

Weaknesses: Williams has a massive ceiling, but overall production has been mostly OK throughout college. He's a bit of a flash player who looks terrific in moments or certain games but disappears for long stretches. He doesn't appear to have the quickest processor, often having stalled-out moments when diagnosing, causing some hesitancies in pursuit. He tends to fire upright out of the stances, limiting his ability to play leveraged, allowing blockers to get underneath his pad level. Pad level and stiffness through his lower body cause him to struggle to change directions. Lacks elite flexibility and bend, shows limited finesse as a rusher, and generally relies on winning with power.

Best Fit: 4-3 DE that can kick inside

Player Ranking (1-100): 87.6 - Williams never quite lived up to his potential statistically, but he certainly showed traits and flashes of brilliance. He has all the physical tools to be great if he can learn to be consistent. His blue-chip characteristics and off-the-field leadership qualities will only further help him. You don't see many kids with his athleticism, length, and power. He's worth a high 1st round pick.

3. Jalon Walker - Georgia - 6'2 245 lbs

Strengths: Walker was mostly a rotational player his first two seasons with the Bulldogs before finally winning a starting role in 2024. Despite having a more limited role in his first two seasons, Walker took advantage of every opportunity greatly. Walker is built with a compact and dense frame and has good overall size and proportional length. Walker has been used in various roles, having played everything from a QB spy to an edge rusher to an off-ball linebacker, showing incredible versatility. Walker is an explosive pass rusher who has shown success from different alignments and can win along the edges or when used as an interior gap blitzer. Heavy-handed and with a diverse set of attack moves enable Walker to win as a rusher. Plays with outstanding effort and motor, playing every snap at 100 mph. Showcases impressive bend and flexion in his lower body to drop his shoulder and get underneath opposing blockers at improbable angles. Noteworthy range and linear burst when used further back as a linebacker, showing the ability to shrink the field with sideline-to-sideline ability. Can stack and shed in pursuit, showing good POP in his hands to work towards blockers and flow to the football. Good overall anchorage power and leverage when taking on blocks along the edges, maintaining good positioning to set the edge. Impressive reps when dropping in coverage, noticeable ability to re-route and engage first contact within contact windows in man coverage reps. Capable of handling assignments against running backs and tight ends in man coverage. He is a very good, forceful tackler who can occasionally lay the wood or securely make extended wrap-up tackles outside his frame.

Weaknesses: Walker had offseason shoulder surgery in 2023. Walker has limited started experience, with only one full season of starting experience. A bit of a tweener that lacks a truly defined position. He likely is limited to an odd front system if he's going to play as an edge player, failing to have ideal size and length dimensions to play with his hand in the dirt. Overall, play recognition skills and ball instincts are just OK at this point, and he's often in catch-up mode, recognizing things too late. This is apparent when he handles drops in zone coverage, failing to drop to appropriate depths while leaving noticeable gaps in coverage.

Best Fit: Edge rusher in either scheme

Player Ranking (1-100): 86.8 - As the son of a football coach, Walker is a high-character, hard-working kid with the athleticism to match. Undoubtedly, he's a gifted pass rusher and should be used that way, regardless of the team he goes to. He has some Micah Parsons and can be successful wherever he's used. He will need further reps and development, but he's impressive. 1st round player.

4. Nic Scourton - Texas A&M - 6'4 280 lbs

Strengths: A former Purdue recruit, Scourton exploded as a sophomore in 2023, finishing with 10 sacks and 15 tackles for loss. Following his sophomore campaign, Scourton transferred to the Aggies, where he played his junior season, showing continued development. Scourton has shown top-end production for two different programs and against elite offensive lines. Scourton has a massive and developed frame, showing the height, length, and density to play in any defensive setup at the next level. Scourton plays mostly on the outside, both in a two and 3-point stance. A violent football player shows the heavy-handedness and upper-body strength to be devastating to blockers. As a rusher, Scourton displays rare flexibility and agility for his size, showing the ability to threaten the outside rush lanes. Sets up subsequent rushes nicely, capable of winning both the outside and inside shoulder of offensive tackles. Features a devastating spin move, utilizing impeccable timing to overset tackles and win the interior rush lane to get into the backfield quickly. Good closing speed and long strides allow him to close cushions in pursuit quickly. Understands how to generate impressive speed-to-power on his bull rush, capable of closing the pocket when he remains leveraged. Maintains good discipline in the running game against misdirection-type plays and RPOs, showing good play recognition abilities and ball location skills. His length is a nuisance for stubby-built blockers, as Scourton commits himself to winning hand placement while controlling blockers to stack and shed.

Weaknesses: Scourton is a tweener with the frame of a defensive tackle but has played most as a defensive end in college. He's far more developed when playing out of a two-point stance, sometimes struggling with his hand in the dirt. In the running game, Scourton fails to keep his pads leveraged, and his hips sink, often struggling to set the edge and maintain positioning. He is a good athlete overall, but Scourton lacks elite quick-twitch out of his stance, often reacting late to the snap. Needs to do a better job of playing leveraged when working out of a two-point stance, playing far too upright, minimizing his opportunities to collapse the pocket. Still developing as a counter-rusher, failing to have a secondary plan if initially blocked. Reliant on winning with either his power or with his spin move, and I'd like to see him develop a better rush arsenal. He's a fairly good tackler, but sometimes he whiffs when approaching ball carriers upright.

Best Fit: Edge rusher in any system

Player Ranking (1-100): 85.4 - Scourton is a stud. He's one of my favorite players to watch in this draft class. His ceiling is massive as he continues to develop both in the running and passing games. His combination of athleticism and size is immense. The fact that he's been dominant in college at 19 and 20 years old is ridiculous. 1st round player.

5. Tyler Baron - Miami - 6'5 260 lbs

Strengths: A former four-star Tennessee recruit, Baron excelled with the Vols for four seasons before transferring to the Hurricanes before the 2024 campaign. Baron has had production everywhere he's been and every season but saved his best season for last with the Hurricanes, easing into a new defense with no ill effects. Featuring a well-developed and proportioned frame, Baron has ideal size requisites to play in any defensive scheme at the next level. Having success along different alignments and in both a 2-point stance and standing up, Baron is a schematically versatile prospect who truly wins wherever he is lined up. Has competed against top-tier competition for two different programs, showing success at both. Baron is a relentless and urgent football player who plays every snap like it's his last. Exploding low off the snap of the ball, Baron sets up 2-way rushes with his ability to win both the outside edges while also having the potential to counter back inside. Generates impressive speed-to-power through his lower half, putting blockers on skates. Has a variety of different pass rush moves he utilizes at his disposal, bringing a clear plan of attack on every rush. Has elastic-like flexibility to threaten improbably wide arcs and dip his shoulder to get underneath even the most leveraged tackles. Has shown the ability to kick inside and generate pass-rush in clear pass-rush situations. Instinctual and highly aware in the run game, Baron has eyes behind his head to always locate the football. Maintains positioning and sets the edge in the running game. Relentless pursuit and hot motor, combined with closing speed, enable him to make several plays from the backside. He has strong hands and an upper body that rarely lets a runner out of his grasp, showing excellent open-field tackling ability.

Weaknesses: Baron's upper body strength is further along than his anchorage power, and he could benefit by continuing to add strength to his legs to anchor better in the running game. Lower body strength will also assist him in bringing a more dynamic power profile to his rushes. He plays every snap at 100 mph and tends to wear out towards the end of games, limiting his effectiveness in playing discipline and taking acute angles to the football. His pads continuously rise mid-play when tired, and he struggles to disengage. While he certainly has a pass-rush arsenal, he can continue to improve his hand tactics when rushing.

Best Fit: Edge rusher in any system

Player Ranking (1-100): 84.7 - Baron is one of my favorite players on tape. You'll rarely see him get washed out of games or not affecting plays. He's constantly working and battling on every snap of the ball. He has a few downsides as a player and should be a Day-1 starter who can significantly improve any defensive line. He's a great pass rusher and a good run-support defensive end. Love this kid. 2nd round player.

6. Kyle Kennard - South Carolina - 6'5 254 lbs

Strengths: Kennard was a 4-year player for Georgia Tech before transferring over to the Gamecocks before his senior season. Kennard exploded during his final campaign in the SEC, finishing atop SEC production metrics, including 16 tackles for loss, 11.5 sacks, and three forced fumbles. Kennard has been used all over the defensive front for the Gamecocks this year as a chesspiece akin to Micah Parsons with the Cowboys. Kennard has an ideal frame to play along the edges, showing schematic and alignment versatility. He has a long and lean body with enough frame room for additional mass. As a rusher, Kennard has twitch for days, showing rare get-off and explosion off the line. He frequently uses his burst with his flexion and bends to challenge to win the arc against tackles. Kennard utilizes various hand tactics to keep his frame clean through contact. He plays with a tireless motor, playing 100 mph on every snap of the ball. When attacking head-on, Kennard can generate significant displacement power with his bull rushes, generating fantastic speed-to-power to put blockers on skates. He also shows success rushing when shading inside, showing good timing and instincts to shoot gaps and penetrate. In the running game, Kennard utilizes his length and powerful hands to stack and shed in pursuit. He's quick to diagnose the development of plays in the backfield, regularly blowing up screens and misdirection-type plays. His motor runs hot in pursuit, making many plays down the field or from the backside. He's been a reliable contributor for five straight seasons for two programs, showing no durability or injury concerns.

Weaknesses: Kennard has a great frame but could benefit from adding more mass and strength to his lower body as he struggles to anchor down in the run game. Kennard can sometimes play recklessly, almost like a chicken without its head. He's quick to shoot gaps, failing always to wait for plays to develop before triggering downhill. He needs to do a better job of diagnosing run-blocking sets in pursuit. When setting the edge, Kennard allows his pads to rise but gets bullied by combo and double teams. As a rusher, Kennard could benefit by adding tools to his tool belt, namely attacking interior lanes. He's a bit of a 1-trick pony who attempts to arc the corner on every rep instead of setting up his subsequent rushes. He's very reliant on winning with his 1st move and could benefit by adding a counter plan to his rushes.

Best Fit: Edge rusher in any system

Player Ranking (1-100): 84.0 - Kennard is a fun player to watch and was a major reason for the South Carolina resurgence on defense. He was unblockable and dominant at times. His success in the SEC bodes well for his future. He's a dynamic combination of explosiveness, motor, and flat-out football player. 2nd round player.

7. Landon Jackson - Arkansas - 6'6 259 lbs

Strengths: A former LSU recruit before transferring to Arkansas and starting for the Razorbacks in the last three seasons. Jackson had his best season as a junior with 14 tackles for loss and 6.5 sacks. Jackson is a versatile defender who plays various roles and alignments for the Razorbacks. He can play both inside and outside and in every kind of scheme. An incredibly well-built defender, Jackson has both the muscled-up frame and vines for arms that are intimidating for offensive linemen. The first thing you'll notice with Jackson is his 1st step explosiveness, regularly exploding off the ball. Hip fluidity and ankle flexion allow him to challenge outside corners against tackles regularly. He is a shifty mover who limits his surface area for blockers, making it difficult to sustain for a long time. Understands how to utilize his hands to keep his frame clean. In the running game, Jackson displays good patience while allowing plays to develop before he crashes down hard. He regularly makes several plays in pursuit, working back toward the ball. Strong hands allow him to wrap up securely in the running game.

Weaknesses: Despite his muscled-up physique, Jackson can struggle against overly powerful blockers that can get both hands on him. He's not a guy who will consistently threaten the pocket with power-rushing moves. Has a bad habit of allowing his pads to rise mid-play, causing him to struggle with leverage. Mostly reliant on winning with speed and could benefit by refining hand usage and developing a larger rush attack when attacking the pocket. Snap anticipation and timing are a bit sporadic, as he's often the last one to get a jump at the line.

Best Fit: 4-3 DE

Player Ranking (1-100): 82.9 - I like Jackson quite a bit. I think he's a very good player against the run and has the explosiveness to continue to get better as a rusher. I love him as a 4-3 LDE in an even front. His frame and length are a true force for offensive tackles. I think he will be a solid starter at the next level. 2nd round player.

8. Mike Green - Marshall - 6'4 248 lbs

Strengths: Green was a 2-year starter for the Thundering Herd, and he exploded during his final season, finishing with double-digit sacks and multiple forced fumbles. Green is a lean, long-edge defender with a large enough frame for continued development. Green has shown his ability to be successful against top-tier opposition, showing up in bigger games for Marshall. An explosive edge rusher, Green combines his snap anticipation with 1st step quickness to immediately challenge and instantly stress offensive tackles. A relentless rusher who brings a wide array of pass-rush moves to the table, Green has a rush plan on every snap. If his initial plan doesn't work, his counter plan brings something else to the offer. Green can convert speed to power, so Green plays with leveraged pads and can put blockers on skates. A former wrestler, Green excels in the hand battles, showing quick and violent hands to shock blockers. He has impressive bend and flexion through his lower body, enabling him to flatten the arc against offensive tackles. Shows good timing and closing speed when used as the looper on stunts, regularly getting home when attacking through the 'A' and 'B' gaps. Plays hard and is relentless in pursuit in the running game, making several plays from the backside. Green has also proven to be a core special teams contributor, playing on all of the units for Marshall.

Weaknesses: Green is a one-season wonder who seemingly came out of nowhere to have the season he did. While he showed impressive film against the better teams he played against this season, he failed to play top-tier competition weekly, taking advantage of favorable matchups. Green must continue to add clean weight and functional strength onto his frame as he is frequently taken out of running plays. He lacks the anchorage abilities and core strength to maintain a strong edge, frequently getting uprooted by combo blocks. Struggles to handle 1 v 1 wrap-up responsibilities as a last line of defense, allowing runners out of his grasp far too frequently. He will need to continue to add more power elements to his game as a pass rusher, relying too much on his speed and twitch.

Best Fit: Edge defender in either scheme

Player Ranking (1-100): 80.7 - It's hard to ignore Mike Green's production this season for Marshall. He was dominant and statistically amongst the best pass rushers in the country. If he maintains his explosiveness while adding much-needed strength and power to his frame, he could be a steal in the late 2nd round.

9. James Pearce Jr - Tennessee - 6'5 243 lbs

Strengths: A 2-year starter for the Volunteers, Pearce blew up immediately as a starting sophomore, finishing with 10 sacks and 15 tackles for loss in the SEC. Pearce is a long, rangy-built edge player with an impressive frame and room for additional development. Comfortable playing both with his hands in the dirt or as a stand-up player, Pearce shows the athleticism to succeed in any defensive structure. At his best when he lines up as a wide-9 rusher, Pearce explodes off the snap of the ball with tremendous twitch and explosion. Overwhelms opposing tackles with his combination of size and length while also having the elastic flexibility through his lower body to win at the top of his arc. Utilizes his speed outside rushes to set up his inside counter moves, keeping tackles playing on their heels. Long strider that closes cushions quickly, getting into the backfield in the blink of an eye. Commits himself to affecting pass plays even when he can't get home, utilizing his length to disrupt the QB's vision. An overwhelming speed-to-power rusher who understands the importance of playing with leverage to maximize power, showcasing a devastating bull rush to put blockers on skates. Uses effectively on stunts, proving to be a dynamic looper who can get home quickly. Impressive lateral mobility and change of directional abilities allow him to handle some zone drops, showing the ability to diagnose and maintain good positioning.

Weaknesses: Pearce has the frame for growth but is still lanky and needs additional development. He routinely gets overwhelmed at the point of attack in the run game, failing to control the edge. He has a bad habit of letting his pads rise in the run game, getting blown off the ball, and then losing his balance when taking on combination blocks. Lower body strength and development need significant work to be a three-down player. He will need to work on his ability to break down blockers in space, failing to disengage in the run game. Very reliant on winning with his speed as a rusher, failing always to understand how to utilize his hands to keep his frame clean. Can be controlled by blockers that can put two hands on him, failing to have ideal counter possibilities. Has had some noteworthy struggles as a reliable tackler.

Best Fit: Edge defender in any scheme

Player Ranking (1-100): 80.3 - Pearce is a very talented and athletic edge defender with the traits of a dynamic pass rusher. He is incredibly explosive, but he doesn't quite know how to fully utilize his traits as a pass rusher other than his burst. In the run game, Pearce will need significant development at the next level and likely need to initially earn snaps as a pass rusher. 2nd round player.

10. Donovan Ezeiruaku - Boston College - 6'2 246 lbs

Strengths: A 3-year starter for the Eagles, Ezeiruaku has been a mainstay for their defense in each of those seasons. Ezeiruaku saved his best season for last, exploding in his final season as a senior in 2024, finishing amongst the top of ACC leaderboards. Ezeiruaku is comfortable playing from several different alignments, as well as playing standing up and with his hand in the dirt. He is a terrific pass rusher who utilizes several hand tactics, including a devastating swim move he uses to perfection. Ezeiruaku has good twitch and explosion off the snap of the ball, coupling quickness, leverage, and snap anticipation to get into the backfield frequently. Challenges offensive tackles in several ways, always playing with a good plan. Has terrific bend and elasticity to dip and threaten the arc at improbable rush angles. Offers a threat as a power rusher, showing the ability to generate speed-to-power and collapse the pocket. In the running game, Ezeiruaku displays the instincts and play recognition skills to remain in good positions while setting the edge. His strong hands and grip power allow him to succceed when working through blocks from tight ends and receivers along the perimeter. Makes decisive decisions and sees things well with his eyes to see run-pass fits before triggering downhill. Plays with a relentless motor and makes several plays in pursuit from the backside. Has shown upside when used in various coverage looks, showing impressive zonal instincts and awareness to handle drops and minimize spacing cushions.

Weaknesses: Ezeiruaku lacks the ideal size and length requisites for many NFL defensive coaches, and his lack of length limits him when attempting to stack and shed. He sometimes gets hung up on blocks, failing to have the length to offer consistent counter ability against tackles that can reach him. Overall, explosive ability is good, but it lacks elite traits. Can get too upright at times when having to go against double teams, regularly getting affected by chips from tight ends. Will need to clean up some of his footwork when handling zonal drops, often taking choppy steps.

Best Fit: Edge rusher in any system

Player Ranking (1-100): 79.8 - I love Ezeiruaku as a football player, especially in an odd front as a stand-up hybrid rusher. He's gotten better and better during his time at Boston College. He started as an OK pass rusher, but he's developed into a terrific rusher with various moves. While he lacks ideal physical traits, the kid's motor, natural pass-rush ability, and toughness are fantastic. He was influential in every game for Boston College this year, even against good competition. 3rd round player.

11. Antwaun Powell-Ryland - Virginia Tech - 6'3 251 lbs

Strengths: A 5th year senior for the Hokies, Powell-Ryland was initially recruited to the Gators, where he began his college career as a rotational player for the first three seasons. Powell-Ryland exploded immediately after transferring to Virginia Tech, finishing with 9.5 sacks and 15 tackles for loss, including three forced fumbles in 2023. In 2024, he had his career year topping all of his 2023 campaign numbers. Powell-Ryland had success rushing from multiple different alignments, including being an interior gap-penetrating linebacker, but he does most of his reps as a stand-up linebacker. Powell-Ryland is a quick-twitch rusher with his best reps utilizing his explosive get-off to attack the exterior shoulder of tackles. He utilizes his bend and ankle flexion to minimize surface area to get underneath blockers and succeed. When rushing head-on, Powell-Ryland's ability to play with leverage pads allows him to succeed as a speed-to-power bull rusher, collapsing the pocket while continuing to churn his legs through impact. He is an unpredictable rusher who displays quick, active hands to shed and keep his frame clean through impact. A relentless motor makes Powell-Ryland a dangerous counter-rusher, frequently getting off on his secondary move. Not content just sacking the QB, Powell-Ryland has shown over and over again his ability to force fumbles, as evidenced by multiple FF each campaign. Effective when used on twists and stunts, showing good timing and closing speed to get home. Powell-Ryland shows more than adequate point-of-attack power in the running game to maintain positioning and leverage against pulling linemen. Highly aware and with disciplined eyes, Powell-Ryland showcases impressive play recognition qualities and is outstanding against RPOs and option-style offenses. Hasn't looked out of place when handling some zone drops, showing impressive lateral mobility and change of directional abilities.

Weaknesses: Powell-Ryland is still growing and developing his frame, and he could benefit from continuing to add clean muscle to his frame. Questions will be asked about why he was such a late bloomer and left Florida after barely getting many opportunities in his first 3 seasons on campus. While he isn't bad per se in the running game, he can be more technically and fundamentally sound with his gap discipline and integrity. He's quick to bail and get downhill, leaving his side of the field exposed at times. Anchorage power and strength is good but isn't elite and he can get bulled by combo blocks to his side of the field. His tackling technique isn't ideal, and he has had some issues wrapping up securely.

Best Fit: 3-4 OLB

Player Ranking (1-100): 79.6 - Powell-Ryland was a pleasant watch on tape. After his final season, putting him in the 1st round discussion is not hard. He was unblockable and completely dominant at times this season. His ability to win rushing the passer is amongst the best in this draft class. His arrow is pointed up, and he's gotten better and better each season. 3rd round player for me.

12. Josaiah Stewart - Michigan - 6'2 245 lbs

Strengths: Stewart was initially recruited to Coastal Carolina in the Sun Belt Conference, where he immediately dominated and set the school's single-season sack record as a true freshman with 12.5 sacks. Following his sophomore campaign, he transferred to Michigan, where he played his final two seasons. He had immediate success at Michigan, showing his ability to compete against the best, saving his best season for last as a senior in 2024. Stewart is an athletically built defender with the muscularity, experience, and density to be a schematically versatile edge defender. Stewart is incredibly explosive, showing tremendous quick-twitch and 1st step burst off the scrimmage line. He frequently challenges outside rush lanes, showing the elastic flexibility and ankle flexion to threaten the outside shoulder of offensive tackles. He has impressive agility and change of directional abilities once he's relied on to get off his mark. Once he wins a rep, his closing speed instantly lets him close down cushions. Has a counter plan on each snap, rarely allowing blockers to sustain blocks. He possesses many hand tactics as a rusher, allowing him to keep his frame clean through impact. A diversified rusher who brings a large pass-rush arsenal and plan to every snap of the ball. Plays with nastiness and toughness, playing with urgency on every ball snap. Disciplined eyes and anticipation allow him to process plays quickly in the backfield, frequently blowing up screens and misdirection-type plays. Does a nice job of breaking down blockers, keeping his eyes glued to the ball carrier while keeping his off-hand free to slow up rushers.

Weaknesses: Stewart has a twitched frame but lacks top-end length and height. While Stewart can handle some coverage responsibilities due to his athleticism and movement skills, it certainly isn't his strong suit. He lacks spatial awareness and zonal instincts to minimize spacing opportunities and recognize plays developing the further he is away from the football. Lacks a power profile and isn't a guy that will consistently dominate with speed-to-power and threaten NFL offensive tackles with a devastating bull rush. Can play a little bit upright in the running game, leaving his chest plate exposed for pulling blockers.

Best Fit: Pass rusher in any scheme

Player Ranking (1-100): 78.9 - Stewart has gotten himself firmly on the NFL map these last two seasons at Michigan. It's hard to ignore his ability to get into the backfield with his rare blend of burst and motor. While he's slightly undersized, it's hard not to love the player. He can play in either scheme, although he might be better in an odd front where he can rush standing up from a 2-point stance. 3rd round player.

13. Princely Umanmielen - Ole Miss - 6'4 260 lbs

Strengths: A former Florida Gator, Umanmielen transferred before his final season and played his final season as a senior for Ole Miss. He has gradually improved throughout college, finally showcasing his former High School upside in 2023 for the Gators, finishing with seven sacks and 12 tackles for loss. Umanmielen has a long and lean physique, carrying little unnecessary body fat. Umanmielen is the definition of explosive, showcasing rare 1st step quickness. Not only is he quick, but his secondary closing bursts allow him to instantly close cushions on runners or QBs. Elastic flexibility manifests throughout his frame, allowing him to move fluidly laterally and vertically. Regularly threatens and challenges the outside shoulder of offensive tackles, showing the ankle flexion to win at improbable angles. Not a 1-trick pony as far as a rusher can win in various ways. He understands how to maximize his frame to generate power, utilizing his lower body explosiveness to create speed-to-power to put blockers on skates. In the running game, Umanmielen has the awareness and instincts to recognize plays develop quickly. Relentless pursuit and motor allow him to sort quickly in the trash, keeping his frame clean when flowing through traffic. Reactionary movement skills and reflexes allow him to win position against blockers quickly. He is a reliable wrap-up tackler who can make plays outside his frame.

Weaknesses: An older prospect who will be 23 years old during his rookie campaign. He has a long and lean physique that lacks the schematic versatility to be a guy who can play with his hand in the dirt. Could benefit by continuing to add additional bulk and strength onto his frame, although it doesn't appear there's a suitable room for much additional muscle. Will allow himself to get eaten up by larger tackles if he isn't playing with appropriate leverage. Sometimes, they can lose gap integrity and discipline in the run game, over-pursuing plays, and lack the patience to let plays develop. He is overly reliant on winning with his speed, attempting to win the outside lane repeatedly, and could benefit from a better rush plan.

Best Fit: 3-4 OLB

Player Ranking (1-100): 78.6 - I like Umanmielen quite a bit, and he's proven to have gotten better and better during his college career. He's an impressive pass rusher with an upside far greater than his college statistics showed. While he's a bit undersized to play in a 4-3 defense, I think he could immediately be a terrific 3-4 OLB for a team. 3rd round player.

14. Jared Ivey - Ole Miss - 6'6 284 lbs

Strengths: Ivey began his career in the ACC with Georgia Tech for two seasons before transferring to Ole Miss and finishing the last three seasons of his career. Ivey has progressively improved throughout college, having his best season in 2024 with fantastic production. Showcasing his power-packed frame with NFL readiness, Ivey has a well-developed physique and good length. Ivey has the size and physical tools to be a schematic and positionally flexible disruptor, showcasing his experience playing all over the defensive front. Ivey's at his best when he's winning with power as a rusher, showing his ability to collapse the pocket and put tackles on skates with his bull rush. A strong upper body allows him to succeed in hand battles with blockers, showcasing diverse hand tactics. Impressive bend for a guy of his size, showing the ability to threaten both the inside and outside shoulders of tackles. He is dynamic when he kicks inside and shoots gaps, showing the ability to play as a 3-technique in clear passing situations. Good closing burst and core strength enable him to succeed as the looper on twists and stunts. In the running game, Ivey plays discipline while showing the point of attack power to maintain the edges. Utilizes his length to extend and lockout, keeping his off-hand free. Recognizes things quickly, showing good ball awareness and high football IQ to adjust quickly and flow to the ball. Works tirelessly in pursuit, chasing down several plays from the backside. A large frame and tackle radius allow him to work out of his frame as a tackler successfully.

Weaknesses: Ivey is a good athlete but lacks the ideal burst and twitch to threaten against more athletic tackles along the edges. Appears to lack a secondary plan as a rusher and is content getting occupied for far too long. Needs to work on his hand usage to disengage and shed against the lineman. Has a habit of firing out of his stance too upright in the running game, presenting too large a surface area for blockers. Takes a lot of plays off and constantly rotates in and out, showing possible conditioning concerns. Significant tightness throughout his lower body is prevalent when he needs to redirect his frame or cross over the face of blockers, failing to threaten on secondary moves.

Best Fit: 4-3 LDE but can play 5-technique DE in a 3-4 or 4-3 DT (3-technique)

Player Ranking (1-100): 78.3 - Ivey has put himself firmly on the draft radar after his stellar final season, dominating in the SEC. His frame makes drafting him incredibly enticing due to his ability to play multiple different positions along the defensive line. He's one of the more versatile players in this draft class. I love him as a 4-3 LDE, and I think he could be great as a secondary rusher for a team. 3rd round player.

15. J.T. Tuimoloau - Ohio State - 6'4 277 llbs

Strengths: A 4-year significant contributor to the Buckeyes defense, Tuimoloau has been a key part of the front four since his freshman season. A consistently reliable player, Tuimoloau shows reliability and constancy in how he plays, rarely missing a snap during his career. A powerfully built edge defender, Tuimoloau showcases density throughout his frame and intriguing length. Experience and frame allow him to be a schematically versatile chess piece for a defense, although he best fits as a 4-3 DE. Power is the name of the game for Tuimoloau, both in the run and passing games. In the run game, Tuimoloau sets his anchor quickly, showcasing his ability to maintain leverage and hold the point of attack, even through double teams. His long arm allows him to lock out and control blockers throughout, keeping his off-hand free. High football IQ allows him to quickly recognize things pre-snap, putting him in good positions to make plays. Tuimoloau displays terrific instincts and awareness post-snap, always locating and working towards the ball. Tuimoloau's power can be overwhelming as a pass rusher, and it is important to understand how to generate speed-to-power to put blockers on skates. Upper body power and strength allow him to shed through blockers, utilizing diverse hand tactics to keep his frame clean. Tuimoloau does a nice job of timing the snap and utilizing good snap instincts to get a good jump at the line of scrimmage frequently.

Weaknesses: While Tuimoloau has had a nice college career, he hasn't proven the ability to be an above-average pass rusher through college. He's a bit of a stiff, straight-line athlete who fails to have any Plan B due to his lack of change of directional ability through his lower half. Plays with a high pad level, limiting his effectiveness to play with balance, frequently being found on the ground. He strictly relies on his power and snap timing to generate a pass rush, and he fails to have secondary quickness or a counter plan as a rusher.

Best Fit: 4-3 DE

Player Ranking (1-100): 77.2 - I like Tuimoloau as a football player. I'm not sure he can play three downs at the next level, but he's an absolute workhorse for the Buckeyes' defense. He makes so many plays, and his physicality and toughness certainly impact and frees up other players on that defense. I think he could be a solid starting LDE in an even front. 3rd round player.

16. Bradyn Swinson - LSU - 6'5 269 lbs

Strengths: Swinson has had a unique college career, playing three seasons with Oregon but transferring to LSU for his final season. He played mostly in his first four seasons in college, rotationally, before finally getting his chance to shine as a senior with LSU. Swinson possesses the frame that evaluators drool over with a power-packed frame and vines for arms. Has experience playing in multiple different defensive setups, showing comfort in both odd and even fronts. Swinson has always had physical tools on his toolbelt, but he's finally showcasing them. As a rusher, Swinson is violent, showing various hand tactics to beat blockers. Has some twitchiness to his movement skills, showing good burst off the line and the closing strides to eat cushions. He Understands how to generate speed-to-power, delivering impressive pushback with his bull rushes. Has the frame and experience to be a matchup problem when kicking inside, showing too much athleticism for interior blockers. In the running game, Swinson impresses with his ability to take on blocks, showing impressive deconstruction ability and POP in his hands. Remains disciplined when setting the edge, reading his keys, and holding the point with his anchorage strength. Looks comfortable when handling some zone coverage looks, maintaining good spatial awareness and limiting cushions. His large frame and wing span enable him to continuously make plays outside his frame, showing reliability as a tackler.

Weaknesses: Swinson is a straight-line guy and struggled when asked to move off his mark or redirect his frame. His noticeable lack of flexibility through his lower half and ankles limits his ability to win in tiny windows or on wide rush lanes. He rushes vertically and could work on his leverage more consistently when attacking the pocket. When Swinson gets his hands on ball carriers, it's generally over, but he takes some poor, overaggressive pursuit angles to the football. He relies on his power and motor to win on rushes and could benefit by adding a large arsenal to his toolbelt.

Best Fit: Edge rusher in either scheme

Player Ranking (1-100): 76.9 - Swinson has improved and saved his best year for last. He has definite tools in his toolbelt with a ceiling for even larger growth. Rare to see guys that have Swinson's size and athleticism while being good in both the running and passing games. While he's a bit of a 1-season wonder, he also showed glimpses at Oregon. I like Swinson and think he could continue to get better with the right coaching staff. 3rd round player.

17. Barryn Sorrell - Texas - 6'4 246 lbs

Strengths: As a 3-year Longhorn starter, Sorrell has been a defensive mainstay during each campaign. Sorrell possesses a terrific next-level frame with long arms and room for additional functional mass. Sorrell is a positionally and schematically versatile edge defender who shows comfort in playing with his hands in the dirt and from a 2-point stance. Sorrell was even asked to kick inside on passing downs and bounce from the left and right sides of the line. Sorrell is a relentless worker who consistently wins on the edge, whether from his initial move or counter move. A twitchy rusher that shows good get-off at the ball snap, immediately challenging to arc the corner against tackles. Sorrell possesses several hand tactics that enable him to have a diversified pass-rush plan on every snap. His upper-body strength, heavy hands, and long-levered frame make it difficult for blockers to control him for long durations. His HOT motor and consistent urgency give him a counter plan if he's initially occupied, making a lot of plays on his secondary move. In the running game, Sorrell utilizes his length to lock out blockers. He quickly identifies and processes things, showing outstanding awareness and play recognition abilities to locate the football. He works tirelessly in pursuit and shows good closing speed to make plays from the backside. He's a reliable open-field tackler who utilizes his entire wingspan to make plays outside his frame. Has shown capabilities and experience to handle zone drops and not look out of place.

Weaknesses: Despite his disruption in almost every game, his overall production has been modest at best, never having top-end statistical production. Sorrell is a good athlete, but he lacks top-end explosiveness off the edge. He can sometimes be a tick late off the snap of the ball, limiting his ability to get off consistently. He's still developing into his frame and could use more weight in his pants, as he lacks top-end anchorage ability to hold up at the point of attack in the run game. He's frequently uprooted and moved out of his spot, failing to sustain and play through combo blocks. His gap instincts and integrity are constantly threatened as he quickly triggers downhill and leaves outside lanes completely exposed. This is particularly exposed on RPOs as QBs often manipulate him, and he will shoot into the backfield, allowing QBs to win consistently along the edges. His lack of lower body power limits him as a power rusher, failing to threaten with his bull rush or threaten stronger tackles consistently.

Best Fit: Edge rusher in any scheme

Player Ranking (1-100): 75.7 - Sorrell is a toolsy rusher with nice traits, albeit not elite. He immediately will offer a team a consistent pass rush, playing on either side of the line of scrimmage. He must improve his overall play strength through his lower body to consistently offer 3-down ability. But boy, does this kid's motor run hot! 3rd round player.

18. Collin Oliver - Oklahoma State - 6'2 240 lbs

Strengths: Oliver exploded onto the scene for the Cowboys in 2021 as a freshman, finishing with 11.5 sacks and 16 total tackles for loss. A hybrid linebacker and defensive end, Oliver plays all over the defensive front 7, being used both in coverage and attacking the pocket. His production during the three seasons before his injury was outstanding, showing reliability and consistent production each campaign. Oliver is an athletically built physical freak of nature with rare explosiveness and twitch. As a rusher, Oliver plays both with his hands in the dirt and in a 2-point stance, showing schematic versatility. He immediately explodes off the snap of the ball, showing outstanding 1st step quickness and explosiveness. Can win in a variety of different ways as a rusher, showing a diverse set of hand tactics. Oliver maintains low pads, allowing him to stay beneath blockers and control them through the snap of the ball, generating devastating power in his bull rushes despite his size.

A natural bender with both ankle flexion and hip flexibility to challenge and attack improbable outside arcs. Plays with a HOT motor, making significant amounts of plays in pursuit or when blockers allow him to disengage. Impressive ball awareness and play recognition skills enable him to locate and find the football quickly. He often beats runners to the spot, winning positioning and leverage. Shows upside as a zone cover linebacker and even as a man-to-man coverage linebacker, showing fluid footwork and spatial awareness. Even when Oliver can't get home on rushes, he's cognizant of getting his hands up to disrupt the QB's vision or swat the ball away. He is a violent tackler who rips at the football, causing several fumbles throughout his time. Does an excellent job of flowing to the football in the run game, showing upper-body strength and toughness at the point of attack to stack and shed in pursuit.

Weaknesses: He suffered a bad right foot injury, causing him to play in only two games in his final season in 2024. He is an undersized pass rusher for the next level, and he will likely be required to gain substantial mass and girth to his frame to hold up for three downs. Lacks ideal amounts of length to play as a 2-gap point of attack DE in a 4-man front and likely will be a better suit for odd fronts. He struggles to set the edge against double teams, getting blown off his position easily due to a lack of lower body anchorage power. He is more of a finesse and athletic rusher than a powerful edge defender, and he will get overwhelmed by the power at the point of attack.

Best Fit: 3-4 OLB

Player Ranking (1-100): 75.2 - There's always a place for good pass rushers on a team, and Oliver is certainly that. His explosive athleticism will enable him to have a potentially successful NFL career. He will likely need to earn additional reps by impressing coaches in preseason and camp. I'd imagine he will initially be a pass-rushing specialist until he can gain additional functional strength and power. 3rd round player.

19. Ashton Gillotte - Louisville - 6'3 275 lbs

Strengths: Gillotte has been a 4-year mainstay of the Cardinals' defensive line but had his rise to stardom in 2023 when he finished with 11 sacks and 15 tackles for loss. Possessing a power-packed frame, Gillotte has terrific density and thickness through his frame. A versatile tone-setter, Gillotte plays with physicality and experience playing along different alignments and stances, showing true schematic and systematic versatility. A load to handle for opposing tackles, Gillotte utilizes his upper body power to stifle with his hands, delivering devastating blows to blockers. He is a quick-twitch rusher who quickly gets off the ball, combining it with his closing bursts. When used on stunts, a weapon frequently attacks the 'A' and 'B' gaps with devastating timing and effectiveness. Generates tremendous speed-to-power due to his lower body explosiveness, capable of closing the pocket in a flash. In the run game, Gillotte is committed to extending and locking out, keeping blockers off his frame. Strength is prevalent throughout his frame, as Gillotte holds the point of attack against pulls and reach blocks. High instincts and awareness allow him to locate and track in pursuit quickly. The motor runs hot on every ball snap, making many plays backside in pursuit.

Weaknesses: After a dominating junior campaign, Gillotte has mostly been underwhelmed through his final campaign, never reaching the heights of his junior season. Tends to rush without a plan, attacking head-on and allowing blockers to control his pads easily. He was frequently all over the defensive front and lacked a defined position. Will get overwhelmed with length, as Gillotte lacks the ideal length for many outside players. Lacks a great counter game, failing to offer any secondary rush if his initial one fails. While explosive, Gillotte isn't an elastic bender who can frequently challenge narrow arcs or get underneath the pads of longer tackles.

Best Fit: LDE in a 4-3 that can kick inside in passing situations

Player Ranking (1-100): 74.2 - Gillotte is a good rusher but isn't an elite number 1 rusher for an NFL defense. Ideally, he'd be suited as an LDE for teams that can hold the point of attack and be a great secondary option to rush the passer. He's a bit of an old-school and hard-nosed kid that can bully offensive tackles. Really good player that will go to war for your defense. 4th round player.

20. Jack Sawyer - Ohio State - 6'5 260 lbs

Strengths: A former five-star recruit, Sawyer has significantly contributed to the Buckeyes defense for the last four seasons. A versatile chess piece for the Buckeyes' defense, Sawyer has moved around to different positions along the defense, playing in the Hybrid Jack position and both RDE and LDE. He's also played both standing up and his hand in the dirt. He is a powerful defender with noticeable length and girth throughout his frame. Sawyer is a tough kid who loves to handle the physical sides of the game, showing the upper-body strength to lock out and keep blockers off his frame in the run game. A relentless and tireless worker, Sawyer makes significant numbers of plays in pursuit. He plays with good gap integrity and discipline, regularly used to set the edge against double teams. Quickly recognizing things pre and post-snap, coupled with lower body power, allows him to maintain assignments, impacting many plays along the perimeters. He is a good straight-line athlete who will use speed-to-power to generate power on his bull rushes. His high football IQ puts him in good positions routinely.

Weaknesses: While Sawyer has been a good player for the Buckeyes defense, he's limited as a pass rusher. While he has good straight-line athleticism, his overall explosiveness and twitch are average. His limited counter ability affects his ability to offer any secondary rush. Lack of ankle flexion and fluid hips causes him to struggle arcing the corner against blockers that can initially mirror him. While he's a good run defender, his overaggressive nature will occasionally fail him, regularly crashing down hard and losing gap integrity against misdirection or counter-type runs.

Best Fit: Rotational DE

Player Ranking (1-100): 74.0 - Sawyer has been a good player for the Buckeyes for the last four seasons. He's limited overall as an athlete, but he can be a nice versatile chess piece for a defense that can have a rotational role. 4th round player.

21. Patrick Payton - Florida State - 6'5 250 lbs

Strengths: A significant contributor for the Seminoles in the last three seasons, Payton had his breakout season in 2023 when he finished with 15 tackles for loss, seven sacks, and two forced fumbles. Payton has an NFL frame with outstanding size and length and enough room for additional growth. Payton rushes as a 5-technique DE, generally playing on the left side of the defense, but he's fully capable of playing in a 2-point stance in 3-4 systems. He's at his best when attacking the outside edges, showing good bend, shoulder dip, and flexibility to capture the edge. Payton possesses a large arsenal of hand tactics that enable him to be freed up along the edges. He works with a tireless and hot motor on every snap of the ball, making several plays in pursuit or on broken-down plays. When he can't get home as a rusher, Payton shows good awareness of disrupting passing lanes, as evidenced by his high passes defended each campaign. In the running game, Payton shows good instincts and block recognition. He utilizes his length to keep his frame clean when working backside while displaying good closing speed to recover and make plays from behind. His length proves to be a hurdle for blockers as he's not easy to control when in pursuit. A solid open-field tackler who is generally reliable in 1 v 1 situations against rushers. Has proven to have success and coverage instincts when dropping in some zone looks, limiting spatial cushions.

Weaknesses: Payton could benefit by adding significant mass and strength to his lower body. Payton is a finesse pass rusher right now that lacks the power profile to win consistently as a rusher. He's a predictable rusher who attempts to arc the corner on every rep in passing situations. He has some burst but lacks elite quick-twitch to challenge better tackles. His lower body lacks significant flexion and change of direction, as he struggles to affect plays when used as a looper on stunts. He sometimes plays recklessly, completely overpursuing plays and taking him out of his gap discipline. Not overly physical in the run game either, struggling to deconstruct in space and consistently set the edge.

Best Fit: Edge rusher in any scheme

Player Ranking (1-100): 73.3 - Payton had a really solid 2023 campaign but had a significant drop-off this year, unfortunately. He likely would have been in the Day 2 discussion, but a disappointing campaign will likely see him get drafted on Day 3. I like Payton as he has terrific attributes, including his size and motor. 4th round player.

22. Jordan Burch - Oregon - 6'6 295 lbs

Strengths: As a 5th-year senior for the Ducks, Burch started his career with South Carolina and contributed in three straight seasons for them before transferring. A densely-built defensive line prospect, Burch has the power throughout his frame and the height to disrupt throwing lanes. A versatile defensive line prospect, Burch has played up the formation, playing along the edges and interior, showing positional and systematic versatility for the next level. A rare athlete for the position, Burch has incredible explosiveness throughout his lower body. A twitchy athlete, Burch exploded out of his stance and showed the ability to threaten inferior athletes constantly. Overwhelms at the point of attack with his power and violent hands. Workout warrior strength is prevalent in his ability to play the run, and he is overwhelmed and disengaging blockers routinely. Keeps his off-hand free when setting the edge, allowing himself to set the edge consistently. He is highly effective when used as the looper to stunt, understanding how to time them with his teammates to get downhill instantly. He showed solid production during each campaign of his career, showing the ability to be a ready-made defender for the next level.

Weaknesses: He comes out of his stance very upright and will need to play better leveraged. Stiffness is prevalent when attacking the edges, and he struggles to change direction or reset his frame if initially occupied. He is very reliant on winning with power rush moves and overwhelming offensive tackles with his size dimensions instead of having a clearly defined pass rush arsenal. Lacks ideal length to challenge longer tackles, failing to win inside hand placement. He is not always disciplined in his manner of play, going 100 mph without always having the necessary technique.

Best Fit: Edge defender that can kick inside on passing downs

Player Ranking (1-100): 73.0 - Burch is a good player who lacks elite characteristics but can compete for rotational snaps early on. Considering his physicality and athleticism, he's been impressive for two big-time college programs and has a massive ceiling. 5th round player.

23. Jalen McLeod - Auburn - 6'1 245 lbs

Strengths: McLeod began his career with Appalachian State in the Sun Belt Conference during his first three seasons before transferring to Auburn to play his final two campaigns. McLeod has improved during his college career, showing significant improvements during each subsequent campaign. Playing in the JACK role for the Tigers' defense, McLeod was entrusted with various tasks, including gap responsibilities in the running game, rushing the passer, and dropping in coverage. Despite being a smaller rusher, McLeod has terrific length proportions and good overall density in his frame. McLeod has successfully rushed from both the right and left sides in a 2-point stance as a rusher. A bendy athlete, McLeod has had his best luck when attacking the outside shoulder of tackles, showing tremendous flexion, shoulder dip, and elastic flexibility through his lower body to win the edge. McLeod has good pop and physicality through his upper body, delivering powerful hands upon impact. Capable of closing the pocket with power, McLeod utilizes his natural leverage advantage to keep his pads down, churn his legs, and push the pocket forward. Further from football, McLeod shows his physicality and toughness when attacking downhill. A violent thumper, McLeod delivers a powerful impact upon contact with ball carriers, frequently ripping at the ball as he brings them down, causing some fumbles. He plays with a smart football IQ, limiting spacing cushions and showing natural zonal instincts when in coverage. McLeod also has extensive experience in special teams throughout his college career.

Weaknesses: Despite a terrific final season as a pass rusher, McLeod's lack of prototypical size could be a factor in limiting him to odd front defenses at the next level. His tweener status will cause some evaluators to struggle to find an ideal position for him. McLeod struggled with an ankle issue during his first season with the Tigers. McLeod needs to widen his rush attack plan and have additional rush alternatives. He can easily get washed out by bigger tackles that can reach his frame, and he fails to offer a counter plan once his frame is reached.

Best Fit: 3-4 OLB

Player Ranking (1-100): 72.8 - McLeod transitioned from the Sun Belt to the SEC with minimal challenges. He's a smart, tough football kid who shows versatility and experience wherever he's used. While he's not an elite athlete, he's a good one who can excel in all game phases. 4th round player.

24. David Walker - Central Arkansas - 6'2 260 lbs

Strengths: As a former high school wide receiver, Walker has transitioned to a top-tier edge rusher for FCS-level Central Arkansas. Walker immediately made an impact from his freshman season onward, posting double-digit sack numbers in two of his three seasons. Walker is a compactly-built edge rusher with a well-built lower half who has experience playing both with his hand in the dirt and as a stand-up 2-point stance linebacker. Walker excels off the blocks, showing a terrific combination of quickness and snap anticipation to explode. He commanded double teams over and over again, showing the ability to blow up plays in the backfield routinely. Weight room strength and explosiveness enable Walker to generate consistent speed-to-power as a rusher, easily collapsing the pocket. A bendable edge rusher with the flexion and shoulder dip to threaten the corner constantly. Has good change of directional abilities and can redirect his frame. Walker has a diversified plan as a rusher, bringing a significant toolbelt to the table. Not just reliant on winning the outside shoulder of tackles, Walker is excellent as a 'B' gap rusher who can shoot the inside shoulder and exploit the space between the tackle and guard. Walker has violent hands that enable him to win most hand battles. A relentless motor and hyper-awareness allow Walker to make many plays in pursuit from the backside. Excellent lower body anchorage power helps Walker to maintain the edge and consistently stay on his feet to win in highly contested situations.

Weaknesses: Walker will have a large learning curve from the FCS level, although he showed flashes when playing against bigger programs. He is still learning the position as he comes from a wide receiver background. Walker lacks elite length for the position and appears to struggle against offensive tackles that can reach his pads. This limits his ability to disengage and play with any consistent counter plan once initially reached. In the running game, Walker is quick to abandon his gap responsibilities, frequently shooting downhill and leaving a part of the field exposed.

Best Fit: 3-4 OLB

Player Ranking (1-100): 72.2 - Walker was a dominant FCS-level player who flashed in every game I watched. He was an unstoppable force at times. He could be a great steal for a team needing a pass rusher early on Day 3 of the draft. He immediately should warrant snaps in nickel situations. 4th round player.

25. Davin Vann - North Carolina State - 6'2 280 lbs

Strengths: Vann is a 4-year starter for the Wolfpack defensive line, improving each campaign. Vann had his best season in 2024, finishing with 14 tackles for loss, 6.5 sacks, and six forced fumbles. Vann is the definition of an iron man, playing in every game since his true freshman season and showing remarkable consistency and toughness. Vann is a stout and compact defender with thick limbs and density through his frame. He's shown the ability to line up, move around, and play different positions, showing positional and schematic versatility. A former state champion wrestler, Vann is an extremely athletic and flexible rusher with impressive physical traits. As a pass rusher, Vann is committed to playing low and winning the leverage battle, consistently threatening to win at the apex of his rushes. He has rare bends, ankle flexion, and elasticity through his frame. He couples his bend with his good 1st step to offer a devastating combination. Vann plays with a HOT motor, working tirelessly on broken-down plays and in pursuit. Vann can threaten as a rusher with power, generating good speed-to-power on his bull rushes. He's proven to be stout at the point of attack, frequently handling combo blocks on the outside while holding his own. He maintains steady gap discipline and rarely is out of position on outside-zone runs. He has the powerful upper body to work through blocks, deconstructing and keeping his frame clean. He quickly recognizes things pre-snap, locating the ball and being in the right position to make plays. A forceful tackler in the run game that shows reliability in wrapping up securely. Vann is a turnover creator and constantly punches and rips at the ball, as evidenced by his 6 forced fumbles this season.

Weaknesses: Vann is a tweener that lacks a truly defined position. He's bounced between playing inside and outside, standing up with his hands in the dirt. Vann has a stout frame with stubby arms, as he lacks the top-end length required by many coaches and scouts. This causes issues when he allows his pads to rise, as he frequently exposes his chest plate to larger tackles that can control his pads. As a pass rusher, Vann relies on winning with speed or with his bull rush and fails to have a defined pass rush plan. He doesn't know how to utilize his hands as a rusher and frequently loses hand battles. If his initial explosive move doesn't work, he has a few fallback options.

> **Best Fit: Edge rusher that can kick inside in passing downs**

Player Ranking (1-100): 71.4 - Vann had a really good season this year for the Wolfpack. He's a good rusher, not a great rusher. He's a good run player but not a great one. He could develop into a starting edge rusher on the strong side, which I think is what would suit him best. 4th round player.

26. Dani Dennis-Sutton - Penn State - 6'5 272 lbs

Strengths: A former 5-star recruit, Dennis-Sutton has gradually earned more and more playing time during his time with the Nittany Lions. Possessing first off the bus size, Dennis-Sutton certainly looks the part with well-chiseled and dense limbs. Dennis-Sutton is comfortable playing standing up or with his hands in the dirt, Showing schematic and positional versatility. Dennis-Sutton possesses a good 1st step in which he combines his snap timing and anticipation to beat tackles with his initial move often. Plays with hair-on-fire urgency on every snap, playing relentlessly as a pass rusher, with multiple coverage sacks on his resume. He is difficult to handle due to his size/power/length, winning inside hand placement against tackles. Has a significant power profile that he utilizes to collapse the pocket when rushing with his bull rush. Wins as a rusher with motor, hands, and a devastating spin move. Dennis-Sutton is at his best in the running game, showcasing impressive point-of-attack strength to seal the edge. He routinely overwhelms, pulling blockers and tight ends along the edges. He plays with full extension, locking out and failing to let tackles control him at the point of attack. Capable of stacking and shedding in pursuit, utilizing impressive upper-body power and hand strength to disengage. He makes a lot of plays in pursuit due to his motor and never-say-die mentality.

Weaknesses: Dennis-Sutton hasn't quite lived up to his former potential and has played mostly in a rotational role during his career. His production level has been modest at best, failing to take over or dominate games. He is prone to abandon his gap responsibilities at moments in the running game, as he frequently fires inside without a backup plan. Lacks the athletic profile to be a counter rusher and is very reliant on his 1st step to win as a rusher. When asked to redirect his frame, overall movement skills are less than ideal, as he has limited agility. He won't be a guy who will consistently offer much as a speed rusher, as his bend and change of direction abilities are modest. Has a bad habit of allowing his pads to rise mid-play, playing far too upright at moments.

Best Fit: 4-3 DE

Player Ranking (1-100): 70.9 - Dennis-Sutton is a good but not great NFL prospect. At this point, he is much farther along in his ability to play the run than he is as a pass rusher. He lacks the explosive twitch to be a dynamic edge player, but his strength and frame will appeal to teams. 4th round player.

27. Fadil Diggs - Syracuse - 6'5 260 lbs

Strengths: Diggs is a former four-star recruit initially recruited to Texas A&M, where he spent four seasons before transferring to Syracuse. Diggs saved his best season for his final one, finishing with 14 tackles for loss and 7.5 sacks for the Orange. Diggs looks the part with outstanding size dimensions, showing good height and density throughout his frame. A versatile chess piece during his college career, Diggs has been used as a linebacker, defensive end, and even defensive tackle. Diggs is a smart football player with terrific instincts and anticipation wherever he's lined up. A reactionary athlete, Diggs recognizes post-snap looks, and quickly diagnoses run/pass fits. He's not easily manipulated and displays good eye discipline in the run game. He stays square in the run game while flowing to the football, maintaining good positioning. A hard-working kid who works tirelessly in pursuit. Diggs has good twitch and bend as a pass rusher to threaten to arc the corner. If he overruns plays, he works hard to recover, never giving up on plays. He displays good timing and core strength to get skinny to attack as a looper on stunts. Diggs displays fluidity and ease of movement in coverage when working in space. He easily transitions and changes directions and has great spatial awareness to maintain leverage on routes.

Weaknesses: Diggs is a tweener that lacks a defined role at the next level. He wins mostly with athleticism and his 'never give up' mentality as a pass rusher. He needs a more varied rush attack, far too often attempting to utilize the same attack method on each snap. He can rush very upright, completely exposing his chest to blockers. In the running game, Diggs's lack of anchorage ability causes him some struggles against double teams and combo blocks. He needs to learn how to use his hands in space to disengage, stack, and shed when flowing to the ball, frequently getting hooked in space.

Best Fit: 3-4 OLB

Player Ranking (1-100): 67.4 - Diggs is a versatile prospect who does mostly everything good but nothing elite. His naturalness in coverage is certainly enticing for 3-4 teams. He will likely need to earn his role as a situational pass rusher/coverage linebacker before proving he can stay on the field during rush downs. While he looks the part, he still needs to get stronger for the next level. 5th round player.

28. Jasheen Davis - Wake Forest - 6'3 253 lbs

Strengths: A former four-star recruit, Davis has been a starter for the Demon Deacons for the last four seasons, showing consistent production during each campaign. Davis plays outside the defense, with experience playing in various alignments. Built with a compact and muscular frame, Davis has good proportional density through his frame. Davis wins mostly with his 1st step, continuously attacking the outside shoulder of tackles. He plays with a relentless motor, playing 100 mph on every snap of the ball. He works tirelessly on broken-down plays and hunts ball carriers and QBs with intent and urgency. He does a nice job of utilizing speed-to-power on his bull rushes, generating good POP and pushback to collapse the pocket. He has various pass rush moves, showing diverse hand tactics. He's also highly effective as a looper on stunts, showing good timing and closing burst to get home. He occasionally rushes as an off-ball linebacker, attacking the 'A' and 'B' gaps, showing the knack to get skinny and disrupt the QB. Davis shows good play recognition skills in the running game and maintains good eye discipline. He stays glued to the ball carrier while working towards the football, showing his upper body strength to fight through blockers and keep his frame clean. He's a reliable and physical tackler that makes runners feel it. Davis has also been used on a number of the special teams' units for the Demon Deacons, showing good experience.

Weaknesses: Davis is a stubby-built athlete who consistently lacks the elite length to win on the perimeter. His lack of length limits him in both phases due to his inability to control the pads of blockers. As an athlete, Davis is a straight-ahead mover and struggles when asked to cross the face of blockers or change directions, having stiff hips and a lack of ideal change of directional abilities. He's forced to frequently take wide angles when attacking the outside shoulder due to his inability to dip and bend. He loves to counter inside on his rushes, leaving his gap assignment vulnerable to deceptive runners that can cut back. His point of attack power is OK, but it isn't great, and he struggles to set a firm edge against double teams and combo blocks. When working in pursuit, Davis will get hooked with minimal abilities to stack and shed in ample time.

Best Fit: 3-4 OLB

Player Ranking (1-100): 66.8 - I like Davis the best in a 3-4 system where he can come screaming off the edge. He lacks the ideal length and gap discipline to play as a 4-3 edge. His athletic traits and consistency every season shows me that he can be a nice role player at the next level. 5th round player.

29. Kaimon Rucker - North Carolina - 6'1 260 lbs

Strengths: Rucker has been a steady player for the Tar Heels defense for five straight seasons, finishing his best season in 2023 with 15 tackles for loss and 8.5 sacks. Rucker is a low center-of-gravity built edge defender with good density and musculature through his frame. Rucker played various alignments for the Tar Heels defense, including playing anywhere from 5-technique to a wide-9 rusher, and he has experience standing up or playing with his hands in the dirt. As a rusher, Rucker combines his snap anticipation with explosive burst off the line of scrimmage to immediately press tackles with his speed. There is noticeable bend and flexion through Rucker's lower body as he can win at the apex of his rush and get underneath the pad of blockers. Rucker is difficult to reach for blockers due to his natural leverage advantage, and he can disengage and shed blockers on the counter. Rucker has heavy hands and brings a varied pass-rush plan on every snap of the ball, winning with power and explosiveness. Rucker is instinctive in the running game, recognizing keys and quickly diagnosing. He's quick to diagnose screens and misdirection-type plays and quickly triggers downhill into the backfield. Rucker plays with a relentless motor and makes several plays in pursuit from the backside. Rucker has experience and has been used in some zone drops, showing good experience and spatial recognition.

Weaknesses: He missed some games in his final season due to fracturing his fibula at the end of the season while injuring his knee earlier. Rucker's size will impede him from being an every-down defensive lineman. He lacks the length and the size to be a true positional fit and has a bit of a tweener shape to him. His tape is very up and down, and he looks unblockable in some games; in others, he struggles to get off blocks. In the running game, Rucker struggles to consistently set the edge, letting ideal anchorage power and core strength. He will get uprooted and washed out against double teams and combo blocks. While he's often good at shedding blocks, he often struggles against longer-levered blockers that can easily control his pads.

Best Fit: Rotational pass rusher in either scheme

Player Ranking (1-100): 66.0 - There's no denying that Rucker is a good pass rusher. He has a knack for getting into the backfield, but the problem is he's inconsistent and lacks an ideal positional fit. He will likely need to earn his shot as a designated pass rusher until he proves he can stay on the field for more snaps. 5th round player.

30. Jah Joyner - Minnesota - 6'5 265 lbs

Strengths: As a 5th-year senior for the Gophers, Joyner has gradually gained more and more snaps throughout his college career. He's played a significant role in the last two seasons, saving his best for last. Joyner is built with the ideal size and frame, and it has a twitched-up frame with rare density and length. Joyner's frame allows him to succeed in both three- and 4-man fronts, showing versatility with schematic and alignment. Joyner will play on the right and left sides and even kick inside in passing situations. A blue-chip prospect who plays with a relentless motor, Joyner makes several effort plays from his never-say-die mentality. Capable of winning on both the outside and inside shoulder of tackles, Joyner utilizes his long strides to close cushions quickly. Joyner makes a lot of plays in the most crucial moments of games, showing rare sustained energy and effort. Heavy hands and a strong upper body allow him to win most hand battles at the line of scrimmage. Joyner works well in combination with his teammates on stunts, showing good timing and instincts to be utilized as the looper. When he can't get home on rushes, Joyner utilizes his length to disrupt and get his hands in the face of QBs. In the running game, Joyner shows good point-of-attack strength and gap discipline. He is a reliable tackler who frequently extends and shrinks his side of the field with his massive wingspan, ripping and tugging at the ball as he brings ball carriers down.

Weaknesses: Joyner had a solid junior season, but unfortunately, he slipped up a bit during his senior season, dropping all metrics. Joyner sits on blocks for far too long as a pass rusher, partly because of his constantly high pad level. He is far below average when it comes to get-off. He fails to shed and disengage from blocks despite his length and upper body power. He frequently overpursues and works too far up the arc as a speed rusher, allowing QBs to step up in the pocket easily. When working laterally, there are clear stiffness concerns; he struggles to change directions and offer any counter plan if his initial rush plan fails. He needs to learn how to utilize his hands and arms to keep his frame clean through contact.

Best Fit: LDE in a 4-3

Player Ranking (1-100): 64.1 - Joyner lacks elite pass-rushing upside. He's an upright rusher who lacks significant twitch and get-off. He's a hardworking kid who has excellent size and length. He will likely be a rotational edge defender at the next level that can occasionally kick inside. 6th round player.

31. R.J. Oben - Duke - 6'3 262 lbs

Strengths: A 6th-year player who played his final season for Notre Dame following a successful 5-year stint with the Blue Devils. Oben comes from good NFL lineage, as he's the son of former NFL OL Roman Oben. As a powerfully built edge defender, Oben has systematic versatility, showing the girth and length of play along the edges on both even and odd fronts. Oben possesses a large and varied pass rush, bringing many different rush plans inside his tool belt. He understands how to utilize his length in running and passing, playing with full extension, and keeping blockers off his frame. Oben has even shown his propensity to kick inside on clear passing plays and generate rush playing as a 3-technique DT. Plays with a relentless and high-energy motor, making several plays in pursuit. Strong awareness and recognition abilities and good lower body power allow him to set the edge in the running game effectively. Shows disciplined eyes and isn't easily fooled by misdirection or RPOs, staying positionally sound at all times. Keeps his hands active even when he can't get home, knocking away many balls. As a tackler, Oben is aggressive, constantly ripping at the ball and forcing several fumbles throughout his time.

Weaknesses: An older prospect who will be a 24-year-old rookie. Oben has stiffness limitations, failing to offer bend, ankle flexion, and hip flexibility, which makes it a constant threat at the next level. When asked to move laterally, Oben's change of directional ability and agility are overtasked. While he has improved as a run player, he still gets needlessly stuck on blocks for far too long. I'd like to see him do a more reliable wrap-up as a tackler, allowing many runners out of his grasp.

Best Fit: Rotational DE

Player Ranking (1-100): 62.9 - Oben didn't quite live up to his potential during his final year at Notre Dame, struggling to make his mark at a bigger program. He's a solid all-around player who must win a spot in training camp. He's not a dynamic, quick-twitch rusher and wins mostly from motor and effort. 6th round player.

32. Quandarrius Robinson - Alabama - 6'5 241 lbs

Strengths: A significant contributor to the defense in the last two seasons, Robinson began starting games for the Tide in 2024, before the injury. A former top high-school recruit, Robinson is a converted safety who has transitioned to playing closer to the line of scrimmage in college. Robinson has a long and rangy physique with vines for arms, making him a difficult matchup for tackles. He has the schematic versatility to play in either scheme, but he has the most experience playing as a linebacker in a 2-point stance. A terrific all-around athlete, Robinson has physical tools in abundance. Exploding off the snap of the ball, Robinson can immediately leave tackles in the dust, possessing both 1st step quickness and the elastic-like flexibility to challenge the arc. He closes on QBs quickly with the long speed that eats up cushions. And while he wins mostly with athleticism, Robinson utilizes his length to keep blockers off his frame. A disciplined edge setter, Robinson shows good read and reactionary skills. He recognizes pre-snap looks and works hard to control the edge and keep containment. He's proven reliable against RPO designs and will maintain positioning and discipline. He works incredibly hard in pursuit, possessing good motor and high urgency. Robinson displays an upside when dropping into coverage, showing good cover awareness and spatial awareness to limit cushions.

Weaknesses: He suffered a season-ending elbow injury during his final season, only playing in 9 games. He's only started five games during college and was mostly a special teams contributor and defensive rotational player his first few seasons. His production has been mostly average, failing to record more than four sacks in a season. Robinson is very lanky and needs to continue adding quality bulk and muscle onto his frame to better assist in the run department. He's often blown off the ball by double teams and combination blocks, failing to anchor down. As a rusher, he's a bit of a 1-trick pony that relies on his speed and could benefit by adding more hand counters to his game. Once he gets reached, he struggles to disengage and offer anything on a counter move.

Best Fit: 3-4 OLB

Player Ranking (1-100): 62.7 - Robinson has abundant physical tools but lacks experience and point-of-attack strength. His size and athleticism can be intriguing, and he could contribute as a rookie as a situational pass rusher. 6th round player.

33. Shemar Turner - Texas A&M - 6'4 285 lbs

Strengths: A four-year contributor to the Aggies defensive front, Turner had his best moments during the 2023 season, finishing with 11 tackles for loss and six sacks. Turner is a big-bodied defender with the schematic and positional versatility to play anywhere on the defensive line. Aggies coaches often used him at both edge positions, but they also bumped him more inside as his frame developed. Turner is an explosive athlete who generates impressive 1st step quickness. He utilizes his twitch to generate speed-to-power, getting underneath the pads of blocks and putting them on skates. Noticeable POP in his hands, showing the upper-body strength and displacement power to offset blockers' hands. He isn't a stiff athlete, showcasing some bend and change of direction to make plays on counter opportunities. Utilizes his length to play with full extension, limiting the opportunity for blockers to control him. In the running game, Turner often uses his club head to engage blockers while keeping his off-hand free to make plays on ball carriers. Has the anchorage strength through his lower half and the point of attack power to hold his own against blockers in run support. Long strides allow him to quickly eat up cushions in pursuit, showcasing a good motor. Length and tackle radius allow him to make plays outside his frame frequently.

Weaknesses: Despite a stellar junior campaign, Turner failed to follow up on it during his senior season. His versatility could be considered a detriment to his growth as he's spent time playing all over the defensive front and lacks a true position for the next level. While he shows flashes of getting low and playing with leverage, he frequently allows his pads to rise mid-play, limiting his success of getting off blocks. Lacks a defined pass rush arsenal or plan, attempting to rely on his power on most snaps. His snap awareness is inconsistent, oftentimes being the lack of one to get a jump at the line. He isn't a great run defender now, and he lacks the ball awareness and play recognition skills to make plays consistently.

Best Fit: Rotational Edge Defender

Player Ranking (1-100): 60.0 - Turner showed glimpses of a good player in 2023 but regressed this season. There are traits with the player, but he will likely need to show his place in training camp and preseason for a team. 6th round player.

34. Elijah Roberts - SMU - 6'4 278 lbs

Strengths: Roberts was initially a highly-regarded four-star recruit for Miami, and he began his career there for three straight seasons before transferring to SMU to play his final two seasons. Roberts had his coming out party in 2023, where he finished with 13 tackles for loss, 10 sacks, and two forced fumbles. Roberts is a stoutly built edge defender with thick limbs and density scattered throughout. He's equally adept at playing with his hands in the dirt or playing in a 2-point stance at the edge of the line of scrimmage. Roberts has moved around and is comfortable playing from different alignments and defensive systems. Roberts is an explosive rusher with good twitch and bursts off the line. Powerful hands and upper body allow him to deliver high-impact blows upon impact, making him a bull to control in the pass-rushing department. He maintains good pad level and leverage when pass rushing, allowing him to convert speed to power to put blockers on skates. His urgency and relentless motor allow him to be effective until the final whistle, working tirelessly in pursuit while making plays from the backside. Strong lower half and anchorage abilities enable him to fight through double teams in the run game. He sets a strong edge and works through blocks well, playing an active role in the running game.

Weaknesses: Coaches and scouts will have concerns about 'why' he didn't contribute much while he was at Miami. He lacked significant opportunities, and when he did, he failed to impress. He took advantage of lesser opposition at SMU and played far better. In the running game, Roberts allows his pads to rise mid-play, making him an easy target for blockers. He gets his hands on many ball carriers but fails to always secure the tackle. Roberts struggled when lined up against bigger blockers during his final season, failing to have an escape plan as a rusher. He needs to develop additional countermoves when his first move fails. While Roberts is twitchy, he lacks elite flexion and hip mobility, which limits his ability to bend consistently and capture the edge.

Best Fit: Edge rusher in either scheme

Player Ranking (1-100): 57.7 - Roberts flashed significantly during the 2023 campaign but had an underwhelming final season. He's had a unique college career where he consistently failed to show he can be a disruptive NFL player. He has a good frame and athleticism but will need additional seasoning. 7th round player.

35. Tyler Batty - BYU - 6'5 275 lbs

Strengths: A significant contributor to the BYU defense during the last 5 seasons, having his best season as a junior in 2023 with 5.5 sacks and two forced fumbles. Possessing a power-packed frame, Batty has a long, durable frame to contribute to the next level immediately. His large frame and experience allow him to contribute along the front and be a scheme fit for different defenses. Batty excels in the running game, displaying terrific anchorage power and strong hands to set the edge. Routinely stacks and sheds when working through blockers, utilizing excellent positioning sense and leverage to win leverage. Powerful pop through his hands and upper-body strength to jolt and displace blockers. Plays with a never-stop motor that allows him to play with urgency on every snap. Excellent awareness and football IQ that can diagnose quickly in the backfield, then flow to the ball. He quickly recognizes misdirection-type plays or screens in the backfield, regularly blowing them up. As a rusher, Batty can utilize his wingspan to disrupt passing lanes and alter throwing trajectories for QBs. He's a power rusher with an impressive power profile, namely his bull rush to close the pocket and put blockers on skates. An impactful tackler that makes runners feel it, delivering tone-setting hits when reaching a ball carrier's frame.

Weaknesses: An older prospect who will be 25 years old right after the NFL Draft. Lacks the finesse and the athleticism to be a great next-level pass rusher. High hipped frame causes him to struggle when changing directions and playing outside his frame. Limited 1st step quickness to threaten vertically. His upright frame, lack of ideal leverage, and lack of bend limit him when attempting to win the edges against more athletic tackles. When kicking inside, Batty gets overwhelmed at the point of attack and fails to offer any upside in winning against double teams and combo blocks in the run game.

Best Fit: Edge rusher in either scheme

Player Ranking (1-100): 56.1 - Batty is a hard-working, physically experienced defender. He's limited athletically, but his motor and football IQ cause him to be an effective player, most notably in the running game. He deserves a shot to win a place for a team. 7th round player.

Top-10 Edge Players:

1. Abdul Carter
2. Mykel Williams
3. Jalon Walker
4. Nic Scourton
5. Tyler Baron
6. Kyle Kennard
7. Landson Jackson
8. Mike Green
9. James Pearce Jr
10. Donovan Ezeiruaku

Chapter 9

Defensive Tackles
(Includes 3-4 DE's)

1. Mason Graham - Michigan - 6'3 320 lbs

Strengths: A 3-year starter for the Wolverines, Graham has been a valuable cog in the Wolverines' defense during each season, showing tremendous consistency and reliability. Comfortable playing all over and at various alignments, Graham has 3-down ability in both odd and even fronts. Built with well-proportioned thickness through his frame, Graham has NFL size and power. As a rusher, he displays good burst and initial quickness out of his stance and can challenge interior blockers from the get-go. His former wrestling prowess is evident in his ability to hand fight and play through blockers. Stays on his feet and plays with excellent leverage, body control, and balance through contact. Possesses a devastating spin move that he has repeatedly shown to get home on rushes. Plays with various hand tactics while displaying a powerful punch that allows him to keep his frame clean while showing the displacement power to collapse the pocket. Dynamic when used on stunts, proving to have the athleticism and closing burst to get home as a looper. Frequently takes on double teams in the running game, allowing his linebackers to flow freely to the football in pursuit. Excellent lower body power allows him to drop his anchor and maintain positioning against combination blocks and double teams. Shows excellent ball awareness and anticipation in the running game, working towards the football while minimizing up openings through the 'A' and 'B' gaps.

Weaknesses: Graham has a stubby build and lacks prototypical height and length thresholds. Can be a little late to react off the snap of the ball, frequently being the last one to get a jump on the ball. Quicker than he is truly explosive, Graham struggles closing down on plays when working backside or in pursuit. He will get overwhelmed at the point of attack against longer blockers that can outreach him, limiting his counter ability to disengage. His wrestling background causes him to get into too many hand battles, taking him out of too many plays due to personal battles. Has noticeable stiffness issues through his lower body, most notably in his hips and ankles, causing him to have some change of directional concerns.

Best Fit: 4-3 DT (3-technique)

Player Ranking (1-100): 88.1 - Graham is a good all-around football player who equally affects the passing and running games. He's an impressive rusher who frequently takes on double teams and causes additional attention from the offense. He's a skillful all-around football player who played like his hair was on fire during every snap of the ball, bringing physicality and toughness to any defense. 1st round player.

2. Tyleik Williams - Ohio State - 6'3 327 lbs

Strengths: A rare 4-year starter for the Buckeyes on the inside, Williams has been a major contributor since his freshman campaign, finishing with five sacks as a true freshman. Williams is built with a muscled-up physique, showing compactness through his upper and lower halves. Rare power is on display for Williams, as he is an absolute load to handle for blockers. Playing several different alignments inside, Wiliams can handle both one and 2-gapping responsibilities, having the lower body anchorage strength to maintain double teams. A high football IQ is on display routinely, regularly showing the ability to locate the ball while showing ball instincts and awareness. Sniffs out screens and misdirection-type runs due to his play recognition abilities. Dynamic 1st step quickness coupled with snap anticipation lets him frequently shoot gaps and generate penetration. Incredibly strong hands and upper body allow him to stack/shed and quickly disengage from blockers. Displacement power in his hands is evident with knock-back power, putting blockers on skates quickly. Even when he can't make the play, Williams' ability to call for double teams opens up opportunities for linebackers to make 1v1 plays in space.

Weaknesses: While Williams is a load to handle in the run game, his effectiveness in the pass-rushing parts of the game isn't nearly as refined. Regularly allowing his pads to rise mid-play, Williams can play too belly-to-belly to truly effective passing plays. He needs to consistently play with a better pad level while increasing his pass-rushing repertoire to be an effective 3-down player. While his upper-body power is top-tier, his length isn't elite. Has some tightness in his lower body, limiting his effectiveness when playing laterally, causing him to struggle to change directions quickly. He is likely only a fit in an even front system, as he lacks the elite range to play in an odd front.

Best Fit: Starting DT (Can play one or 3-technique)

Player Ranking (1-100): 85.4 - I love Williams as a player in a 4-3-type defensive setup. His ability to impact games and plays is outstanding. He is a dynamic player against the run, impacting both inside and outside runs. He has rare quickness for a guy his size, getting in the backfield far more than you'd expect. While he isn't an elite pass-rushing DT, he has the explosiveness and the power to contribute. His experience and success against top-tier competition make me confident he will be a good starter at the next level. 1st round player.

3. Walter Nolen - Ole Miss - 6'4 290 lbs

Strengths: A former consensus five-star recruit, Nolen began his career with Texas A&M for two seasons before transferring to Ole Miss for his final season in 2024. Nolen saved his best for last with the Rebels, proving his upside while beginning to showcase his talent. Nolen has been kicked around all over the defensive front for both the Rebels and the Aggies, showing the ability to line up anywhere from defensive end to nose tackle. Shows the capability to win in various ways depending on where he's aligned, showing schematic versatility. Nolen is at his best when playing inside on a slanted front, where he can utilize his burst and core flexibility to win inside narrow gaps and get into the backfield. When firing low out of his stance, Nolen showcases impressive speed-to-power capabilities to collapse the pocket and put blockers on skates, especially when he's lined up outside. Has a varied pass rush arsenal, including several hand tactics to keep blockers guessing. Not just a straight-line athlete, Nolen can change directions, showing impressive lateral mobility for a guy of his size. In the running game, Nolen is capable of 2-gapping, showing good point-of-attack power to sustain combo blocks and double teams while being a difficult guy to move off his spot. Maintains sound assignment and positioning on run fits, keeping his eyes fixated on the ball carrier. Does a nice job stacking and shedding in pursuit, showing impressive POP in his hands to keep his frame clean when working towards the ball carrier. He is a violent tackler who utilizes his entire wingspan to make plays outside his frame.

Weaknesses: Can occasionally be a little late to react to the snap of the ball, failing to display ideal snap timing and anticipation. Nolen plays at inconsistent pad level; sometimes it's great, and sometimes he fires way too upright out of his stance. Questions will be asked about why he failed to produce early on in his college career. There are moments when his motor runs hot and cold, appearing to lack top-end conditioning. He can quickly give up his chest plate, allowing offensive linemen to control him throughout a play. Needs to develop a counter plan as a rusher, getting washed out of too many plays without any noticeable way to get off.

Best Fit: 4-3 DT (3-technique) or 3-4 DE (5-technique)

Player Ranking (1-100): 84.1 - Nolen is a highly-touted prospect who displays the talent level only to get better and better as a football player. He's a great blend of athleticism and point-of-attack power. He's a 3-down player who is just as good in the running game as in the passing game. 2nd round player.

4. Kenneth Grant - Michigan - 6'3 339 lbs

Strengths: A dominant starter in the Wolverines' last two seasons, Grant has had stellar production playing in the heart of the Michigan defense. A mountain of a man, Grant has the size and girth to be a dominant force in any defense system at the next level. Grant is a rare physical specimen who shows outstanding movement skills for a man of his size. Featuring a good burst, Grant explodes off the snap of the ball, instantly pressing the line of scrimmage. Impressive flexibility and flexion allow him to threaten in minimal space. Lateral movement skills allow him to funnel and flow to the ball along the perimeter, showcasing noticeable agility and change of direction. Grant is not just an athlete but a powerful man who requires committed blockers, often dominating when on an island. Has a large toolbelt of hand tactics to work and breakdown blockers, showing quick and active hands to keep his frame clean. Commands double teams in a clear passing situation, showing the speed-to-power to collapse the pocket. He does an excellent job of getting his hands off to disrupt the QBs vision when he can't get home, with several pass deflections each season. Capable of playing anywhere from a 0-technique nose tackle to a 5-technique DE in a 3-man front. Sees plays developing quickly, showing good play recognition traits to diagnose. Good anchorage strength to hold up in the running game, capable of handling two-gap responsibilities. A reliable open-field tackler that makes runners feel it, showing impressive closing speed to make plays backside.

Weaknesses: Grant could struggle to play 3-downs at the next level due to his size and lack of ideal motor. He's far more advanced as a pass rusher than in the running game, frequently getting washed out of plays due to poor leverage. His instincts and snap anticipation often leave something to be desired, as he frequently gets a late jump on the ball. He must continue diversifying his pass-rush attack plan, far too often relying on his power and bullrush to close the pocket.

Best Fit: 3-4 DE or 4-3 DT (1-technique)

Player Ranking (1-100): 83.9 - Grant is a big-bodied space-eating physical specimen. Make no mistake, this is NOT a run-stuffing nose tackle. He is a guy who can generate significant power and movement skills in the passing game. He's better as a pass rusher than he is currently as a run player. 2nd round player.

5. Deone Walker - Kentucky - 6'6 345 lbs

Strengths: A 3-year starter for the Wildcats since his true freshman campaign, Walker exploded into NFL Draft talk following his 2023 campaign, in which he finished with 7.5 sacks and 13 tackles for loss. Walker is a massive h with incredible size, length, and girth. A former basketball player shows it in how he plays, showing rare mobility and change of directional skills for a man of his size. Comfortable playing all over the defensive front, even playing some as a standup linebacker, Walker has the experience to handle different alignments with success. Exploding off the snap of the ball, Walker displays good snap anticipation and 1st step quickness to challenge blockers instantly. Power throughout his frame enables him to collapse the pocket with speed-to-power rushes. Constantly required double teams when rushing from the interior on passing situations. Heavy hands and a powerful upper body create displacement against both interior blockers and even tackles. Walker is not just a bull rusher; he has diverse pass-rush skills and moves that he utilizes to keep blockers second-guessing. Not just a 2-down player, Walker displays the traits of a successful 3-down player at the next level. When he doesn't win initially, Walker displays relentless hand tactics to win most hand combats to knock blockers backward and cause them off-balanced. Capable of shooting gaps when used on twists and stunts to generate backfield pressure and make plays behind the line of scrimmage. In the running game, Walker has a 2-gap upside with his wingspan and point-of-attack power combination. Impressive lateral agility to disengage while keeping his head on a swivel to locate the football.

Weaknesses: Walker had a terrific sophomore campaign in 2023. Still, he didn't improve on that, and he regressed significantly on the stat line and film, especially against the top-tier competition that he had competed against in 2024. Walker's conditioning will be a problem with the amount of weight he carries, causing him to struggle to stay on the field. He has an inconsistent ability to navigate and get off blocks; at times, he can do it, but other times, he gets hooked for far too long. His biggest issue in the running and passing game is his leverage issues, constantly firing upright. Better leveraged blockers will stay underneath his pads and sustain him for long durations. This is most notable in combo and double-team blocks. Lack of elite anchorage power is exposed due to pad level, getting knocked off the ball in the run game.

Best Fit: Nose Tackle in either scheme

Player Ranking (1-100): 83.4 - Walker looked like a Top-10 pick during the 2023 season. Unfortunately, he significantly regressed and was a bit exposed at times. He will need to play at a better weight, allowing him to stay on the field. He has ridiculous ability for a man of his size. Has a massive ceiling, and with the right coaching, he could be great. 2nd round player.

6. T.J. Sanders - South Carolina - 6'5 300 lbs

Strengths: A 3-year significant contributor for the Gamecocks in the interior of their front, Sanders has extensive experience competing against top-tier competition. Sanders had his best season as a sophomore in 2023, finishing with 43 tackles and 4.5 sacks. A physically imposing defender, Sanders looks the part with a massive twitched-up frame showing the length and the height to disrupt QBs passing lanes. He is an aggressive blue-chip prospect who has worked his tail off to get where he is, as he was only a former three-star recruit. Plays every snap like it's his last, showing aggressiveness and 'hair is on fire' urgency. Has twitchiness to his game, showing a good initial burst off the snap of the ball, and he couples that with impressive snap anticipation. Commits himself to playing leveraged in the passing game, getting underneath the pads of blockers and putting them on skates. Understands how to generate rolling power through his lower half, generating impressive speed-to-power explosion. Can make plays outside of his frame, showing reliability as a tackler. Excellent deconstruction abilities when working in the run game, fighting through blockers and disengaging routinely. Violent in pursuit, working relentlessly back toward the football. Has an internal GPS, even with his back towards the football, knowing exactly where the ball is at all times. Equally adept in both the running and passing games. With a large ceiling and proper development, expect him to get better and better.

Weaknesses: Sanders, after a tremendous 2023 season, hasn't quite lived up to his former billing in 2024 with far less production. While he's a handful as a pass rusher, Sanders lacks a pass-rush arsenal or a defined array of pass-rush moves. Tends to rush upright on occasion, leaving his chest plate completely exposed. He is more explosive than powerful and has some anchorage concerns when attempting to 2-gap. He will get overwhelmed at the point of attack when handling double teams.

Best Fit: 4-3 DT (3-technique)

Player Ranking (1-100): 82.8 - I like Sanders quite a bit as a gap penetrating 3-technique. Noticeably, his lower body has some room for growth and strength. But he's a handful who can make plays in the backfield, running and passing games. His instincts, anticipation, and explosiveness are enticing. He's a true 3-down DT that can be very disruptive. 2nd round player.

7. Derrick Harmon - Oregon - 6'5 310 lbs

Strengths: A 2-year starter for Michigan State, Harmon transferred to Oregon following his 2023 campaign. Harmon had his best career for the Ducks in 2024, improving his production and overall quality of play. A long-levered interior prospect with both the height and the length to be effective in any scheme at the next level. Harmon has shown the ability to play along the defensive front, showing success at various alignments. Harmon's length makes him very difficult to control for blockers, locking out offensive linemen and controlling them through the duration. Explosive off the blocks, Harmon reads the game intelligently, quickly diagnosing between run and pass and triggering downhill. Play recognition allows him to sniff out plays in the backfield, rarely getting fooled by RPOs or option-style plays. Harmon can sidestep defenders in the passing game or attack them head-on with a devastating bull rush. He is relentless as a rusher, showing impressive counter abilities with his violent hands and urgent play style. Harmon is difficult to control in the running game, easily disengaging against blockers when stacking and shedding. He can hold his own against double teams, showing impressive anchorage abilities and core strength. Good block recognition abilities with his understanding of reading blocking schemes while displaying reactionary reflexes. He is relentless in pursuit of his ability to make plays from the backside and must be accounted for at all times.

Weaknesses: Harmon is built with a high-hipped frame, limiting his ability to change directional movements. This limits him against athletic quarterbacks who can easily evade him when asking him to play sideways. His overall pad level is inconsistent, frequently allowing his pads to rise throughout the play. He gets into the backfield often and doesn't make as many plays as expected for someone constantly around the ball. Will need to continue to refine and develop a larger pass-rush arsenal to be effective on three downs.

Best Fit: 4-3 DT (1-technique) or 3-4 DE (5-technique)

Player Ranking (1-100): 81.4 - Harmon is a good all-around interior prospect who can disrupt the game. While I'd like him to finish more plays, he's a solid football player who lacks a significant weakness. While he's not a top-tier athlete, his length and point-of-attack power are difficult to deal with. He certainly has three down upside and should be a Day 1 starter for a team. 2nd round player.

8. Shemar Stewart - Texas A&M - 6'6 290 lbs

Strengths: A former five-star recruit for the Aggies, Stewart has been a Texas A&M defensive front's mainstay during the last three seasons. Stewart displays a power-packed frame with outstanding length and muscle in abundance. He's proven to be a versatile cog for the defense, playing all over the defensive line at every position. Stewart's versatility will appeal to any defensive scheme at the next level, offering the ability to play on both odd and even fronts. As an outside-edge player, Stewart has proven his ability to stand up or play with his hands in the dirt. Displaying good twitch and an explosive 1st step, Stewart immediately threatens the outside shoulder of offensive tackles, showing good bend for his size. He has a dynamic bull rush as he regularly collapses the pocket, capable of putting offensive tackles on skates. Stewart has a good arsenal of pass-rush moves at his disposal. His length enables him to control the pads of blockers, showcasing outstanding knockback power through his upper body. His ability to kick inside in passing situations allows him to utilize his explosiveness to shoot gaps and challenge inferior guards and centers. Stewart is a hardworking presence who plays with urgency and a HOT motor on every snap. He's also proven iron-man durability, not missing one game during his college career. He is also one of the youngest players in this draft class, at only 21 years of age.

Weaknesses: Despite Stewart's physical accolades, he's only had 4.5 sacks and 12 tackles for loss during his three-year career. His moving around to various positions has prevented him from having a defined position, and he's a bit of a 'jack of all trades master of none.' His frame will make playing with leverage a constant battle for Stewart as he frequently allows his pads to rise mid-play. In the running game, Stewart lacks ideal point-of-attack power through his lower body, and he's frequently uprooted against double teams and combo blocks. Stewart misses too many chances to make plays as he's always around the ball, but he fails to always securely wrap up and finish plays.

> Best Fit: 3-4 DE or 4-3 DT (3-technique)

Player Ranking (1-100): 81.1 - While Stewart played mostly on the outside in college, his frame and length can allow him to be a nightmare mismatch on the inside. Either way, his scheme versatility will be enticing to all defenses. He has a legit chance to be a much better NFL player than he was in college. His stats don't indicate how disruptive he was at times. 2nd round player.

9. Alfred Collins - Texas - 6'5 320 lbs

Strengths: A former top five-star high school recruit, Collins has played a major role for the Longhorns defensive front for the last five seasons, getting significant snaps since his freshman season. Collins is a long and powerfully built interior defender with positional flexibility for a defensive line. Played in both three and 4-man fronts in college, showing comfort and experience for multiple schemes and at different alignments. Possessing a rare ceiling, Collins has untapped potential due to his rare blend of athleticism and frame. Collins can overwhelm at the point of attack with his upper-body power and strong hands to shed against blockers. As a rusher, Collins utilizes impressive speed-to-power to generate impressive power through his lower body to close the pocket with his devastating bull rush. Quickly closes down with an impressive blend of twitch and closing speed. Commits himself to winning inside hand leverage against squatty interior blockers who can't match him with length. Has the anchorage power to play in both one and 2-gap systems, understanding how to win positioning and leverage to open up opportunities for teammates. Used effectively on stunts and twists, understanding how to shoot gaps while remaining skinny through narrow windows. Maintains good gap integrity and awareness in the running game. Locates the ball quickly in the run game, working his way back towards the football and making plays in pursuit. His motor runs HOT and shows good down-after-down relentlessness and aggressiveness.

Weaknesses: Despite having 5 years of experience in a major college program, Collins has a lot of potential with significant room for growth. As a rusher, he's a bit of a headless chicken who lacks a defined plan or skillset when setting up his rushes. A very upright rusher that ditches his stance immediately after the snap. Will get hung up on blocks for far too long, lacking any secondary ability to disengage. Plays far too belly to belly, leaving his chest completely exposed and bouncing off blockers. While he has the power to handle 2-gap systems, his lack of leverage limits him when handling double teams. He is not a consistently reliable tackler, allowing runners to stay on their feet too often when he gets his hands on them.

Best Fit: 3-4 DE or 4-3 DT

Player Ranking (1-100): 80.7 - There's the possibility with Collins that he might finally get it and be a dominant interior defender at the next level. His positional flexibility and frame make him attractive in any defensive system. He has flashes of it but fails to show it consistently. But there's an intriguing skillset with the player. 2nd round player.

10. Ty Robinson - Nebraska - 6'6 310 lbs

Strengths: As a 6th-year senior, Robinson has started for the Cornhuskers in the last three seasons. Robinson began getting significant play time as a redshirt freshman, starting in several games that year. His reliability and sturdiness have proven invaluable, having not missed a game in four straight seasons. Robinson exploded during his final campaign with the Cornhuskers, posting six sacks and 11 tackles for loss, a rare production for an inside player. Possessing a rare frame, Robinson has a twitched-up and developed frame with vines for arms, allowing him to be a dominant inside force. Robinson is a scheme-versatile and alignment-versatile prospect who has played all over the defensive formation for the Cornhuskers. He appeals to both three and 4-man front teams. Robinson is a physical throwback player, playing every snap like his last. He frequently requires double teams due to his overwhelming power and length, dominating at the point of attack. In the passing game, Robinson wins mostly with power, locking out offensive linemen and driving them backward with his continued leg drive. He also displays an array of hand tactics, showing quick and violent hands to disengage when attacking downhill. He shows good initial quickness off the blocks and can shoot gaps quickly in a slanted front. In the running game, Robinson displays terrific anticipation and vision. He keeps his eyes glued to the ball carrier while flowing to the action. His massive wingspan enables him to close gaps and make plays from the backside, showing reliability as a tackler. Robinson is an immovable force against combo blocks and double teams, dropping his anchor and absorbing contact.

Weaknesses: An older prospect who will be 24 years old during his rookie NFL season. Robinson is a what-you-see, what-you-get player who is likely fully maxed out in body composition and athletic characteristics. He will need to continue broadening his ability as a pass rusher and not rely on winning, namely with power. Robinson tends to get into many personal battles, taking him out of the action. When asked to change direction or redirect his frame, he struggles, showing clear tightness and a lack of flexibility through his lower half. His frame makes it difficult to play with leverage, and he constantly battles with the upright pad level and keeps his frame overly exposed. Robinson plays 100 mph and is prone to getting out of breath and exhausted as games wear on, but he could benefit from continued conditioning.

> **Best Fit: 4-3 DT (1-technique) or 3-4 DE (4 or 5-technique)**

Player Ranking (1-100): 80.1 - Robinson is a fun football player. He has to be an absolute nightmare to match up against because he LOVES the trenches and getting dirty. He must be accounted for on every play and makes many plays for an interior player. 2nd round player.

11. Howard Cross III - Notre Dame - 6'1 288 lbs

Strengths: A rare 6th-year senior for the Fighting Irish, Cross has been a significant contributor on the defensive line for the last four seasons. The son of former NY Giants great Howard Cross Jr, Howard III has an excellent NFL pedigree and is a former state champion wrestler. Cross is a shorter but compactly built interior defender who has bounced around successfully at different alignments. Cross has produced steady production against top-tier opposition in the last four seasons. Cross showcases a quick 1st step as a pass rusher, enabling him to slip gaps and be a force on twists and stunts. His former wrestling experience is evidenced by his ability to utilize his hands, winning most hand battles and consistently getting into the backfield. He can win with power by keeping his legs churning and collapsing the pocket. Has more than enough lateral quickness and agility to change directions and is effective when working on slanted fronts. Impressive all-around closing speed allows him to chase down plays and close quickly on QBs. His motor runs hot on every single play, generating coverage sacks due to his relentless work ethic and never-stop mentality. Cross understands how to maintain leverage and balance through contact in the running game. He plays with terrific technique to slip blocks and locate ball carriers. He is a force due to his combination of leverage and natural lower-body power to consistently win at the point of attack, rarely getting moved out of his spot.

Weaknesses: An older prospect who will be 24 years old at the start of his rookie season. He lacks the ideal frame and length to play in an odd front system, as he likely will need to play in an even front. Lack of length causes him to struggle to disengage as a pass rusher on counter moves; if his initial move doesn't win out, he can sit on blocks for a long time. Cross can sometimes play too aggressively, attempting to shoot gaps and overrun plays, taking him out of his gap assignment. His limited tackle radius limits his overall range, failing to make significant plays outside his frame.

> **Best Fit: 4-3 DT (1 or 3-technique)**

Player Ranking (1-100): 79.4 - Cross is a high-floor and low-ceiling prospect who most certainly will earn a role for a team at the next level. While he lacks elite traits, his work ethic and ability to affect plays consistently is impressive. He 100% has starter potential and is equally adept in the passing and running games. He gets into the backfield a LOT and is an absolute load to deal with. 3rd round player.

12. Darius Alexander - Toledo - 6'4 320 lbs

Strengths: A dominant force for Toledo in the last three seasons, Alexander had his best season in 2023, finishing with six tackles for loss and four sacks. Built with a power-packed frame and vines for arms, Alexander meets size thresholds to play in any system at the next level. Comfortable aligning as a nose tackle, 3-technique, or a 3-4 DE, Alexander succeeds wherever he's put. Alexander has outstanding explosiveness and athleticism, possessing incredibly light and agile feet. He generates terrific get-offs to challenge interior linemen, immediately putting them in recovery mode. Not just quick, Alexander has a diversified rush plan with a large variety of moves. With jarring power in his upper body, Alexander can generate outstanding raw power to uproot and deconstruct blockers. When dropping his pads, he showcases the ability to generate impressive speed-to-power to put blockers on skates and close the pocket. Noticeable lower body flexibility and agility enable Alexander to cross the face of blockers and play laterally successfully. Capable of being a 1-gap penetrator with his ability to utilize core strength and explosive quickness to explode through narrow gaps. He works tirelessly at all times, and this is especially evident when working back towards the football. His closing speed is rare, regularly making plays down the field or on the opposite side. His tackle radius lets him condense multiple gaps, limiting available openings for backs in the game. He's a sturdy football player who has played almost every game in the last four seasons with no lingering injury concerns.

Weaknesses: Alexander hasn't competed against consistent top-tier competition. He gives up leverage in the run game, allowing his pads to rise. This causes him to struggle to anchor against combo blocks and double teams, regularly getting moved off his spot and struggling with his balance. His upper body strength is further advanced than his lower body strength. He tends to get into too many personal battles in the run game, losing track of the ball carrier and overpursuing plays. He doesn't always read and anticipate blocking schemes, is frequently susceptible to cut blocks, and often runs into things without properly anticipating.

Best Fit: 4-3 DT (1 or 3-technique) or 3-4 DE (4 or 5-technique)

Player Ranking (1-100): 79.7 - Alexander is an incredibly disruptive football player who shows up far more often than his stat line would suggest. He's a dynamic interior pass rusher with abundant twitch and explosiveness. As a rookie, he should immediately press for snaps. 3rd round player.

13. J.J. Pegues - Ole Miss - 6'2 324 lbs

Strengths: Pegues began his career at Auburn for two seasons before transferring to Ole Miss for his final three campaigns. Pegues started his career at tight end for the Tigers before transitioning into a full-time defensive tackle during his sophomore season. Pegues has gotten better and better playing on the inside, having his best season to date in 2024 with 14 tackles for loss and 3.5 sacks. Pegues has a rare skillset and has been used heavily as a red-zone rush threat, with seven touchdowns rushing the ball, proving his versatility and athleticism. Pegues has a good build for the next level, showing good twitch and proportional density through his frame. His skill set and experience make him attractive to teams playing on both even and odd fronts, as he can succeed across the line. Pegues is an athletic mover who can immediately press linemen with his initial quickness and movement skills. When he can't get into the backfield, Pegues does a good job getting his hands up to disrupt the QBs vision. When handling single blocks, Pegues can bend and get underneath their pads and force QBs off their spot. Lower body looseness and lateral agility are present as Pegues can work well in slanted fronts and cross the face of blockers. When collapsing the pocket, Pegues shows good lower body strength to churn his legs to clog up rush lanes. He keeps his head on a swivel in the running game, recognizing pre-snap looks and frequently diagnosing in the backfield. He works tirelessly in pursuit, showing good effort, and can make plays from the backside.

Weaknesses: While Pegues has the physical skillset for continued refinement, he needs additional technical acuity and finesse. At the snap of the ball, Pegues can sometimes be a tick late, allowing blockers to get a head start. He's frequently without a plan as a rusher, allowing himself to get pushed around like a bowling bowl. He needs to learn to utilize his hands when attacking the pocket, frequently allowing blockers into his frame. He appears to lack top-end length, which limits his ability to control the point of attack. While his overall power profile is good, he struggles consistently playing through double teams and combo blocks in the run game, and he will get uprooted and moved out of his gap assignment due to poor leverage.

Best Fit: 3-4 DE or 4-3 DT (1 or 3-technique)

Player Ranking (1-100): 79.2 - Pegues had an outstanding season for Ole Miss this season. His versatility and athleticism will bode well as he continues refining his interior disruptor game. Pegues is equally good in the run and the passing phases and has proven disruptive. 3rd round player.

14. LT Overton - Alabama - 6'5 285 lbs

Strengths: A former unanimous five-star high school football player, Overton began his career with the Aggies, where he was a 2-year rotational player. Following his sophomore season in 2023, Overton transferred to Alabama, where he had his best season in 2024. Overton has prototypical size and length, allowing him to have success playing on the outside and inside. Overton has been moved all over the place for both teams, playing in several different alignments. Overton is a dynamic athlete with impressive directional skills and agility for a man of his size, but he is completely overwhelming when playing inside. He is capable of winning with both finesse and power. Overton is extremely twitchy as a pass rusher and can challenge blockers' inside and outside shoulders. His explosiveness is evident when used as the stunt looper, showcasing impressive closing speed to shoot gaps. He brings a varied and large pass-rush arsenal to the table. His motor and counter ability allow him to succeed on the secondary move. Capable of collapsing the pocket with speed-to-power on his bull rushes. In both the run and passing games, he understands how to utilize his hands, possessing quick and active hands to control and disengage. A gap filler in the running game that shows good awareness and play recognition skills. Works tirelessly in pursuit, making several plays from the backside.

Weaknesses: Overton's on-field success has never matched his overall athleticism, failing to impress greatly before his final season at Alabama. He has been a tweener throughout college, rarely playing meaningful snaps at a set position as he's been bounced around at various weight classes. His snap timing and awareness aren't ideal, as he's frequently the last one to get a jump at the line of scrimmage. As a rusher, his flexion through his lower body limits him when working the outside, failing to arc the corner in narrow windows. He misses far more tackles than you like to see for a defender, failing always to secure. He can be overly reliant on winning with his athleticism, failing to always play with good technique. He explodes from his upright stance, rarely playing with the ideal pad level.

Best Fit: 3-4 DE (5-technique) but can play as a 4-3 LDE.

Player Ranking (1-100): 78.5 - Overton has a massive ceiling but is still incredibly raw as a prospect. He could end up being a Pro-Bowler, but he could also be a rotational defender for a team. He certainly has traits, but he needs to continue to get more refined as he did at Alabama this past season. I love seeing him play on the inside in passing situations, as his athleticism completely overwhelms. 3rd round player.

15. Omarr Norman-Lott - Tennessee - 6'3 315 lbs

Strengths: Norman-Lott began his career with Arizona State for the first three seasons, proving to be a reliable producer in each of his last two seasons there. He transferred to Tennessee before the 2023 campaign, starting in his last two seasons in the SEC for the Vols. Norman-Lott is a powerful man who has grown into his frame increasingly and has experience playing all over the line of scrimmage. At Arizona State, he frequently played in a 2-point stance along the edges, but he's transitioned to playing on the inside for Tennessee. Norman-Lott is a relentless pass rusher who successfully attacks the pocket from different alignments. He combines his snap anticipation with his 1st step quickness to immediately threaten blockers. He utilizes his natural pad level and strong hand placement to dominate the leverage battle and maintain control through the snap. Good lateral ability and lower body flexibility to cross the face of blockers and threaten laterally or in slanted fronts. He brings a diversified rush plan to the table, showcasing an array of hand tactics. He plays 100 mph on every snap, working tirelessly in pursuit. He shows advanced block recognition skills and can diagnose pre- and post-snap. He has shown the ability to blow up screens and outside-zone runs in the backfield. In the running game, Norman-Lott utilizes his upper-body power to stack and shed. He's capable of quickly slipping blocks while working back toward the football. He makes several plays in pursuit, regularly chasing down from the backside and showing impressive closing speed.

Weaknesses: Norman-Lott is a big man who has gained mass quickly and could benefit by continuing to refine his frame while adding power and cleaning up his sloppy weight. His effectiveness in the running game is significantly weaker than his ability to affect clear passing downs. His upper body is further along functionally than his lower body, as he struggles to consistently drop his anchor and maintain positioning in the run game. He gets easily uprooted and moved off his spot by combo blocks. He's had some nagging injury concerns, causing him to miss game time in multiple seasons. He wears down towards the end of the game, causing his leverage and technique to suffer. His gap awareness and integrity are frequently compromised as he ditches his assignment to trigger downhill. As a pass rusher, Norman-Lott needs to do a better job bringing a counter plan to the table, as he relies strictly on his initial move to generate pressure.

Best Fit: 4-3 DT (1 or 3-technique) or 3-4 DE (4 or 5-technique)

Player Ranking (1-100): 78.2 - Norman-Lott is an impressive pass rusher from inside alignments. His motor, 1st step, and upper body power enable him to be disruptive frequently. As he continues to refine his frame and gain functional strength through his lower body, he will get better and better. I think he's completely versatile and should be a 3-down player at the next level. 3rd round player.

16. Ty Hamilton - Ohio State - 6'3 295 lbs

Strengths: As a 5th-year senior, Hamilton has been a steady force on Buckeye's defensive front for the last four seasons. With iron-man durability, Hamilton has shown the ability to stay on the field throughout his career with no injury history. Hamilton is built with a power-packed frame, showing outstanding density and strength. Hamilton can play in any defensive system and has schematic and positional flexibility. Hamilton is a dominant force in the running game, proving to be unstoppable for single blockers. It's rare to see an interior player throw guys to the ground as much as Hamilton did over and over again. He's best utilized in a 2-gap role where he can consistently use his anticipation and anchorage power to hold the point of attack. Hamilton is quick to recognize blocking schemes and understands how to break down blockers, frequently working through them. His upper-body strength and hands deliver devastating hits to blockers, forcing them into recovery mode. He plays with a relentless motor and routinely puts effort into broken-down plays until the final whistle. He always stays square and leveraged, showing good body control and balance. As a pass rusher, Hamilton has noticeable twitch and 1st step quickness. He's best, though, when playing with power, as he's proven to be a dominant bull rusher. He keeps his legs churning through impact and can collapse the pocket. Hamilton is a reliable form tackler who can extend and make plays outside his frame.

Weaknesses: Hamilton's pass-rushing production has been mostly minimal, with few sacks and plays behind the line of scrimmage. He lacks any defined pass-rush plan other than winning with power. He needs to understand how to utilize his hands better to disengage and offer a diversified rush plan if he wants to stay on the field for three downs. He's often stonewalled on his initial move and lacks a counter plan. Hamilton has stiffness concerns in his lower body, and he struggles when asked to move off his spot or change directions, making him easy to avoid for running QBs.

Best Fit: Nose tackle in either scheme

Player Ranking (1-100): 77.9 - Hamilton is one of this draft class's best pure run stuffers. He's got an incredibly powerful trunk, and he's virtually unmovable. He's not just 'there,' but he makes plays consistently. He will make a run defense better. I'd like to see Hamilton continue utilizing his explosive twitch to assist more in the pass-rush department. 3rd round player.

17. Tyrion Ingram-Dawkins - Georgia - 6'5 300 lbs

Strengths: Ingram-Dawkins is a former five-star high school player for the Bulldogs who finally lived up to his bill during his junior season in 2024, finishing with eight tackles for loss and three sacks. Ingram-Dawkins is a powerfully built defender with a muscled-up physique and impressive workout strength. Capable of playing all along the defensive front, Ingram-Dawkins shows comfort at various alignments and could be a scheme fit for any defense at the next level. Ingram-Dawkins is a bull to deal with for blockers, showing outstanding point-of-attack strength through his frame. In the passing game, Ingram-Dawkins does a terrific job of utilizing speed-to-power to close the pocket with his bull rush. His violent upper body, coupled with his length, enables him to control the pads of blockers, utilizing the push/pull technique to devastating effect. In the running game, Ingram-Dawkins shines the brightest. Displaying terrific instincts, Ingram-Dawkins always keeps his eyes fixated on the backfield. He maintains good leverage and body positioning to control the point of attack. He displays the lower body anchorage power, balance, and lateral agility to handle 2-gap assignments effectively. Against RPOs, Ingram-Dawkins maintains sound discipline and gap integrity. He reads blocking schemes well and can move lineman off their spots when deconstructing blocks. He plays with good lockout and extension, not allowing blockers to reach his pads. He is a forceful tackler who utilizes his entire tackle radius to make plays outside his frame, showing good wrap-up technique. He plays with a tireless motor and works hard when pursuing plays from the backside.

Weaknesses: Ingram-Dawkins is a 1-year starter with less than ideal experience. He's struggled with repeated injury issues during his first three seasons and missed a lot of game time. As a pass rusher, Ingram-Dawkins can often rush very upright, limiting his ability to play leveraged. He consistently fails to show ideal amounts of flexibility or bend to challenge as a rusher. Ingram-Dawkins is a 1-trick pony as a rusher, relying solely on his power profile. He lacks any counter plan if he's initially occupied. Not an overly explosive rusher and will likely be limited to a 2-down role at the next level.

> **Best Fit: Nose Tackle or 3-4 DE**

Player Ranking (1-100): 77.7 - Ingram-Dawkins has a bright future ahead of him, and he's only 21 years old. While he lacks elite athleticism and the ability to be a consistent presence as a pass rusher, he's an impressive contributor in the run game. He can thrive in several defense roles and should appeal to most defenses. 3rd round player.

18. DeMonte Capehart - Clemson - 6'5 315 lbs

Strengths: A 5th year senior for the Tigers, Capehart took over as a significant contributor during his redshirt sophomore campaign in 2022. Capehart is a massive player, displaying rare strength and power throughout his long-levered frame. Capehart has experience playing all over the interior of the Tigers' defensive line, showing schematic versatility for the next level. Capehart shows a good initial burst out of his stance in the passing game. Long arms and a powerful lower body enable him to win inside hand placement to control blockers, putting them on skates and being capable of closing the pocket when playing with leveraged pads. In the running game, Capehart is a dominant interior force. Impressive lower body power and core strength allow him to handle 2-gap assignments, rarely getting uprooted from his spot. Keeps his head on a swivel at all times, showing good processing abilities while being highly aware when the ball carrier is. Strong and powerful hands allow him to displace blockers, constantly stacking and shedding in pursuit. Capable of clearing pathways to running backs, showing rare physical strength and power when in pursuit. Plays with impressive leverage in the running game, making him an immovable force for interior blockers, fully capable of sustaining combo blocks.

Weaknesses: Capehart has been mostly a rotational player for the Tigers in each of the last three seasons, rarely staying on the field for an entire series. Capehart's overall production as a pass rusher has been modest at best, failing to offer little in the pass rush department. Their hand technique and pass-rush arsenal will need to be developed so that he can assist in anything other than early downs for a team. Capehart flashes good leverage at times but constantly allows his pads to rise as a bull rusher, limiting his ability to collapse the pocket consistently.

> **Best Fit: Nose Tackle in a 4-3 or 3-4**

Player Ranking (1-100): 76.2 - Capehart is a physically imposing and incredibly powerful man with outstanding success in the running game. While he's likely limited to a 2-down player at the next level, he can majorly impact early downs. 3rd round player.

19. Yahya Black - Iowa - 6'5 315 lbs

Strengths: Black, a 5th-year senior for the Hawkeyes, has been a 2-year starter who has excelled in various alignments for the Hawkeyes' defensive front. Comfortable playing as a 0-technique nose tackle or kicking to the 1, 2, 3, or 4-technique. His versatility allows him to be systematically and schematically versatile for any NFL defense. Black is a massively built man with incredible size and length, making him a difficult assignment for interior blockers. As a rusher, Black can completely collapse the pocket with speed-to-power, putting blockers on skates and pushing them backward. His powerful upper body and heavy hands are capable of completely disarming blockers. Understands how to work in twists and stunts with his teammates, allowing the looper to get free releases through the 'A' and 'B' gaps. He does a terrific job of getting his hands up to disrupt the QBs vision or knock down the pass if he can't get home. Black dominates in the running game, playing with a terrific lock-out extension. Capable of 2-gapping, Black showcases outstanding ball awareness and point-of-attack power. His powerful lower body enables him to win positioning against double teams, rarely getting moved off his spot. Understands how to stack and shed blockers, keeping his off-hand clean to slow up runners. Works tirelessly in pursuit, regularly making plays from the backside or along the perimeter.

Weaknesses: While Black has shown he can occasionally contribute as a rusher, he lacks the skillset to be a regular 3-down player. His only skills as a rusher come from bull rushing, failing to have any pass-rush arsenal at his disposal other than power. Black's pad level is a continual problem due to his frame, firing out of his stance far too upright. Black was rotated in and out of games quite a bit, allowing him always to stay fresh and make some wonders about his conditioning. Movement skills and burst are OK, but they fail to threaten blockers with finesse or explosion.

Best Fit: DT in either scheme (0 or 1-technique)

Player Ranking (1-100): 75.5 - Black is an enormous man with incredible power throughout his frame. His ability to generate double teams and collapse the pocket opens up opportunities for others despite him not having stellar production. He's dominant in the running game, immediately upgrading a defense's run defense. 3rd round player.

20. Jay Toia - UCLA - 6'3 325 lbs

Strengths: As a 3-year starter for the Bruins, Toia has been a mainstay in the center of the defensive front. Built with an enormous frame, Toia has the height and girth to be a dominant interior defender. A versatile interior defensive tackle who can play all over the front and at different alignments and schemes. Not just a 'space-eater,' Toia has rare 1st step explosiveness and twitch to shoot gaps and immediately generate backfield pressure and stress interior blockers. Does an excellent job of working through narrow gaps, showing impressive core flexibility to get skinny and plug gaps. Quick and active hands allow him to keep his frame clean when working through combination blocks in the run game. Shows impressive lateral agility and change of directional abilities to flow to the ball. Good football intelligence and play recognition skills, enabling him to win positioning and leverage. Possesses a high sense of awareness of his surroundings, quickly locating and working toward the football. Can close the pocket with his bull rush, generating impressive speed-to-power to put skaters on blocks. In the running game, Toia utilizes his upper body strength and aggressiveness to control the point of attack with inside hand placement. He does a nice job of stacking and shedding in pursuit. Keeps his off-hand free when flowing to the football, slowing down runners along the perimeters.

Weaknesses: Toia is likely a 2-down player at the next level who lacks consistent production despite having the physical tools to succeed. Despite his size, Toia lacks the ideal proportional length. Fires out of his stance too high, allowing defenders to control him throughout the snap. Lacks a counter plan or any secondary quickness, getting hooked on blocks for too long. Lacks a top-end motor as he was often taken off the field on key 3rd downs and in obvious passing situations. His lower body power is average at best, and he struggles to anchor against double teams, getting moved off the ball far too easily.

> **Best Fit: DT in either scheme**

Player Ranking (1-100): 74.7 - Toia is a solid, penetrating defensive tackle that can win in various alignments. His schematic versatility allows him to be a fit for more defenses. While he lacks ideal length and didn't consistently produce in college, he has the skills to improve as a player. 4th round player.

21. Aeneas Peebles - Virginia Tech - 6'1 286 lbs

Strengths: Peeble was initially recruited to Duke, where he played for four seasons before transferring over to Virginia Tech for his final season. Peebles has produced solid for four straight campaigns, showing consistency, experience, and sturdiness to stay on the field. Peebles is an alignment versatile interior defender, lining up all over the defensive front for both Duke and Virginia Tech. Built with a low center of gravity frame with excellent frame density and compactness. He's at his best when he can be a 1-gap penetrator, as he has terrific get-off and twitch. He combines his 1st step quickness with good snap anticipation to immediately threaten guards and center upon snap of the ball. His advanced hand tactics and usage enable him to shed quickly, bringing a varied power pass-rush arsenal. Peebles utilizes his natural leverage advantage to control the point of attack, regularly winning as a bull rusher and is capable of collapsing the pocket. Peebles isn't a stiff athlete, showing the ability to succeed in slanted fronts, good lateral agility, and change of direction. In the running game, Peebles's high football IQ enables him to get a good read of developing plays, regularly maintaining good positioning and spatial sense. He routinely diagnoses plays in the backfield and shows the ability to flow to the ball. Peebles plays with a hair-on-fire mentality and urgency on every snap, working tirelessly in pursuit and on broken-down plays.

Weaknesses: While Peebles has shown the ability to 2-gap, he lacks elite anchorage strength to win positioning against double teams and combo blocks consistently. Despite having a natural leverage advantage, he sometimes allows his pads to rise mid-play and get uprooted off his spot. Peebles has great density but lacks ideal height and wingspan proportions, limiting his effectiveness or upside in playing in an odd front. Peebles relies on winning with his initial move as a rusher and lacks a counter plan if initially occupied, lacking the length to shed consistently. Limited to a power rush plan, lacking significant offerings as a finesse rusher. His limited tackle radius causes him to struggle to consistently make plays outside his frame, regularly allowing runners to run past him.

> **Best Fit: 4-3 DT (3 or 1-technique)**

Player Ranking (1-100): 74.2 - Peebles is a good 1-gap penetrator with terrific twitch. He is a solid pass rusher that should stay on the field for all three downs. He lacks ideal measurables and lower body strength to be a 2-gap player, but in a 4-3 system, he should immediately contribute to a rotation. 4th round player.

22. Simeon Barrow Jr - Miami - 6'3 290 lbs

Strengths: As a 5th-year senior for the Hurricanes, Barrow initially began his career at Michigan State for four seasons, starting in 30 games for the Spartans. Barrow has had a career of stellar production for an interior defender but had his best year with the Hurricanes in 2024, finishing with 5.5 sacks and eight tackles for loss, including one forced fumble. Barrow has experience playing up and down the defensive formation, including over the center, on the edges, and as a three and 4-technique. As a rusher, Barrow displays good initial burst and quickness out of the blocks. He combines his twitch with good snap anticipation and reactionary quickness to press the lineman immediately off the snap. He utilizes his natural leverage advantage to control blockers by getting underneath their pads, and he uses his quick and active hands to swipe away blockers. Barrow displays outstanding anticipation and instincts in the run-and-screen game, regularly sniffing out plays for negative yardage. He recognizes blocking schemes and shows advanced eye discipline. He's fantastic in the trenches with his ability to sustain positioning and anchor down. He often requires double teams and combo blocks due to his natural low center of gravity and lower body power. His motor runs HOT on every play, regularly chasing down plays from the backside. Barrow has proven to be a dynamic special teams' contributor, blocking multiple kicks during his career.

Weaknesses: Barrow lacks an ideal frame and might be limited to even fronts at the next level. He has a stubby build that lacks ideal length and height measurables while also lacking significant room for additional development. His lack of ideal measurables limits him when attempting to work on counter moves, and he fails to have the secondary quickness and length to disengage. He's reliant on winning off the snap of the ball, and if blockers can reach his frame, his ability to affect the play is generally over. He struggles when plays go away from his frame, lacking the tackle radius to close down rush lanes. He often allows runners out of his grasp if he can't reach them with his full frame.

Best Fit: 4-3 DT (1 or 3-technique)

Player Ranking (1-100): 73.0 - Barrow had a terrific year this year for the Hurricanes. While he lacks the frame and traits to be a dynamic 3-down player, he can certainly impact a defense. He's been productive in the Big Ten and ACC for four straight seasons, showing iron-man reliability and toughness. He's an absolute beast in the running game and can affect the pass in moments. 4th round player.

23. Joshua Farmer - Florida State - 6'3 318 lbs

Strengths: A 2-year starter for the Seminoles that has played a major role in the last three seasons for the defensive line. Farmer is a well-built prospect with good density and proportional length. Farmer has played all over the defensive line, having extensive experience playing at different alignments. This will give Farmer the upside of playing in multiple schemes at the next level. As a pass rusher, Farmer has shown the ability to be disruptive with three down upside for the next level. He flashes low pads off the snap of the ball, utilizing good leverage when attacking downhill. He utilizes his leverage and speed-to-power explosiveness to put blockers on skates with his bull rush. Farmer is a twitchy rusher with good get-off and movement skills off the snap of the ball. Violent upper body and diverse hand tactics give Farmer many moves to diversify his rush attack. Farmer showcases loose limbs and flexion through his lower body, enabling him to win in narrow gaps and dip his shoulder to win the outside shoulder of guards and centers. Farmer utilizes his length in the running game to lock out blockers from reaching his pads. He shows good awareness and play instincts to locate and flow towards the ball. He has the pop in his upper body to keep his frame clean through impact. Farmer has good closing speed when flowing to the football and makes a high volume of plays in pursuit.

Weaknesses: Farmer underwent surgery for his thumb at the end of the 2023 campaign. Farmer relies on winning on his initial move as a pass rusher; if he doesn't win quickly, he will sit on blocks for a long duration. He lacks a significant counter plan. While Farmer sometimes plays with great leverage, other times, he allows his pads to rise significantly. Farmer needs to continue to add functional strength through his lower body as he struggles anchoring in the run game. He's frequently blown off the ball against double teams and combo blocks, failing to sustain positioning. He can quickly abandon his gap responsibilities, leaving lanes susceptible and completely exposed.

Best Fit: 4-3 DT (3-technique)

Player Ranking (1-100): 71.7 - Farmer is best as a 1-gap penetrator who can utilize his quickness and burst to get into the backfield. His production has been very steady over the last three seasons. His ability to rush the passer will serve him as a three-down player. He needs to get better in the run game. 4th round player.

24. Saivion Jones - LSU - 6'5 280 lbs

Strengths: A significant contributor to the Tigers' defense in the last three seasons, Jones has proven ironman reliability. Capable of playing all over the defensive front, Jones shows the positional flexibility to be intriguing in both odd and even fronts. He's been used at different alignments with varying degrees of success. Jones has a prototypical power-packed frame with outstanding length and muscularity throughout the frame. His motor runs hot on every play, playing each snap like it's his last, showing outstanding energy and hustle. Jones excels in the run game with his ability to play with instincts and play recognition skills. He recognizes blocking schemes while keeping his eyes fixated on the backfield. His anchor power is good, enabling him to fight through pulls and down blocks without getting displaced. His strong upper body and hands enable him to work through blocks, showing good stack and shed abilities. He works tirelessly in pursuit, showing good recovery speed to close down plays from the backside. As a pass rusher, Jones shows a good 1st step to put tackles in recovery mode immediately. He keeps his legs churning when bull rushing, showing the ability to collapse the pocket. He uses a wide array of hand tactics to keep blockers guessing. He shows good timing on loops and stunts, regularly getting into the backfield. Jones will only be 21 years old on draft night.

Weaknesses: Despite Jones being a 2.5-year starter for the Tigers, his overall production has been mostly modest, failing to eclipse 4.5 sacks in any campaign. He's still a raw pass rusher that lacks enough tools in the arsenal. He fires high out of his stance, exposing his chest plate to blockers to win inside-hand leverage. He lacks a counter plan as a rusher if his initial plan doesn't work out, failing to utilize his hands properly. He's not a bendy athlete who can capture the edge or get underneath tackles. He's often slow to fire off the ball, lacking ideal reactionary reflexes. There is noticeable stiffness throughout his lower body, lacking flexion, and a change of directional skills. He has an interior defender frame but has mostly played on the outside in college and might be forced to kick inside at the next level.

Best Fit: 3-4 DE (4 or 5-technique) or 4-3 DT (3-technique)

Player Ranking (1-100): 71.2 - Jones is an intriguing prospect with a 'first off the bus' size. He will immediately blow teams away with his frame and length, but he fails to impressive consistently enough for me as a pass rusher. There are developmental traits, but I think he'd best be served kicking inside and playing as a 3-4 DE or 4-3 DT. 4th round player.

25. Omari Thomas - Tennessee - 6'4 325 lbs

Strengths: As a 5th-year senior for the Vols, Thomas has been a mainstay on the Tennessee defense each season, proving sturdiness and reliability. A physical specimen, Thomas has a massive frame with thick limbs, good length, and outstanding density throughout his frame. Thomas had his best season in 2024, finishing with six tackles for loss and four passes defended. Thomas is a highly experienced college football player who has played in 60 games, starting in 40. Comfortable playing in various alignments, Thomas is an interior disruptor with schematic versatility for the next level. As a rusher, Thomas displays good twitch and explosiveness off the snap. He displays good core flexibility to get skinny and squeeze between the gaps. He showcases good bend and lateral movement skills, enabling him to cross the face of blockers and win on linear pathways to the ball. Thomas uses violent hand gestures and displays good punching skills and a strong upper body to knock blockers backward. When he can't get home, Thomas commits himself to getting his hands up and knocking the ball down. Thomas works hard in the running game, eating gaps and space in the middle of the defense. He works tirelessly in pursuit and has enough athleticism to chase down runners from the backside.

Weaknesses: An older prospect who will be 24 years old early in his rookie season. Thomas has to deal with poor pad levels repeatedly in both game phases. In the passing game, Thomas completely exposes his chest plate, making it very difficult for him to get off on secondary moves. He allows the lineman to control the leverage battle, limiting his chance to win with power. He lacks the counter ability to threaten on his secondary move consistently. In the running game, Thomas's pad level causes him to get caught flat-footed while allowing pulling blockers to fit their hands easily. He struggles against double teams and combo blocks, lacking the top-end anchorage strength to maintain positioning.

Best Fit: 4-3 DT (3-technique) or 3-4 DE (4 or 5-technique)

Player Ranking (1-100): 70.2 - Thomas has the frame and the power to be successful in any defensive setup at the next level. As a former four-star high school prospect, I know there is clear talent here. He's competed against the best competition and more than held his own. While he lacks top-end talent, he should earn a nice role as an all-around interior disruptor. 4th round player.

26. Tonka Hemingway - South Carolina - 6'3 288 lbs

Strengths: As a 5th-year senior for the Gamecocks, Hemingway has been a disruptive presence for South Carolina in the last five campaigns. A sturdy and reliable presence, Hemingway has proven to have iron-man-like health, rarely missing a snap in the last five seasons. Hemingway has a long and powerful frame, possessing vines for arms and proportional size and girth. An explosive athlete, Hemingway displays good twitch and burst off the line of scrimmage, capable of getting in the backfield instantly. His experience has proven reliable, playing a wide variety of different alignments on the defense's interior. As a pass rusher, Hemingway utilizes his core strength and quickness to get skinny. His powerful upper body works tirelessly in hand fights, utilizing various pass-rush moves. He recognizes things quickly in the backfield, displaying rapid-like reflexes to sniff out zone runs and screens. When he can't get home as a rusher, Hemingway does a terrific job of getting his hands up to be disruptive to the QB's vision, with several passes defended each season. In the running game, Hemingway plays with a relentless motor. His anchor strength allows him to handle combo blocks and double teams, displaying good contact balance. He displays the quickness to beat blockers to landmarks, closing out cushions with his tackle radius. When taking on blocks, Hemingway can stack and shed in pursuit.

Weaknesses: Hemingway is an older prospect who will be 24 years old during his rookie season. While he displays good athleticism, he lacks the elite twitch and change of directional abilities to be a dynamic pass rusher at the next level. He fails to have the ideal mass and size on his frame and struggles when asked to handle 2-gap responsibilities against double teams and combo blocks. As a rusher, Hemingway relies on winning with his initial move, and he fails significant counter abilities if his initial plan is blocked. Hemingway is more of a finesse interior player and lacks the power profile to collapse the pocket. Hemingway has struggled to break down as a reliable tackler in space, frequently letting runners stay on their feet through contact. He's had issues maintaining his gap integrity in the run game, frequently ditching contain.

Best Fit: 4-3 DT (3-technique)

Player Ranking (1-100): 69.3 - Hemingway has had two seasons of 4+ sacks, which makes me think he can certainly have a role as a 1-gap penetrating defensive tackle, best equipped as a 3-technique. He has good twitch and movement skills but lacks the dominant size and power profile. 5th round player.

27. Nazir Stackhouse - Georgia - 6'3 320 lbs

Strengths: A 5-year contributor to the Bulldogs defense and 3-year starter, Stackhouse has had a solid college career with extensive experience. Stackhouse is built with a power-packed frame, capable of handling 2-gapping responsibilities at the next level. More than just a space eater, Stackhouse shows high levels of football IQ to sniff out plays post-snap. A difficult body to move, Stackhouse has a powerful frame that works relentlessly hard in all areas of the game. Never content being sustained, Stackhouse always looks for an available opening on the counter. Impressive when utilized in short-yardage situations, Stackhouse forces backs to often look for a differing opening. As a pass rusher, Stackhouse showcases his lower body drive and power to put blockers on skates and close pockets. His length, coupled with his explosive power, causes difficulties for shorter and squattier built blockers who can't win leverage. A reliable and consistent contributor, Stackhouse has been on the field almost every game since his freshman campaign.

Weaknesses: An older prospect who will be 23 years old on draft day. Stackhouse will be limited to 2-down responsibilities at the next level, failing to offer consistent pass rush in obvious passing situations. His overaggressive nature causes him to play unbalanced, often caught lunging and being knocked to his feet. Very slow reaction times lead to him frequently being the last guy on the line of scrimmage to react, always in catch-up mode after. When moving laterally, Stackhouse appears stuck in the mud, failing to redirect his frame. Doesn't always locate the ball well, gets into personal battles, and is completely taken out of the play. Throughout his time in Georgia, his production has been very minimal.

Best Fit: Nose Tackle (Can play zero or 1-Technique)

Player Ranking (1-100): 68.9 - Stackhouse is a better athlete than you'd expect for a man of his size. In the NFL of yesterday, his draft stock would be higher. However, considering his lack of production and 3-down abilities, Stackhouse will be limited to the next level. He can serve as a rotational 2-gapping DT for the right system. 5th round player.

28. Vernon Broughton - Texas - 6'4 305 lbs

Strengths: As a 5th-year senior for the Longhorns defensive front, Broughton has gotten better and better during each season. He's saved his best season for last, finishing with four sacks, five tackles for loss, and two forced fumbles in his final campaign in 2024. While Broughton was mostly used as a rotational player his first few seasons, he proved this year, along with Alfred Collins, that he could be a dominating disruptor at various alignments along the front. Broughton displays a good frame, showing proportional size and strength throughout his frame. He excels as a 1-gap penetrator, showcasing his outstanding 1st-step quickness to shoot gaps and close quickly on plays. He does a good job of playing leveraged with good flexibility and bend to get underneath center and guards. Broughton displays a wide variety of different pass rush moves, showing advanced and violent hand techniques. Broughton can generate speed-to-power on his bull rushes, particularly when lined up along the edges. If he's initially occupied, Broughton shows good counter ability with the impressive change of directional skills to offer a secondary plan as a rusher. In the running game, Broughton utilizes his size and power to anchor down and take on blocks. His length enables him to play with full extension, rarely letting blockers into his frame. His violent hands and strong upper body enable Broughton to succeed in shedding and making plays in the run game. He works tirelessly in pursuit, running several plays down from the backside. He is a reliable open-field tackler who rarely allows runners out of his grasp if he reaches them.

Weaknesses: Broughton has had one year of stellar production in 2024, failing to impress in his previous seasons with the Longhorns. While he's improved in the run game, he still has significant work. He frequently fires off the ball with high pads, enabling blockers to reach his frame. His lower body lacks the ideal anchorage power for double teams and combo blocks. He's often uprooted and moved off the ball when handling 2-gap assignments. He doesn't appear always to recognize run/pass fits at times, lacking ideal play recognition skills and instincts.

Best Fit: 4-3 DT (3-technique)

Player Ranking (1-100): 68.7 - Broughton was impressive this season for the Longhorns. He's got a great blend of size and athleticism. While he lacks significant starting experience, his upside is through the roof with continued development. He's far better as a pass rusher than a run player, but he could develop into a nice starter. 5th round player.

29. Eric Gregory - Arkansas - 6'4 320 lbs

Strengths: As a 6th-year senior for the Razorbacks, Gregory has been a mainstay for the defensive front for the last five seasons, staying on the field for four straight seasons and showing iron-man reliability. He saved his best season for last, finishing with over 40 tackles and three sacks in 2024. Gregory came onto campus as a defensive end but has bulked up to play on the inside. Gregory has shown versatility and can be used anywhere coaches ask him to play, both inside and outside. Gregory shows the flexibility to be used in any defensive setup at the next level. Gregory has active hands at the snap of the ball, showing good POP and displacement power to put blockers on skates. He works well in a 1-gap system as a gap penetrator, showing good core flexibility and initial quickness. He has a steady supply of pass-rush moves, mostly by his violent hands and powerful upper body. He moves well laterally, showing good change of direction and agility to redirect his frame. Gregory displays terrific ball awareness in the running game and always works back toward the ball carrier. He can work through blockers, stacking, and shedding to make the play. He works tirelessly in pursuit and makes plays at all levels of the field. A reliable open-field tackler that brings ball carriers down with aggression and physicality, making them feel it.

Weaknesses: An older prospect who will be 25 years old during his rookie season. Unfortunately, some of Gregory's weight is bad, slowing him down significantly. His lower body is behind in terms of strength and power. He struggles to anchor against double teams and combo blocks and frequently gets moved off his spot. His poor leverage and pad level exacerbated this lower body strength limitation. He allows blockers to frequently reach his pads, limiting his ability to maintain positioning. He needs a better attack plan when rushing the quarterback, frequently utilizing the same rush on every play despite having a good arsenal.

Best Fit: 4-3 DT (3-technique)

Player Ranking (1-100): 68.3 - Gregory has been a solid player for four seasons. If he can clean up some of his poor weight and add some of his former explosiveness back, he can contribute to a defensive line rotation. He's looked solid at times! 5th round player.

30. Rylie Mills - Notre Dame - 6'5 295 lbs

Strengths: As a 5th-year graduate student for the Irish, Mills has extensive experience and has generated significant snaps since his freshman campaign in 2020. A steady performer who has been reliable and consistent in each campaign, showing improvements on tape during each subsequent season. Mills possesses a lean and muscled-up proportioned frame with the schematic and positional flexibility to play in both 3-man- and 4-man fronts. Has moved from playing some 5-technique in an odd front early in his career to playing more two and 3-technique consistently the last couple of seasons. Mills has noticeable athleticism and twitch to his frame, allowing him to shoot gaps and be dangerous on stunts. Long strider that takes good angles to the football in pursuit and when closing on the QB. Powerful upper body with many hand tactics to attack the pocket differently. Very disciplined eyes with internal GPS that allows him to quickly locate the football and work back towards it. Acceleration and closing speed allow him to make plays along the boundaries in pursuit. A relentless motor that tires defenders out on counter moves or on broken-down plays. Keeps defenders off of his frame in the running game, playing with full extension. Can stack and shed in the running game with good upper-body power. Noticeable weight room strength is present through his lower body, allowing him to win at the point of attack and seal edges when playing along the edges. A reliable wrap-up tackler that can make plays outside of his frame. Has extensive experience on all the different special teams' units offering upside for the next level.

Weaknesses: An older prospect who will be a 24-year-old rookie. Struggles with constant leverage concerns, playing far too upright. He was far too content playing belly-to-belly and getting bounced off blocks, constantly exposing his frame. Lacks any secondary pass rush moves to offer anything on the counter. Needs to have a better pass-rush plan. Gets stuck and hangs up on blocks for long durations of play. Not an overly bendy athlete and lacks the core flexibility to win in narrow windows. Has some hip tightness when asked to redirect his frame, showing a noticeable lack of change of direction skills.

Best Fit: 4-3 DT (3-tech) or 3-4 DE (5-tech)

Player Ranking (1-100): 66.9 - Mills is an experienced and tough kid who has some enticing athleticism to match. While he doesn't always showcase his athleticism on the football field, he shows developmental upside for continued growth. His biggest challenge will be playing with leverage and keeping his pads down. 5th round player.

31. Thor Griffith - Louisville - 6'2 320 lbs

Strengths: A 3-year starter for FCS-Level Harvard University before transferring to Louisville for his final year. Griffith was dominant at Harvard, finishing with 13.5 sacks, 33.5 tackles for loss, and 132 tackles in three years. Griffith has experience playing all over the defensive formation, having experience in both three and 4-man fronts. He's played as a true NT or a 5-technique DE in a 3-man front. Griffith utilizes his natural leverage advantage to stay leveraged through the ball snap, getting under the pads of blockers. Griffith is incredibly explosive in short bursts and utilizes it in conjunction with his snap anticipation and timing to get into the backfield. He is violent in how he plays, showing good upper-body power and strength to disengage consistently. His counter ability manifests as his motor never stops working, showing his secondary ability as a rusher. Can generate speed-to-power as a rusher, getting explosive power through his legs. The very powerful lower half enables Griffith to sit on blocks in the running game, rarely getting moved off of his spot in the run game. Processes things in the backfield quickly, showing impressive ball instincts and awareness. A tough kid who plays with a relentless mean streak, staying square and in control. Has some lateral movement skills, showing the balance and agility to stay on his feet while changing directions.

Weaknesses: While Griffith wasn't bad per se at Louisville, he failed to impress against better competition. Lacks the ideal and length measurables to fit in a 3-man system and will likely be better suited in an even front system for the next level. Griffith relied on his dominant athleticism to consistently win against Ivy League schools and will need to continue to refine his pass rush arsenal to excel against better competition. He wasn't always a reliable open-field tackler and missed several plays he should have made.

Best Fit: 4-3 DT (3 or 1-Technique in a 4-3 Defense)

Player Ranking (1-100): 65.5 - Griffith is a guy you take a chance on for additional development at the next level. He has rare physical traits and LOVES football. Unfortunately, he didn't have the same impact against better competition and will likely need continued NFL refinement. But the kid is strong as an ox and has rare explosiveness. 5th round player.

32. Jermayne Lole - Texas - 6'3 315lbs

Strengths: As a 6th-year senior at Texas this past season, Lole began his career at Arizona State for three seasons before transferring to Louisville and eventually to Texas. Lole is a stout and low center-of-gravity-built interior defender who has bounced around at various alignments and spots on the inside. Lole moves with explosive quickness and twitch off the snap of the ball, immediately putting lineman under pressure to recover. He utilizes his natural advantage to get underneath the pad of blockers, which can collapse the pocket with lower-body drive. With his initial POP, Lole's outstanding upper-body strength gives him significant displacement power. He's a force that shows good agility and change of directional ability, allowing him to work up and down the line of scrimmage. His bend and flexion allow him to be effective when working as a 1-gap penetrator, frequently getting underneath the pads of centers and guards. Lole shows good patience in the running game and maintains gap discipline throughout. He's capable of shooting gaps and making plays in the backfield. He has disciplined eyes, quickly locates the ball, and works his backside in pursuit. Lole plays with a HOT motor and remains urgent on every snap.

Weaknesses: Lole has had two season-ending issues in his upper body. His last three seasons in college were significantly underwhelming after three stellar seasons at Arizona State. His stubby build limits his ability to get blockers off his frame, frequently allowing blockers to reach his pads. He struggles against longer-levered blockers that can reach him. If he doesn't win as a pass rusher with his initial move, he fails to offer a counter offering as a rusher. Lole continuously gets washed out of plays in the running game when handling double teams and combo blocks. He lacks a consistent anchor and appears to wear down in the run game.

Best Fit: 4-3 DT (3-technique)

Player Ranking (1-100): 63.7 - Lole has impressive physical attributes, but he's unfortunately too inconsistent. He has some fantastic tape in which he looks unblockable. But other times, he looks like a limited defender. His tape for the last three seasons leaves something to be desired. But there are traits here. He looked devastating at times at Arizona State. He's worth a gamble in the 6th round.

33. C.J. West - Indiana - 6'2 330 lbs

Strengths: A 4-year player and multi-year starter for MAC-Conference Program Kent State, West transferred to Indiana for his final season in 2024. West has been a steady player for four straight seasons, showing iron-man durability, and rarely misses a game throughout his career. West is a physically imposing athlete, displaying a wide and compact bowling-bowl-shaped frame. Comfortably playing on three- and 4-man fronts, West has shown versatility in positional and alignment by playing all over the interior front of defensive lines. West shows surprising athleticism and twitches off the snap of the ball. He possesses violent and powerful hands, utilizing various hand tactics to keep his frame clean while he attacks the pocket. He utilizes his natural leverage to stay underneath the pads of blockers, controlling them at the point of attack. In the running game, West shows good lateral agility and change of direction to work across the face of blockers in slanted fronts. When splitting double teams, West shows the core flexibility to get skinny by narrowly closing gaps to get into the backfield. West utilizes his violent hands to work through blocks in pursuit, showing good stack and shed abilities. He possesses a relentless motor that works hard to chase down plays in pursuit, showing good recovery speed.

Weaknesses: West's tape this year was a regression from his former levels at Kent State, proving the jump from the MAC to the Big Ten was a sizeable one for West. He is frequently late off the snap of the ball, lacking ideal reaction time and snap awareness. He struggles frequently with high pads, both in the running and passing phases of the game. In the run game, he fails to provide the anchorage ability to the point of attack power to play as a 2-gapper. He gets displaced by double teams and combo blocks. His hand usage is inconsistent, with his hands frequently being located too high and too far outside. For being a larger man, West has struggles consistently wrapping up. He's frequently an ankle swiper that misses in space. West lacks a significant power profile as a pass rusher and struggles to collapse the pocket with his bull rush.

Best Fit: 4-3 DT (1 or 3-technique)

Player Ranking (1-100): 62.4 - West has been good and just OK at times this year for Indiana. He's a noteworthy athlete for his size but lacks the point-of-attack power to be a consistent run-stuffer. He's likely best suited for a 4-3 system, which won't require a 2-gap or play in too much space. 6th round player.

34. Cam Jackson - Florida - 6'5 342 lbs

Strengths: Jackon began his career with Memphis for the first three seasons, playing a major role for their defensive front during his final two seasons there. After his third season, Jackson transferred to Florida, where he started his final two seasons for the Gators. Jackson has been a versatile chess piece for the Gators front that has played anywhere on the interior, including as a 0-technique nose tackle and a 3-technique one-gap penetrator. Jackson is a massive man with a thick frame, long arms, and a powerful lower body. Jackson utilizes his size well, especially in the running game. His size alone enables him to hold his ground and block multiple gaps, clogging running lanes for backs. He has the natural force and strength to anchor down, making it difficult for single blockers to move him off his spot. Their outstanding upper body and hand strength enable them to dominate hand battles, frequently overwhelming blockers at the point of attack. He reads the game well, staying in a good position while showing anticipation to be in a good position to make plays. He keeps his head on a swivel and locates the ball well, showing good pursuit and effort to make the play when he's away from the ball. In the passing game, Jackson does a good job of utilizing his arms to lock blockers out and utilize his leg drive to generate some pushback as a bull rusher. At times, a noteworthy lateral twitch is out of his stance, and he combines that with above-average snap anticipation. He's generally a very good and reliable tackler who can make plays outside of his frame.

Weaknesses: Jackson needs significant conditioning upgrades, and he could benefit by cleaning up some of his sloppy weight around his midsection. His frame makes it difficult to sustain effort and intensity down after down, as he was repeatedly rotated in and out of games. His production throughout college was mostly in the run game, with very few plays made behind the line of scrimmage. He is likely limited to a 2-down role at the next level as he offers little as a rusher outside of power. Despite his size, Jackson still lacks elite power, as you'd expect, and will get routinely overwhelmed against double teams and combo blocks.

Best Fit: Nose Tackle

Player Ranking (1-100): 61.0 - Jackson, at this point, is a limited 2-down player with a nice frame for continued development. If he can clean up some of his weight, he can maximize his overall upside, and it may give him more explosive qualities. 6th round player.

35. Akheem Mesidor - Miami - 6'3 280 lbs

Strengths: As a 5th-year senior, Mesidor began his career with the Mountaineers for two seasons before transferring to Miami for his final three seasons. His first year with the Hurricanes was his most impressive in 2022, where he finished with 11 tackles for loss and seven sacks. He is a versatile defensive line prospect with systematic and positionally flexibility, allowing him to play inside and outside and in various alignments to succeed. Mesidor is an athletic mover who plays with the twitch to be effective in all areas of the game, as evidenced by his high tackles-for-loss production. With great quickness out of the blocks, Mesidor utilizes his explosiveness and short-area bursts to get into the backfield quickly. His hands were violent, allowing him to shed when working towards the ball carrier, showing good upper-body strength. Recognizes things quickly in the backfield, keeping his eyes glued on the ball carrier, and works back towards it. Mesidor has some flexibility to his lower half on the edge, showing the ability to dip and bend around the edges. Commits himself to getting his hands up on plays he can't get home, disrupting the QB sight lines.

Weaknesses: An older prospect who will be 24 years old on draft day. Missed most of the 2023 season due to a foot injury. Appeared to lose some of his explosiveness following his injury, causing him to have far less production in his final season. Mesidor likely projects inside for most evaluators, but he's undersized when playing as a true DT. Power isn't a strong suit for Mesidor as he's likely only a fit in a 1-gap system where he can attack the pocket solely. While he's certainly explosive, Mesidor lacks a defined pass-rush arsenal when attacking the pocket and is overly reliant on winning with his explosiveness. He gets overwhelmed at the point of attack, failing to have the ideal lower body strength to hold the point of attack. In pursuit, Mesidor's aggressive nature causes him to take over aggressive pathways to the football.

Best Fit: 4-3 DT (3-technique) or can play as an oversized LDE

Player Ranking (1-100): 58.9 - Mesidor has some traits and has succeeded in two programs. Unfortunately, he doesn't look the same player since his foot injury. If he can return to his 2022 self, he can be a great rotational piece for a defensive setup. 7th round player.

36. Patrick Jenkins - Tulane - 6'2 305 lbs

Strengths: A former four-star recruit for TCU, Jenkins played two seasons for the Horned Frogs before transferring to Tulane for his final three seasons. Jenkins has extensive college experience, playing in nearly 60 games throughout college. Jenkins has a well-developed frame with little unnecessary weight. Jenkins had his best season in 2023 for Tulane, finishing with 12 tackles for loss and 5.5 sacks. Jenkins has shown the ability to move up and down the defensive front, playing at different alignments. Jenkins is best when used as a 1-gap penetrator, utilizing his explosive twitch and quickness off the snap of the ball. Jenkins understands how to use his natural leverage advantage to get underneath the pad level of blockers and get skinny through narrow gaps to be disruptive. Good lateral agility and bend enable Jenkins to offer secondary options as a counter-rusher if his initial move fails. Jenkins carries a good arsenal of pass-rushing moves and diverse hand tactics. When closing on a play, Jenkins flashes good explosiveness and speed to close cushions. Jenkins plays with a hot motor, urgency, and intent on every snap. In the running game, Jenkins plays with good diagnostic abilities to recognize movement in the backfield.

Weaknesses: Jenkins hasn't competed against many top-tier offensive lines, and when he did, he appeared to struggle significantly with the jump of competition. Jenkins has a bit of a stubby build and lacks the length and range to be a 2-gapper. His timing and snap anticipation can be erratic, as he's frequently a tick late off the snap of the ball. He lacks an ideal lower-body power profile and will get uprooted and blown off the ball on double teams and combo blocks. He doesn't consistently know how to utilize his hands when flowing to the ball in the game, frequently getting hooked with no recourse. Jenkins isn't always a secure tackler and often allows backs out of his grasp once he reaches them.

Best Fit: 4-3 DT (3-technique)

Player Ranking (1-100): 58.4 - Jenkins has noticeable twitch in his frame, and he's relentless as a pass rusher. He's had success for three straight seasons and has shown good reliability. He lacks the necessary strength and power in his lower body to hold up on 1st and 2nd downs, but he can be a good situational pass rusher early on. 7th round player.

37. Cam Horsley - Boston College - 6'3 306 lbs

Strengths: As a 5th-year senior for the Eagles, Horsley has played in practically every game of his college career, immediately contributing as a true freshman. The definition of reliable and sturdy is that Horsley has a power-packed frame with outstanding density and size. Horsley values teams that play in both 3 and 4-man fronts, showing schematic and alignment versatility. Horsley was frequently tasked with 2-gapping, showing his impressive point of attack power and anchorage strength. An immovable force that drops his anchor shows a relentless nature to power through and still affects the running game. His upper-body strength and active hands enable him to shed and disengage quickly. He keeps his head on a swivel and works back towards the ball carrier in pursuit. Horsley displays snap anticipation and a good initial burst off the line of scrimmage in the passing game to press lineman. His heavy hands and vice-like grip strength allow him to knock back and then control blockers initially. He also has shown an ability to close the pocket with his steady leg drive, showing impressive speed-to-power.

Weaknesses: Horsley was consistently taken off the field in passing situations, proving he has little three-down value. His pass-rushing production and plays behind the line of scrimmage have been inconsequential at best. He lacks any pass-rushing repertoire other than the repeated bullrush attempts. Once stuck on a block, he lacks the secondary quickness and countermoves to offer an alternative plan. He is a straight-line athlete with clear stiffness and range issues when playing outside his frame.

Best Fit: Nose Tackle in either scheme

Player Ranking (1-100): 57.1 - Horsley is a bull in the run game with terrific power and strength. He, unfortunately, offers little to nothing in passing situations other than an occasional bull rush that threatens. He has a nice frame, and his experience and durability are enticing traits. 7th round player.

38. Joe Evans - UTSA - 6'3 335 lbs

Strengths: A former LSU recruit who played three seasons for the Tigers before transferring to UTSA at the All-American Athletic Conference. Evans has started in the last two seasons, proving to be a reliable defensive presence in the middle of the UTSA defense. Evans has extensive experience playing in the SEC for three seasons and now in the AAC, playing excessive college football against big-time competition. A powerful man, Evans has outstanding density and strength through his frame. Evans could play in the odd front for UTSA as the nose tackle and as the four and 5-technique on the outside. His versatility will serve him well at the next level. Evans displays good get-off upon snap of the ball, showing the ability to penetrate and split double teams. He has a variety of pass-rush moves with his hands, and he has a powerful initial punch to displace linemen in the passing game. He's capable of collapsing the pocket with his bull rush, as he shows good lower body strength to drive forward. Evans is a space-eater in the running game that frequently requires double teams. He utilizes his off-hand to extend and keep blockers off his frame so he can keep his dominant hand free in the run game. A reliable open-field tackler that wraps up securely. He shows good effort and relentless urgency in pursuit, making plays routinely from the backside.

Weaknesses: An older prospect that will be 24 years old on draft weekend. Evans suffered a season-ending lower-body injury early in his final season, only playing in a handful of games. Evans is likely a 2-down player at the next level, as he's a limited pass rusher. That was evidenced by his lack of statistical production each campaign. His pass-rush variety relies on his bull rush and violent hands, but he lacks the redirect ability to win on his counter move if initially occupied. His pad level is a constant concern as he allows blockers to easily reach his pads when attacking in pass sets. While powerful, Evans lacks elite core strength and lower body anchorage power as he's frequently uprooted against combo blocks and double teams in the running game.

Best Fit: 3-4 DE (4 or 5-technique) or 4-3 DT (1-technique)

Player Ranking (1-100): 54.8 - Evans' injury and age will likely cause him to go undrafted. He's a good football player with a nice skill set but lacks 3-down ability at the next level. He will have to carve a role for a team as a 1st and 2nd down run stuffer. Undrafted free agent.

39. Tommy Akingbesote - Maryland - 6'4 316 lbs

Strengths: A 4th-year player for the Terrapins who has started games in the last three seasons. Akingbesote is a big-bodied interior defender with the athleticism and the length to be effective in different defensive setups while playing in different alignments. A former high school basketball player, Akingbesote, only began playing football as a junior in high school, proving to have a high ceiling with additional development. A quick mover, Akingbesote fires off the snap of the ball with a noticeable twitch. Can control blockers with his upper body, winning reps with his length and motor. Can reach the backfield with good north/south closing speed and snap anticipation. Works hard when working backside, proving to play with a HOT motor. Appears to recognize things quickly, showing good anticipation and play recognition skills.

Weaknesses: Akingbesote's overall ball production numbers have been modest, failing to change and alter games consistently. While he's worked hard to put on muscle the last few years, he's still a little undersized to play as a 2-gap nose tackle at the next level. The lack of an ideal power profile limits him when fighting through combo blocks and double teams, and he fails to have ideal core strength and lower body anchorage power. Plays very upright, failing to keep his pads leveraged through contact. Likely a 2-down player at the next level who fails to impact plays in the passing game. Their limited pass-rush arsenal and lateral movement skills cause him to struggle when asked to move off his spot. He has no secondary counter plan and doesn't quite know how to utilize his hands or deconstruct blockers.

Best Fit: 3-4 DE or 4-3 DT

Player Ranking (1-100): 54.3 - Akingbesote has some upside with a nice frame and impressive overall athleticism. Considering his newness to playing football, he's made great strides already, and there's reason to think his NFL game could be better than college. Undrafted free agent.

40. Jamaree Caldwell - Oregon - 6'1 325 lbs

Strengths: Caldwell has had a long road to where he is currently. He started at JUCO before transferring to Houston for two seasons before eventually ending up at Oregon for his final campaign. Caldwell came into talks in 2023 after posting nine tackles for loss and 6.5 sacks for Houston, proving to be a disruptive interior presence for them. Caldwell is a short and stout center gravity defender who utilizes his natural leverage advantage over blockers. He's moved all over defensive lines and has experience playing anywhere from 0-technique to 5-technique. Caldwell is the hard-working blue-chip prospect who wins with his consistently urgent motor and immovable frame. In the running game, Caldwell proves his ability to consistently eat up blocks, frequently requiring double teams and combo blocks. He possesses active and heavy hands combined with good linear explosiveness, enabling him to slip blocks and make plays outside his frame. He's adept at reading things in the backfield and showing good play recognition pre-snap. In the passing game, Caldwell has a good initial burst, which enables him to generate good speed-to-power to put blockers on skates.

Weaknesses: After a stellar season at Houston in 2023, Caldwell fell way off the map in 2024 with a disappointing Oregon season. The increased competition levels likely caused him some struggles. While Caldwell is good in the running game, he's more of a space eater than a disruptive run stuffer. He struggles consistently anchoring against double teams and will get uprooted. He has a bad habit of allowing his pads to rise mid-play, increasing his surface area and making him an easier target to block. He has a bit of a stubby build, lacking elite length to extend and make plays outside his frame. Caldwell is limited to a bull rush and a few limited hand tactics in the passing game. He lacks finesse or counter plans to hit attacks and will likely be a 2-down player at the next level.

Best Fit: 3-4 DE (4 or 5-technique)

Player Ranking (1-100): 54.1 - Caldwell likely would have been drafted if he came out after the 2023 season, but unfortunately, his campaign this year caused additional concerns. He will have to earn his place likely in training camp. Undrafted free agent.

Top-10 Defensive Tackles:

1. Mason Graham
2. Tyleik Williams
3. Walter Nolen
4. Kenneth Grant
5. Deone Walker
6. T.J. Sanders
7. Derrick Harmon
8. Shemar Stewart
9. Alfred Collins
10. Ty Robinson

Chapter 10

Middle Linebackers
(MIKE Linebackers in 3-4 or 4-3)

1. Danny Stutsman - Oklahoma - 6'3 229 lbs

Strengths: A 3-year starter for the Sooners as a linebacker, Stutsman has been a mainstay for their defense, exploding immediately during his first year of starting as a sophomore. In his first year starting, he finished with 125 tackles, 11 tackles for loss, three sacks, and two interceptions. A long and rangy athletically-built linebacker who displays the size to play both off or on-ball linebacker, and has played at each of the LB spots for the Sooners. A tackling machine, Stutsman utilizes his key and diagnostic ability to be in a position to make plays constantly. Length and strength allow him to make plays outside of his frame frequently. A natural football player, Stutsman plays like he loves the game in all areas. He shows tremendous instincts and physicality, bringing intensity to whatever defense he plays on. Power is manifest throughout his frame, displaying rare POP in his hands, frequently displacing blockers and putting them on their butts. A relentless motor that plays with a quick downhill trigger. He is a reliable open-field tackler that makes runners feel his hits. A very good athlete who plays with range when playing north/south or east/west. Capable of playing on an island as a MIKE linebacker or in dime packages as the only LB on the field. He is an impressive blitzer when used to attack the blocker, minimizing his surface areas when attacking both the A and B gaps. Has some bendiness to the way he rushes, capable of arcing the corner as a speed rusher. Short-area bursts and above-average long speed allow him to make up ground and close cushions quickly. A signal caller for the defense that plays the game with high intelligence, recognizing looks pre-snap while adjusting the defensive set-up.

Weaknesses: His overaggressive nature will lead to him taking some poor pursuit angles due to his quick trigger. Can be easily manipulated by play-fakes and misdirection-type runs where he will crash hard. His eyes, when triggering approach, blockers with a fearless 'blow them up' approach rather than always having a plan to stack/shed more efficiently. His height will cause him to get in trouble when approaching ball carriers, attempting to wrap up too upright, which can cause some missed tackles.

Best Fit: ILB in either scheme but can play outside as well

Player Ranking (1-100): 83.7 - I absolutely love Stutsman as a football player. He's a dynamic, reliable, and hard-nosed football player that will make any defense better and more physical. While he's not perfect as a prospect, and NFL evaluators will push him further down boards due to not elite athleticism, they are going to be making a major mistake. Watch the tape on this kid; he just makes plays. 2nd round player.

2. Chris Paul Jr - Ole Miss - 6'1 235 lbs

Strengths: Initially recruited to play for Arkansas, Paul transferred to Ole Miss following his sophomore campaign. A highly experienced starter for two big-time SEC programs, Paul has started in each of the last two seasons while playing a major role as a sophomore for Arkansas as well. Paul exploded in his final season at Ole Miss, finishing with nearly 90 tackles, 11 tackles for loss, 3.5 sacks, and 1 interception. Paul is an athletically built interior linebacker that plays with physicality and athleticism. The definition of a sideline-to-sideline football player, Paul plays with terrific range and closing speed in all phases. In the running game, Paul shows the ability to quickly diagnose and identify, shooting downhill quickly. He diagnoses blocking schemes quickly, taking on blockers with a good pad level and an urgent hair-on-fire mentality. He plays with springiness when working through blockers, sifting through space with ease. He plays with good patience and discipline in the run game, maintaining good gap integrity. He works tirelessly from the backside and makes several plays on the other side of the field from pure hustle. He is a trustworthy open-field tackler who wraps up securely while bringing his feet through contact, rarely missing an opportunity to finish a play. Paul is a natural in coverage, showing fluidity and spatial awareness. He has a natural feel for passing windows and minimizes spacing opportunities. He's always aware of the QB's eyes, keying in and maintaining sound positioning. He has the burst and anticipation to undercut underneath throws in coverage, competing at the catch point or knocking the ball away. Paul is an instinctual football player who brings energy, intelligence, and urgency to a defense.

Weaknesses: Paul lacks ideal measurables, failing to reach ideal length and weight thresholds for interior linebackers. His lack of length causes him to struggle in space when working through longer-levered blockers, failing to disengage consistently. As a rusher, Paul lacks the natural traits and the pass rush variety to offer much other than a gap shooter. He's a bit upright and stiff when attacking as a rusher, lacking bend and flexion to win in narrow gaps. As an aggressive pursuer of football, Paul can sometimes take aggressive pathways to the football, leaving him out of position. When playing in man coverage, Paul has a tendency to get caught ball-watching, causing him to bite on double moves and play-action.

Best Fit: ILB in either scheme

Player Ranking (1-100): 83.2 - Paul is an urgent and intense football player who will improve a defense. His athleticism and downhill mentality are fun to watch! He's a natural in zone coverage and displays the upside to get better in man coverage. He should instantly compete to start on the inside for both odd and even front defenses. 2nd round player.

3. Lander Barton - Utah - 6'4 236 lbs

Strengths: Barton has been a reliable and steady contributor to the Utah defense for each of the last three seasons, getting progressively better during each campaign. Built with a long-levered frame, showcasing good length and room for additional growth and muscle. Coming from a long lineage of successful athletes in his family, Barton is no exception. An instinctual and physically imposing linebacker with excessive comfort in all game phases. Has the football IQ and frame to be successful in any defensive system. An easy mover that shows the free-flowing range and closing burst to shrink the field considerably. Barton excels in coverage, routinely handling man coverage responsibilities against TEs and RBs, staying in phase with them on in-breaking routes. Barton possesses loose limbs, allowing himself to flip his hips and change directions easily, rarely needing to slow down. Barton has excellent play recognition abilities in zone coverage and an understanding of spatial concepts to minimize cushions. He understands how to utilize his hands in coverage, limiting spacing opportunities while being physical at the catch point. Impressive ball production in each of the last two seasons, with multiple interceptions. In the running game, Barton quickly attacks downhill and blows up plays in the backfield. He plays fearlessly when attacking pulling linemen, routinely blowing them up or disengaging. He knows when to be patient in moments, stay disciplined, and always remain on the ball of his feet. In pursuit, Barton's speed and closing bursts allow him to make a number of plays from the backside, playing with a relentless motor on every snap and rarely getting caught in the trash.

Weaknesses: Barton suffered a season-ending leg injury in the 2023 campaign, causing him to miss half the season. He has a longer and rangier build and could benefit by continuing to add clean muscle onto his frame, namely his lower body. Barton has some hesitations when shooting downhill in the run game in moments, causing him to be a little late to plays. Barton can get washed out of plays when linemen can get two hands on him. His aggressive nature causes him to take some poor pursuit angles at moments. Generally, he's a good tackler, but he can get a little lazy with his technique of trying to bump runners down with his shoulder. As a pass rusher, Barton is limited, failing to affect consistently when working between the 'A' and 'B' gaps. He will need to develop a larger arsenal to be successful. In coverage, Barton is prone to get caught peeking into the backfield at times, granting some separation prior to the release of the ball.

Best Fit: 4-3 MIKE or 3-4 ILB

Player Ranking (1-100): 81.4 - Barton is a good all-around football player who has been steady when he's been on the field. He's still relatively inexperienced, having been mostly a rotational player his freshman season and missing most of his sophomore campaign. He's a stellar athlete who has the frame and natural instincts to get better and better. 2nd round player.

4. Nickolas Martin - Oklahoma State - 6'0 220 lbs

Strengths: Martin exploded onto the scene in the Big 12 during his sophomore campaign in 2023, in which he finished with 140 tackles, 16 tackles for loss, six sacks, two interceptions, and one forced fumble. He appeared to be continuing where he was in 2024 before the injury. An athletically-built interior linebacker, Martin has played primarily as the MIKE linebacker in the heart of the Cowboys' defense. Martin is the definition of a heat-seeking missile who plays every snap like it's his last, showing unrelenting effort and motor. Martin utilizes his rare burst and closing speed in the running game to frequently trigger quickly. He quickly recognizes things in the backfield, looking for cues while showing reactionary reflexes to get a head start on blockers. As a pass rusher, Martin has again shown terrific upside in his ability to attack both along the edges and through 'A' and 'B' gaps. He displays rare sideline-to-sideline range, allowing him to cover acres of space, even when playing as a standalone linebacker in subpackages. His lower body explosiveness and closing speed allow him to arrive at contact both with ball carriers and blockers with power and gusto, delivering impressive pop. He is a reliable open-field tackler that makes runners feel his impact. He's handled various roles for the defense, having success wherever he's used. As a QB-spy, Martin shows impressive diagnostic abilities, timing, and lateral mobility to limit mobile QBs at all sides of the field. In coverage, Martin has handled extensive zone and even man looks. He can carry tight ends up the field in man coverage, staying attached at all levels. Martin's natural instincts, route recognition skills, and spatial awareness enable him to limit cushions in the zone.

Weaknesses: Martin missed the second half of his final season with a right knee issue. His medical will be very important at the next level. Martin is certainly "undersized" compared to most MIKE linebackers, and there will be questions as to whether he can hold up in that role at the next level. He's not a guy you want constantly taking on and deconstructing blockers in space, as he's far better playing through open space. His aggressive mentality can sometimes take a hit when he takes aggressive pursuit angles to the football, taking him out of some plays. He's mostly been a one-season wonder who has only played in one full season in his entire 4-year college career. Very reliant on his athleticism, and needs to do a better job of balancing his reactionary abilities with patience as plays develop. While he's mostly a good tackler, he has a tendency to go for the big hit or arrive a little too upright into tackle attempts.

Best Fit: Hybrid LB in any scheme

Player Ranking (1-100): 80.9 - Martin is one of this draft class's most exciting and fun players. His 2023 tape is unreal. He's all over the place. He will make a defense faster, more physical, and more versatile. His ability to play three downs and have an impact in both coverage and rushing the passer is rare. As long as his medical checks out, he should go in the 2nd round.

5. Jeffrey Bassa - Oregon - 6'2 230 lbs

Strengths: Bassa has had a stellar college career with the Ducks, immediately impressing and winning significant games as a freshman. Bassa started his career as a safety before transitioning to playing as an interior linebacker for the Ducks. A terrific athlete, Bassa shows smooth movement skills and change of direction skills to cover large chunks of grass. His former safety experience is evident in how he plays the game, excelling in the coverage areas of playing linebacker. Bassa has an advanced understanding of route concepts, spatial awareness, and route recognition and can handle both man and zone looks. Lateral twitch and speed allow Bassa even to handle man coverage assignments against slot receivers and tight ends across the field. He's aggressive through routes and shows good ball skills and timing upon the balls' delivery, frequently attacking and jumping routes. Disciplined eyes and pre-snap awareness give Bassa an edge for plays in the running game, frequently calling and adjusting before the snap of the ball. His instincts and his short-area bursts enable him to trigger and close quickly into the backfield. He shows good timing and burst when used as a blitzer on 3rd downs, frequently shooting gaps and affecting QBs' passing lanes. Bassa has proven to be a reliable special teams contributor throughout his time in college, playing on all of the coverage units.

Weaknesses: Bassa struggled in his final season due to an ankle injury that caused coaches to limit his snaps in some games. Bassa looks more like a safety than an interior linebacker in how he is built and lacks significant room for growth. He struggles to handle some of the physical components of playing inside, as he lacks an ideal point of attack strength and a wingspan. He struggles at times disengaging and stacking/shedding quickly when in pursuit, frequently getting hooked with minimal ways to disengage. His lack of anchorage strength and power through his lower body causes him to get bullied by combo blocks and double teams, frequently getting uprooted. His tackle radius is limited, and he struggles when plays run outside of his frame. He's prone to some false steps in coverage, sometimes triggering downhill on play-action plays and getting fooled by deceptive QBs.

Best Fit: ILB in either scheme

Player Ranking (1-100): 80.2 - Bassa is a good football player who has played in many games, especially big games for the Ducks the last few seasons. While I'd like to see him continue to get stronger, his coverage instincts are fantastic for an interior linebacker. He could also easily play WILL linebacker, but I think his future could be especially bright playing inside. 2nd round player.

6. Jack Kiser - Notre Dame - 6'2 231 lbs

Strengths: A 6th year senior and team captain for the Irish, Kiser has had a fantastic college career, proving to have an extensive college resume. Kiser had his best season as a senior, starting every game and finishing with 90 tackles, two sacks, and two forced fumbles. Kiser displays leadership traits in abundance as he was the heart and soul of the Irish defense in 2024. Kiser has good proportional density and length and features a well-built and compact frame. Comfortable playing both in the middle of the linebacker committee or as the chase and run weakside linebacker, Kiser has the instincts and football intelligence to do both. Kiser is a highly intelligent diagnoser that recognizes looks pre-snap. His quick trigger and reactionary quickness allow him to get downhill in a flash, beating blockers to landmarks in the run game. He displays outstanding physicality and toughness, capable of stacking and shedding in space. He's a fluid mover who is at his best when he's freely flowing to the ball, navigating through traffic, and taking acute pursuit angles to the ball carrier. He always maintains sound discipline and gap integrity, rarely being out of position. Kiser is a tackling machine that rarely lets runners out of his grasp, proving to use outstanding wrap-up technique and all of his tackle radius. Kiser has proven an effective gap shooter on passing downs, showing good timing and bursts to get into the backfield. Comfortable using different coverage schemes, Kiser has good positional sense, cover awareness, and understanding of route concepts. Kiser has extensive special teams experience and has been one of the most reliable contributors in the last few seasons.

Weaknesses: Kiser will be 25 years old as a rookie, likely limiting his longevity at the next level. His overall athleticism and range are average, and he fails to have ideal sideline-to-sideline abilities. His lower body is not as developed as his upper body, and he can struggle to play through blocks against pulling linemen. In coverage, Kiser lacks the agility, change of direction, and twitchy reflexes to minimize spacing against better athletes in man coverage. He often drifts too deep in zone looks, enabling large cushions to be found by tight ends and backs. He could benefit as a blitzer by doing a better job of disguising pre-snap, often giving away the defensive setup before the snap. Overall, he struggles when tasked with playing in too much space.

Best Fit: ILB in either scheme but can play weakside as well

Player Ranking (1-100): 77.6 - Kiser's age and ideal athleticism will cause him to get drafted lower than he should. I have no doubt Kiser will play an immediate role in defense and special teams for a team. His intelligence, toughness, and reliable tackling ability will immediately improve a defense. A high floor and low ceiling prospect. 3rd round player.

7. Kobe King - Penn State - 6'1 243 lbs

Strengths: A 2-year starter and defensive team leader, King has been the heart and soul of the Nittany Lions' defenses. A stout and physically imposing inside backer, King has good density and muscle on his frame. King exploded in his final season in 2024, finishing with 97 tackles, nine tackles for loss, and three sacks. A smart and cerebral linebacker, King excels in the running game. Quickly reading his keys and diagnosing, King gets downhill in an instant. He's a forceful thumper who brings the hammer as a tackler. King can be a chase-and-run linebacker or a stack-and-shed linebacker, showing the upper-body physicality to deconstruct when working in space. He plays with a relentless motor, showing urgency and intensity on every snap of the ball. He's quick to recognize things in the backfield, blowing up screens or running plays behind the line of scrimmage. A reliable open-field tackler that rarely misses a key stop. He's often used effectively as a QB spy, maintaining good discipline on RPOs and minimizing the damage done by mobile QBs. He displays a good trigger while taking acute angles to the ball carrier. King has improved his spatial awareness in the passing game while minimizing possible throwing lanes. He shows good agility and change of direction to stay on the hip pocket of tight ends and running backs in the flats. King is an effective blitzer who does his best work when attacking the 'A" gap, showing good timing and instincts.

Weaknesses: King lacks ideal measurements for an inside linebacker, failing to meet length thresholds. He's often too quick to jump downhill, overpursuing plays and taking himself out of the frame. He's quick to bite on eye candy in the backfield, not always recognizing play-action and misdirection-type plays. He struggles when consistently asked to play in too much space, lacking top-end range and speed. In coverage, he appears to struggle with footwork when working through transitions. While he's a good tackler, he often approaches ball carriers upright and allows them to pick up additional yardage after contact.

Best Fit: ILB in either scheme

Player Ranking (1-100): 75.9 - King should immediately be a core special teams contributor for a defense. While he lacks elite range and size, he makes up for it with heart and toughness. He is a schematically versatile prospect who should appeal to any team that wants a smart and physical thumper. 3rd round player.

8. Jay Higgins - Iowa - 6'0 232 lbs

Strengths: As a 5th-year senior and 2-year starter in the center of the Hawkeyes defense, Higgins has shown NFL characteristics when playing in the Big Ten. Higgins set the world on fire in 2023, finishing atop production numbers in the Big Ten regarding solo and assisted tackles. Higgins is the heart and soul of the Hawkeyes defense, showing incredible football IQ and instincts. Processes things quickly in the backfield, utilizing terrific anticipation and ball awareness skills to locate the football and be in the right positions to make plays. His frame manifests power as he works through blocks and maintains positioning against blockers. Stays low and leveraged through blockers, showing impressive lower-body strength to anchor against pulling blockers. Plays with a relentless motor on every snap of the ball, playing like every snap is his last. A tackling machine that cleans up plays all over the field, showing open-field reliability and wrap-up technique. Utilizes torque from his lower body to deliver big hits to unsuspecting targets. Proves to offer reliability as a cover linebacker, understanding his assignment while maintaining good zonal instincts and spacing. The defense leader was relied upon to signal call and adjust the defense. He is a terrific special teams contributor who was used heavily during his first few seasons on campus.

Weaknesses: Higgins is an undersized linebacker who fails to meet some NFL defenses' height, weight, and length thresholds. Struggles to stack and shedding in traffic, lacking the length to keep his frame clean. A limited athlete that offers OK straight-line speed but is very limited laterally to cover significant amounts of ground. Lower body tightness and lack of hip mobility cause him to struggle to flip his hips and be relied upon to handle man coverage responsibilities. The lack of quick twitch and bursts limits his ability to make plays in the backfield. Not a guy that will threaten as a blitzer due to lack of closing speed and burst.

Best Fit: ILB in any scheme and special teams

Player Ranking (1-100): 74.2 - Higgins is a limited athlete who will likely serve in a special teams role immediately for a team. While he offers the potential to assist in clear running situations, he's likely not a 3-down player at the next level. High floor but low ceiling prospect that lacks the traits for significant upside. 4th round player.

9. Jamon Dumas-Johnson - Kentucky - 6'1 235 lbs

Strengths: A 2-year starter and multi-year national champion with Georgia before transferring over to the Wildcats for his final season. Dumas-Johnson is a stout and compactly-built interior linebacker with the frame and NFL body armor to withstand playing in the same position at the next level. A 'jack of all trades,' Dumas-Johnson shows comfort and vast experience in both coverages and the running game. Natural instincts and ball-processing abilities allow him to keep his eyes glued to the backfield, showing good initial quickness to get downhill in an instant. His motor runs hot on every play, showing good pursuit. Plays with reckless abandonment and isn't afraid to lay the wood. Excellent when used as an 'A' gap blitzer with high amounts of sack totals each campaign despite playing as a middle linebacker. Dumas-Johnson shows good fundamentals and awareness skills in coverage while limiting spacing for running backs and tight ends. He always keeps his feet active, rarely getting caught flat-footed when receivers attempt to force him to change directions. In the running game, Dumas-Johnson shows aggressive physicality to fight through blocks coupled with the spatial awareness to sort through traffic, keeping his frame clean. He is a big game performer who has played some of his best games against the best competition.

Weaknesses: He missed the end of his final season with Georgia due to breaking his left forearm. The medical will be very important for Dumas-Johnson in his evaluation for the NFL scouts. Dumas-Johnson's consistently wrapping up ball carriers is far lower than you'd like to see for a middle linebacker. While he's experienced in all phases of play, Dumas-Johnson doesn't have the athleticism or natural movement skills to handle man coverage situations at the next level. Not an overly rangy linebacker who can play in acres of space and could be limited to odd front defenses or playing as an outside backer at the next level.

Best Fit: Middle LB in a 3-4 system or 4-3 SAM

Player Ranking (1-100): 73.9 - Dumas-Johnson is a good all-around football player who lacks a true elite characteristic. He likely would have lost his starting gig if he had stayed in Georgia, which is why he likely transferred to Kentucky. He will have to earn his keep on special teams and in a rotational way during his rookie campaign. 4th round player.

10. Demetrius Knight Jr - South Carolina - 6'2 245 lbs

Strengths: Knight has had a 6-year college career, beginning with four seasons with Georgia Tech. He struggled with some injuries and didn't see the field regularly until he transferred to Charlotte. He starred for Charlotte in 2023, finishing with 96 tackles, three interceptions, and six tackles for loss. He then transferred to South Carolina for his final campaign in 2024, continuing his success in the SEC with another stellar campaign. Knight is a compactly built linebacker that has good proportional length and density. A former high school QB, Knight has proven to be a versatile player throughout his time in college, playing at each linebacker spot. He's likely best suited inside as he has both the size and the physicality to excel there. The leader of the Gamecocks defense, Knight is a hardworking and physical downhill thumper. His film study enables him to read things quickly pre-snap, adjusting and altering the defense. Knight maintains good patience while he allows plays to develop in the running game. He maintains good positioning and understands when to trigger and shoot downhill. He has good upper body strength and pop in his hands to jolt blockers that come into his frame. A clean-up tackler that appears to always be there to finish the play. He can play sideline to sideline, possessing the anticipation to beat runners to the spot. His former QB experience allows him to thrive in coverage, possessing good recognition and zone instincts. He minimizes spacing cushions and can compete at the catch point.

Weaknesses: Knight is an older prospect who will be 25 years old on draft night. Questions will be asked about his lack of playtime and injuries at Georgia Tech for four seasons. Knight is a good athlete but lacks the elite twitch to succeed when playing on an island. He appears to have some lower body tightness that limits him when crossing the field and changing directions. He plays upright and fails to sink in his hips when working out of a backpedal. His pad level can cause him to struggle when approaching ball carriers, failing to wrap up securely. He's susceptible to double moves and falling victim to pre-snap motion, causing him to trigger downhill and causing him to get out of position. He flashes good physicality when playing through blockers, but at times, he is easily taken out of plays far too easily.

Best Fit: ILB in either scheme

Player Ranking (1-100): 73.0 - Knight was a good player in the SEC this year. He brings physicality, football IQ, and a blue-chip quality to the defensive side of the ball. He lacks the elite traits to be a dynamic game-changer, but he should immediately win snaps on special teams and offer a backup option at inside linebacker. 4th round player.

11. Jason Henderson - Old Dominion - 6'1 225 lbs

Strengths: A 4-year starter for the Monarchs who has set school records for tackling, proving to be one of the most prestigious tacklers in NCAA history. Henderson had his best season in 2023 with 170 tackles, including 20 tackles for loss and 4.5 sacks. Henderson is a downhill thumper that shows the natural instincts and high football IQ teams want from their linebackers. Tasked with various coverage assignments and through different defensive set-ups, Henderson hasn't looked out of place. Recognizes things quickly, showing good play recognition abilities coupled with 'shot out of a cannon' reaction times. Can blow up things in the backfield, including outside run plays of screens routinely. Has a rare knack for locating and finding the football, showing hyper-awareness. A HOT motor that plays the game with reckless abandon on every play, making plays in pursuit across the field or even vertically 20+ yards away. Despite being an undersized linebacker, Henderson certainly doesn't play like it, willing to go toe to toe against bigger ball carriers and blockers. Excellent fundamentals and wrap-up technique rarely cause him to miss a tackle. Takes acute angles in pursuit with few wasted steps. In coverage, Henderson shows an advanced understanding of route concepts while doing a nice job of competing at the catch point. A natural leader that shows toughness and heart on every snap. Has extensive special teams upside and can immediately play a role there for a team.

Weaknesses: He suffered a season-ending knee injury in the Monarch's finale of the 2023 campaign, causing his final season to be somewhat limited. His medical evaluation will be very important. Henderson lacks the ideal requisite size dimensions for an interior football player, causing many to feel he's more of an off-ball linebacker. His lack of size limits his ability to stack/shed against bigger blockers and get hooked on blocks. Not a great lateral-moving athlete, showing some stiffness when tasked with changing directions or handling man coverage duties. Quick in short bursts but isn't an overly rangy linebacker with a lack of top-end speed. Has competed against lesser competition, allowing him to post gaudy production statistics. While his pass-rush production is there, he lacks the bend or the twitchiness to be anything other than a gap-penetrating blitzer at the next level.

> **Best Fit: 3-4 ILB or 4-3 WILL**

Player Ranking (1-100): 70.3 - I like Henderson as he was the heart and soul of that Monarchs defense. I worry about his injury, but if he checks out 100%, he can immediately be a key special teams contributor for a defense. His knack for finding the football is rare, and he's certainly a guy worth having despite having some athletic/size limitations. To me, his best fits are as an inside linebacker in a 3-4 defense or kicked outside as an off-ball linebacker in a 4-3. 4th round player.

12. Eugene Asante - Auburn - 6'1 219 lbs

Strengths: As a rare 6th-year senior, Asante started his career in North Carolina before transferring to play for the Tigers in 2022. Asante exploded in 2023 for the Tigers, finishing with 86 tackles, 9 tackles for loss, and 5 sacks. Asante is a long and lean linebacker prospect who has shown the ability to be effective in all game phases. His frame shows the upside for continued growth and development. Asante is a good athlete who excels as a chase and run linebacker. In the running game, Asante utilizes his length and range to make plays from sideline to sideline. He's quick to beat blockers to spots at the 2nd level, showing good acceleration and closing bursts. A capable blitzer that has shown success attacking both the 'A' and 'B' gaps or attacking along the edges. Plays with a relentless motor, and he makes a number of plays in pursuit from the backside. In coverage, Asante shows a good understanding of zone looks with impressive zonal instincts and awareness. His length can cause challenges at the catch point for receivers, allowing him to be disruptive when the ball is in the air.

Weaknesses: After having a stellar campaign in 2023, Asante's 2024 campaign was a bit disappointing overall in terms of production and consistency. Asante missed most of his first year with Auburn after struggling with injuries. His slim frame limits him when handling some of the physical components of playing on-ball linebacker. His biggest concern is his lack of point-of-attack power. He consistently gets hung up on blocks with no exit plan, lacking the strength in his upper body to stack/shed. Asante lacks ideal processing abilities and can be slightly late in responding to things. When he's playing further away from the football, he struggles to play with sound discipline and is quick to trigger. This causes them to be baited by quarterbacks and can cause them to bite on double-moves or misdirection-type running plays.

Best Fit: ILB in any scheme

Player Ranking (1-100): 55.8 - Asante has played a lot of years in college and has extensive experience. He's going to have to earn his chances on special teams initially. I worry his lack of elite instincts, football IQ, and functional strength will limit his chances of being a contributor early on. But with development, there is a chance he can make a roster at the next level. 7th round player.

13. Shaun Dolac - Buffalo - 6'1 225 lbs

Strengths: A former walk-on, Dolac has had an impressive college career and has had to work his way up the ranks with Buffalo in the MAC Conference. Dolac's production throughout the school has been outstanding, leading many statistical categories during the last three seasons. He is a smart blue-chip prospect who excels in the mental parts of the game, utilizing his diagnostic abilities to trigger and get downhill quickly. An instinctual football player who has impressive football acumen while clearly being a film junkie, often being two steps ahead of the offense. A tackling machine that has a knack for locating the football and flowing towards it. A reliable open-field tackler that wraps up securely while laying the wood in moments. He does a nice job of flowing to the football and working through blockers, showing impressive POP with his hands to keep his frame clean. A good blitzer that works through both the 'A' and 'B' gaps with good timing and disguise ability. Plays with a relentless motor on every snap of the ball, making many plays in pursuit. Has shown cover instincts when used in various zone looks, understanding route concepts while minimizing cushions in the middle of the field.

Weaknesses: Missed most of the 2023 campaign due to an injury. Dolac hasn't competed against top-tier competition throughout college and will have a major jump at the next level. An undersized kid who lacks the frame, power, and length to be a prototypical linebacker at the next level. While he has the mental acuity to succeed, he lacks the physical intangibles that show room for substantial growth. The lack of range limits him when asked to take on assignments in both coverages and when playing in subpackages.

Best Fit: Developmental MLB in either scheme and special teams

Player Ranking (1-100): 53.6 - Dolac is a tough-nosed kid that I wouldn't bet against. While he lacks the physical traits to excite evaluators, writing him off would be a disservice after his terrific college career. This kid deserves a legitimate chance and will likely have to do it on special teams. Undrafted free agent.

Top-10 Middle Linebackers:

1. Danny Stutsman
2. Chris Paul Jr
3. Lander Barton
4. Nickolas Martin
5. Jeffrey Bassa
6. Jack Kiser
7. Kobe King
8. Jay Higgins
9. Jamon Dumas-Johnson
10. Demetrius Knight Jr

Chapter 11

Outside Linebackers
(Strong Side or Weak Side)

1. Jihaad Campbell - Alabama - 6'3 244 lbs

Strengths: A 2-year starter for the Tide, Campbell has proven to be a versatile chess piece for the Tide defense in the last two campaigns. Campbell is built with ideal proportions, providing a compact frame with excellent length. Capable of lining up at various positions, Campbell's versatility enables him to be used on the line of scrimmage or as an off-ball linebacker. A read-and-react linebacker, Campbell has proven to be a tackling machine. Displaying terrific movement skills and short-area bursts, Campbell utilizes his eyes to break, diagnose, and trigger. A former high school pass rusher, Campbell proved his ability to affect the pocket this year when attacking both the 'A' gap and when working as an edge rusher along the perimeter. His 1st step burst, and his ability to bend and capture the edge cause him to stress the outside shoulder of tackles. In the running game, Campbell shows natural instincts and sideline-to-sideline abilities to chase and pursue. A massive tackle radius enables him to flow to the ball while keeping his frame clean, shortening the field. Has extensive experience in coverage situations, including both man and zone. In the zone, Campbell displays good route instincts and a natural feel of route combinations, remaining in good positions while minimizing openings. Utilizes excellent timing and closing speed to attack the football and challenge at the catch point. Has the ability to handle some man coverage responsibilities, providing experience covering both tight ends and running backs out of the backfield. A terrific leader, Campbell has proven to be an excellent locker-room character for the entire team. He is a standout special teams contributor who has played on all the units throughout his time.

Weaknesses: Campbell is a bit of a tweener who lacks a true identity as a football player, being used all over the line of scrimmage. As a pass rusher, Campbell relies on his twitch and speed to get home, rarely altering his ability to attack the pocket. His overall play strength in the running game is just OK, as he is frequently handled by tight ends in the running game, failing to break down blockers consistently. In pursuit, Campbell's overzealous tendencies cause him to take poor pursuit angles and too many false steps, taking him out of plays. While he is generally a good tackler, he approaches ball carriers very upright and is often a drag-down tackler that allows additional yardage after contact. In coverage, there appear to be some stiffness concerns when working through transitions in man coverage, often needing to gear down when changing directions.

Best Fit: 4-3 WILL or 3-4 OLB

Player Ranking (1-100): 84.9 - Campbell is a dynamic athlete who is ALWAYS around the football. Some parts of his game need tuning up, but his athleticism and instincts will allow him to be a valuable defensive chess piece for a defensive coordinator at the next level. He has all the intangibles you want in a football player. 2nd round player.

2. Deontae Lawson - Alabama - 6'2 239 lbs

Strengths: Lawson is a former top four-star recruit who has been a team captain for the Tide. A 2-year starter that has been a major factor for the Tide defense in the last three seasons, showing improvement during each campaign. Lawson has an athletically built profile and has worked hard to gain functional mass during the last few seasons. He's played mostly on the inside for the Tide, but he will likely be projected to the outside at the next level. In the running game, Lawson displays good instincts and burst allowing him to quickly drop his trigger. He displays a good overall sideline-to-sideline range that enables him to make plays at all levels of the field. He loves playing downhill and approaches ball carriers with a thump, displaying impressive pop when attacking them head-on. He works well in space, sorting through the trash while minimizing contact with pulling linemen. He's adept at attacking the pocket as an additional rusher from the outside and when shooting gaps on the inside. He times the snap count well and minimizes surface area to be disruptive. When used in coverage, Lawson displays fluidity and anticipation. He's experienced playing both in soft zones and in man coverage. He does a good job of anticipating routes and showing good recognition abilities. He will quickly close down at the catch point, showing a good knack for knocking the ball away and being disruptive. Lawson has been Tide's vital core special teams contributor throughout the last three seasons.

Weaknesses: Lawson has struggled with a variety of injury concerns during the last three seasons, causing him to miss games in each campaign. In his final season, he suffered a bad knee injury, and his medical evaluation will be important in when he can return. Lawson can be reckless as a tackler, often going to the big hit instead of reliably wrapping up. In pursuit, he frequently takes over aggressive pathways to the football, taking himself out of plays. Lawson isn't a guy who is going to consistently play through blocks; he lacks the length and the point-of-attack strength to consistently stack/shed in space. His frame and play strength are limited to play on the inside, and he will likely be best served as an outside backer in an even front. Lawson was frequently exposed when playing in man coverage, granting significant separation against tight ends and running backs.

Best Fit: 4-3 SAM or WILL

Player Ranking (1-100): 84.4 - Lawson is a rangy athlete with sideline-to-sideline abilities. While I worry about his current injury and his ability to stay on the field, there's no denying he can help a football team. He would best be used as an off-ball linebacker in a 4-3. He can play either as a SAM or a WILL. He 100% should be used to attack the pocket on 3rd downs, as he has a knack for doing it. 2nd round player.

3. Carson Schwesinger - UCLA - 6'2 225 lbs

Strengths: As a 1-year starter and former walk-on for the Bruins, Schwesinger waited for his chance to come, and it finally came in 2024. Schwesinger played primarily as a special teams contributor and reserve linebacker his first two seasons on campus. A defensive leader, Schwesinger has impressive attributes to transition to the next level. Built with a long-levered frame, Schwesinger has good proportional length and height. While he played on the inside for the Bruins, he likely will transition to an outside linebacker role in a 4-3 defense. Schwesinger exploded in his only season starting, finishing with nearly 150 tackles, four sacks, two interceptions, and one forced fumble. Schwesinger is a smart and instinctual football player who recognizes things quickly in the backfield. His quick trigger and electric athleticism enable him to beat blockers to landmarks in the running game. A true sideline-to-sideline athlete, Schwesinger has impressive fluidity throughout his frame to flip his hips and work towards the ball. He recognizes blocking schemes and understands how to avoid and slip blocks in space. He quickly locates and anticipates post-snap, utilizing his twitchy reflexes and acceleration to trigger downhill. He is a tackling machine that utilizes all his tackle radius to extend and make plays outside his frame. A secure open-field tackler that shows good wrap-up technique. Schwesinger plays with a HOT motor and is a magnet to the football, playing with natural instincts. He shows upside as a blitzer, regularly shooting through the 'A' gap and closing quickly to affect the throw. In coverage, Schwesinger utilizes his high IQ and coverage instincts to take away leverage on underneath routes by backs and tight ends. When dropping to deeper depths, Schwesinger understands how to minimize spacing cushions while keeping his eyes glued to the QB to attack the football in the air. A top-end special teams player that immediately can be used on all coverage units.

Weaknesses: Schwesinger has only 1-year of starting experience, and in his first two seasons, he didn't see the field often. His frame is somewhat limited at the next level, as he has a high-cut torso with minimal room for additional growth. He's still ironing out the game's mental aspects, as his 100 mph nature can sometimes get him in trouble. He's quick to trigger downhill while being fooled by pre-snap and post-snap looks in the backfield, taking him out of position in coverage. His overaggressive pursuit lanes can lead to him being out of position in the run game, overrunning plays. While working in the run game, Schwesinger struggles to stack and shed against bigger blockers and will likely have to transition to a free-flowing LB role at the next level. His overall anchorage power will be challenged at the next level, as he's frequently uprooted by pulling blockers. While generally good in coverage, he's prone to getting grabby at the top of routes.

Best Fit: 4-3 WILL

Player Ranking (1-100): 84.1 - Schwesinger is a blue-chip prospect who has athletic traits to match. His work ethic and leadership qualities will be a great match at the next level. He needs more experience, and his frame is somewhat limited, but it shouldn't stop him from being a potential Day-1 starter at WILL linebacker for a 4-3 defense. 2nd round player.

4. Barrett Carter - Clemson - 6'1 220 lbs

Strengths: A 3-year starter and former five-star high school recruit for the Tigers, Carter immediately rose to stardom after a tremendous sophomore campaign in which he finished with over 70 tackles, 5.5 sacks, 2 interceptions, and 2 forced fumbles. Carter is built in the shape of a modern-day linebacker, with a lean physique that shows the frame as a 3-down player at the next level. A jack of all trades type, Carter excels at being used as a versatile chess piece for the TIgers' defense. Comfortable playing in man coverage against running backs and TEs, Carter shows ease of movement and reliability in coverage settings. A tremendous athlete, Carter displays impressive vertical and lateral range, which allows him to make plays at all levels of defense. Reactionary and quick to diagnose, Carter can immediately trigger downhill, routinely blowing up screens and plays in the backfield. High football IQ allows him to signal calls and adjust the defense, putting himself in good positions to make plays post-snap. An excellent blitzer with excellent short-area bursts, allowing him to be effective in attacking the outside as well as the interior gaps of the defense. Carter works well in space, keeping his frame clean while honing in on the ball carrier, never letting them out of his sight, even through traffic.

Weaknesses: Carter played mostly in an ILB role for the Tiger's defense and played in subpackages, but there's no denying he's substantially undersized to play that role at the next level. Lack of size and functional size will sometimes get him in trouble when handling stacking/shedding consistently, as he's far better at playing in space. He will get overwhelmed if blockers can get two hands on him. While his coverage movement skills are superb, he looks slightly out of place when handling zone situations, regularly leaving too much space. His tackling ability isn't great due to poor technique and leverage when approaching ball carriers. He regularly allows runners to gain additional yardage after contact and often needs help bringing ball carriers to the ground.

Best Fit: 4-3 OLB (WILL)

Player Ranking (1-100): 83.0 - Carter is an explosive player who will immediately be an awesome special teams contributor in addition to gaining snaps as a subpackage linebacker. I like him best when he's used on the outside, where he can freeflow to the ball. His instincts, range, and athleticism are all excellent. A very good player for the modern-day NFL. 2nd round player.

5. Smael Mondon Jr - Georgia - 6'3 225 lbs

Strengths: A former five-star high school recruit, Mondon has significantly contributed to the Bulldog's defense in the last three seasons. He's played in various roles, both on and off-ball linebacker, showing the size and athleticism to be effective in either role. Mondon is an elite athlete for the linebacker position, showing the athleticism and range to play in man coverage against slot receivers on occasion or play as a standalone dime linebacker in acres of space. Highly effective when used attacking the interior of the pocket as an A-gap blitzer, Mondon's quick-twitch and closing speed are rare. Length allows Mondon to close gaps quickly or shorten the field, regularly extending and making plays outside of his frame in both coverage and in the running game. Has fluidity in the way he moves laterally, showing good change of direction and loose limbs. High football IQ allows him to see plays before they develop, utilizing excellent read/react abilities to beat ball carriers to the action. He is a reliable wrap-up tackler who utilizes good fundamentals, refusing to let the ball carriers out of his grasp.

Weaknesses: Mondon's ceiling is huge, but he's nowhere near reaching it and is still quite raw. He's still developing into his frame, and at this point, he's undersized and could benefit from additional bulk. While his athleticism and closing bursts are terrific, he sometimes hesitates in processing, causing him to be late to the ball. He gets caught ball-watching in coverage, leaving some distance between him and his assignment. For as long as he is, he's not a guy who will frequently fight through blocks and get stuck for far too long. He's not a natural pass rusher who will consistently threaten from different alignments, failing only to make his mark as a blitzer.

Best Fit: 4-3 OLB (WILL)

Player Ranking (1-100): 81.3 - It's rare to have guys like Mondon make it too far in the draft despite being a bit raw. While Mondon has gotten better in each season, he's not quite a game-changer yet. He will likely earn his mark immediately in the NFL as a special teams player as he learns to contribute more and more on defense. I'd like to see him play as a WILL linebacker, as that'll allow him to play in space while allowing him to best use his athleticism. 2nd round player.

6. Tyreem Powell - Rutgers - 6'4 255 lbs

Strengths: A 3-year starter for the Scarlett Knights, Powell has proven to be a playmaking off-ball linebacker with impressive success against the better competition. Powell is built with a sizeable frame, almost reminiscent of a defensive end. His size and wingspan enable him to be used in a hybrid role with success in coverage, rushing the passer, and attacking in the run game. In the running game, Powell attacks gaps and plays with a downhill nature. He quickly locates ball carriers and funnels runners to the outside, maintaining good positioning and leverage. A noteworthy athlete with a nose for the ball, showing good closing speed and all-around range. He has improved each season in his ability to stack and shed in pursuit, working through contact from pulling linemen well. He moves well in pursuit, showing recovery speed and long strides to close cushions quickly. A natural pass coverage linebacker with excessive experience in both zone and man. He's capable of carrying running backs and tight ends up the field, staying in phase every step of the way. Powell maintains good spatial sense in zone drops and drops to proper depths to limit cushions. His length and pass awareness allow him to close cushions and minimize windows so that QB can fit them into congested parts of the field. Powell has a lot of experience in the various special teams' units. As a pass rusher, Powell is mostly a gap shooter who does a good job of timing the snap count and utilizing his speed to get skinny in tight windows. He is a reliable open-field tackler, utilizing his entire wingspan to make plays outside his frame.

Weaknesses: Powell had some injury concerns in high school and required two neck surgeries. He's a little bit of a tweener that lacks a true position. Some evaluators might view him as a defensive end, and others as a linebacker. He could benefit by refining his frame and adding functional strength, mostly through his upper body, to play better through blockers. He frequently plays with a high pad level in the running game, limiting his effectiveness in changing directions suddenly. In pursuit, Powell tends to take overly aggressive pathways to the football, which takes him out of plays. In coverage, Powell fails to make enough plays despite being close. He always fails to locate the ball with his back to the ball and loses track of receivers at moments.

Best Fit: 4-3 OLB (WILL)

Player Ranking (1-100): 79.4 - Powell is a jack-of-all-trades Swiss-army knife football player. He isn't great at any one thing, but he's good at everything. His athleticism and size are intriguing for flexible defensive coordinators. His upside is good with continued development. 3rd round player.

7. Shemar James - Florida - 6'1 229 lbs

Strengths: A former five-star high school prospect, James has been a mainstay of the Gator's defense in the last three seasons. James returned from his season-ending injury in 2023 to have his best season in 2024, finishing with 64 tackles, four tackles for loss, two sacks, and one interception. Possessing a lean and chiseled physique, James has good proportional length with virtually zero body fat. A former two-way athlete in high school, James' former wide receiver experience enables him to play the linebacker defense with instincts and football intelligence. Playing in the heart of the defense, James can play in acres of space, displaying terrific all-around athleticism and burst. Frequently tasked with handling full-field responsibilities, James showcases ideal anticipation, range, and lateral fluidity to play as a stand-alone linebacker. In the running game, James senses things quickly, triggering downhill with the ability to blow things up in the backfield. His closing burst is an extreme asset when attacking in the backfield, utilizing it to be a nightmare for QBs on blitzes through the 'A' and 'B' gaps. James plays with a relentless motor and works hard to chase plays down from the backside. James shows his ability to minimize spacing cushions when tasked with zone looks in coverage. He reads the game well and has good recognition skills and advanced route pattern recognition.

Weaknesses: James missed the second half of the 2023 season after needing surgery to repair his dislocated kneecap. James has only started one full season in college and lacks significant starting experience. While he played as a middle linebacker for the Gators, his lack of ideal size and bulk will likely limit him to an outside role at the next level. Lack of strength and anchorage ability cause him to struggle when playing through blocks, frequently getting stuck without any ability to deconstruct consistently. His downhill nature causes him to overpursue plays, taking him into the wrong gap and lacking proper gap discipline. As a tackler, James can be inconsistent. When he has room to operate, he can be a forceful thumper, but when he doesn't have momentum, he tends to approach ball carriers high, often requiring assistance from his teammates.

Best Fit: 4-3 WILL

Player Ranking (1-100): 78.0 - James is a highly skilled, twitchy linebacker with a massive ceiling. While he lacks ideal bulk and strength, he has outstanding athleticism and range. I think he's best suited to play on the outside, as he can more easily freely flow to the ball. 3rd round player.

8. Cody Simon - Ohio State - 6'2 235 lbs

Strengths: As a 5th-year senior, Simon has been a major part of Buckeye's defense for the last four seasons, showing outstanding durability and reliability. Simon had his best season in his final campaign, proving his upside after several seasons of being mostly a rotational player. Simon is a highly intelligent football player who has been bounced around at different linebacker positions, showing the experience of playing at MIKE, SAM, or WILL. Simon's been at his best when attacking the pocket, showing good snap anticipation and core flexibility to shoot gaps and live in the backfield. He is a natural at attacking the 'A' and 'B' gaps as a blitzer, showing impressive closing speed and burst. He has a good feel for developing plays, showing impressive anticipation and instincts in the running game. He triggers quickly, reading and diagnosing with rapid-like reflexes. A rangy athlete with more than enough athleticism and closing speed to play the full field. He is a hard-working blue-chip prospect who utilizes his urgent mentality to constantly find and locate the football. In coverage, Simon has shown the ability to handle zone drops while minimizing spacing opportunities in the middle of the field, showing smoothness and fluidity through his lower body. He is a reliable open-field tackler who can lay the wood head-on, extend it, and make plays outside his frame. A team leader who brings natural leadership and work ethic to a defense.

Weaknesses: Simon lacks the ideal frame to play as MIKE at the next level. He lacks significant muscle, and his frame is limited to additional growth. His length is less than ideal, and he struggles when having to play through blockers, frequently getting hooked with no recourse. He's mostly been a role player throughout college, and questions will be asked as to why he didn't start games earlier in his career. He's been bounced around quite a bit, lacking a truly defined role for the next level. Simon can be too quick to abandon his gap assignment, frequently triggering downhill and leaving lanes vulnerable.

Best Fit: SAM Linebacker in a 4-3 or 3-4 MIKE. Special teams' standout

Player Ranking (1-100): 77.6 - Simon had a really stellar season this past season. He proved he can carry the load and has the athleticism to succeed at the next level. While his frame is limited, his football IQ and athleticism combination should serve him well. He will immediately be a stud on special teams. 3rd round player.

9. Cody Lindenberg - Minnesota - 6'3 235 lbs

Strengths: Lindenberg is a 3-year starter for the Gophers that saved his best season for last, finishing with nearly 100 tackles and 5 tackles for loss during his final campaign. Lindenberg possesses an NFL frame, showing good length and power throughout his frame. Lindenberg is a film junkie, and it's obvious the way he plays football. He quickly recognizes pre-snap looks, enabling him to anticipate and be around the football constantly. He does a terrific job of disguising defensive looks. While Lindenberg played mostly off-ball linebacker, he has the skill set to play inside. In the running game, Lindenberg reads his keys and quickly diagnoses. His quick and aggressive trigger shows the downhill mentality to blow up plays in the backfield. His length allows him to play through blocks, keeping his frame clean as he sorts in space. A large tackle radius allows him to close perimeter rush lanes, utilizing his entire radius to make plays outside his frame. A reliable wrap-up tackler that utilizes good form and technique. He plays with sound technique and discipline, rarely being out of position or biting down hard on misdirection-type plays. Lindenberg has an impressive range and can play on an island in subpackages. He has a good understanding of zonal concepts, minimizing space and cushions against complex offensive systems. When in coverage, Lindenberg stays locked into the backfield while keeping his eyes fixated on the QB. He has natural movement skills, showing fluidity through his hips, and can turn and run with tight ends up the seams or in the flats. When taking any false steps in coverage, Lindenberg's recovery quickness allows him to work back and close ground.

Weaknesses: Missed the first seven games of the 2023 campaign with a leg injury. Lindenberg has also missed game time during the 2021 campaign. He will have some durability concerns at the next level, as he's struggled to stay healthy throughout his career. He has a tendency to take aggressive pursuit angles, leading to missed opportunities in space. While Lindenberg has shown terrific ability in zone, his man coverage skills are still in progress. He lacks the ideal change of direction movements, and when having to handle quicker running backs out of the backfield, he struggles when playing on a linear plane. He is generally good when playing through blocks, but his upright nature sometimes limits him when deconstructing against bigger pulling blockers.

Best Fit: 4-3 SAM or 3-4 MIKE

Player Ranking (1-100): 76.5 - Lindenberg is a positionally versatile linebacker that can be used at multiple different linebacker positions. He has 3-down upside with his ability to cover. His downhill and urgent mentality will serve him well. His football IQ and physicality will make his defense better if he stays healthy. 3rd round pick.

10. DeShawn Pace - Central Florida - 6'2 218 lbs

Strengths: A 3-year starter for Cincinnati before transferring to Central Florida before his final season in 2024. Pace has been impressive throughout college, showing rare positional versatility to be used as a defensive chess piece for two different teams. Built with a safety physique but a linebacker mentality, Pace has good overall toughness and physicality on his frame. Pace is a rangy athlete who shows sideline-to-sideline range and can handle full-field responsibilities. Can change directions fluidly and seamlessly without needing to gear down to flip his hips. Reads the game instinctually and without hesitation, seeing things before they develop. Plays with a relentless hair-on-fire motor, playing every snap like it's his last with full urgency. His click-and-close abilities are terrific, shooting out of a cannon to get downhill. Plays far bigger than his listed weight, showing outstanding toughness and physicality. A violent thumper in run support that makes ballcarriers feel it. Utilizes his large wingspan to shrink the field and make comfortable wrap-up tackles outside of his frame. Acceleration and closing speed allow Pace to be dynamic in pursuit as he makes plays backside. He takes good pursuit angles to the football, rarely playing undisciplined and recklessly. Physical when taking on blockers, showing the ability to take them on head-on or beat them to the action. Showcases upside as a gap shooter when attacking the pocket, showing good timing and burst off the line. Pace is at his best in coverage, showing the ability to handle zonal drops or man coverage assignments against tight ends or running backs. His length allows him to be disruptive within contact windows or at the catch point, showing natural cover instincts at the catch point to make plays on the ball. Outstanding ball production in coverage, both with passes defended and interceptions.

Weaknesses: Pace is a tweener that lacks a truly defined position. Although he plays bigger than his size indicates, he will likely struggle to handle block deconstruction regularly as an on-ball linebacker at his size, and he will need to be covered up by bigger linebackers and defensive tackles so he can flow to the football freely. Pace tends to beat receivers to the spot, often grabbing them or making contact before the balls' arrival, and he could be prone to get some defensive penalties at the next level.

Best Fit: Hybrid off-ball linebacker

Player Ranking (1-100): 73.2 - Pace is such a fun player to watch with how he can dictate the game and be around the football on practically every play. Pace can be a stud if he can get drafted by the right coaching staff that can fully utilize his skillset. He's at his best when he's freely flowing to the football. His coverage abilities are truly terrific as well. 4th round player.

11. Francisco Mauigoa - Miami - 6'3 230 lbs

Strengths: Initially recruited to Washington State, Mauigoa began his career with the Cougars for the first two seasons before transferring to Miami following the 2022 campaign. Mauigoa has been a steady starter in the heart of the Hurricanes in the last two seasons, showing outstanding production during each campaign. Mauigoa is a long and athletically built interior linebacker used to playing on all three downs. While he is on the leaner side, Mauigoa has enough bulk on his frame for continued development. An instinctual athlete, Mauigoa processes things rapidly, utilizing his instincts and reflexes to recognize looks in the backfield. He wastes no time in triggering downhill, showing impressive quickness and closing speed to blow up plays in the backfield routinely. When attacking downhill, Mauigoa shows the ability to both slip blockers or play through them, showing good upper body strength to stack/shed. Natural movement skills and change of directional ability lend themselves to a 3-down linebacker. Mauigoa is a savvy pass rusher who consistently can rush the passer from both the 'A' and 'B' gaps and along the edges. He's used effectively as a looper in key passing situations, showing good timing and instincts to get home. Mauigoa plays with a HOT motor, showing the ability to play fast but with good discipline in his assignments. He takes sound angles in pursuit, rarely taking himself out of plays. His motor and blue-chip nature allows him to make significant plays from the backside.

Weaknesses: Mauigoa is a tweener who lacks the ideal size and frame requirements to play as an on-ball linebacker at the next level, and he could benefit from additional mass being added. He can sometimes struggle with his pad level when playing in space, frequently approaching both ball carriers and blockers very upright, limiting his success in playing through contact. As a tackler, he frequently needs additional help or he grants yards after first contact. Mauigoa is quicker than he is fast and lacks the ideal range and top-end speed to handle significant man coverage responsibilities.

Best Fit: 4-3 OLB (WILL)

Player Ranking (1-100): 70.4 - Mauigoa has impressive tape in the last two seasons at Miami and his final season with Washington State. He's a tough kid with impressive instincts and football intelligence, giving him linebacker flexibility. He could excel as WILL but also play an inside role. 4th round player.

12. Oluwafemi Oladejo - UCLA - 6'3 240 lbs

Strengths: Oladejo began his career with Cal for two seasons before transferring over to play his final two seasons with UCLA. Oladejo is a hybrid defender who began mostly as an interior linebacker before transferring to playing more of a hybrid DE/off-ball linebacker this season and was responsible for several assignments in the USC system. Oladejo has a muscled-up and dense frame with proportional length. Oladejo is a natural athlete who has twitch and bursts in abundance. A smart football player who picks up things quickly and will handle whatever the coaching staff entrusted him to do. Oladejo is at his best in the running game, showing terrific anticipation and play-recognition abilities to blow up plays in the backfield. He diagnoses quickly and trusts his eyes, dropping his trigger and getting downhill. He plays with a hair-on-fire urgency and relentlessness, running 100 mph on every snap. He makes several plays from the backside in pursuit, showing good closing speed. He does a good job of flowing to the football in space, working through traffic, and finding clean pathways. When he has to work through blocks, Oladejo shows impressive POP and upper-body strength to play through and still make plays. As a pass rusher, Oladejo does his best work when shooting through the 'B' gap, showing good timing and core flexibility to get skinny and effect plays in the backfield. He's been tasked to handle a number of different coverage assignments, but he is at his best in zone drops. He keys in on the backfield while remaining glued to the QB's eyes. He drops to proper depths and disrupts passing lanes routinely. A physical kid who loves contact and is generally a very good wrap-up tackler. A blue-chip prospect with the right mentality and hardworking nature that will continue to get better.

Weaknesses: Oladejo is very raw and is being tasked to do things that he's never done before. He was asked to attack the pocket significantly this season, and while he showed glimpses, he needs significant developmental work. His hand usage and pass rush plan are severely lacking as he will need additional development. He's an upright rusher with high pads, limiting his effectiveness as a bull rusher. He routinely allows blockers to reach his frame, as he lacks top-end length and consistent leverage. He is not an overly bendable athlete with elasticity and flexion, as he appears to have some stiffness when playing on linear pathways.

Best Fit: 4-3 SAM or 3-4 OLB

Player Ranking (1-100): 66.8 - Oladejo is still incredibly raw, but he flashes significant physical attributes. As he gains experience playing in all phases, he will improve. I like him best as an off-ball SAM linebacker. He's good at taking on blocks and can assist the pass rush department with key passing downs. 5th round player.

13. Khari Coleman - Ole Miss - 6'2 224 lbs

Strengths: Coleman began his career at TCU for three seasons before transferring to the Rebels and playing his final three campaigns in the SEC for Ole Miss. Coleman is a hybrid football player who initially began his career playing mostly as an outside edge rusher before playing more of a role-diverse linebacker for the Rebels. His best skill is his versatility, proving to be effective in many phases, such as rushing the passer and in coverage. Despite Coleman's undersized frame, he maximizes it with physical play, playing far bigger than his listed size. As a rusher, Coleman shows good twitch and burst off the edges, bending underneath the outside shoulder of tackles and having success as a speed rusher. When playing from depth, Coleman shows the ranginess and the downhill ability to trigger to shrink the field. He often beats blockers to the action at the 2nd level, taking acute diagnostic angles to the football to make the play. He plays with a 'hair on fire' urgency, showing good closing speed to make plays at all levels of the field. His natural instincts and anticipation allow him to find and locate the football, always being spotted around the ball. In coverage, Coleman shows ease of movement and natural coverage skills. He displays good instincts and spatial awareness to minimize cushions when in zone. He reads the quarterback's eyes in the backfield and makes plays on the ball. He's shown the ability to handle running backs and tight ends in man coverage assignments at moments as well.

Weaknesses: Coleman had his best season in his first season at Ole Miss and has gradually regressed in the two subsequent seasons. He's mostly been a rotational player throughout college who will come on the field in clear passing situations, rarely playing down after down. Coleman has a tweener build, lacking the ideal functional strength and size to play as a true linebacker. He lacks a true identity as a football player and will likely need to be drafted by a defensive mind that has a specific role in mind. In the running game, Coleman is more of an 'avoid' player than someone who will consistently take on blocks. He tends to be a drag-down tackler who relies on grabbing and pulling down rather than utilizing proper wrap-up fundamentals. His urgency and downhill mentality can sometimes be reckless, often crashing down hard and biting on RPOs and play-action plays. In coverage, Coleman's lack of size and wingspan limits him when lined up against bigger TEs who can easily box him out at the catch point.

Best Fit: Developmental WILL Linebacker in a 4-3 system and special teams

Player Ranking (1-100): 60.3 - Coleman shows athletic traits, but he's still a major work in progress despite 5 years of college football. He needs a defined role at the next level to continue refining the necessary traits to play there. His best attributes are in coverage and when rushing the passer. 6th round player.

Top-10 Outside Linebackers:

1. Jihaad Campbell
2. Deontae Lawson
3. Carson Schwesinger
4. Barrett Carter
5. Smael Mondon Jr
6. Tyreem Powell
7. Shemar James

8. Cody Simon
9. Cody Lindenberg
10. DeShawn Pace

Chapter 12

Cornerbacks

1. Travis Hunter Jr - Colorado - 6'1 185 lbs

Strengths: A former five-star and number-one high school prospect in the country, Hunter began his career at Jackson State, playing for two seasons in the FCS before transferring to Colorado and playing his final two seasons. One of the best two-way athletes we've ever seen in college football, offering tremendous upside as both a cornerback and a wide receiver. Hunter has a long, lean physique and more than enough room on his frame for additional clean muscle. As a corner, Hunter is silky smooth. Comfortable handling inside and outside duties, Hunter gets in the face of receivers mirroring their everyone movement while playing with supreme confidence. Rare fluidity and transitional quickness allow him to stay in the hip pocket of receivers, rarely giving them an inch of space. Have never seen a defensive back cover lateral routes, nor is Hunter capable of handling receivers on an island. Possesses stellar footwork out of his backpedal and then easily flips his hips with little need to gear down. Plays corner like a receiver with the ball in the air, showing rare ball skills and hip-point ability to time the balls' arrival to perfection. Eye discipline and route awareness allow him to see things developing quickly. A physical and willing tackle who will blow up screens or run in the backfield. As a receiver, Hunter is dynamic when playing both as a 'Z' and in the slot. Plays with suddenness and route deception, keeping cornerbacks guessing at every step. He is a very comfortable hands' catcher who easily extends and makes plays away from his frame. Body control allows him to adjust and contort his body to adjust to badly thrown balls. Dynamic change of directional abilities with the ball in his hands, rarely allowing the 1st defender to get two hands on him. Alters his route tempo and speeds at various points of his stem, showcasing the secondary gear to create spacing at the top of his routes. His incredible conditioning and stamina have allowed him to play 120+ snaps per game throughout college.

Weaknesses: As a corner, Hunter is a baiter who plays the position like a gambler, daring QBs to throw in his direction. Most times, it works effectively, but there are times when it bites him. His thin frame causes him to struggle to bring ball carriers down 1v1 at moments, often being more of a drag-down tackler against bigger backs. He could benefit by adding additional muscle to his frame to handle better and more possession-style receivers that can reach or box him out at the catch point. Tends to get a bit grabby in coverage when panicked. Would like to see him break down blockers better when in space, tending to get hung up on blocks for far too long. As a receiver, he lacks the jamming technique and upper-body strength within contact windows and will struggle being asked to play on the line of scrimmage against bigger defensive backs. He may be forced to play mostly one position at the next level.

Best Fit: Dynamic two-way player who should get significant snaps at both CB and WR

Player Ranking (1-100): 93.7 - One of my favorite players I've ever evaluated, Hunter is dynamic at both corner and receiver. I could see people thinking his upside is better at one position or another, but it's like splitting hairs. If I had to say, I'd likely say he's SLIGHTLY better as a corner. Even with that being said, he should still get reps at both positions. This kid will completely change a team. Top-3 pick.

2. Will Johnson - Michigan - 6'2 202 lbs

Strengths: As a highly experienced and decorated national champion, Wolverines coaches entrusted Johnson with a varied and heavy workload for defense in the last few seasons as the starter. Often tasked with shutting down the opposing team's number receiver, Johnson has the comfort and alpha mentality to be a top-tier NFL corner. Built with prototypical boundary corner height, weight, and length, Johnson can match up athletically and size-wise with the bigger NFL possession receivers. Comfortable in any defensive alignment, Johnson is experienced in press-man, off-man, and zone corner, as coaches often ask him to play differently in different games. While he played mostly as a boundary corner, Johnson would kick inside as well. Johnson is a rare athlete for his size, displaying both fluid lateral movement to mirror in space and long speed to handle speedsters on vertical planes. He is a technician in how he plays, proving to have advanced technique and footwork through his backpedal. As a cover corner, he challenges receivers at every level of the route with his hands and physicality. Johnson gets right in the face of receivers when playing in press to disrupt and re-route with physicality and violent hands. When further away from the ball, Johnson utilizes his route recognition skills to diagnose and trigger, timing the ball's arrival perfectly to swipe at the receiver's hands at precisely the right moment. Displays excellent instincts and spatial awareness, limiting zone cushions and possible openings at all levels. Sees things quickly with a lightning processor, showing tremendous click and close abilities. Former high school receiving prowess is evident in how he attacks the football down the field, proving to have success to high point and easily track the ball. Plays with urgency and a HOT motor, rarely giving up on plays while proving to be a terrific teammate to make plays in pursuit. Has good timing and natural instincts as a slot blitzer, proving to get home and frequently disrupt the QB's vision.

Weaknesses: The main concern with Johnson is his overaggressive nature, leading to almost all of his problems. He has a bad habit of grabbing when panicked, getting several poor defensive penalties. His overagggression in coverage will sometimes bait him into triggering on double moves and play-action as he always attempts to make a play on the ball. He doesn't always get his head turned down the field in coverage and prefers playing with his back to the ball to minimize spacing cushions. While violent and willing in run support, he often approaches ball carriers upright, causing him to bounce off tackle attempts or lead to unnecessary additional yardage after contact.

Best Fit: Starting Boundary Corner in any scheme

Player Ranking (1-100): 85.6 - Johnson is an experienced and NFL-ready corner with the size thresholds and athleticism to succeed at the next level. While I'd like to see him improve in run support while reducing his penalties, he's a good corner. I don't think he has elite traits, but he should be a solid starter for years to come. 1st round player.

3. Jahdae Barron - Texas - 5'11 194 lbs

Strengths: As a 5th-year senior for the Longhorns, Barron began generating significant amounts of snaps as a sophomore before transitioning to the full-time starter on defense in 2022 as a junior. Barron is the definition of versatile, having played the STAR position for the Longhorns' defense, getting moved all over the defensive front. Despite his smaller physique, Barron excels wherever he's moved to and plays with a relentless physicality, bringing urgency to every snap. Even when the Longhorns' defense struggled early in his career, Barron still showed up and battled. A former track athlete, Barron's explosiveness and quick twitch allow him to beat receivers and backs to the spot routinely. High football IQ and reactionary abilities enable Barron to see plays developing before they even develop. Rare key and diagnostic abilities are present, in addition to exceptional instincts. Excels in zone coverage looks, showing exceptional route and play awareness to trigger downhill and limit spacing. Has the comfort of playing in the box closer to the line of scrimmage, playing through blockers with toughness. Movement skills and loose limbs allow him to handle nickel coverage opportunities, showing elastic flexibility when asked to flip his hips and change direction. Will attack routes at the top with physicality and impressive timing, competing at the catch point. His motor and anticipatory skills allow him to deliver big hits to ball carriers, catching unsuspected receivers off guard. Loves assisting in run support, playing with tenacity and the never-say-die mentality to play through blocks and escape block attempts.

Weaknesses: Barron has the aggression and physicality in run support, but he can take over aggressive pathways to the football. This causes him to take some poor angles, allowing unnecessary additional yardage. It also causes him to miss some tackles due to always attempting to take the big hit. He's a bit undersized and will struggle against longer targets that can box him out at the catch point. Gets a little jittery when the ball is in the air when he's in coverage, often grabbing receivers at the top of routes. Lacks a truly defined position, as he's bounced all over the defensive front for Texas.

Best Fit: Versatile Corner who can play safety as well

Player Ranking (1-100): 85.0 - It's hard not to love Barron as a prospect. He's been the heart and soul of the Texas defense the last couple of seasons, and he's done so much for them. He brings so much intensity and the love of football to the game you can't help but love watching him play. 1st round player.

4. Shavon Revel Jr - East Carolina - 6'3 193 lbs

Strengths: Revel Jr transferred to East Carolina from Louisburg College before the 2022 season. For East Carolina, he only started one full season in 2023, in which he exploded, finishing with 12 pass breakups in addition to being a major special teams contributor, blocking two kicks. The first thing that stands out with Revel is his frame, which displays vines for arms and excellent height, allowing him to match up against the biggest of NFL targets. Revel has experience playing press, off-man, and in some zone looks but excels the most in press. A former track athlete in high school, Revel is a very good straight-line athlete, showing the ability to stay in phase with receivers constantly on vertical routes. Even if Revel is initially beaten, his recovery speed is exceptional, allowing him to recover quickly and challenge at the catch point. Revel challenges essentially everything, making every throw in his direction a dogfight for receivers, as evidenced by his 12-pass breakups. For being the top player on his defense, teams threw at him a lot, allowing him to be tested, which showcased his ability. Not a tall and stiff athlete, Revel can easily move laterally, showing fluidity throughout his lower half when changing directions. Plays far more physically than you'd expect; Revel plays with fearlessness and a downhill nature when attacking in the run game. He plays with terrific pursuit, never giving up on plays and regularly making plays backside. Has showcased some impressive abilities to be used as a blitzer, showing good timing and instincts when used.

Weaknesses: Unfortunately, Revel tore his ACL early in his final season and is only playing in a few games this year for the Pirates. His rehabilitation will likely go into the early parts of his rookie season next year and could impair him early on for a team. Rose to stardom quickly and only had 1 season of starting experience and could be labeled a 1-season wonder. Long and lean physique that could benefit by adding some additional muscle onto his frame. Would like to see him finish a few more interception opportunities, failing to hang on to several opportunities he had securely. He can sometimes get too handsy at the catch point, and it will get called at the next level. Has a bad habit of not always getting his head turned down the field, limiting his opportunities to make plays on the ball.

Best Fit: Starting CB

Player Ranking (1-100): 84.7 - If Revel proves he's fully healthy again, I could see teams taking him early. Considering how quickly he rose to stardom and his lack of experience against top-tier competition, I have some concerns. His frame and athleticism are incredibly enticing for NFL evaluators, and I think he will experience some growing pains early on at the next level. I'd feel comfortable taking him in the 2nd round.

5. Denzel Burke - Ohio State - 6'0 189 lbs

Strengths: A rare 4-year starter, Burke took over one of the Buckeyes starting spots immediately as a true freshman. Built with NFL size and length, Burke has the prototypical frame to play in any defensive setup at the next level. Burke has displayed consistent production and reliability for the Buckeyes all 4 seasons of his campaign, seemingly getting better each year. A twitchy-built corner, Burke displays the fluidity and short-area bursts to excel in coverage and the running game. Burke quickly sees things and uses his eyes and instincts to explode to the ball, closing gaps quickly. Burke shows sticky coverage skills, and ease of lateral mobility allows him to minimize spacing opportunities for targets. Recovery quickness allows him to quickly close cushions with his hands inside the contact windows if he misses. Forces QBs to make extremely tight window throws if attempting to throw against him. High football IQ allows him to recognize route concepts, showing good awareness and anticipation at all points of the stem. He is very comfortable in various coverage schemes but appears most confident in press man, where he can utilize his length and agility to limit spacing. Impressive ball skills that will challenge receivers in the air and red-zone situations.

Weaknesses: In the running game, Burke routinely plays too high, approaching ball carriers too upright, failing to wrap up securely. A little bit of a gambler in coverage that attempts to make the big play, sometimes whiffing on the ball, causing big plays behind him. Will sometimes completely miss with his hands inside the contact windows, allowing some spacing opportunity off the snap of the ball. Can struggle at times against larger targets that can reach him or outmuscle him in contested situations. Quicker than fast, Burke lacks the elite long speed in straight-line situations when playing on an island. He doesn't always get his head turned when his back is towards the ball, which will lead to some PI calls at the next level.

Best Fit: Starting Boundary Corner in any scheme

Player Ranking (1-100): 84.0 - Burke will be a good starting CB at the next level. While I don't think he's an elite corner due to his questionable tackling skills and lack of top-tier speed, he will be an immediate starter. His vast starting experience playing for a big program will be incredibly helpful for him. He rarely made a bad mistake for the Buckeyes in 4 years of starting. 2nd round player.

6. Benjamin Morrison - Notre Dame - 6'0 190 lbs

Strengths: Morrison, a team campaign for the Fighting Irish, has been a starter for the last three seasons since his true freshman campaign. A decorated college football player, Morrison is highly experienced and developed for the college level, showing NFL readiness. Morrison instantly atop Division I leaders as a true freshman, finishing with six interceptions. A versatile defender, Morrison has shown comfort in playing both outside and inside while also having comfort in different defensive looks. He's at his best in off-man coverage, where he can utilize his terrific short-area quickness and disciplined eyes to win positioning and stay attached to the hip pocket of opposing receivers. A very good natural cover corner that stays in control and balanced throughout routes. Impressive read and reaction skills allow him to jump quickly on the ball, quickly closing down and making plays underneath. High IQ and route recognition allow him to showcase his down-the-field awareness and ball skills, as evidenced by his impressive ball production numbers. Has a good feel for developing routes and seeing things quickly. Attacks and tracks the ball downfield like a wide receiver, showing high-point ability. Good timing and physicality at the catch point, timing the balls' arrival well to make plays. A willing run support corner despite being smaller, showing physicality and 'want' when it comes to getting downhill and making a big tackle.

Weaknesses: Morrison struggles when handling press duties against bigger receivers due to a lack of elite strength, size, or length, often getting bullied on the line of scrimmage and giving up too much ground. Has some issues in transitions, especially when receivers challenge him laterally, appearing to have some hip tightness when asked to change directions. He has good speed but is not a great speedster, and he will struggle to make up ground if he initially grants any. Has a bad habit of grabbing when panicked, often getting overly physical down the field, leading to penalties. His overaggressive nature sometimes leads to him peaking into the backfield, granting separation behind him.

Best Fit: Starting Boundary Corner

Player Ranking (1-100): 83.1 - I like Morrison as an off-man or zone cover corner. He has natural ball skills and is highly experienced against some current NFL receivers. While he lacks 'elite' traits, he can compete to be an immediate starter for a team. 2nd round player.

7. Trey Amos - Ole Miss - 6'1 197 lbs

Strengths: He began his career in Louisiana for three seasons, where he played for three seasons before transferring to Alabama, where he played in a rotational role. Then, finally, he switched to Ole Miss for his final season of eligibility, where he won a starting job. Amos saved his best season for last, where he got a chance to shine against top-tier competition, finishing with the best all-around production. Amos is a long and rangy prospect with the height and wingspan to disrupt receivers at all levels. Comfortable playing in press-man, as well as off-man and in zone looks. Amos challenges receivers when in press at the line of scrimmage, disrupting route timing and limiting their ability to release effectively. Maximizes contact windows, roughing up undersized receivers with confidence. When playing off or in the zone, Amos shows good route recognition skills to shoot downhill quickly when attacking the ball. A smooth and fluid mover, Amos maintains good positioning through routes while staying in phase with receivers. His excellent ball skills, awareness, and body control allow him to challenge himself at the catch point constantly. Reads receiver cues down the field to time the balls' arrival to perfection. An alpha dog that plays with self-assured confidence to challenge receivers at all levels. Aggressive and physical in run support and on screens, frequently blowing them up in the backfield. Has the traits to be a good blitzing cornerback, showing impressive timing and short-area bursts to get into the backfield.

Weaknesses: An older prospect who will be 23 years old on draft day. Amos is a gambler, and this causes him to bite on double moves or get caught ball-watching and leaving major spacing behind him down the field at moments. Amos can be overly physical at the top of routes, often grabbing at the top. A good athlete, but Amos doesn't appear to have top-end long speed or ideal change of direction skills. He will grant some separation on lateral in-breaking routes due to hip tightness and upright playing nature. While physical in run support, Amos frequently approaches upright and is more of a drag-down tackler than someone who approaches with good tackling fundamentals.

Best Fit: Press-man Boundary Corner

Player Ranking (1-100): 82.2 - Amos was impressive at Ole Miss this year, showing the ability to be a reliable starter. He had moments at Alabama but, unfortunately, played mostly in a rotational way. Amos has a great mix of ball skills, physicality, and size. I like the confidence and swagger he plays with. He has a chance to earn a major role immediately as a rookie. 2nd round player.

8. Maxwell Hairston - Kentucky - 6'1 186 lbs

Strengths: Hairston was a 2-year starter for the Wildcats, and he immediately showcased his ability as a starter in 2023, finishing atop the SEC with five interceptions and two returned for touchdowns. Hairston is a long, rangy corner with good measurables and room on his frame for additional growth. Comfortable handling different scheme looks, Hairston has extensive experience in both zone and man looks. A high-IQ football player, Hairston excels at reading and diagnosing pre and post-snap. Hairson can recognize route concepts in the zone, allowing him to precisely read his keys, diagnose, and trigger downhill immediately. His natural ball skills and reactionary quickness allow him to constantly be disruptive at the catch point, timing the ball's arrival to perfection. He utilizes his length to be disruptive through contact windows and throughout the stem of receivers. In press coverage, Hairston shows fluidity and natural flexibility to allow him to mix and match receivers on vertical and lateral routes. He stays aggressive throughout routes while remaining opportunistic and staying glued to the QB's eyes. Terrific short-area quickness and recovery abilities allow him to close any ground quickly. In the running game, Hairston stays aggressive while working downhill and is willing to sacrifice his body to deliver big hits. Has shown impressive upside when used as a blitzer off the edge, showing good timing and burst to affect the play.

Weaknesses: Hairston is only a 2-year starter and is still learning and growing. He has some technique work that needs refinement, most of it when playing press-man. He has a bad habit of getting caught flat-footed and opening up his hips on shorter routes, granting easy leverage to receivers. He will need to clean up some of his footwork when working out of his backpedal, taking too many wasted steps. His lack of size and power can cause him to struggle against bigger-possession receivers who can box him out at the catch point. Has had some penalty concerns throughout college. Quicker than he is fast, Hairston will get challenged vertically against better athletes who have him for speed. His eye discipline in coverage isn't always great, as he can be baited for discerning quarterbacks, which can get him triggering downhill on double moves and play-action. Lacks of power and strength limit him in the run game, as he cannot fight through blockers, easily getting uprooted off his position. Can struggle to break down as a tackler in open-field situations.

Best Fit: Boundary Corner in Zone or Off-Man Scheme

Player Ranking (1-100): 81.0 - Hairston is a natural playmaker with many big plays in the last two years. He has natural instincts and is always around the football. He will have some growing pains, but he will have some terrific moments as well. 2nd round player.

9. Darien Porter - Iowa State - 6'4 185 lbs

Strengths: A former high school wide receiver, Porter has transitioned into playing corner the last few seasons for the Cyclone, starting in his last two seasons. Porter is built with an exceptional frame, showing rare height and vines for arms. A former high school track athlete, Porter has set 200- and 400 records, showing exceptional athleticism. He's been a terrific core special teams' maven during college, with several blocked punts on his resume. As a corner, Porter has shown experience playing in various coverage setups, including man, off-man, and in-zone looks. Porter most excels when playing press-man where he can utilize his length to disrupt and re-route receivers. He maintains physicality through all levels of the stem, showing good route recognition abilities as helped by his former receiver pedigree. When playing in man coverage, Porter stays in phase with receivers on vertical planes, rarely allowing separation vertically. If granting any separation, Porter's closing speed and recovery enable him to recover lost ground quickly. He has a natural feel for redirecting routes and maintaining leverage. When playing in zone or off-man, Porter shows an advanced understanding of route combinations while maintaining proper depths and following the QBs eyes at all times. His short-area click and close ability allows him to jump routes and make plays on the ball. He's a quick processor with a high motor that sees things developing quickly, blowing up screens and minimizing yards again after contact.

Weaknesses: Porter has not even started in two full seasons of college football and is still learning and developing his craft. While he's a quick study, he will need to continue to be refined in a new position. Porter needs to continue refining and maximizing functional strength and mass on his frame as he lacks much bulk and body armor, limiting his ability in the running game. He lacks physicality and aggressiveness when taking on blockers, showing hesitancy at times, likely due to his thinner physique. Porter plays better against bigger receivers than shorter ones, as he struggles against shifty receivers that can cause him to lose leverage and expose his hip tightness when forcing him to play on lateral planes. He can sometimes get caught ball-watching in the backfield and grant separation against double moves. He has a bad habit of getting grabby when beaten in coverage and needs to balance the right amount of physicality in coverage.

Best Fit: Outside press-man corner and special teams

Player Ranking (1-100): 79.9 - Porter is a versatile, do-everything football player with a massive ceiling. He's not quite as refined yet as you'd hope, but he has the potential to be a stellar top-tier corner in the right system. His combination of size, length, and speed is highly coveted. 3rd round player.

10. Jason Marshall Jr - Florida - 6'0 200 lbs

Strengths: A former five-star high school prospect who took over as a starting cornerback for the Gators during his freshman campaign, not looking back for the last four seasons. Marshall looks like the part with a great NFL frame, displaying the ideal height and length for an NFL boundary corner. Marshall has the experience to play in different types of defensive setups, looking comfortable in both off-man and press-man. Marshall is a read-and-react athlete with good recognition abilities and twitchiness to close cushions fast. Has the physicality and length you like to see for a college player, regularly manning up against larger targets and competing for everything. Has high amounts of passes defended each campaign, showing terrific awareness and strong hands to perfect the balls' arrival. Excellent in contested situations, understanding how to play physically at all levels of a route without getting called for penalties. Looks in control on every snap of the ball, matching receivers stride for stride and allowing limited movement in both vertical and lateral settings. Has very good patience and discipline, rarely getting caught on double moves or in play-action settings. Has the alpha dog mentality you like to see in corners, regularly matching up against the team's top offensive player.

Weaknesses: Despite Marshall's physicality in coverage, his lack of physicality is evident in the running game, which he doesn't always appear interested in. He gets stuck on blocks, failing to shed and make plays in pursuit. He also utilizes poor wrap-up technique, often needing assistance bringing ball carriers to the ground due to his upright nature in approaching ball carriers. A good athlete, but Marshall isn't a top-tier vertical athlete and will struggle against the speedsters at the next level who can challenge him vertically. Despite getting his hands on many balls throughout college, he misses too many opportunities to intercept the ball, dropping some easy opportunities.

Best Fit: Starting Boundary Corner

Player Ranking (1-100): 79.5 - Marshall is a good outside corner who utilizes his length and size to be a constant menace for opposing receivers. He makes receivers fight and battle for every catch and shows the size thresholds that NFL evaluators like to see in corners to match up against possession receivers at the next level. 3rd round player.

11. Domani Jackson - Alabama - 6'1 190 lbs

Strengths: A former 5-star USC recruit who stayed with the Trojans for two seasons before transferring to Alabama and playing his final season with the Tide. Possessing prototypical NFL corner size and length to play along the boundaries, Jackson has additional room on his frame for more muscle. Jackson is a rare athlete for the cornerback position, showing outstanding speed and transitional quickness to mirror the best of them. A track athlete in high school, Jackson set state records in the 100 meters. Comfortable playing in off-man, zone, and press-man, Jackson is versatile and comfortable in any defensive system. Jackson is smooth throughout his backpedal and transitions, as he stays attached to the hip pocket of opposing receivers. Can flip his hips without gearing down when challenged on linear planes. Sees things quickly, showing impressive short-area quickness and click-and-close ability to make plays on the ball. A technically sound defender that stays patient, in control, and balanced throughout the duration of a play. He was rarely challenged vertically due to his speed, and when he was, he rarely allowed an inch. Repeatedly was used as a blitzer, showing good timing and burst to affect the throw. He is a physical and willing run support player who shows a quick trigger and isn't afraid to put his body on the line to make a big hit.

Weaknesses: He has had some durability issues in college and high school, including a bad knee injury in high school. His overall production was minimal throughout college, failing to showcase the ball skills or playmaking abilities he did in high school. In coverage, Jackson gets caught on his heels against quicker receivers who will challenge him underneath, repeatedly giving up inside leverage. He shows willingness to run support but fails to disengage and get off blocks when working towards the ball carrier.

Best Fit: Off-man or Zone Corner

Player Ranking (1-100): 79.3 - The skies are the limit for Jackson as a football player, as he has the athleticism and size to match up against any next-level receiving target. While he hasn't made as many plays in college as you'd think, considering his make-up, he shows the traits for continued refinement. He had his best season during his final campaign at Alabama. As long as he checks out OK medically, he should be a 3rd round player.

12. Zy Alexander - LSU - 6'2 194 lbs

Strengths: Alexander transferred to LSU after playing three seasons for Southeastern Louisiana in the FCS. Alexander has proven to be a shutdown corner for the Tigers in the last two seasons. Alexander is built with a long-levered frame, including good overall length and size. He has room on his frame for additional growth. Adept and comfortable playing various coverage schemes, including off-man, man, and zone coverage. Alexander is at his best when playing in man coverage on the boundary, utilizing his silky smooth movement skills to mirror down the field. Alexander has natural movement skills, including change of direction and agility. He stays in the hip pocket of receivers throughout, rarely granting separation. He's disruptive with his long arms through the stems of receivers and plays through receivers' hands at the catch point. He's perfectly comfortable with his back to the ball on deeper routes and maintains good positioning. He utilizes good anticipation and timing to time the balls' arrival to perfection. Alexander showcases good cover awareness, football IQ, and ball-tracking skills in zone and off-man looks. He's had multiple interceptions every college season and even led the FCS in one campaign. His click-and-close abilities enable him to jump routes and close cushions quickly. He maximizes his frame with physicality in the run game, proving to have a downhill nature. He's a reliable tackler who will sacrifice his frame to stay square against bigger backs.

Weaknesses: Alexander tore his ACL during the 2023 season, causing him to miss the last few games of the regular season. He also misses some game time in his final campaign with a concussion. He hasn't played a full college football season since playing for Southeastern Louisiana. In man coverage, Alexander keeps his back towards, not always playing the ball. He can be overly aggressive in zone looks and attempt to jump routes that are out of his reach, allowing big plays from behind. He doesn't appear as comfortable in zone and can allow big cushions. He's mostly a reliable tackler, but he can sometimes resort to back technique when he jumps at ankles. He's still a bit thin and needs to grow and develop his frame more. In press coverage, Alexander can be a little too soft with his jam technique and giving up free releases. He lacks top-end deep speed and can be challenging on vertical routes, lacking recovery abilities.

Best Fit: Boundary outside corner

Player Ranking (1-100): 78.8 - Alexander has shown shutdown potential as an outside corner. While he lacks elite physical attributes, he's smart and possesses natural coverage ability. I worry about his ability to stay healthy consistently, but he's been very good for LSU during the last two seasons. 3rd round player.

13. Ra'Mello Dotson - Kansas - 6'1 176 lbs

Strengths: As a 5th-year senior and 4-year starter for the Jayhawks, Dotson is a highly experienced corner player with major success in the Big-12 in the last 4 years. Dotson is a ball magnet, showing incredible ball production during the last four seasons. Dotson plays primarily as a boundary corner outside, generally on the defense's left side. He's most comfortable in zone and off-man looks, preferring to play further away from the football while facing the action. Dotson is impressive in size and has vines for arms, allowing himself to stay physical within contact windows and at the catch point. Utilizes good leverage technique with the sidelines, utilizing body positioning to shrink the field. His large wingspan makes it difficult for receivers to outmuscle him at the catch point due to his frequently timing the balls' arrival to perfection. Has excellent read and react skills, enabling him to utilize his short-area quickness to close quickly on the ball. Has a knack for reading routes and understanding route concepts, often beating receivers to the spot and winning the ball. His natural ball skills allow him to compete frequently and high-point the football down the field. Stays in control throughout the play, playing on the balls of his feet and willing to get downhill quickly. Willing and instinctual in run support, showing good awareness to find and locate the football and work towards it quickly.

Weaknesses: While long and rangy, he lacks ideal girth and muscle on his frame and could use additional bulk. Lack of size and body armor causes him to make some business decisions in run support, often ankle biting and failing to wrap up securely. Struggles in press situations or when playing with his back to the football, giving up sizeable cushions and failing to utilize proper jam technique. He is better in short spaces than vertical settings and will struggle on double moves or guys who can challenge him up the field. Gets caught ball-watching due to frequently attempting to jump routes. When asked to flip his hips and work out of his backpedal, he shows some stiffness through his lower half.

Best Fit: Developmental Zone Corner

Player Ranking (1-100): 78.6 - Dotson has some impressive traits, notably his ball skills. His experience and length could make him a valuable player for a team looking for a heavy zone-look defensive front. He should 100% improve his physicality and functional strength to be an every-down player. 3rd round player.

14. Azareyeh'h Thomas - Florida State - 6'2 198 lbs

Strengths: Thomas, a 1-year starter for the Seminoles, had a stellar season playing mostly on the boundary for the Florida State defense. Thomas is built with terrific overall size, impressive height, and vines for arms. Thomas is adept and experienced playing in press-man, off-man, and further back in zone looks. When in press-man, Thomas utilizes his length to be disruptive within contact windows, re-routing and messing up receiver timing. He's got smooth and fluid footwork that enables him to work in and out of breaks while staying on the hip pocket of receivers. He always remains patient and on the balls of his feet while minimizing spacing opportunities. When playing off-man and zone, Thomas keeps his eyes fixated on the QB's eyes while displaying good instincts and spatial awareness. He displays impressive eye discipline and quickly recognizes developing plays to trigger down and close. His reactionary quickness and closing burst enable him to contest and fight for things at the catch point, showing good timing and ball skills. On down-the-field routes, Thomas displays impressive body control and adjusts his body to make plays on the ball. He rarely is fooled by double moves or play-action type plays. A willing participant in the run game that shows toughness and aggression to trigger and blow up plays. An impressive blitzer that has been used repeatedly to time the snap count to get in the backfield, regularly affecting the throw. A highly experienced special teams contributor with extensive experience in various units.

Weaknesses: Thomas is a 1-year starter who fails to have expensive experience, which sometimes shows. Thomas is willing to play the running game but struggles to disengage from stalk blocks. When he approaches ball carriers, he attacks them upright and attempts to drag them down by their upper body. He's not a reliable open-field tackler. Thomas is a good athlete but lacks elite foot quickness and will grant separation against receivers that can get him playing on linear planes. He lacks elite hip mobility and change of direction skills against the savvier route runners. He gets his hands on many balls but fails to turn them into turnovers, with only two interceptions during his three seasons combined.

Best Fit: Outside press-man boundary corner

Player Ranking (1-100): 78.1 - Thomas is a versatile defender who has played all the different corner spots and is playing safely at times. He's a natural cover corner with great size that has some rawness to his overall game, but he's got terrific upside. He rarely allows separation but must refine some of his techniques and gain experience. 3rd round player.

15. Jacob Parrish - Kansas State - 5'10 198 lbs

Strengths: A 2-year starter for the Wildcats, Parrish had his breakout year in 2023, in which he finished with four interceptions and nine passes defended. Parris, a starter on the boundary, has the experience to play any of the corner spots, both inside and outside. While he played mostly in man coverage situations, Parris also shows versatility and the upside of playing in zone and off-man situations. Parris is a fluid and smooth moving corner that easily moves in and out of transitions. In man coverage, he stays attached to the hip pocket of receivers while barely allowing them an inch throughout their stems. He maintains physicality and aggressiveness at every phase, understanding what he can and cannot get away with. He plays with hyper-aggressiveness and a fiery demeanor, seemingly daring QBs to throw in his direction. He has lightning-quick feet with little wasted motion throughout his backpedal, and he's perfectly comfortable playing on an island. If he grants any separation, Parris has the recovery quickness to regain lost steps. Parris uses his key and diagnostic abilities and advanced processing abilities to recognize looks quickly when playing in zone. He has advanced spatial awareness, which allows him to minimize spacing cushions. He plays with instincts and lightning-quick reflexes that allow him to click close, and break on routes in a flash. In the running game, Parris shows good willingness and a quick trigger that allows him to find the football quickly. He's known to break up screens and underneath routes, identifying post-snap looks quickly. A willing and physical tackler who utilizes good wrap-up abilities.

Weaknesses: Parris has obvious size concerns that will likely limit him at the next level, possibly pushing him to strictly nickel duties. He struggles with bigger receivers who can dominate him at the catch point, utilizing their frames to box him out. Parris is quicker than he is fast and could struggle against elite vertical receivers at the next level. When in man coverage, Parris can be caught peeking into the backfield, making him susceptible to double moves and play-action. He tends to get too grabby at the top of routes, although he got away with it mostly in college. In the running game, Parris will get swallowed up by bigger bodies that can reach him at the next level. He lacks the upper-body strength to disengage and play through contact consistently.

Best Fit: Nickel corner and special teams

Player Ranking (1-100): 77.9 - Parris is a really good all-around cover corner that, unfortunately, has size restrictions. He's got a knack for big plays and finding the football. His versatility in playing in different defensive systems should bode well. He should immediately be a top-notch special teams contributor while adding some defensive snaps early on. 3rd round player.

16. Dorian Strong - Virginia Tech - 6'1 185 lbs

Strengths: A 5th-year senior for the Hokies, Strong has significant experience, starting games as a true freshman in 2020. Strong had his best season in 2023 after returning from his injury, finishing with three interceptions and eight passes defended. Strong has experience in various coverage looks but is at his best when playing in press-man as a boundary corner. A natural cover guy, Strong possesses both the fluidity and the transitional quickness to minimize spacing at all levels of routes. Above-average change of direction with very few wasted steps when crossing the field. Excellent ball awareness and instincts enable Strong to beat receivers to set points, closing on plays quickly and utilizing excellent timing and strong hands to disrupt at the catch point. Strong quickly closes down and makes plays on the ball if granting any separation down the field.

Has the click/close and the route recognition skills to be used in zone coverage looks, minimizing spatial cushions. Tracks the ball down the field like a receiver, showing flexible body control and strong hands to win in contested situations. Stays under control at all times, rarely panicking or getting handsy down the field. Plays bigger than his size indicate utilizing his long arms to play through the hands of receivers on contested catches. He has improved each season as a corner, improving his weak points. Will compete for everything, showing the alpha mentality and the self-confidence to handle 1v1 assignments on an island.

Weaknesses: He suffered a season-ending hand injury in 2022, causing him to miss most of the season. Quick than he is fast, Strong appears to lack top-end speed and will grant some separation on vertical routes. While he has above-average length, Strong is very slim and his size limits his ability to play physical. This causes him to struggle against bigger possessions receivers that can outmuscle him through various points of their stem, most noticeably at the top. Very passive and hesitant in run support, lacking the necessary physicality and willingness to assist. He is either an ankle biter, jumping at the feet or receivers, or he attempts to drag down from the top, allowing additional yardage after contact.

Best Fit: Outside Boundary Corner, Ideally in a Press-Man System

Player Ranking (1-100): 77.3 - Strong is a highly experienced, natural cover guy with impressive movement skills. The concern with Strong will be his size and physicality translating to the next level. He is a complete liability in run support at this point. If he can improve with coaching, he can be a starter at the next level. 3rd round player.

17. Jabbar Muhammad - Oregon - 5'10 183 lbs

Strengths: Muhammad is a 5th-year senior who has played for three different programs: Oklahoma State, Washington, and finally, Oregon. He had his best season in 2023 with Washington, where he finished with nearly 50 tackles, five tackles for loss, two sacks, three interceptions, and a conference-leading 16 passes defended. Muhammad has extensive experience playing in various looks and defensive setups. Muhammad has the most success in playing off-man and zone, where he can utilize his route recognition skills to remain on the balls of his feet and close down quickly. Comfortable playing both inside and outside, Muhammad plays bigger than his size. He's a highly intelligent and instinctual cover guy who recognizes things quickly, displaying tremendous quick and close as evidenced by the amount of passes he breaks up. He always remains patient through the receiver route, remaining in the hip pocket of opposing receivers. Noteworthy ball skills and tracking abilities to high point and attack the ball precisely at the right moment. Has both the short area bursts and the lateral movement skills to mirror on in-breaking routes. Fearless and physical in run support, remaining hyper-aware while quickly triggering downhill. An impressive blitzer that can time the snap count while disguising to reach home or significantly affect the throw.

Weaknesses: Muhammad has significant size and length limitations that could force him to be limited to a nickel corner only at the next level. Lack of length and size causes him to struggle against bigger possession receivers that can box him out at the catch point. While Muhammad is quick, he struggles against speedier receivers that can challenge him vertically, lacking elite long speed. His lack of size and upright nature in run support causes him to bounce off runners in moments, failing to wrap up securely. He struggles to play with his back to the ball and will grant separation due to frequently getting caught peeking into the backfield. Doesn't always play disciplined and can be baited by QBs into falling for play-action and double moves.

Best Fit: Nickel corner

Player Ranking (1-100): 76.0 - Muhammad is a sticky corner who makes plays wherever he's lined up. He's limited size-wise, but there's no denying he's a playmaker. He should be able to fight for snaps immediately for a defense, and I wouldn't hesitate to use him occasionally on the outside. 3rd round player.

18. O'Donnell Fortune - South Carolina - 6'1 185 lbs

Strengths: Fortune is a 2-year starter for the Gamecocks who has played a major role in the defense during the last three seasons. Fortune is a long and rangy athlete with terrific all-around movement skills and length to be disruptive. While he has some experience in press-man, Fortune plays the bulk of his snaps as a boundary corner in an off-man system. A smooth and agile mover, Fortune stays balanced and patient through route stems. He eases in and out of transitions with quick feet and a fluid backpedal. He remains hyper-alert and on the balls of his feet, waiting for the precise moment to attack. His short-area quickness and closing ability are fantastic. He regularly challenges and makes plays on the ball. If he grants a reception, he's there immediately for minimal damage. Fortune has proven to have natural ball skills and is a real ball hawk when the ball is in the air, as evidenced by his seven interceptions, and high passes defended the last three seasons. He tracks the ball seamlessly, showing innate timing and anticipation. He plays with an attacker's mindset and shows calmness and patience, never panicking when the ball is released. He displays short-area quickness and the long speed to challenge receivers vertically while granting little separation. He plays with an alpha dog mentality and self-assured confidence on every snap of the ball. He's proven to be a reliable and effective blitzer from the outside, showing great burst and timing. He diagnoses things quickly in the backfield and will drop his trigger, showing twitchy reflexes.

Weaknesses: Fortune is lanky, and his lack of bulk and functional strength limits him significantly when playing against bigger receivers. He's frequently bullied at the catch point against receivers who can utilize their frame to box him out. In the running game and tackling department, Fortune has sometimes proven to be a liability. He struggles to disengage from physical stalk blockers. He regularly takes overly aggressive angles in pursuit, taking him out of plays. And when he makes contact with bigger ball carriers, he often needs assistance to finish the job. In coverage, Fortune can sometimes get baited by QBs in their ability to utilize play-fakes and double moves to catch him biting down.

Best Fit: Boundary corner

Player Ranking (1-100): 75.6 - Fortune is a smooth, fluid mover with natural ball skills. He needs to get significantly stronger to get on the field. But I was impressed watching his footwork and reactionary movement skills. He is already a solid cover corner with the frame to develop continually. 3rd round player.

19. Cobee Bryant - Kansas - 6'0 175 lbs

Strengths: A significant contributor since his freshman campaign, Bryant has had a stellar college career, appearing to love the brightest lights in the biggest moments for the Jayhawks defense. Bryant is a long and rangy-built corner with the experience to handle inside and outside duties. His ball production has been outstanding during his college career, with multiple interceptions every season of his career, as well as multiple return touchdowns. A natural-born playmaker, Bryant is comfortable in press-man or zone, showing he can succeed further away from the football. Bryant utilizes his diagnostic abilities to flow towards the football in zone, showing excellent play recognition abilities and instincts. Bryant is a smooth mover that plays on the balls of his feet at all times, quickly recognizing looks and triggers downhill to click and close. In press coverage, Bryant is confident to get in receivers' faces to re-route them and disrupt them at the line of scrimmage. He utilizes his length throughout the stem of receivers, showing good physicality at the top of routes to disrupt the timing of the ball. He's excellent down the field, showing the ability to locate and track, regularly making plays in the air. A willing assister in the running game, Bryant shows fearlessness in taking on backs in the hole or chasing them down from the backside. Bryant has extensive experience on special teams, offering upside on several units.

Weaknesses: Bryant is very thin and can cause some struggles against bigger possession-style receivers that can outmuscle him at the line of scrimmage or the top of routes. He could benefit by adding more strength and weight onto his frame to better assist in the running game. He fails to fight through blocks, regularly getting hooked without the ability to disengage. The worry is that gaining too much weight could slow him down further, and he already lacks top-end speed to challenge receivers up vertical planes. His overaggressive nature causes him to take some poor pursuit lanes. Bryant is best in straight lines and has lower body stiffness when playing laterally, needing to gear down when he needs to flip his hips.

Best Fit: Developmental corner

Player Ranking (1-100): 74.9 - I like Bryant and think he has developmental upside. He's a big-time playmaker with natural instincts to find and locate the football. While he needs continued development regarding his frame, I think he has traits that should work in his favor with the right coaching. 4th round player.

20. Thaddeus Dixon - Washington - 6'1 187 lbs

Strengths: A former JUCO prospect, Dixon has been a starter for the Huskies defense in the last two seasons. While playing mostly as a boundary corner, Dixon also has some experience kicking inside and playing in the slot. Dixon is a long and rangy corner with vines for arms, allowing him to succeed against bigger next-level possession-based receivers. Comfortable in various coverage setups, Dixon played mostly in press-man at Washington but has shown the ability to play in a Cover-3 zone system and off-man. Dixon is disruptive and violent off the line of scrimmage, loving to get in the face of receivers and disrupt them at the line of scrimmage. He maintains physicality throughout routes, understanding what he can and cannot get away. He has the vertical speed to stay in stride with receivers who attempt to run deep routes, recovering quickly if he loses any ground. Dixon has surprising hip mobility and agility when working laterally, minimizing spacing opportunities against shallower routes. When in zone or off-man coverage, Dixon displays eye discipline and cover awareness to maintain positioning and stay on the balls of his feet at all times. He times the balls' arrival to perfection, utilizing his length to knock balls away and play through receivers' hands.

He tracks the ball effortlessly down the field, showing body control and natural ball skills. In the running game, Dixon shows good aggressiveness and willingness to assist.

Weaknesses: When in press, Dixon can sometimes miss with his jam technique, allowing easy releases. He tends to get grabby at all levels of route stems, and while he got away with it quite a bit in college, he could have a harder time at the next level. Dixon is a wiry-built corner and could benefit by adding more mass to his frame. While willing in the run game, Dixon has difficulty playing through blockers in pursuit. He lacks the upper-body strength to stack and shed consistently. In man coverage, Dixon takes some false steps out of his backpedal, getting caught flat-footed in transition. He has some noticeable stiffness concerns through his ankles and lower body, limiting his change of directional abilities.

> **Best Fit: Cover-3 corner or Press-man corner**

Player Ranking (1-100): 74.7 - Dixon has had some really good tape the last two seasons. While he hasn't gotten a lot of recognition, there's a player here. He has the size, athleticism, and natural coverage instincts. He'd be perfect for a team that played in a prominent cover-3 system. 4th round player.

21. Will Lee III - Texas A&M - 6'3 190 lbs

Strengths: Lee started his college career at Iowa Western Community College for two seasons before transferring to Kansas State for one season and, eventually, his final year with the Aggies. Lee has extensive starting experience, starting all 4 seasons of his college career, showing good durability and reliability. Built with a terrific frame, possessing vines for arms and more than enough room for additional mass. Lee has experience playing at every receiver spot, inside and outside. He's also highly experienced playing in press-man, off-man, and zone looks. Lee utilizes his length to be disruptive when in press-man situations, showing the ability to re-route. He maximizes physicality within contact windows and through receiver stems. He's a fluid mover who works in and out of his backpedal with quick feet and impressive hip flexibility. He stays on the hip pocket of receivers, showing good balance and discipline on double moves to remain in a good position. His length and quickness allow him to disrupt lateral and in-breaking routes. His click and close abilities are highlighted when playing in zone or off-man, showing timing and anticipation to time the balls' arrival to perfection. Lee possesses natural ball skills and tracking abilities, as evidenced by his multiple interceptions each campaign and high passes defended every season. Lee is impressive in the running game, showing good competitive toughness and aggressiveness and quickly triggering down. He utilizes his length to work through blockers and to close down his side of the field. He's a reliable open-field tackler who maximizes his tackle radius on every snap, ripping at the ball as he brings ball carriers down.

Weaknesses: Lee can be overly physical at the top of routes, frequently getting grabby and called for PIs. While he has a good frame, Lee is still lanky and could benefit by maximizing his frame with additional mass. He lacks top-end speed and will grant separation on vertical routes against better athletes. Lee is a gambler when playing in off-man and zone coverage, attempting to jump routes and sometimes granting too many cushions. He lacks ideal spatial awareness and instincts when playing in zone, leaving large gaps of spacing by him. He had several plays in which he could have finished with interceptions this past year, but he failed to capitalize on them. While mostly smooth, his tall and upright frame can struggle and transition issues against smaller and quicker receivers.

Best Fit: Press-man corner

Player Ranking (1-100): 74.1 - Lee was stellar for the Aggies this season. He's a natural ball hawk with good man coverage skills, terrific length, and good physicality at every level. His reliability in tackling situations will bode well for him to have an instant impact on special teams. 4th round player.

22. Quincy Riley - Louisville - 6'0 195 lbs

Strengths: A 6th-year senior for the Tigers, he initially began his career at Middle Tennessee State before transferring to Louisville to play his final two seasons, which he started for the Tigers. A highly experienced defensive back who has played in various defensive setups while handling both inside and outside duties. Teams often relied upon Riley to move upon the opposing team's number-one receiver to shadow them. Riley is a long and rangy built corner that has the vines for arms to be disruptive at all levels. Riley's length and aggressive nature allow him to disrupt and alter route tempo and timing when handling press responsibilities. He moves fluidly laterally, showing an impressive change of directional abilities to mirror in space. A former track athlete who can stay with the best NFL athletes up the field. Riley's instincts and ball skills are on full display as a zone corner or when playing off-man, as evidenced by his terrific ball production numbers in each campaign. Showing terrific route anticipation and recognition skills with an advanced understanding of route concepts, Riley reads things quickly and often beats receivers to the action. His mental processing skills, in combination with his rapid reflexes, allow him to trigger downhill quickly, showing excellent short-area quickness and burst. His large radius allows him to fight for everything at the catch point, showing innate timing to disrupt at the catch point and time the balls' arrival. A physical football player who shows aggressiveness and willingness in run support. Has extensive special teams upside and was a return specialist in high school.

Weaknesses: An older prospect who will be 24 years old a few weeks after the NFL draft. He's slightly undersized and could use additional muscle and girth onto his frame to better hold up against possession-based receivers. While willing to support, he frequently gets hung up on blocks for too long, lacking any counter plan. When working out of his backpedal, footwork can sometimes be clunky, wasting too many steps and struggling to flip his hips. Sometimes will get too aggressive down the field in coverage, often getting grabby at the top of routes or outside contact windows.

Best Fit: Versatile corner

Player Ranking (1-100): 73.6 - Riley could be one of the steals of the draft. Has the athleticism, experience, and length to be a nice player at the next level. While he needs to show he can consistently succeed against better levels of competition, he certainly has the traits and the ball skills. 4th round player.

23. Jermari Harris - Iowa - 6'0 185 lbs

Strengths: Harris is a 5th-year senior for the Hawkeyes that has started since midway through the 2021 campaign. He immediately became a success as a starter, finishing the 2021 campaign with 34 tackles and four interceptions. Despite missing a full season for injury, Harris showed no ill effects, coming back strong in 2023. Harris has the ideal frame to play as a boundary corner at the next level, showing prototypical height and length. He possesses the frame to handle the more physical NFL 'X' receivers. While experienced in various coverage setups, Harris is at his best as a press man. When in press, Harris is a frequent disruptor for receivers. He turns every rep into a physical battle, getting the better of receivers both at the line of scrimmage and down the field. Harris is very comfortable playing with his back to the ball. Harris shows impressive ball skills and tracking abilities to make plays on the ball, as evidenced by his high pass scores defended each campaign. Click and close quickness is a strength for Harris, as he can minimize openings in a flash. His experience is present in his style of play, showing excellent veteran-like savvy in how he finds and maintains positioning throughout the stem. Harris is tough and willing to trigger downhill and wrap-up ball carriers in the running game.

Weaknesses: They suffered a season-ending injury, causing Harris to miss the 2022 season. Then, he was suspended for two games due to sports wagering. Will be a 25-year-old rookie. Harris is likely limited to playing on the outside in defenses that play heavy man defense as he lacks the processing abilities and instincts to play facing the action. Harris isn't a great straight-line speed athlete and will struggle against the speedy NFL receivers who will challenge him vertically. Can get a bit grabby against better athletes, attempting to minimize their separation. Lacks separation quickness against nuanced route-runners that can get him turned inside out. While willing in run support, Harris lacks the point-of-attack strength and toughness to go through blocks.

Best Fit: Potential Starting CB

Player Ranking (1-100): 72.9 - Harris is a good football player who isn't great in any one attribute. He will have to showcase his abilities in training camp. I think in the right scheme, Harris won't look out of place. He's a smart and savvy corner who rarely gets beat badly. 4th round player.

24. Upton Stout - Western Kentucky - 5'9 182 lbs

Strengths: Stout began his career at North Texas for two seasons before transferring to Western Kentucky. Stout has played a versatile role for the Hilltoppers in the last three seasons, playing both in the nickel and on the outside. Stout is an undersized but extremely twitchy corner with the most success in nickel situations. His ball production has been stellar during each campaign, constantly showing the reflexes and instincts to be around the football. Stout utilizes his aggressive and physical mentality to disrupt receivers through contact windows and at the catch point when lined up in the slot. He's very fluid when working out his backpedal, showing ease of motion and natural flexibility. He easily flips his hips, demonstrating terrific agility and change of direction movement skills. He's sticky in man coverage, staying on the hip pocket of slot receivers throughout their stems. Stout has an advanced understanding of route concepts and good recognition skills when playing off-man or in zone, allowing him to anticipate, click, and close quickly. His ability to drive on underneath routes and get his hands on the ball is stellar, as evidenced by his multiple return touchdowns in college. Despite being an undersized corner, Stout plays like the biggest guy on the field with his intensity and fearless mentality. He never shies away from contact and will play through blockers in the run game, stacking and shedding in space. He's a terrific tackler who utilizes good wrap-up technique, rarely missing an opportunity in pursuit.

Weaknesses: Struggled with injuries in two different seasons, causing him to miss half of the 2021 campaign and half of the 2023 campaign. Stout has obvious height and length concerns that limit his ability to match up against bigger possession-based receivers. He will get boxed out at the top of routes by larger targets that he can't match for length or size. Will be limited to nickel duties only at the next level. Stout is quick in short spurts but lacks the top-end speed to challenge against vertical targets, as he will grant separation on up-the-field routes. He hasn't competed against many NFL athletes throughout college.

Best Fit: Nickel Corner

Player Ranking (1-100): 70.1 - Stout's mentality and urgency is unparalleled for a defensive back. His football IQ and downhill nature are shocking, considering his smaller stature. He's a sticky corner that shows natural coverage skills and recognition in all coverage looks. I wouldn't be surprised to see Stout win a role on defense during his rookie season. 4th round player.

25. Mac McWilliams - Central Florida - 5'10 185 lbs

Strengths: As a 5th-year senior at UCF, McWilliams started his career with UAB for the first four seasons before transferring to UCF for his final season of eligibility. McWilliams is a highly experienced and decorated football player who has excelled at both programs. McWilliams also has extensive return experience at both colleges and in high school. McWilliams has experience in different coverage looks, but he's at his best in man coverage. Comfortable playing both outside and inside, McWilliams likely is best suited inside at the next level. McWilliams, A fluid-moving athlete, shows silky smooth footwork as he eases out of his backpedal. He's sticky in coverage, attaching himself to the hip pocket of opposing receivers throughout their stems. His very good foot quickness and hip mobility enable him to be outstanding on shorter and intermediate shallow patterns, regularly jumping routes, and being disruptive. He plays far more physical than his listed size would indicate, showing good toughness at the line of scrimmage and the catch point. McWilliams has impressive ball skills, regularly timing the balls' arrival to perfection to play through the receiver's hands at exactly the right moment. McWilliams shows good instincts when playing in off-man or zone looks and can trigger underneath quickly. He's a willing support tackler who will sacrifice his body to take on ball carriers. He shows upside as a blitzer, regularly used to attack from the nickel.

Weaknesses: McWilliams's size constraints will likely limit him to playing on the inside at the next level. He hasn't competed against many top-tier receivers during his college career. He's struggled with repeated nagging injury concerns and has only played in one full season. While willing to run support, his lack of functional strength and length limits his ability to disengage and play through blocks. Despite his ball skills and passes defended, he doesn't finish plays with enough turnovers, considering. McWilliams is quicker than he is fast and will be challenged against speedier long stride receivers that will challenge him vertically.

Best Fit: Nickel corner and return specialist

Player Ranking (1-100): 69.4 - McWilliams is a fiery corner that plays with swagger and a scrappy nature. While he lacks ideal size and straight-line speed, he makes up for it with his alpha dog mentality. He has a chance to be a solid contributor at the next level. 5th round player.

26. Korie Black - Oklahoma State - 6'0 185 lbs

Strengths: Black has been a 3-year starter for the Cowboys, playing in almost every game in the last 4 seasons, showing iron-man durability. Black had his best season in his final season in 2024, finishing with three interceptions and 36 tackles. Black is a long and rangy corner with experience playing in various coverage setups for the Cowboys, including press-man, off-man, and in-zone. He also frequently bumps into the nickel in passing situations. Black is an explosive athlete with natural twitch and acceleration off the line of scrimmage. He utilizes his length to be disruptive at the line of scrimmage when in press. He also utilizes physicality throughout route stems and understands what he can and cannot get away with. His movement skills are fluid and natural, and he shows good hip mobility and agility when needed to cross the field. A former track athlete, Black plays with self-assured confidence and often grants some separation to bait QBs into throwing in his direction. He maintains stickiness in coverage both on linear and vertical planes. When playing further off the line, Black shows impressive click and close ability to anticipate breaks and underneath routes. He times the balls' arrival to perfection, playing through the hands of the receiver. A defensive leader who was often responsible for adjusting and signal calling on the back end of the defense. Black has been a significant special teams contributor, playing on the block coverage units with some big plays during his time.

Weaknesses: Black has a thin physique, and he has difficulty playing to the levels of physicality required in the running game. He consistently struggles to disengage from blocks, failing to play through blockers. When approaching ball carriers, he's frequently upright and bounces off tackle attempts or attempts to ankle swipe with little success. Black tends to get overly handsy at the top of routes in coverage. While he got away with it in college, he will likely get called more at the next level. Black gets his hands on many balls due to his coverage and natural ball skills, but he doesn't finish plays with interceptions nearly as much as he should. His hands are a liability, and he's had some poor drops. Black can struggle against receivers who can outmuscle him at the line of scrimmage or at the catch point.

Best Fit: Versatile corner that can play in any system

Player Ranking (1-100): 67.9 - Black is a good athlete with natural coverage abilities. His wiry physique needs additional development and functional mass to stay on the field consistently. He lacks a significant weakness in coverage, and QBs frequently avoided him the last couple of seasons in the Big 12. 5th round player.

27. Justin Walley - Minnesota - 5'11 195 lbs

Strengths: Walley has been a mainstay for the Golden Gophers for the last four seasons, starting the last 3.5 seasons consecutively. He has iron-man reliability, having not missed one game of his college career. Walley is a lean, athletically built corner who plays far bigger than his listed size. Walley has bounced around to different defensive systems and has extensive experience playing in man, off-man, and zone coverage. He appears the most comfortable in zone or off-man coverage, allowing him to utilize his natural feel of spacing and anticipation to break on routes. Walley is an instinctual athlete with a great feel for developing routes, completely understanding route concepts and where he needs to be. Walley sees things quickly and shows reactionary and twitchy movement skills, allowing him to click and close instantly, as evidenced by his high passes defended each campaign. A fluid mover, Walley moves well in short spurs, showing flexible hips and good change of direction. In man coverage, Walley minimizes spaces on underneath routes, matching stride for stride against receivers. He plays physical at the catch point, showing terrific timing to play through the hands of receivers to make plays on the ball. Despite Walley being a smaller corner, he can get vertical and challenge larger receivers at the high point, showing impressive leaping abilities. Walley is physical and competitive in the running game, showing fearlessness and a downhill mentality. Walley is generally a secure wrap-up tackler who rarely lets runners out of his grapes.

Weaknesses: Walley lacks ideal measurables both in the height and length department to play on the boundary at the next level. While Walley has good twitch and quickness, he lacks top-end speed, will get challenged, and struggles to minimize separation against elite NFL athletes. When playing man coverage, Walley tends to open up his hips too early, allowing receivers the head start to win on double moves or vertical routes. In the running game, Walley routinely attacks with overaggressive pursuit lanes, leading him to overrunning plays. He can struggle when attempting to stack and shed against larger receivers.

> **Best Fit: Zone or off-man cover corner that can play inside or outside**

Player Ranking (1-100): 65.9 - Walley is a highly experienced and smart football player who has good instincts and cover awareness. While he lacks elite physical attributes and size, he makes up for it in the mental areas. Walley should have a chance to be a role player for a defense while being a special teams stud. 5th round player.

28. Tommi Hill - Nebraska - 6'0 205 lbs

Strengths: Hill was initially recruited by Arizona State, where he began his career before transferring to Nebraska following his rookie season. Hill has transitioned back and forth between playing receiver and cornerback before finally settling on playing corner the last two seasons. Hill has proven to be a reliable defensive stalworth for the Cornhuskers in the last three seasons. He had his best season as a junior in 2023 with terrific ball production, including four interceptions and 13 passes defended. Hill is NFL-sized and possesses a large enough frame for continued growth and development. The former receiver's background is on display when playing corner, showcasing the impressive ability to read and process things when playing further from the football. While he has experience playing in various coverage schemes, Hill is at his best in zone. Hill has outstanding ball skills and ball awareness, allowing him to close cushions in the blink of an eye. Utilizes his innate instincts and play recognition skills to trigger quickly against the pass, showing impressive timing to arrive at precisely the right moment to make plays on the ball. Has the strength and the frame to match up well against NFL corners, showing the physicality and the length to be disruptive at all levels of a route. Hill is a willing tackler who is fearless when triggering downhill to assist in run support. Hill has extensive experience as a kickoff return specialist.

Weaknesses: Unfortunately, Hill is unpolished in all aspects of playing corner, as he has been bounced around and utilized at various spots. He failed to capitalize on his stellar 2023 campaign with a lackluster final season. He lacks the refinement and the technique to play as a press corner, as he looks far more comfortable further away from the football. Lacks great foot speed and will be challenged by better NFL athletes that take him vertically. Appears to have some lower body stiffness that minimizes his ability to stay attached and in phase with receivers on in-breaking routes, granting them leverage and separation.

> **Best Fit: Developmental Corner**

Player Ranking (1-100): 64.2 - Hill looked very good at times for Nebraska, and at other times, he looked subpar. He gives up a lot of plays in coverage and will likely have continued growing pains as he gets more comfortable playing cornerback at the next level. He has a chance if a coach will give him time to continue growing, as he has some traits. 6th round player.

29. Bilhal Kone - Western Michigan - 6'2 190 lbs

Strengths: Kone played two years of college football at Iowa Central Community College before transferring to Indiana State and eventually to Western Michigan for his final two seasons. Kone is a long and rangy corner with vines for arms, enabling him to be used in various coverage schemes. He has the frame for continued development as a boundary press corner but has a propensity for success when playing zone. Kone flashes quick feet and smooth fluidity through his backpedal when working in press. He remains patient through stems while staying in control. A long strider that matches and stays on the hip pocket of receivers well in man coverage. His long strides enable him to recover quickly when he initially grants separation. Kone keeps his eyes fixed on the quarterback in zone coverage, displaying good instincts and cover awareness. He recognizes zone concepts and has a good feel for developing routes. He times the ball's arrival to perfection, frequently jumping routes or at least being disruptive at the catch point. If he gives up receptions, he utilizes his tackle radius to limit the damage done afterward. He works tirelessly in pursuit in the run game, and he makes a lot of tackles from the backside. An experienced special teams contributor who plays on every unit.

Weaknesses: Kone missed the second half of the 2022 campaign after dealing with an injury. He possesses a lean and lanky frame, which could use additional development and pass. He struggles to disengage in pursuit in the running game, lacking top-end strength and pop. While willing in run support, he approaches ball carriers upright and allows additional yardage after contact. When in press, Kone fails to initiate ideal jam technique, often allowing free releases for receivers. He can struggle against shorter and shiftier receivers that can get him turned inside out, as he lacks elite change of direction and agility on lateral routes. His overall athleticism and speed are good, but he is short of being in the upper echelon of corners.

Best Fit: Zone corner with developmental press upside

Player Ranking (1-100): 62.4 - Kone has a terrific frame and length that coaches covet. Unfortunately, he lacks technical refinement as a press corner and functional strength. He has a chance to get better and better with additional coaching. He will battle for a roster spot. 6th round player.

30. Jordan Hancock - Ohio State - 6'1 194 lbs

Strengths: Hancock played mostly as a role player during his first couple of seasons on campus before transitioning to gaining starts in his junior campaign. Hancock is a versatile chess piece for the Buckeyes defense that has moved all over the defensive backfield from corner to safety to nickel and has success in whichever role he's been used. Hancock is a wiry corner of good height with enough room on his frame for additional mass. Hancock has shown terrific natural coverage ability, whether playing man, off-man, or in-zone looks. When lined up in man, Hancock shows his ease of movement. He's got fluidity in abundance, easily transitioning in and out of breaks while remaining in the hip pocket of receivers. He's quick and explosive in short segments and utilizes his reactionary movement skills to minimize spacing and recover quickly. Hancock displays high football IQ and route recognition abilities when playing off-man and zone. He's quick to see plays developing while keeping his eyes fixated on the QB. He communicates effectively from the defensive backfield pre-snap. He has a knack for creating turnovers and making plays on the ball, forcing four fumbles and three interceptions in the last two seasons. Hancock adds upside as a highly effective slot blitzer that utilizes impressive timing, anticipation, and closing burst to get home.

Weaknesses: Hancock struggled with minor injury concerns during his first two seasons, which caused him to miss some game time. While he has good height, Hancock lacks ideal proportional length and can struggle against longer receivers that can outreach him. His lack of length is also obvious in the running game, as he fails to disengage and shed when pursuing ball carriers. While willing to assist in the run game, Hancock is ineffective in offering much assistance. He routinely bounces off ball carriers or allows them additional yardage after contact. Hancock lacks ideal functional strength and could benefit by continuing to refine and add bulk to his frame. Hancock tends to open up too quickly in coverage situations, granting receivers easy leverage opportunities to separate. He's not a natural ball tracker with his back to the target and tends to get grabby at the top of routes.

Best Fit: Versatile all-around developmental corner

Player Ranking (1-100): 61.9 - There's no denying Hancock has some terrific traits that should carry over to the next level. He lacks experience and strength through his frame. If he can continue to add quality bulk and offer something in the run game, Hancock could develop into a nice defensive chess piece, as he did in college. 6th round player.

31. Brandon Adams - Central Florida - 6'3 180 lbs

Strengths: A significant contributor in the last four seasons, Adams had his best season as a senior, improving his ball production. Adams displays a long-levered frame with vines for arms, allowing him to succeed in press-man. While he's best at press man, he also shows experience playing in both zone and off-man. Excelling at the line of scrimmage, Adams utilizes his length to disrupt and re-route receivers at the line of scrimmage. A fluid mover that eases out of his backpedal, showing impressive lateral mobility and change of directional abilities to mirror on shorter to intermediate routes. If he initially gives an easy release, his movement skills and recovery quickness allow him to recover quickly. Good overall play recognition skills, showing an advanced understanding of route concepts. He isn't easily fooled or manipulated by play-action or double moves, staying attached to the hip pocket of receivers. A long strider who has good long speed, enabling him to stay in phase with receivers on vertical routes. Times the balls' arrival to perfection, showing good physicality at the catch point. Has extensive experience on all the special teams' units, showing upside for that phase at the next level.

Weaknesses: Adams is rangy and thin, and he could benefit by continuing to add functional strength and power to his frame. His lack of strength is evident in his lack of confidence in run support, and he sometimes looks disinterested and uncommitted. He fails to stack and shed in pursuit, regularly getting hung up by tight ends along the edges. When in pursuit, he takes poor angles constantly, leading to bigger plays than necessary. He has had constant penalty concerns throughout college, getting overaggressive at the line of scrimmage and past contact windows. He gets very grabby when panicked, and this will need to be continually coached out of him. He can take too many false steps when further from the ball, lacking zone instincts and naturalness. His overall ball skills and production have been underwhelming throughout college. He quickly gives up free releases and easy access to underneath routes and slants.

Best Fit: Developmental Boundary Corner

Player Ranking (1-100): 61.4 - Adams has talent no doubt. His issues stem from discipline, lack of coaching, and overall experience. If he can continue to be refined while maximizing his length and movement skills, he can win some reps as a rookie to play on the outside. 6th round player.

32. Fentrell Cypress - Florida State - 6'0 188 lbs

Strengths: Cypress was a 4-year player for Virginia before transferring over to Florida State before the 2023 campaign. Cypress had his best season with Virginia in 2022, finishing atop the ACC with 14 passes defended. Cypress is a highly experienced cornerback prospect who has seen it all and played in various coverage systems. Cypress is a lean, long corner with good proportional length and enough room on his frame for additional mass. In man coverage, Cypress shows good patience and smooth footwork out of his backpedal. He matches stride for stride with receivers, with little wasted motion. He's competitive at the line of scrimmage and isn't afraid to get in the face and be disruptive. His track background enables him to challenge top-end speedsters, granting them little separation. Cypress communicates well with his teammates to minimize spatial cushions when playing in zone looks. He's quick to recognize route concepts, and his click-and-close abilities allow him to trigger down and compete at the catch point. His twitchy reflexes and reactionary athleticism enable him to constantly be around the football, proving to have ball hawk traits. In the running game, Cypress is willing and arrives quickly at the party. He shows hyper-aggressiveness and will work through blocks with urgency. Despite being undersized, Cypress shows a willingness to wrap up securely. Cypress has extensive special teams experience and can be an asset on all the units at the next level.

Weaknesses: An older prospect who will be 24 years old shortly following the draft. Despite Cypress' six seasons in college football, he's only had one career interception. He gets his hands on many balls but doesn't finish them with turnovers, calling into question his ball skills and hands. Cypress lacks ideal bulk and body armor on his frame, and he struggles against bigger possession receivers who can outmuscle him at the line of scrimmage, at the catch point, and in the run game. Despite his straight-line speed, Cypress has some stiffness concerns when working laterally, allowing quicker receivers to win inside leverage on him, and frequently gives up short to intermediate routes. Cypress can lose track of the ball when challenged vertically, as he's frequently caught looking into the backfield. When attacking downhill in the run game, Cypress frequently takes aggressive pathways to the ball, taking him out of play.

Best Fit: Developmental boundary corner that can play in any defensive system

Player Ranking (1-100): 59.1 - Cypress has the mentality, football IQ, and athleticism to excel at the next level. The main problem is he needs to get stronger. His lack of functional strength and power limits him in college and will likely be a bigger detriment at the next level. There are definite traits there to work with. 7th round player.

33. Zah Frazier - UTSA - 6'3 185 lbs

Strengths: A former JUCO All-American, Frazier has played with UTSA in the Conference USA for the last three seasons. Frazier is a long and lean cornerback prospect with extensive college experience between three different programs. Frazier is experienced playing in different defensive systems, but he appears to be most comfortable playing off-man and zone. While Frazier is still raw, he's shown continuous improvement during each campaign. Frazier is a top-tier athlete with terrific long speed to match up against NFL athletes. If he initially grants any separation, Frazier utilizes another gear to close cushions and recover ground. He repeatedly does this on vertical routes, closing cushions with long strides. Frazier's wingspan makes it challenging for receivers, utilizing contact windows well if he's in man coverage. When playing further back, Frazier shows ball skills and innate timing while utilizing his length to play through the receiver's hands and be disruptive. A natural ball tracker, Frazier remains in control without panicking when the ball is in the air. Frazier's closing burst and length on underneath routes enable him to jump routes and close quickly. He appears to be a smart football player who recognizes and sees things quickly, having an advanced understanding of zone concepts.

Weaknesses: Frazier is an older prospect who will be 25 years old during his rookie season. His thin and wiry frame causes him to have issues when the game gets physical. He repeatedly plays upright in the running game, limiting his ability to make tackles upon impact. He gets stuck on blocks without the upper-body strength to disengage consistently. In coverage, Frazier is faster than he is quick and appears to have some lower body stiffness concerns when playing on linear planes. When asked to cross his face and redirect his hips against shorter and more agile receivers, he struggles.

Best Fit: Developmental zone corner

Player Ranking (1-100): 57.3 - Frazier is a great straight-line athlete with impressive athleticism and length. The worry is he will be 24 years old and lack functional strength through his frame. His ceiling for growth is likely diminished, considering his age. 7th round player.

34. Tahveon Nicholson - Louisville - 5'11 180 lbs

Strengths: Nicholson played for Illinois three seasons before transferring to Louisville and playing his final season for the Tigers. Nicholson is an athletically built boundary corner that has a good proportional length. Comfortable playing in various coverage setups, Nicholson has experience playing in zone, man, and off-man looks. Nicholson is most comfortable handling press-man responsibilities, showing good physicality and fluidity in man coverage. Nicholson is smooth out of his backpedal, wasting little motion, and stays attached to the hip pocket of his target. He does a terrific job of staying stride for stride, mirroring every move. Nicholson's physical style of play enables him to utilize an aggressive jam technique at the line of scrimmage to disrupt while also maximizing physicality within contact windows. When playing further from the football, Nicholson's ability to diagnose and read things is amplified, showing good diagnostic abilities. He maintains good communication with his teammates while keeping his eyes fixated on the QB's arm motion. He displays good click and close ability, quickly anticipating underneath and in-breaking routes to trigger downhill. In the running game, Nicholson is a willing participant who shows good physicality and has sometimes laid the wood.

Weaknesses: While Nicholson has good overall length disruptions, he lacks ideal bulk and height through his frame. He struggles against bigger possession receivers who can utilize this body to frame at the catch point. While Nicholson is a good athlete in smaller spaces, he lacks the top-end speed to challenge elite vertical receivers on up-field routes. He appears to have stiffness issues when changing directions quickly, causing him to grant separation against more nuanced smaller receivers. While Nicholson has gotten his hands on many balls, he fails to take advantage of opportunities with turnovers. He's only had two interceptions throughout his career. Nicholson's size limits him when working towards the ball carriers, as he frequently gets stuck on blocks with minimal ideas on how to stack and shed consistently.

Best Fit: Developmental boundary corner

Player Ranking (1-100): 54.8 - Nicholson is a solid cover corner, if nothing else. His length and movement skills enable him to mimic receivers' shadows. He lacks the physicality, size, and explosive qualities to be a starter at the next level. He could develop into a nice backup. Undrafted free agent.

35. Toriano Pride Jr - Missouri - 5'10 190 lbs

Strengths: Pride began his career with Clemson before transferring to Missouri before his final season in college as a junior. Pride is a smaller but athletically built corner that excels in short spaces. Comfortable playing in any defensive system, Pride has experience in press-man, off-man, and in-zone looks. He's also more than comfortable to play inside and outside. Pride shows silky smooth footwork when playing in man coverage, enabling him to work with minimal wasted steps. Excellent fluidity and change of directional skills allow Pride to stay sticky in coverage, remaining in the hip pocket of receivers. Pride displays good instincts and play-recognition abilities to sniff things out when playing off-man or in zone. He remains patient while staying on the balls of his feet, always ready to trigger. He's quick to jump routes and play through the hands of receivers upon the receipt of the ball. On down-the-field routes, Pride showcases good overall ball skills with flexible body control to adjust and attack the football. Despite being smaller, Pride can challenge vertically and high points against bigger targets. In the running game, Pride displays the reactionary quickness and the trigger to get downhill. He's quick to react to screens and misdirection-type plays.

Weaknesses: Pride is a severely undersized corner that lacks the length and size combination to play on the outside at the next level. He's likely limited to slot duties solely. While Pride is explosive in short bursts, he lacks the top-end speed to stay vertical with better athletes. Pride is sticky in coverage, but he repeatedly gets boxed out at the catch point against bigger receivers. While Pride shows instincts in the run game, he lacks the frame and the point-of-attack power to play through blockers, frequently getting stuck. He fails to wrap up securely, regularly allowing runners to break tackles after getting his hands on them.

Best Fit: Nickel corner and special teams

Player Ranking (1-100): 54.3 - Pride is a good short-area athlete who has been mostly a role player throughout college, both at Clemson and Missouri. He doesn't consistently stay on the field and lacks ideal consistent experience. Undrafted free agent.

Top-10 Cornerbacks:

1. Travis Hunter
2. Will Johnson
3. Jahdae Barron
4. Shavon Revel Jr
5. Denzel Burke
6. Benjamin Morrison
7. Trey Amos
8. Maxwell Hairston
9. Darien Porter
10. Jason Marshall Jr

Chapter 13

Safeties

1. Malaki Starks - Georgia - 6'1 205 lbs

Strengths: Starks has been a mainstay of the vaunted Bulldogs' defense in the last three campaigns, showing outstanding production and reliability while competing against top-tier competition. Starks is a former five-star high school recruit who was previously a track and field star and two-position high school football player. Starks is built with a nice blend of length and size, with room on his frame for continued development. Starks has been a versatile safety in various coverage assignments, from handling slot duties to playing further away from the football. Stark's high IQ and intangibles allow him to be successful wherever he is used. Former track athleticism is displayed in coverage, staying with receivers on vertical routes. Fluidity and lower body springiness allow him to easily mirror in space, showing rare changes in direction and hip mobility. Starks shows natural ball skills down the field in coverage, timing the balls' arrival perfectly to attack the football. Excellent ball awareness and high-point ability to attack the football in the air. When he can't snatch it, he does an excellent job of knocking it away or disrupting the receiver's vision. A reliable last line of defense, Starks utilizes good physicality and competitive toughness to bring ball carriers to the ground by hook or crook. He isn't shy about triggering in the running game when playing closer to the run of scrimmage, showing good short-area quickness and closing speed. When flowing to the football, Starks take acute angles in pursuit while showing the ability to break down tackles in space. Has a good feel and understanding of zone looks, showing excellent spatial instincts and recognition skills to limit spacing opportunities.

Weaknesses: Starks had offseason shoulder surgery following his sophomore campaign in 2023. He can have mental lapses that appear to cause hesitancy when closing on the ball or making a play, perhaps due to self-confidence. Highly aggressive mentality that intelligent QBs can sometimes bait on double moves and play-action plays down the field. Will get confused at times against more complicated route concepts, seemingly getting out of position in moments. While he's a mostly reliable tackler, he can approach ball carriers upright, leading to additional yards after contact.

Best Fit: Versatile Starting Safety

Player Ranking (1-100): 85.9 - I like Starks, but not as much as other evaluators do. He is reliable, highly intelligent, and tremendously athletic. He doesn't flash as much as I'd like for someone of his skill set. While the skies are the limit for Starks, I don't think he's an immediate top-end safety at the next level, but he certainly has the tools to become that. 1st round player.

2. Nick Emmanwori - South Carolina - 6'3 227 lbs

Strengths: A 3-year starter at safety for the Gamecocks, Emmanwori has improved progressively during each campaign, showing the rare ability to start as a true freshman. Built with rare size throughout his frame, showing incredible density and muscularity to enable him to handle the physicality at the next level.

Emmanwori is a versatile defender who can line up in various coverage packages, including playing significantly in the nickel. In coverage, Emmanwori shows movement skills and athleticism in handling tight ends and slot receivers. A terrific athlete, Emmanwori showcases the long speed to challenge receivers on vertical planes when playing in deeper halves. Maintains good leverage and positioning when working in and out of transitions, showing quick feet and agile hips to limit spacing for receivers. Impressive ball awareness and skills when playing further away from the ball enable him to time, judge the balls' arrival, and make plays. When playing closer to the line of scrimmage, Emmanwori shows good key and diagnostic skills to trigger downhill and make plays on the ball carrier. Appears to have advanced football understanding and IQ, regularly diagnosing and recognizing pre-snap looks. A physical player in run support that shows zero hesitancy when triggering downhill, giving up little after first contact with ball carriers. Takes acute pursuit angles to the football when flowing to the opposite side of the field. Excellent wrap-up reliability in the open field, rarely missing a tackle. Has the range and the speed to handle Cover-2 responsibilities when playing further from the ball, maintaining disciplined eyes to read the QB's arm motion and eyes.

Weaknesses: Emmanwori is faster than quick and could struggle to handle coverage responsibilities on an island against shorter, quicker targets that can get him turned inside-out. When working out of his backpedal in man coverage, he appears to take too many false and choppy steps, limiting his ability to stay in phase. Doesn't always process things quickly, at times having some mental lapses, causing him to be in catch-up mode. For being a bigger guy, he gets stuck on blocks when in pursuit far too easily. Emmanwori can get a bit grabby and panicky in deeper coverage responsibilities, causing him to get called for penalties. Lacks the explosive twitch and reactionary quickness to play as a center fielder in a single-high defensive setup.

Best Fit: Box Safety

Player Ranking (1-100): 84.0 - Emmanwori is a physical downhill thumper most comfortable playing closer to the line of scrimmage. While he has the athleticism and the length to play further from the football, he's best used as a versatile nickel/safety hybrid that can handle coverage responsibilities closer to the line of scrimmage. 2nd round player.

3. Xavier Watts - Notre Dame - 6'0 203 lbs

Strengths: A converted wide receiver for the Fighting Irish who began his career at receiver before transitioning to linebacker and then eventually safety. Watts had his coming out party in 2023, finishing with over 50 tackles, 7 interceptions, and 1 forced fumble, and winning the Bronko Nagurski Trophy for the country's best defensive player. Watts is muscled up with density and thickness throughout his frame. Comfortable playing closer to the line of scrimmage or being used in the deeper halves of the field playing in coverage. Watts is at his best facing the action where he can utilize his rare key and diagnostic abilities to close down on plays quickly. His former receiver qualities manifest in how he understands offenses, showing excellent play recognition and awareness of route concepts. His nose for the football is evident in his ability to make big plays in the biggest moments, showcasing rare ball skills and GPS location abilities. His versatility allows him to disguise coverages and be used as a defensive chess piece all over the defensive front. Disciplined eyes enable him to stay in position on double moves or play-action plays, rarely getting fooled by deceptive QBs. A quick processor lets him sort through the trash while taking acute angles to the football in pursuit. His outstanding athleticism allows him to close quickly, especially in short areas. Loose limbs enable him to change direction fluidly and flip his hips when needing to play laterally. Former linebacker skills are evident in how he plays with physicality, triggering downhill and laying the wood against receivers and running backs. A hard worker with outstanding character and blue-chip qualities to continue refining and improving despite having minimal experience in a new position.

Weaknesses: Watts is still raw as a safety and is continuing to be refined regarding different coverage aspects of playing safety. Hasn't had to handle significant amounts of man coverage assignments and looks to need continued refinement. Quicker than he is fast, Watts lacked top-end range and speed. A big hitter, constantly looking to lay the wood, swings, and misses at times, leading to big plays on whiffed open-field tackle attempts.

Best Fit: Versatile Starting Safety

Player Ranking (1-100): 83.4 - Watts is a play-making ball hawk with an enormous ceiling. He's incredibly smart, explosive, and tough. He should immediately make an NFL defense faster and more physical. 2nd round player. I love this kid.

4. Billy Bowman Jr - Oklahoma - 5'10 200 lbs

Strengths: A rare 4-year starter at nickel cornerback/safety for the Sooners, Bowman is a highly experienced and seasoned defensive back. He had his best season as a junior when he finished with Big-12 leading six interceptions and three returning for touchdowns. Despite Bowman's lack of ideal measurables, he has a densely-cut frame with sufficient muscle to withstand the NFL rigors. Bowman has handled various coverage responsibilities, playing both in deeper coverages as a single-high or coming inside and playing as a nickel corner. A natural playmaker, Bowman has rare diagnostic abilities and instincts. Showcases the ability to track the ball down the field, and high point against larger targets. Very fluid movement skills enable him to easily cross the field without losing any built-up momentum. Despite his size, Bowman has been used to handling man coverage against larger targets, including tight ends, and he shows the propensity and physicality to have success. Watches the receiver's eyes and arms to time the balls' arrival to perfection, fighting through the catch point to make plays down the field. High IQ allows him to diagnose before the snap of the ball and then utilize his click/close ability to get downhill and blow up plays. Excellent awareness of different coverage alignments, showing advanced understanding of route concepts. Bowman has been a core special teams player for the Sooners and has experience on all the units. Dynamic in the open field when returning interceptions, showing upside as a return specialist.

Weaknesses: Bowman's lack of height and length will likely limit him and take him off the board for many defensive coaches at the next level. He can get lazy with his wrapping-up abilities, frequently attempting to rip at the ball and force a fumble instead of getting the ball carrier down. Limited length will cause him to struggle to compete at the catch point against larger targets despite being willing and aggressive. His overaggressive nature often leads him to crash down hard on double moves, which leads to him getting baited by discerning QBs.

Best Fit: Versatile Starting Safety

Player Ranking (1-100): 81.0 - I love Bowman as a player, and he certainly has some Antoine Winfield Jr in his game. A physical enforcer that has an advanced understanding of coverages. He is a great and easy mover, allowing him to play with range at any spot a defensive coordinator wants to use. He is certainly a bit aggressive and could benefit by getting a little more reliable as a tackler, but the kid is a playmaker! 2nd round player.

5. Kevin Winston Jr - Penn State - 6'2 205 lbs

Strengths: Winston sprang onto the NFL draft scene following his stellar sophomore campaign in 2023, which saw him have over 60 tackles and three tackles for loss. Built with a prototypical NFL physique, Winston has a long and wiry frame that allows him to match up against bigger NFL targets. Winston is a versatile safety who has handled various responsibilities, including playing as a single-high, cover-2, or handling subpackage linebacker responsibilities. Winston brings a nasty punch and aggressive mentality to the safety position, showing the physicality and downhill nature you like to see from a safety. Disciplined eyes and good instincts allow him to read his keys and quickly diagnose. His diagnostic abilities allow him to take acute angles to the football in pursuit, showing the closing burst to limit yardage. Attacks the football at precisely the right moment, showing impressive tracking ability and ball skills. A fluid-moving athlete who is capable of challenging receivers vertically as well as laterally. Good overall recovery speed to close down any cushions quickly. In coverage, Winston utilizes his length to disrupt and alter the timing for receivers out of their stance. He is a terrific tackler who takes every opportunity seriously, showing comfort in extending and making plays outside his frame.

Weaknesses: Winston missed most of the 2024 season with a partially torn ACL. Winston has played in minimal games and has little starting experience, having only started one full season in 2023. Winston lacks ideal functional strength throughout his frame. He could benefit by adding clean weight to his frame to give himself additional body armor for his physical style of play. While a mostly very secure tackler, Winston has a tendency to approach ball carriers very upright, causing them to pick up additional yards after contact. Doesn't always get his head turned in coverage and will likely get called for pass interference at the next level. He is prone to playing overaggressively at times and will get caught having some lapses in coverage.

Best Fit: Versatile Starting Safety

Player Ranking (1-100): 80.2 - Winston likely would have been drafted as high as the 1st round with another good year of film. His injury and lack of overall experience cause some concern for evaluators, including myself. His tape from 2023 was stellar. His athleticism, range, and physical make-up allow him to be used in various ways for a defense. 2nd round player.

6. Lathan Ransom - Ohio State - 6'1 210 lbs

Strengths: A 5th year senior for the Buckeyes who has been a mainstay of their defense during the last four seasons. Ransom is built with a tough, rugged frame, showing NFL muscularity and density. Experienced at playing all over the Buckeyes defense, including as a deep halves safety or closer to the line of scrimmage. Ransom is an urgent downhill safety that excels when playing closer to the line of scrimmage. His high IQ and good play recognition abilities allow him to shoot downhill in a flash, and he shows terrific short-area quickness and closing speed. Instincts and read/react abilities allow him to shoot gaps and be a nuisance in the backfield, both in the running game and when used to blitz through 'A' and 'B' gaps. He is a violent thumper who will fight through blockers, generating excellent pop through his upper body. He is unafraid of sacrificing his body and putting the big hit on unsuspecting receivers. Ransom shows the physicality through stems to re-route and be disruptive when in coverage. Shows good patience, rarely getting fooled by play-fakes or double moves. A reliable open-field tackler that will make plays in space. Always goes for the football when making tackles, as evidenced by his high forced fumbles each campaign. He was a special teams contributor on multiple units and blocked multiple punts during his career.

Weaknesses: He suffered a Lisfranc tear towards the end of the 2023 campaign, causing him to miss the last several games of the season. While Ransom can handle some coverage assignments, he's not ideally used in man coverage situations on an island. He struggles mirroring, as his lower body has noticeable tightness concerns when asked to change directions. Has to slow down when flipping his hips, causing him to lose built-up speed and will grant separation. He is better in short bursts than in long vertical settings, as he lacks top-end long speed. Struggles with his back to the ball in coverage, failing to get his head turned around. His overall ball skills are OK, but he lacks the anticipation and timing to challenge when the balls are in the air. Generally a good tackler, but there are moments he plays upright, and he's more concerned with making the big hit with his shoulders than bringing ball carriers down reliably. Has had some penalty concerns when used in coverage.

Best Fit: Box safety

Player Ranking (1-100): 79.2 - Ransom is a highly experienced safety who has the football IQ and physicality to excel in defense. He will immediately be a terrific special teams contributor while showing coaches he deserves to play some defense snaps. He will get exposed in deep coverage and is far closer to the line of scrimmage as a box safety. 3rd round player.

7. Andrew Mukuba - Texas - 6'0 185 lbs

Strengths: A 3-year starter at Clemson before transferring over and playing his final year with the Longhorns. Mububa is an experienced safety prospect who has played all over the defensive setup with two big-time college programs. Mububa is an athletically built athlete with the physical traits to be a versatile defensive puzzle piece for an NFL defensive coach. Comfortable playing in nice coverage or lining up as a Cover-2 safety, Mububa makes a difference wherever he is lined up. A quick-twitch mover, Mukuba uses his rare key and diagnostic abilities and impressive athleticism to click/close instantly. Will trigger quickly when recognizing a running play, showing fearlessness and toughness at all levels. When playing further away from the ball, Mububa maintains disciplined eyes while keeping his eyes glued to the backfield. Highly advanced ball skills and tracking ability enable him to locate the ball quickly and make plays at the catch point. In man coverage, Mukuba shows fluidity throughout his lower half and change of direction abilities to mirror receivers at all points of their routes. Plays bigger than his size suggests, as Mukuba has had some big-time hits when targets come across the middle of the field.

Weaknesses: Mukuba has been moved around throughout college so much that he lacks a true position for the next level. For safety, he is undersized and lacks the ideal body armor to play closer to the line of scrimmage. Lack of length and height will minimize his chances of handling coverage opportunities against larger possession receivers or tight ends. As a guy always around the ball, I'd have liked to see Mukuba make more plays on the ball, as his interception numbers have been modest at best. A little too aggressive sometimes in pursuit, leading to poor pursuit angles and missed opportunities to make plays. Mukuba has had significant tackling issues throughout his career, although he has improved during his final campaign considerably.

Best Fit: Versatile Coverage Safety

Player Ranking (1-100): 78.9 - Mukuba has been a really good college football career with two programs and in four straight seasons. He's party safety and partly cornerback and has the athleticism to do either well. He's a little undersized for safety, although that'll likely be his position for most teams. I'd like to see him play as an FS who can occasionally handle slot duties at the next level. 3rd round player.

8. Jonas Sanker - Virginia - 6'1 210 lbs

Strengths: As a 3-year starter for the Cavaliers, Sanker has been a mainstay on both special teams and defense during his college career. While versed in play in several different alignments, including at nickel, free safety, in the box, and further from the football, Sanker does his best work playing closer to the line of scrimmage. Sanker has a good frame with functional length and muscularity. He is a blue-chip prospect who works his tail off and plays with a hot motor on every snap of the play, bringing urgency and energy to a defense. Sanker is a good athlete who moves well, especially in short spurts, showing impressive click and close abilities. Sanker reads the game well in the running game, trusting his eyes and triggering downhill. He regularly sniffs out plays in the backfield, possessing a natural nose for the football. He takes reliable pursuit pathways to the football, regularly in a good position to make the play. A terrific tackler, Sanker has had over 200 yards the last two seasons, rarely missing an opportunity if he gets his hands on ball carriers. He utilizes the ideal wrap-up technique but is also aggressive in attempting to rip the ball out. Sanker displays good ball skills in coverage due to his anticipation, timing, and reactionary reflexes. He regularly attacks the football at the right moment and plays through the receiver's hands to knock the ball out or affect the play. He's at his best in zone looks, where he can utilize his understanding of route concepts to maintain proper spacing and trigger down underneath routes. Sanker has proven to be a good blitzer that utilizes good snap anticipation and timing to affect plays. He is a sturdy football player who has stayed mostly healthy throughout his career.

Weaknesses: Sanker struggles to find deeper coverage opportunities when he's further away from football. He lacks the top-end speed to be utilized as a last line of defense, and he appears to have some hip tightness concerns that cause him to struggle when changing directions quickly. Sanker needs to be a better finisher when he gets his hands on the ball, only having two career intercepts despite the high amount of passes defended each campaign. In pursuit, Sanker struggles to play through blockers. He regularly gets stuck on blocks with minimal opportunities to disengage.

Best Fit: Box Safety

Player Ranking (1-100): 78.0 - I absolutely love Sanker as a football player. He's around the football constantly, possesses instincts, and his reliability in tackling is superb. He will immediately be a top-notch special teams contributor. But I think he will win a starting spot quickly as a safety. 3rd round player.

9. Xavier Nwankpa - Iowa - 6'2 215 lbs

Strengths: A former 5-star high school prospect, Nwankpa has started for the Hawkeyes in the last two seasons. Built with an impressive frame, showing good muscle density and proportional length, Nwankpa displays the physical traits scouts and coaches drool over. In the last couple of seasons, Nwankpa has been used in various ways, including playing as the robber (cloud safety), single-high, cover-2 safety, and in the box. Nwankpa is a natural playmaker and is always around the football field, as evidenced by his 16 interceptions in high school. A terrific all-around athlete who displays both the long speed and the short-area acceleration to play at any alignment. His fluidity is evident in coverage, turning, and running with the best athletes, showing elite fluidity and lower body springiness. Nwankpa played his best when deployed as the robber, allowing him to utilize his football IQ to identify and process. His closing speed and trigger abilities made him a forceful thumper who continuously found the football. He will challenge at the top of routes, showing good timing and awareness to be disruptive and play through the hands of a receiver. Nwankpa is a physical tone-setter who utilizes his entire frame to shrink the field, regularly making plays outside his frame. He can close large cushions quickly, showing full-field range when playing further from the ball.

Weaknesses: While Nwankpa was utilized at times in man coverage duties, it's the weakest part of his game. He struggles to move fluidity out of a backpedal and will take too many false steps. He will grant open, easy leverage to quick receivers that can get him to open up his hips too quickly. While Nwankpa has shown impressive physicality in the run game, he's not adept at playing through blockers. He will frequently get hooked and fail to have any consistent deconstruct abilities. His upper body needs additional functional strength as he struggles to win hand fights when sorting through the trash in the middle of the field. When playing in zone and off-man coverage, Nwankpa sometimes loses track of his assignment, staring too long into the backfield. He takes very aggressive pathways to the football, but sometimes he takes himself out of plays.

Best Fit: Versatile Coverage Safety

Player Ranking (1-100): 77.1 - Nwankpa is an athlete still developing and raw in many respects. His ceiling is through the roof! If he can continue to gain experience while refining some of his weaknesses, he should 100% be a quality starter in this league. 3rd round player.

10. Sebastian Castro - Iowa - 5'11 205 lbs

Strengths: A 5th-year senior for the Hawkeyes, Castro has been a valuable starter for the last three seasons, improving in each subsequent campaign. With a stout and compact frame, Castro is built with good thickness through his frame to allow him to succeed in his physical brand of football. Casto has been used in various roles, including playing in the nickel, as a safety, and as an outside linebacker; Castro is a jack of all-trades defensive chess piece. As a cover corner, Castro maintains sticky coverage against slot receivers. He shows the twitch and the lateral mobility to mirror and remain in the hip pocket of receivers, rarely letting them breathe. Experienced playing both press-man and zone, Castro is at his best when he can play in zone looks due to his football IQ and processing abilities. His play recognition skills and ball instincts are second to none, showing rare key and diagnostic abilities. Prior to the development of the play, Castro locks his eyes in and triggers downhill in a flash, showing rare closing speed to blow up plays. He routinely blows up screens and plays in the backfield due to his instincts and recognition skills. A playmaker who is constantly around the football, showing ball skills and ball tracking abilities when playing further away from the football. Click and close, and ball timing allows him to arrive at the ball at the precise moment to knock it away. A downhill thumper in run support, Castro triggers quickly and regularly brings down ball carriers significantly bigger than him. He shows a relentless motor in pursuit, fighting off blockers and showing impressive upper-body strength to disengage and still make the play. An excellent special teams contributor with excessive experience in the various coverage units.

Weaknesses: An older prospect who will turn 25 early in his rookie season. Lacks the ideal size requisites to play in height and length on the outside, likely limiting him to nickel or box safety duties at the next level. Castro is quicker than he is fast, lacking the ideal long speed and range to cover significant parts of the field when playing further away from the football. He will struggle in man coverage assignments against tight ends or possession receivers that can reach or box him out. Has overaggressive tendencies and will attempt to jump routes frequently, making him susceptible to double moves and play-action.

Best Fit: Box safety and special teams

Player Ranking (1-100): 76.6 - Castro's age and his size will likely drop him a bit. Please make no mistake, though; this kid makes plays when he's on the field. He will immediately be a dynamic special teams contributor. Defensive coaches will figure out a way to get him on the field. 3rd round player.

11. Rod Moore - Michigan - 6'0 198 lbs

Strengths: A significant contributor for three straight seasons for the Wolverines before his injury, Moore has proven to be a reliable leader of the defense. Moore is an incredibly knowledgeable and smart football player who can be used in various ways for defense. Comfortable playing in a single-high setup in addition to playing closer to the line of scrimmage. Looks the part in any way he is used, showcasing plus technique and confidence. He's quick to see things developing pre-snap, allowing himself to be in good positions on every snap. When he recognizes a run, he's quick to trigger downhill and assist in the run game, even when playing deep. He is a very fluid-moving athlete who displays elastic-like flexibility through his frame to swivel his hips, effortlessly change directions, and cross the field, minimizing wasted motion. Very comfortable handling man coverage opportunities in the slot against tight ends or running backs. Ball skills are prevalent, especially when plays are in front of him, frequently showing the ability to disrupt at the catch point. He was a core special teams contributor to the Wolverines and was used on all their units throughout college.

Weaknesses: Moore tore his ACL during spring practices, causing him to miss his final season. Recovering from his injury could require some time before he's fully ready. A long and lean frame can cause him to struggle when handling NFL levels of physicality. Functional strength isn't ideal for Moore in any area. While a willing tackler, he isn't already reliable and can struggle to wrap up against bigger ball carriers. Has some difficulties working through space if a blocker can reach him, as he likely won't be able to disengage. Quicker than he is fast and lacks the recovery speed to make up ground if he bites on double moves.

Best Fit: Coverage Safety and Special Teams

Player Ranking (1-100): 75.9 - Moore is the type of guy you take a chance on in the 3rd round of the draft. His tape is closer to 2nd round, but unfortunately, his ACL injury is a cause for concern. It could significantly alter his NFL career if he loses any mobility or athleticism, especially laterally. He could be a great steal for a team in the 3rd round, as he's a well-rounded coverage safety who, at the very least, will be a core special teams contributor.

12. Craig Woodson - Cal - 6'0 210 lbs

Strengths: A 5th-year senior and 3-year starter for Cal, Woodson is a highly experienced and versatile chess piece for the Golden Bears' defense. Woodson is built with an NFL frame, possessing proportional length and body armor. Woodson has extensive experience playing throughout the defensive backfield, including playing in the slot, single-high, cover-2 halves safety, as a zone patrolling safety, and in the box. Woodson, a fluid athlete, shows outstanding change of direction and loose hips. Woodson shows good overall upside when playing in the deeper parts of the field, displaying cover awareness, range, and anticipation. He can attack and track the ball from depth, utilizing impressive quickness and timing. He remains patient and calm down the field, rarely panicking. He can time the balls' arrival to perfection, playing through receivers' hands. When playing closer to the line of scrimmage, Woodson has an instinctual knack for being around the football. He's excellent against running quarterbacks, rarely letting them out of his sightlines. He has a good feel for attacking the pocket as a blitzer, showing good timing and burst. He always keeps his eye fixated on the backfield, showing good anticipation and feel for developing routes. His trigger is quick, getting downhill, and blowing up plays routinely. Woodson isn't afraid to plug holes in the run game, proving to be a forceful tackler that runs his feet through contact, securely wrapping up. His ball skills when playing shallow or from deeper depths are good, finishing the last three seasons with about 20 passes defended and five interceptions.

Weaknesses: Woodson is an older prospect who will be 24 years old on draft night. He lacks elite range and is much quicker than he is fast. He's a little too overconfident in his pursuit angles at times, taking overly aggressive pathways to the ball, which either causes him to be behind the play or too far in front of the play. In zone coverage, Woodson lacks elite spatial awareness and instincts. He's frequently too deep or too shallow, causing him to leave large openings to receivers. In the running game, Woodson struggles consistently to disengage from blockers. He is excellent when he has clean pathways to the ball, but when he doesn't, he really struggles to make plays.

Best Fit: Versatile Coverage Safety

Player Ranking (1-100): 75.0 - I really like Woodson as a football player. He's smart, has good ball skills, is a great tackler, and is versatile. While his age limits his overall potential for growth, I think he can immediately play an important role at the next level. I wouldn't be surprised if Woodson gets a chance to be a starter during his rookie season. 3rd round player.

13. Malachi Moore - Alabama - 6'0 182 lbs

Strengths: A 5-year contributor to the Tide's defense, Moore has been a defense captain in the last two seasons. Moore has been the versatile chess piece for the Tide's defense, used in all positions and setups, including deeper or closer to the line of scrimmage. Moore excels in coverage looks, showing familiarity with zone concepts and playing in the nickel position. Incredibly intelligent, Moore recognizes pre-snap looks, putting himself in good positions and often aligning the defense correctly. An instinctual athlete who possesses a fast processor, allowing him to sniff out plays and diagnose frequently. Plays with fearlessness despite being a smaller safety, proving to be a good and reliable open-field tackler. He's not afraid of coming up and laying the wood on bigger ball carriers at times. In pursuit, Moore has a keen sense of angles, taking aggressive but good pathways to the football. He is at his best when he can play facing the action, showing a natural ability to click and get close to the football. Has noticeable fluidity throughout his frame, showing good agility and lateral mobility when asked to change directions and flip his hips. Has a plus upside as he's been a multi-year special teams contributor with experience on multiple units.

Weaknesses: An older prospect who will be 24 years old when the NFL season starts. While he's experienced in man coverage opportunities, he appears to lack confidence against speedier receivers as he often gets grabby down the field. Quicker than he is fast, Moore doesn't have the top-end speed to match receivers stride for stride. His lack of range limits him from playing in single-high looks for the next level, as he lacks elite end range. He is occasionally susceptible to double-moves in zone looks, as he is often caught peeking into the backfield. He is a little bit small for the safety position and has had some little injury concerns throughout his time. While willing in the running game, lack of power and POP causes him to get hung up on blocks.

Best Fit: Versatile Safety

Player Ranking (1-100): 74.2 - Moore is a highly experienced and versatile safety for the Tide defense that can be an immediate contributor on special teams. I worry about his lack of size and average to below-average athleticism. His best attributes are his football IQ and natural instincts, which could earn him a starting job. 4th round player.

14. Jaylen Reed - Penn State - 6'0 210 lbs

Strengths: A 2-year starter for the Nittany Lions, Reed had a terrific final campaign in 2024, finishing with nearly 100 tackles, three interceptions, and 2.5 sacks. Reed possesses a good overall frame for the position, featuring good proportional length and density through his frame. Comfortable being tasked in various ways, Reed has played both in deeper coverage and playing closer to the line of scrimmage. His football IQ and film study enable him to see things before their development. Reed excels most when he can trigger downhill, showcasing good read and react abilities to trigger and close. He recognizes run fits quickly, playing on the balls of his feet with the ability to make big hits on backs. Reed is not just a big hitter; he shows good, reliable wrap-up abilities to make plays outside his frame. He takes acute angles to the football, understanding how to sort through traffic to keep his frame clean. He plays positionally sound, showcasing good gap integrity in the running game, allowing him to be around the ball frequently. Reed keeps his eyes glued in the backfield when playing further away from the ball. He quickly recognizes route concepts while maintaining proper depths when in zone coverage. Reed possesses good ball skills to attack the football immediately, maintaining good cover awareness and timing. Reed has been a terrific special teams contributor for Penn State since his freshman campaign, with vast experience on all the units.

Weaknesses: While Reed has experience playing further from the ball, he struggles when asked to play on an island. He lacks the elite range and movement skills to be tasked with playing sideline-to-sideline. If asked to handle man coverage responsibilities, there appears to be noticeable stiffness through his lower body. He struggles when asked to flip his hips and change directions without gearing down. His trigger can be too quick sometimes, causing him to be out of position when he reads improperly. As a blitzer, Reed needs to hide his disguises better, frequently being late to the party.

Best Fit: Free Safety that is best playing closer to the line of scrimmage

Player Ranking (1-100): 74.0 - Reed had a solid final season for the Nittany Lions and greatly helped their defense. His versatility and football IQ will serve a team well. His ability to be a major factor on special teams immediately for a team will be a major selling point. 4th round player.

15. Hunter Wohler - Wisconsin - 6'2 211 lbs

Strengths: A 2-year starter at safety for the Badgers, Wohler rose into draft discussions following his stellar junior campaign in 2023, finishing with 120 tackles, six tackles for loss, and two interceptions. Wohler is a highly experienced safety who plays in various coverage looks, including cover-2, single-high, cover-3, in-the-box, nickel, and as a subpackage linebacker. Wohler has NFL size, possessing outstanding density and a large frame that can handle the rigors of NFL physicality. Wohler is a downhill and aggressive football player who loves to drop his trigger when playing from all different depths. He brings an intense physical presence to defense and shows good short-area quickness and closing speed. He's a tackle machine that utilizes his instincts and play recognition abilities to shoot downhill. He keeps his eyes glued to the backfield and will blow up plays before they develop. He stays square in the hole, showcasing terrific wrap-up abilities, and isn't afraid to lay the wood at times. In coverage settings, Wohler has handled various man and zone looks. He can handle RBs, TE, and even receivers in man situations. He has a good feel when keeping the action in front of him in zone looks, sensing his surroundings well, and showing a good feel for route combinations. Wohler has proven to be a reliable blitzer when attacking from the slot, utilizing good snap anticipation and timing.

Weaknesses: Wohler lacks the top-end range and speed to handle full-field assignments in deeper parts of the field. He appears to have significant tightness concerns in his lower body that limit him when asked to play laterally or flip his hips. He's quick to bite on double moves and play-action, taking too many false steps and will grant separation. In man coverage, Wohler struggles against quicker and shiftier receivers that can keep him turned inside out. In run support, Wohler struggles to get off contact and will get hooked by pulling linemen without any ability to disengage.

Best Fit: Box safety

Player Ranking (1-100): 73.0 - Wohler is a physical thumper who shows the natural instincts to always be around the football. His experience and motor will serve him well at the next level. He will immediately be a dynamic special teams player while he shows he can hold a place on defense. 4th round player.

16. Maxen Hook - Toledo - 6'0 210 lbs

Strengths: A 4-year starter for MAC-Conference program Toledo, Hook has been a steady and consistent performer for four straight seasons, winning numerous awards in the MAC. Built with a lean and athletic frame, Hook has above-average muscularity and density on his frame. Comfortable playing in several alignments, Hook has extensive experience in cover-2 looks, slot duties, and playing in the box. Hook is a smart football player with an internal GPS that always finds the football. He plays with suddenness and urgency on every snap, showing outstanding awareness and short-area quickness to close quickly on plays. Hook maintains a good sense of his surroundings while limiting spatial cushions when in coverage. His click-and-close abilities enable him to cut off throwing lanes and make plays on the football. Hook is a disciplined and patient safety that maintains good positioning while allowing plays to develop with a keen sense of what's going on. He stays on the ball of his feet and has rapid-like reflexes that enable him to anticipate and beat the action. Hook is a violent and physical football player who isn't afraid to lay his body on the line in the running game. He's a terrific open-field tackler who rarely lets runners out of his grasp. Hook was a core special teams player for Toledo during his first few seasons and will likely win his chance there initially.

Weaknesses: The biggest concern for Hook is his lack of consistent playing against top-tier competition. When handling man coverage responsibilities, Hook lacks the traits to do that at the next level. He is a north/south athlete who shows tightness concerns throughout his lower body, limiting his ability to play laterally and flip his hips when in coverage. He lacks the range to play as a stand-alone single-high safety at the next level and will likely be best used in a zone-style system when he can stay closer to the line of scrimmage. Hook takes very aggressive pathways to the football, sometimes taking overly aggressive lanes that take him out of plays. In run support, Hook will struggle to break down blockers, frequently getting hung up without the ability to disengage.

Best Fit: Developmental Safety and Special Teams contributor

Player Ranking (1-100): 71.5 - Hook's tape is impressive. He's always around the football field and looks great in moments. He's a tackling machine that is a terrific last line of defense. My concern is his overall athleticism and range when transitioning to the next level. He will likely have to win reps on special teams before he's given a chance on defense. 4th round player.

17. Caleb Ransaw - Tulane - 5'11 194 lbs

Strengths: Ransaw began his career with Troy, where he started in his final season with them in 2023 before transferring over to Tulane with his head coach. Ransaw is a highly experienced defensive back who has played all over the defensive backfield, including playing as an outside corner, in the slot, and finally, as a versatile safety for Tulane. Ransaw is an athletically built defender with good overall size and proportional length. Ransaw is a good fit for today's NFL safeties, having the experience to play various coverage roles. A highly nuanced football player who reads and reacts to the game well, Ransaw can come into the box and handle nickel responsibilities. A rapid athlete who moves best in short bursts and shows good click and close abilities. Noticeable flexibility and lower body movement skills enable him to flip his hips and minimize spacing against shorter, shiftier slot receivers. Ransaw seems to excel most when playing zone safety, as he can shadow his area of the field and play closer to the line of scrimmage. His physicality is far better than you'd think for his size, as he is a terrific last line of defense that routinely wraps up.

Weaknesses: His overall ball skills and production have been minimal, with only one career interception despite significant snaps in the last three seasons. He hasn't consistently competed against top-tier competition throughout his college career. His frame is small, and he appears to be close to being fully maxed out. Has been mostly a Swiss army knife player who lacks a defined position at the next level. Quicker than he is fast, Ransaw lacks the closing speed to handle playing further from the football in a Cover-2 or Single-High system. He struggles when further away from the football, lacking the necessary anticipation, instincts, and range.

Best Fit: Zone safety closer to the line of scrimmage that can cover

Player Ranking (1-100): 69.8 - Ransaw is a physical kid who moves well in a small space. His tackling reliability and versatility will immediately give him a chance to make an NFL roster. He will be a dynamic special teams contributor on Day 1. 5th round player.

18. Jaylin Smith - USC - 5'11 190 lbs

Strengths: A chesspiece for the Trojans' defense in each of the last four seasons, Smith shows incredible experience and versatility. Smith has been a starter in the last two seasons, having back-to-back impressive seasons. Smith has bounced between playing safety and corner, playing mostly as a nickel safety in 2023 and playing as an outside corner in 2024. Smith is an athletic and leanly-built defender who excels in instincts, anticipation, and football IQ. In coverage, he's best further away from the line of scrimmage. He excels in off-man and zone, where he can utilize his diagnostic abilities and understanding of route concepts to succeed. In zone coverage, Smith's zonal instincts and spatial understanding enable him to limit openings and space. A smooth mover in coverage, Smith stays on the balls of his feet at all times and remains patient through routes, rarely getting exposed on play-action or double moves. He plays with a relentless motor and urgency on every snap, proving good lateral mobility and short-area quickness to close cushions quickly. When he grants a reception, Smith limits yardage after contact, almost always bringing the ball carrier down immediately. Smith is outstanding in the running game, sacrificing his body and playing far bigger than his listed size would suggest. He's a reliable open-field tackler who utilizes his entire frame to make plays. Shows upside when attacking the pocket as a slot blitzer, utilizing good timing and anticipation to affect plays.

Weaknesses: Smith has athletic and physical limitations for the next level. He lacks the ideal size and length thresholds to play as an outside corner. He will likely be limited to playing as a nickel safety or in a zone-safety hybrid scheme. Smith frequently struggles against larger targets that can consistently win inside leverage against him. He is routinely boxed out at the catch point and lacks the physicality to win in contested settings. Smith is quicker in short spaces and struggles when asked to play in acres of space. He lacks the vertical twitch to handle covering receivers on an island, frequently allowing separation on vertical routes. He is not a typical safety that you'll want to play in deeper halves, and he would struggle to play in Cover-2 or single-high as he lacks the range for it.

Best Fit: Hybrid safety that can come up and handle nickel duties

Player Ranking (1-100): 67.1 - Smith is a good football player but not a great athlete. He will earn his stripes on special teams for a team while proving he can play some snaps on defense. 5th round player.

19. Dante Trader - Maryland - 5'11 202 lbs

Strengths: Trader is a multi-sport athlete at Maryland who also plays lacrosse. A smart and instinctual football player, Trader has started at safety in the last three seasons, showing reliability and durability to stay on the field. His production throughout each campaign has improved, proving to be a quick read. Trader is a smaller but athletically built safety with extensive experience playing various roles for the Terrapins, from stacking in the box to nickel duties to playing as a single high. Trader most excels facing the action when he can utilize his feel for the game to make plays. Trader has a nice blend of quick feet, anticipation, and route recognition abilities to see and react quickly. Trader recognizes route concepts when playing in coverage while using good timing and ball skills to arrive at the ball at exactly the right moment. He's capable of jumping routes and beating receivers to the spot. He's clearly a film junkie as he's always around the football, proving to have a high football IQ and work ethic. Trader identifies things quickly in the running game and shows zero hesitation when triggering downhill. He is a terrific tackler who drives his feet through contact, showing reliability in open-field scenarios. When plays are away from Trader, he takes acute pursuit angles to the football to make plays.

Weaknesses: Trader is an undersized safety that lacks ideal measurables, both in mass and length. He could utilize more functional strength and mass on his frame to better hold up the physical components at the next level. Trader is a far better athlete in small spaces than he is further away from the football. He's not a guy that you'll want handling man coverage assignments on an island down the field as he consistently grants separation on vertical routes, lacking top-end vertical speed. His man coverage skills are below average as he lacks the elastic fluidity through his frame to change directions and minimize spacing against savvy route runners. Trader is a 'close but not cigar' player who is around the football field a lot but doesn't make nearly as many plays as he should.

Best Fit: Box safety

Player Ranking (1-100): 66.2 - Trader is a good all-around athlete that lacks elite traits. He will immediately be a special teams maven for a team while proving that he can earn more and more snaps on defense. 5th round player.

20. Zion Childress - Kentucky - 6'0 194 lbs

Strengths: A rare 5-year significant contributor in college football, Childress began his career at Texas State in the Sun Belt conference before playing three seasons for Kentucky. Childress has a long, athletically built frame that has shown versatility throughout the defensive backfield. Childress will line up deep, play in the middle of the field as a zone safety, or come up and handle nickel duties. Childress is a noteworthy athlete with the range and the speed to play from depth or handle man coverage assignments. Childress displays quick feet, agility, and fluidity throughout his lower half when playing in man. He stays attached and remains sticky at all times. When further away from the ball, Childress displays the instincts and the football IQ to identify and process things quickly. He communicates well with his teammates when playing on the back end, maintaining calmness and patience. He quickly recognizes things in the backfield and will drop his trigger to assist in run support, proving to be a reliable tackler with a knack for ripping and punching at the ball to create turnovers. His closing burst and short-area quickness cause him to be a nuisance on underneath routes and screens, frequently being disruptive around the line of scrimmage. His length enables him to shrink one side of the field, regularly extending and making plays outside his frame.

Weaknesses: Despite his extensive experience, Childress has only one career interception. His long and lean frame could use additional mass and functional strength. He lacks elite ball skills and doesn't come up with enough turnovers when given a chance. He has some issues in transition, taking some wasted motion when working out of a backpedal in coverage. Generally, he's a reliable tackler, but he tends to be a drag down tackler that allows additional yardage after contact. He struggles when working in space and playing through blocks, frequently getting stuck and unable to disengage.

Best Fit: Versatile Coverage Safety

Player Ranking (1-100): 66.0 - Childress is built more like a corner than he is truly a safety. He's a versatile coverage safety who can handle various coverage responsibilities. He needs to get stronger and improve in the run game, but he 100% can get better with additional development. 5th round player.

21. Rayuan Lane III - Navy - 5'10 197 lbs

Strengths: Lane has been a starter for the Midshipmen for the last 3.5 seasons, starting in every game. His iron-man durability has served him well, gaining extensive experience. Lane is an athletically built safety who displays tremendous athleticism and was a former 3-sport high school athlete. Comfortable playing in the nickel, dropping deep as a coverage safety, or playing in the box. Lane is the defensive leader and signal caller, possessing outstanding football IQ and play-recognition abilities. When playing from depth, Lane shows his impressive range and closing speed. He can cover the full field, displaying good anticipation and cover awareness. His film study is apparent, as he's frequently in position to make plays, beating receivers to the spot. He anticipates in-breaking routes and can click and close with very good short-area quickness. He does a good job of playing through the receiver's hands at the catch point, evidenced by his high passes defended totals each campaign. Lane possesses good straight-line speed and can handle nickel assignments against quicker and agile receivers. He mirrors in space, showing silky smooth lateral agility and change of directional skills. Lane has natural ball skills and tracks them well, covering them from deeper positions and showing innate timing to attack the football. He's had multiple returns for touchdowns the last couple of seasons and is a natural playmaker. In the running game, Lane triggers quickly and isn't afraid to lay the wood. He works tirelessly in pursuit and will make plays from the backside, regularly tracking down receivers or runners from behind. Lane has experience on special teams and is one of the best gunners in college football.

Weaknesses: One of Lane's biggest concerns is his competition levels, as he hasn't consistently competed against many elite offenses. His frame is less than ideal for safety, and he lacks the height and length many teams covet. Lane has difficulty disengaging when in run support as he stacks and sheds in pursuit, getting hooked on blockers. In coverage, Lane struggles against bigger possession-based receivers, and he will grant them inside leverage and utilize their frames to box him out. He's a gambler in coverage and is susceptible to double moves and overpursuing plays, leading to him giving up several big plays when covering on an island.

Best Fit: Versatile Coverage Safety

Player Ranking (1-100): 65.5 - Lane is a good athlete with natural movement and ball skills. He's given up some big plays in coverage but has the football IQ and movement skills to excel at the next level. He has the range to play from depth while occasionally playing inside and covering the slot. He holds incredible value on special teams. 5th round player.

22. Malik Verdon - Iowa State - 6'4 220 lbs

Strengths: Verdon is a 2-year starter for the Cyclones, and he has been greatly impressed when he's been able to stay on the field. He had his best season in his final year in 2024, finishing with 76 tackles, one interception, and two forced fumbles. Verdon has a massive frame for the position, displaying vines for arms and good overall muscularity and density. Fully capable of playing closer to the line of scrimmage or in the deeper parts of the field, Verdon has good football intelligence and athleticism to be used anywhere. Verdon is a terrific athlete who quickly utilizes his long strides to eat up massive cushions. Verdon displays the range and the anticipation to close cushions and recover lost ground when playing in the deeper halves. He's comfortable playing with his back to the ball, showing natural coverage awareness and ball skills down the field. He quickly recognizes run fits when playing from depth, triggering quickly and getting downhill instantly. His length allows him to easily make up ground to the ball carrier, regularly closing perimeter rush lanes and extending to make plays outside his frame. He takes acute angles to the football, wasting limited motion. Verdon is a reliable open-field tackler who showcases good physicality and toughness in the run game. The Cyclone's defense played a lot of zone looks, asking Verdon to play in cloud coverage, and he appears to have good spatial awareness and ball recognition skills.

Weaknesses: Verdon has struggled with repeated injury concerns throughout his 4-year college career, missing game time every season. Verdon's biggest issue is playing through blocks in the run game, struggling to disengage against pulling blockers. He regularly gets overwhelmed at the point of attack and struggles to consistently play through contact due to his upright frame, allowing more leveraged defenders to control him. While Verdon is straight-line fast, he has some stiffness concerns when asked to play laterally. He often needs to gear down when tasked with changing direction, sometimes allowing some separation. He's better in deeper coverage than he is closer to the line of scrimmage and struggles to minimize spacing when handling slot receivers.

Best Fit: Coverage safety

Player Ranking (1-100): 64.6 - Verdon has always looked excellent this season. He has the range to play as a deeper halves safety, but he is still quite raw and lacks ideal amounts of experience. If his medical checks out OK and he improves in the running game, he could be a fun developmental project with a huge ceiling. 6th round player.

23. Shilo Sanders - Colorado - 6'0 195 lbs

Strengths: The other son of NFL Hall of Famer Deion, Shilo, is another talented son with great NFL genes. Sanders has had a long and storied college career, initially beginning in South Carolina, following his father to Jackson State and then eventually Colorado. Sanders had his best season in 2023, where he finished with 70 tackles, one interception returned for a touchdown, and four forced fumbles. Sanders has experience in various looks throughout his college career, but he's played mostly as a deeper halves cover safety for Colorado the last couple of seasons. Sanders is an instinctual football player who utilizes his play-recognition abilities and anticipation to constantly be around football. Sanders isn't content just being around the ball; he's always trying to create turnovers. Sanders is at his best in a halves defense in which he takes his side of the field, showing good range and coverage ability while facing the action. A fluid mover that displays loose hips and good agility to play on linear pathways. His football IQ and short-area quickness allow him to time the balls' arrival to perfection, regularly playing through receivers' hands. Smith shows good physicality and a downhill mentality in the running game, dropping his trigger quickly. He's not afraid to lay the wood and deliver a big hit to a runner or a receiver.

Weaknesses: Sanders will be 25 years old on draft night. Sanders has had continuous injury concerns over the last few seasons, including tearing his ACL, a finger injury, shoulder surgery, and a forearm concern. His medical will be very important during the pre-draft process. He's also been involved in an ongoing legal battle after an alleged assault charge from when he was 15 years old. Sanders is a long, wiry-built safety lacking prototypical density and body armor to play at the next level. Sanders is a flashy prospect who looks like a 1st rounder in some games, and in other games, he looks like an undrafted free agent. While willing in the run game, Sanders struggles to shed and make plays in pursuit consistently. His man coverage skills need refinement and tuning up if he wants to offer nickel upside. Sanders is a good athlete but lacks top-tier athleticism and vertical speed and will struggle in too much space on an island.

Best Fit: Versatile Coverage Safety

Player Ranking (1-100): 62.4 - Sanders has an uphill battle between his injury and off-the-field concerns. He can get drafted earlier if those are quelled by the interview/medical process. His play has been erratic in his final season. Undoubtedly, he's talented, but can he put it all together? 6th round player.

24. Alijah Clark - Syracuse - 6'1 187 lbs

Strengths: Clark was immediately thrust into the starting role for the Orange after transferring from Rutgers following his freshman campaign. A 3-year starter, Clark has played as a 'boundary safety' for the Orange, who handles various tasks for the defense. Clark is a long and rangy defensive back with room on his frame for continued development. Clark has a versatile skillset to play at the next level. Often tasked with handling man coverage responsibilities, Clark shows silky smooth movement skills when asked to play laterally on an island. He maintains good shadow coverage while minimizing available openings against targets across the middle. His competitive demeanor and good timing enable him to be disruptive at the catch point, frequently timing the balls' arrival to perfection. He displays good short-area and transitional quickness, enabling him to close cushions quickly. He is a finisher who routinely wraps up and brings his coverage assignment down immediately after receipt of the ball. When playing from depth, Clark senses things quickly in the backfield and triggers fast, showing the ability to blow up plays and deliver big hits. He plays far bigger than his listed size, showing fearlessness and physicality. A significant special teams contributor has been used on most of the coverage units.

Weaknesses: Clark was suspended for a violation of team rules in 2023. Clark is a tweener who lacks a true position. Clark is far more experienced playing closer to the line of scrimmage than he is playing on the deeper end of the defense. He lacks ideal range and coverage instincts when playing from depth and is much better in more condensed areas of the field. His slight frame could benefit by adding more bulk and muscle. He struggles when working through blockers in space, lacking the upper-body strength to stack and shed. Despite being in good positions to make plays, Clark lacks reliable hands and missed some opportunities to come away with the ball.

Best Fit: Box safety or outside corner

Player Ranking (1-100): 61.4 - Clark has a cornerback frame that has played mostly a hybrid safety role for the Orange. He looks most comfortable playing closer to the line of scrimmage. He can be used as an outside boundary corner or a box safety. His versatility should serve him well at the next level. 6th round player.

25. Emmanuel McNeil-Warren - Toledo - 6'2 202 lbs

Strengths: A 2-year starter for MAC-Conference program Toledo, McNeil-Warren has been a versatile chesspiece for the Rockets in each campaign. Built with an ideal safeties frame, McNeil-Warren has terrific length and enough room on his frame for additional bulk. He's adept at playing several roles, from single-high, as a nickel corner, in the box, cover-2 safety, and as a zone safety in cover-3 looks. McNeil is a turnover machine, forcing five fumbles and intercepting the ball 3 times during the last two campaigns. His natural instincts and awareness allow him to always be around the football. McNeil-Warren shows fluidity and oily hips in coverage, allowing him to handle assignments against quicker slot receivers. He quickly closes down with a good closing burst if he initially gives any movement. He's best when playing as a shallow zone safety, allowing him to utilize his diagnostic abilities and route anticipatory skills to jump routes and attack downhill. His short-area quickness and click/close abilities enable him to continuously challenge routes at the catch point, playing through the receivers' hands. He frequently baits QBs into throwing in his direction before triggering downhill. McNeil-Warren enjoys the physical components of playing football and loves attacking in the run game. He stays square when attacking bigger backs in the hole, showing fearlessness and good wrap-up abilities.

Weaknesses: McNeil-Warren hasn't competed against top-tier opposition regularly. He missed several games during his final season with an undisclosed injury. He only has 1.5 years of starting experience at the MAC level and will need additional seasoning and refinement. McNeil-Warren frequently takes overly aggressive pathways to the football in the run game, taking him out of plays. He lacks the physical traits to play in the deeper halves of the field at the next level. His overall range and top-end speed are good but aren't great. He's quicker in short spurts than he is truly fast.

Best Fit: Zone safety that is best closer to the line of scrimmage

Player Ranking (1-100): 58.4 - McNeil-Warren's tape was impressive. His lack of experience, high-end athleticism, and large transition to the NFL will likely cause him to drop in the draft further than his talent says he should. He could be a solid developmental safety with time and experience. 7th round player.

26. Yam Banks - Ole Miss - 5'11 210 lbs

Strengths: Banks was a 3-year starter for South Alabama in the Sun Belt Conference before transferring over to Ole Miss for his final campaign. Banks rose to prominence following his 2022 campaign in which he led the Sun Belt with six interceptions and 11 passes defended. Banks has an NFL frame, showing good compactness and density through his frame. While Banks played mostly in the nickel for South Alabama, the Ole Miss coaches tasked him with playing in various coverage setups. He played in the deeper parts of the field in a cover-2 system and closer to the line of scrimmage as a subpackage linebacker. Banks is at his best in nickel duties, as he can line up in man coverage and handle slot receivers. He's a fluid mover that displays good quickness in bursts. Banks can play on a linear plane and show smooth fluidity and flexible hips in coverage. He maintains good positions while staying attached to the receiver's hip pocket. Banks shows the instincts and the anticipation to read and diagnose when playing further off the ball. Banks times the balls' arrival and shows the physicality and downhill nature to attack the football. A natural ball tracker when facing the action, Banks has good overall ball skills and can win in 50/50 challenges despite being on the smaller side. Banks utilizes his compact frame and physical style to trigger downhill quickly in the run game.

Weaknesses: Unfortunately, following the Bank 2022 campaign, his production has gradually declined. He had a disappointing season at Ole Miss this season, sometimes getting taken off the field. Banks lacks ideal length, and this limits him when playing in coverage. He's frequently boxed out at the catch point against bigger targets. His length also causes him issues when working toward the football in the run game. He struggles stacking and shedding in pursuit and sits on blocks for far too long. Banks tends to attempt to ankle swipe as a tackler and miss his fair share of open-field tackles. He lacks top-end range to play further away from the football and is likely best used in a nickel role.

Best Fit: Zone safety that can play in the nickel

Player Ranking (1-100): 54.8 - Banks looked great at South Alabama, but he had a disappointing season for Ole Miss this season. He was frequently taken off the field and greatly failed to impress against better competition. He showed natural ball skills and coverage ability in the Sun Belt, which could show that there's still upside to the player. Undrafted free agent.

Top-10 Safeties:

1. Malaki Starks
2. Nick Emmanwori
3. Xavier Watts
4. Billy Bowman Jr
5. Kevin Winston Jr
6. Lathan Ransom
7. Andrew Mukuba
8. Jonas Sanker
9. Xavier Nwankpa
10. Sebastian Castro

Conclusion

As I mentioned at the very beginning of my introduction, use this guide as a resource, not just for the 2025 NFL Draft but also for the future. Take a look at it in a year, two years, or ten years down the road.

I do my absolute best to start evaluating these guys as soon as possible so I can get this draft guide out ASAP. I don't want to be swayed by pre-draft workouts. I want to be influenced by the most important thing BY FAR: the tape!

Maybe you'll be confused by some of my write-ups or rankings. Remember this: I finished this guide in late January! And I don't regret that at all. It's actually worked to my advantage every year of my guide.

Also, keep in mind that I don't have access to medicals, interviews with coaches, or other pre-draft festivities. My rankings are strictly based on the players' play, not any of the intangibles and off-the-field stuff. It's impossible to know that stuff.

I truly hope you love my guide, whether you're a beginner digging into the draft for the first year or if you're an obsessive draft head like me!

I'm sure there will be guys that I miss in this guide that I don't review, not due to laziness, but likely since they were late risers and I didn't get a chance to review or write up their evaluation before the draft.

I truly, more than anything else, hope you see the time, effort, and detail I put into every single evaluation. The research I do on every one of these players is beyond extensive. I use every single available resource, contact, and article I can find to write up the most fact-oriented and accurate report possible. Of course, it's possible there could be some errors. Please be understanding :)

As I say in every guide, if you guys have any questions, please message me on Twitter at my handle: @DTPDraftScout.

Once again, I have to say thank you so much from the bottom of my heart. I could never have turned this fun little side hobby into a full-time gig if it weren't for you!

If you could all do me a favor and PLEASE leave me a review on Amazon, it would mean the absolute world to me! And as always, thanks to every last one of you guys for grabbing my draft guide. If any of you need help with anything in the future, let me know, and I'd be more than honored to help you out.

Honestly, Daniel Parlegreco

Glossary of Terms

0 Technique (Zero Technique DT) – A DT who is required to play two different gaps. They are lined up directly over the center. They can be in a 3-4 or a 4-3 system. They are the biggest guys on the defensive side of the ball. They are generally extremely powerful and clog the middle of the field. They generally are not required to rush the passer, nor are they very good at it. They are also called nose tackles as well.

1 Technique (One Technique DT) – A DT that generally is required to take on multiple blockers and open things up for his fellow defensive lineman. They play on either one of the outside shoulders of the center and are not directly over the center like a 0 technique. They generally are also referred to as nose tackles as well. A 1 technique is always partnered up with a 3 technique DT as well. The 1 technique is more powerful, stronger and a better player against the run. The 3 technique is more explosive and a better pass rusher.

2 Technique (Two Technique DT) – A DT that plays head up directly over the guard. They have more gap assignments and are generally required to handle both the 'A' gap between the guard and the center in addition to the 'B' gap between the guard and the tackle. They are usually required to be incredibly stout and constantly take on double teams.

3 Technique (Three Tech DT) – Plays on the outside shoulder of either guard. They are the penetrating and more explosive DT that is a better pass rusher. They don't have much responsibility in the way of gap control, and generally are 1-gap players. Think of guys like Warren Sapp and Aaron Donald.

3-4 OLB – Plays mostly on the line of scrimmage but standing up on the outside. These guys are generally your best pass rushers in a 3-4 system. They can be used in coverage at times as well. They are similar to 4-3 DE's but differ because of the defensive scheme your defense employs. 4-3 DE's are required to put their hands on the ground and are relied upon to be generally bigger, longer and stronger against the run. Depending on the defensive coaches and their philosophies, most guys are capable of playing either as a 4-3 DE or a 3-4 OLB depending on what defensive system your team plays.

4-3 OLB – These guys aren't your pass rushers. They consist of both the Will linebacker and the Sam linebacker. The Will (Weak Side) is generally the more athletic, sideline to sideline LB who is faster and can cover better. The Will plays on the weak side of the formation. The Sam (Strong Side) linebacker is the guy that's asked to play closer to the line of scrimmage to play the run more. They play on the strong side of the formation.

Cover 2 – Two deep-lying safeties who each cover half of the field.

Cover 3 – Rather than covering ½ the field like a Cover 2, a Cover 3 requires 3 deep playing guys who each takes a 3rd of the field.

Dime Defense – Has 6 defensive backs on the field, only 1 linebacker and 4 rushers on the line. Used in passing situations or long yardage situations.

JUCO – Transferred from a junior college program.

Mike Linebacker – Quite simply the middle linebacker on your team.

Nickel Defense – Has 5 defensive backs on the field, 2 linebackers and 4 rushers on the line of scrimmage. Used in passing situations or when teams are in 3 receiver sets.

Nickel Linebacker – When a team is playing in nickel, there are 2 linebackers on the field. These linebackers are the best on the team in space, and can really cover and run.

Quick Twitch (Twitchy) – Meaning a guy who is explosive off the snap of the ball. They possess above-average quick-twitch fibers, meaning they are more explosive in their lower bodies.

Rangy – Good length but lacks great bulk on his frame. Almost like a wiry-built guy who lacks the ideal weight on his frame

RPO – A popular new term in the NFL referring to run pass option plays. It's when the QB goes to the line of scrimmage with both a run and a pass play. He generally decides based on the defensive look whether to run or pass

Sam Linebacker (Strong Side Linebacker) – Stronger, bigger guy who is required to play closer to the line of scrimmage. Generally, has more assignments in the run game.

Single High Safety – Deep covering safety who plays deep by himself and covers the entire field. Generally is a safety who plays with outstanding range and instincts. Think Earl Thomas.

Slot Cornerback (Nickel Corner) – A cornerback who plays inside and covers the receivers closest to the line of scrimmage. These cornerbacks are usually smaller, quicker and more agile.

Sub-packages – Any package which is different from your base defense. Your base defense is either a 3-4 or a 4-3. Every team has sub-packages that are generally required to be used in certain game situations, such as nickel or dime defense. Most teams in the NFL play in their sub-package almost 50% of the time.

Will Linebacker (Weak Side Linebacker) - More athletic outside linebacker who plays on the weak side of the formation in a 4-3 defense.

100 Big Board

1. Travis Hunter
2. Abdul Carter
3. Cameron Ward
4. Ashton Jeanty
5. Tyler Warren
6. Tetairoa McMillan
7. Mason Graham
8. Will Campbell
9. Mykel Williams
10. Kelvin Banks
11. Jalon Walker
12. Tre Harris
13. Harold Fannin Jr
14. Josh Conerly Jr
15. Jaxson Dart
16. Savion Williams
17. Josh Simmons
18. Malaki Starks
19. Donovan Jackson
20. Will Johnson
21. Luther Burden III
22. Nic Scourton
23. Tyleik Williams
24. Colston Loveland
25. Jahdae Barron

26. Jihaad Campbell
27. Aireontae Ersery
28. Tyler Baron
29. Shavon Revel Jr
30. Tyler Booker
31. Deontae Lawson
32. Emeka Egbuka
33. Jake Briningstool
34. Walter Nolen
35. Carson Schwesinger
36. Shedeur Sanders
37. Tate Ratledge
38. Kyle Kennard
39. Denzel Burke
40. Nick Emmanwori
41. Omarion Hampton
42. Kenneth Grant
43. Danny Stutsman
44. Deone Walker
45. Xavier Watts
46. Ajani Cornelius
47. Chris Paul Jr
48. Benjamin Morrison
49. TreVeyon Henderson
50. Armand Membou
51. Barrett Carter
52. Wyatt Milum

53. Landon Jackson
54. T.J. Sanders
55. Tez Johnson
56. Oronde Gadsden II
57. Cameron Williams
58. Trey Amos
59. Emery Jones
60. Jalen Milroe
61. Jonah Savaiinaea
62. Kaleb Johnson
63. Anthony Belton
64. Derrick Harmon
65. Lander Barton
66. Smael Mondon Jr
67. Shemar Stewart
68. Maxwell Hairston
69. Billy Bowman Jr
70. Isaiah Bond
71. Nickolas Martin
72. Grey Zabel
73. Mike Green
74. Alfred Collins
75. Elic Ayomanor
76. James Pearce Jr
77. Jeffrey Bassa
78. Kevin Winston Jr
79. Ty Robinson

80. Earnest Green III
81. Darien Porter
82. Donovan Ezeiruaku
83. Darius Alexander
84. Antwaun Powell-Ryland
85. Jason Marshall Jr
86. Howard Cross III
87. Tyreem Powell
88. Quinshon Judkins
89. Domani Jackson
90. J.J. Pegues
91. Lathan Ransom
92. Xavier Restrepo
93. Luke Kandra
94. Josaiah Stewart
95. Andrew Mukuba
96. Zy Alexander
97. Princely Umanmielen
98. Re'Mello Dotson
99. LT Overton
100. Quinn Ewers

Index

A

Abdul Carter, 125
Aeneas Peebles, 170
Aireontae Ersery, 91
Ajani Cornelius, 92
Akheem Mesidor, 180
Alan Bowman, 15
Alfred Collins, 160
Alijah Clark, 254
Andrew Mukuba, 241
Anthony Belton, 94
Antwane Wells Jr, 61
Antwaun Powell-Ryland, 134
Arian Smith, 57
Armand Membou, 92
Ashton Gillotte, 140
Ashton Jeanty, 17
Azareyeh'h Thomas, 219

B

Barrett Carter, 199
Barryn Sorrell, 139
Benjamin Morrison, 212
Benjamin Yurosek, 80
Bhayshul Tuten, 31
Bilhal Kone, 231
Billy Bowman Jr, 239
Bradyn Swinson, 138
Brandon Adams, 232
Brandon Crenshaw-Dickson, 98
Brashard Smith, 25
Bru McCoy, 66
Bryson Nesbit, 78

C

C.J. West, 179
Caden Prieskorn, 79
Caleb Ransaw, 249
Cam Horsley, 181
Cam Jackson, 179
Cam Miller, 14
Cameron Skattebo, 28
Cameron Ward, 3
Cameron Williams, 93
Carson Schwesinger, 198
Carson Vinson, 105
Charles Grant, 98
Chase Lundt, 103
Chimere Dike, 68
Chris Paul Jr, 186
CJ Dippre, 86
Clay Webb, 113
Cobee Bryant, 223
Cody Lindenberg, 203
Cody Simon, 202
Collin Oliver, 139
Colston Loveland, 72
Connor Colby, 120
Cooper Mays, 123
Corey Kiner, 38
Craig Woodson, 245

D

Damien Martinez, 29
Dani Dennis, 145
Danny Stutsman, 185
Dante Trader, 250
Darien Porter, 215
Darius Alexander, 163
David Walker, 144
Davin Vann, 144
Demetrius Knight Jr, 192
DeMonte Capehart, 168
Denzel Burke, 212
Deone Walker, 157
Deontae Lawson, 197
Derrick Harmon, 158
DeShawn Pace, 203
Devin Neal, 26
Dillon Gabriel, 9
DJ Giddens, 27
DJ Uiagalelei, 12
Domani Jackson, 217
Dominic Lovett, 66
Donovan Edwards, 30
Donovan Ezeiruaku, 133
Donovan Jackson, 107
Dorian Strong, 221
Drew Kendall, 122
Dylan Fairchild, 112
Dylan Sampson, 21

E

Earnest Green III, 95
Eli Stowers, 82
Elic Ayomanor, 49
Elijah Arroyo, 78
Elijah Badger, 65
Elijah Roberts, 151
Emeka Egbuka, 47
Emery Jones Jr, 94
Emmanuel McNeil-Warren, 255
Eric Gregory, 176
Eugene Asante, 194

F

Fadil Diggs, 146
Fentrell Cypress, 233
Francisco Mauigoa, 204

G

Garrett Dellinger, 118
Gavin Bartholomew, 83
Gee Scott Jr, 84
Gerald Mincey, 105
Grey Zabel, 111
Gunnar Helm, 75

H

Harold Fannin Jr, 72
Hollin Pierce, 101
Howard Cross III, 162
Hunter Dekkers, 15
Hunter Wohler, 247

I

Isaiah Bond, 48

J

J.J. Pegues, 163
J.T. Tuimoloau, 137
Ja'Corey Brooks, 62
Ja'Quinden Jackson, 40
Jabbar Muhammad, 222
Jack Bech, 52

Jack Kiser, 189
Jack Nelson, 96
Jack Sawyer, 141
Jackson Hawes, 82
Jackson Slater, 119
Jacob Gideon, 124
Jacob Parrish, 220
Jah Joyner, 148
Jahdae Barron, 210
Jake Briningstool, 73
Jake Majors, 117
Jalen McLeod, 143
Jalen Milroe, 5
Jalen Rivers, 115
Jalen Royals, 50
Jalen Travis, 101
Jalon Walker, 127
Jamaree Caldwell, 183
James Pearce, 132
Jamon Dumas-Johnson, 191
Jared Ivey, 136
Jared Wilson, 113
Jarquez Hunter, 22
Jasheen Davis, 147
Jason Henderson, 193
Jason Marshall Jr, 216
Jaxson Dart, 4
Jay Higgins, 191
Jay Toia, 169
Jayden Higgins, 60
Jaydn Ott, 35
Jaydon Blue, 41
Jaylen Reed, 247
Jaylin Lane, 64
Jaylin Noel, 58
Jaylin Smith, 249
Jeffrey Bassa, 188
Jermari Harris, 226
Jermayne Lole, 178
Jihaad Campbell, 196
Jimmy Horn Jr, 68
Jo'quavious Marks, 23
Joe Evans, 182
John Campbell Jr, 104
Jonah Monheim, 114
Jonah Savaiinaea, 110
Jonas Sanker, 242
Jordan Burch, 142
Jordan Hancock, 231
Jordan James, 32
Josaiah Stewart, 135
Josh Conerly Jr, 89
Josh Fryar, 103
Josh Simmons, 90

Joshua Farmer, 171
Joshua Gray, 121
Justin Walley, 229

K

Kaden Prather, 63
Kaimon Rucker, 147
Kaleb Johnson, 19
Kalel Mullings, 23
Kelvin Banks Jr, 89
Kenneth Grant, 156
Kevin Winston Jr, 240
Khari Coleman, 206
Kobe Hudson, 63
Kobe King, 190
Korie Black, 228
Kurtis Rourke, 8
Kyle Kennard, 130
Kyle McCord, 7
Kyle Williams, 58
Kyren Lacy, 56

L

Lander Barton, 186
Landon Jackson, 131
Lathan Ransom, 241
LeQuint Allen Jr, 33
Logan Brown, 100
LT Overton, 164
Luke Kandra, 111
Luke Lachey, 81
Luther Burden III, 46

M

Mac McWilliams, 228
Malachi Moore, 246
Malaki Starks, 237
Malik Verdon, 252
Marcus Mbow, 97
Marcus Wehr, 117
Marcus Yarns, 40
Mason Graham, 154
Mason Taylor, 76
Matthew Golden, 51
Max Brosmer, 10
Maxen Hook, 248
Maxwell Hairston, 214
Mike Green, 131
Miles Frazier, 115
Mitchell Evans, 86
Moliki Matavao, 85

Mykel Williams, 126

N

Nate Carter, 39
Nate Noel, 37
Nazir Stackhouse, 174
Nic Scourton, 128
Nick Emmanwori, 238
Nick Nash, 59
Nickolas Martin, 187

O

O'Donnell Fortune, 222
Ollie Gordon II, 29
Oluwafemi Oladejo, 205
Omari Thomas, 173
Omarion Hampton, 18
Omarr Norman-Lott, 165
Oronde Gadsden II, 74
Oscar Delp, 77
Ozzy Trapilo, 99

P

Pat Bryant, 54
Patrick Jenkins, 181
Patrick Payton, 141
Peny Boone, 42
Phil Mafah, 35
Princely Umanmielen, 136

Q

Quandarrius Robinson, 150
Quincy Riley, 225
Quinn Ewers, 6
Quinshon Judkins, 20

R

R.J. Oben, 149
Ra'Mello Dotson, 218
Raheim Sanders, 34
Rayuan Lane III, 251
Ricky White III, 54
Riley Leonard, 11
RJ Harvey, 24
Rod Moore, 244
Roman Hemby, 42
Rylie Mills, 177

S

Saivion Jones, 172
Savion Williams, 45
Sebastian Castro, 244
Seth McLaughlin, 119
Shaun Dolac, 195
Shavon Revel Jr, 211
Shedeur Sanders, 4
Shemar James, 201
Shemar Stewart, 159
Shemar Turner, 150
Shilo Sanders, 253
Simeon Barrow Jr, 171
Smael Mondon Jr, 200

T

T.J. Sanders, 158
Tahj Brooks, 33
Tahveon Nicholson, 235
Tai Felton, 53
Tate Ratledge, 108
Terrance Ferguson, 75
Tetairoa McMillan, 44
Tez Johnson, 48
Thaddeus Dixon, 224
Theo Wease Jr, 67
Thor Griffith, 177
Tommi Hill, 230
Tommy Akingbesote, 183
Tonka Hemingway, 174
Toriano Pride Jr, 235
Tory Horton, 55
Travis Hunter Jr, 208
Tre Harris, 45
Tre Stewart, 36
TreVeyon Henderson, 19
Trevor Etienne, 37
Trey Amos, 213
Ty Hamilton, 166
Ty Robinson, 161
Tyleik Williams, 155
Tyler Baron, 129
Tyler Batty, 152
Tyler Booker, 108
Tyler Shough, 10
Tyler Warren, 71
Tyreem Powell, 200
Tyrion Ingram-Dawkins, 167

U

Upton Stout, 227

V

Vernon Broughton, 175

W

Walter Nolen, 155
Weston Franklin, 116
Will Campbell, 88
Will Howard, 8
Will Johnson, 209
Will Lee III, 225
Will Rogers, 13
Will Sheppard, 61
Willie Lampkin, 121
Wyatt Milum, 109

X

Xavier Nwankpa, 243
Xavier Restrepo, 50
Xavier Truss, 102
Xavier Watts, 238

Y

Yahya Black, 169
Yam Banks, 255

Z

Zah Frazier, 234
Zakhari Franklin, 69
Zion Childress, 251
Zy Alexander, 217

Made in the USA
Coppell, TX
10 April 2025

48104300R00142